A PHOTOGRAPHIC
ENCYCLOPEDIA
OF
BIRDS

Text by Richard Coomber
Designed by Philip Clucas
Photography from Planet Earth by
    J. Brian Alker, K. and K. Amman, Sean T. Avery,
    A.P. Barnes, D. Barrett, Richard Beales,
    J.R. Bracegirdle, Jim Brandenburg, Franz J. Camenzind,
    Philip Chapman, H. Charles, Mary Clay,
    Martin Coleman, Richard Coomber, Jim Damaske,
    B.N.S. Deo, Georgette Douwma, John Downer,
    Geoff du Feu, Sue Earle, John Fawcett, Paolo Fioratti,
    Michael Fogden, D. Robert Franz, Werner Frei,
    R.T. French, C.B. Frith, D.W. Frith, Dr Peter Gasson,
    Daniel W. Gotshall, Nick Greaves, Hans Christian Heap,
    Julian Hector, Chris Howes, David Kjaer, Ford Kristo,
    Ken Lucas, Gillian Lythgoe, John Lythgoe,
    Richard Matthews, Mark Mattock,
    David Jesse McChesney, Roger Mear, F.C. Millington,
    Colin Pennycuick, Doug Perrine, David Phillips,
    Howard Platt, David A. Ponton, Mike Potts,
    Jorge Provenza, P.N. Raven, David Rootes, Andy Rouse,
    David E. Rowley, Rod Salm, Keith Scholey,
    Jonathan P. Scott, Nancy Sefton, Anup Shah,
    Manoj Shah, William M. Smithey, Jr,
    Bernadette Spiegel, Nicholas Tapp, P.V. Tearle,
    Nigel Tucker, John Waters, Margaret Welby,
    Alex Williams, Joyce Wilson and Rodney Wood.
Commissioning Editor: Andrew Preston
Publishing Assistant: Edward Doling
Editorial: Gill Waugh
Production: Ruth Arthur, David Proffit and Sally Connolly
Director of Production: Gerald Hughes
Director of Publishing: David Gibbon

CLB 2422
© 1990 Colour Library Books Ltd., Godalming, Surrey, England.
This edition published in 1990 by Gallery Books,
an imprint of W.H. Smith, Inc.
112 Madison Avenue, New York, New York 10016.
Printed and bound in Italy.
All rights reserved.
ISBN 0 8317 2801 9
Gallery Books are available for bulk purchase for sales promotions
and premium use. For details write or telephone
the Manager of Special Sales, W.H. Smith, Publishers, Inc.,
112 Madison Avenue, New York, New York 10016. (212) 532-6600.

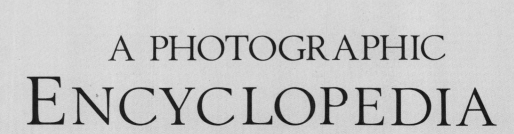

A PHOTOGRAPHIC
ENCYCLOPEDIA
OF
BIRDS

· RICHARD · COOMBER ·

GALLERY BOOKS
An Imprint of W. H. Smith Publishers Inc.
112 Madison Avenue
New York City 10016

CONTENTS

Facing page: a Silver Gull, Australia.

INTRODUCTION

The *Encyclopaedia of Birds* covers 180 bird families, many of which are illustrated in the 400 coloured photographs that accompany the text. In the World today there are about 8,950 species of birds, but in reality there could be more or less because of the discrepancies between various lists.

The systematics of the World's birds have been placed under the microscope, and analysis of their DNA either confirms or rejects long held beliefs about the relationships between families. At present no single checklist incorporates such changes, so for this volume I have followed the sequence used by Howard and Moore in *A complete checklist of the Birds of the World*. This was published in 1980, and although I understand that an updated edition is in preparation, it is not yet available. Some changes have been incorporated in more recently publish works, including the handbooks of the Birds of Africa and South America, but these are only appearing at the rate of about one volume every two years and will not be complete several years to come.

The sequence of birds follows a set pattern rather like a family tree, or in the modern idiom, a computer's disk-filing system. At the top, or in the root directory is:

Class: BIRDS – made up of 27 Orders or groups of related birds; the largest being the *Passeriformes*. **Order** These groupings contain 180 families.

Family Each family contains a single genus or several genera. The relationship between the members becoming close with each sub-division. It is on the families that the sections of this book are based.

Genus Within each genus is one or more species; members of a genus are obviously related to one another.

Species Each is given two names – a popular name, often in English, and a scientific name. The scientific name is the international language for any form of life; the name American Robin is also known as *Turdus migratorius*; far easier than remembering that in Dutch it is the *Roodborstlijster*, in French it becomes *Merle migrateur* and in German *Wanderdrossel*!

Sub-species Some species are sub-divided where certain populations have evolved distinct races within the species.

The sections of this book include the following information, which varies slightly in its presentation within certain families, for it is on the families of birds that this book is based. The number of species are divided in different genera, but the number of species that comprise an individual genus is not shown, for otherwise the sections would just be a list of names and numbers. I have not gone in to the details of bird song, display or colours of eggs, for there are just too many combinations for a book of this nature.

Within each section, one can read about the **distribution** of the family and its preferred **habitat**; a **description** of some genera or species; details of their **movements**, whether **migratory** or **sedentary**; their **diet** and **breeding biology**. In some cases one will find information about **extinct** and currently **endangered** birds.

The *Encyclopaedia of Birds* is intended as a reference book, where one can enjoy the pictures and read the text relating to particular bird families. I hope it is a book that will create an increased awareness of the birds at home and abroad.

First page: a Leaden Flycatcher. Title page: (left) a
Red-browed Firetail, (inset left) a Blue-crested
Flycatcher and (inset right) a Rainbow Lorikeet.
Facing page: a Rainbow Bee-eater and (above)
an African Jacana.

OSTRICH

Order: *Struthioniformes*
Family: *Struthionidae*
the genus *Struthio* contains a single
species *Struthio camelus*.

Ratites are the group of flightless birds that live mainly on the major land masses across the Southern Hemisphere. They are birds without breast bones or 'keels'.

Of the ten Ratitae species, it is only the Ostrich *Struthio camelus* that occurs north of the Equator and this, the largest, is perhaps the most familiar flightless bird to people living in Europe and North America. We tend to think of Ostriches putting their heads in the sand to avoid trouble, but this notion is far from the truth. They have excellent eyesight and on sensing danger they can run at speeds up to 45 mph. (72 km/h.) or even faster in short bursts.

Ostriches are mainly vegetarians eating leaves and roots and are to be found on the plains of Africa sharing the pastures with gazelles, zebra and other species of game. They can be found in deserts and savannahs and formerly extended across the Middle East and into Arabia. Following the spread of firearms since World War I, the Ostrich has declined markedly and is now almost certainly extinct in this part of its range. A decline has also taken place in the western Sahara, so now it is only in East and Southern Africa that the species remains common. Even there the bulk of the populations live within the great national parks of the region.

The large, black-bodied male Ostrich can weigh up to 345 lb. (156 kg.) and stands some 8 ft. (2.4 m.) tall. Those birds of the northern and southern subspecies have blue thighs, whereas males from Central Kenya south to the Zambezi have pink thighs. Females are more lightly built and their grey-brown plumage recalls their South American relatives, the Rheas *Rhea spp.*, but that species has three toes compared with the Ostrich, which has only two. Ostriches are record-breakers several times over holding the titles of heaviest, tallest, fastest running bird.

Breeding is often associated with the onset of the rains. New growth provides not only food, but cover, which helps protect the small chicks when they are most vulnerable to predation. A group of Ostriches consists of a male and a major female plus up to six minor females, who often lay in the nest after the major female has completed her clutch. The male incubates the 25 or so eggs, relieved by a female when he needs to feed. The egg can weigh up to 3 lb. (1.5 kg.) and is the largest laid by any bird. Unlike other species of birds the young Ostrich does not have an egg-tooth with which to break through the egg shell. Instead it is able to crack the shell by muscle pressure alone! After the first few weeks of life they have few natural enemies, as they can outrun most of the predatory species occurring in the same areas. Ostrich eggs are a valuable source of food for many animals in Africa, from Lion *Leo panthera* to Egyptian Vulture *Neophron perenopterus*, who has learnt to break abandoned eggs by throwing stones at them! The shell of the highly prized egg is used as a water carrier by native peoples such as the Bushmen of southern Africa. The young Ostriches grow quickly although it takes about 12 months for the young birds to become full grown reaching breeding age in 3-4 years.

RHEAS

Order: Rheiformes
Family: Rheidae
two genera, *Rhea* and *Pterocnemia*, each
containing a single species.

There are two species of Rhea to be found in South America, where they are the counterparts of the Ostrich *Struthio camelus* in Africa. Both the rheas and the Ostrich share a common ancestor dating back before the breakup of the great island continent, Gondwanaland.

The Common or Greater Rhea *Rhea americana* occurs in

Left: an Ostrich chick takes its first look at the world outside the egg. Ostrich eggs are the largest produced by any living bird and take about 40 days to hatch. They are incubated mainly by the male with occasional assistance from the female. After hatching, chicks take 12 months to become fully grown.

north-eastern Brazil, south to central Argentina. It prefers tall grass and more bushy habitat than the Ostrich and nests on dry ground close to marshes or rivers. Farther south and west the Common Rhea is replaced by the closely related Darwin's Rhea *Pterocnemia pennata*. This species is smaller and has white spots on an otherwise similar lax grey-brown plumage. The distribution takes it from southern Argentina and Chile north to the Andean plateau in Peru and Bolivia. There is an interesting story relating to the discovery of this bird by Charles Darwin during his monumental voyage on H.M.S. *Beagle*. At dinner one evening he realised that the structure of the leg bone eaten at the table was not the same as those eaten earlier on the journey! And so Darwin's Rhea became known to science.

The male Common Rhea can reach 5 ft. (1.5 m.) in height and weigh up to 55 lb. (25 kg.). The sexes are similar, although the female tends to be slightly smaller. They have excellent eyesight and are constantly on the look out for danger, although once fully grown they have few enemies other than man. It can out run all but a gaucho on horseback,

Above: in the Little Karoo, South Africa, a male Ostrich pants in the heat of the midday sun. A fully grown male stands about 8ft. high and has been clocked at speeds of up to 45 mph. Ostriches were formerly more widespread, but their numbers have been reduced by modern hunting methods.

who traditionally hunt the Rhea by throwing a *bolas*, which consists of three balls joined by rope. The *bolas* entwines itself around the legs of the fleeing bird, bringing it helplessly crashing to the ground. Throughout their range Rheas have declined at the hand of man and are now only to be found in remote areas or in those places where they are afforded protection.

Rheas are largely vegetarian, but also will eat insects such as grasshoppers and small mammals: Out of the breeding season the species gather in flocks and groups of 20-25 can be found feeding with deer and domestic cattle.

Females are prolific egg layers and up to 80 eggs have been found in a single nest, although it would have been the minor females, associating with the male, who laid many of these. The nest is just a scrape, lined with grass, in the ground and the male undertakes the incubation that can last at least five weeks. On hatching, the down-covered active young eat insects for the first few days. They grow faster than young Ostriches as they are fully grown in five months, although it is two years before they become sexually mature.

Above: fighting male Ostriches in Zimbabwe show their muscular legs and rudimentary wings during a contest over a female. The Common Rhea (left) is the more widespread of the two species of rhea, a flightless family confined to South America. Like the other large, flightless birds they have loose plumage and run well to escape danger.

9

CASSOWARIES
Order: *Casuariiformes*
Family: *Casuariidae*
the genus *Casuarius* contains three species.

Cassowaries are to be found in north-eastern Queensland in Australia and New Guinea, which lies to the north. They are birds of the tropical rain forests where they inhabit areas close to streams and in forest clearings.

The Southern or Double-wattled Cassowary *Casuarius casuarius* occurs in Queensland and New Guinea, whilst confined to New Guinea and neighbouring islands are the Dwarf *C. bennetti* and One-wattled *C. unappendiculatus*

with its powerful legs and feet. During the breeding season, they can be particularly dangerous and there are a number of well documented cases in which people have been killed in defensive attacks by cassowaries.

Cassowaries of all three species are elusive birds in their native jungle habitat and are most often to be found singly or in pairs. Breeding coincides with the main fruiting period of forest trees, so that fallen fruit on the jungle floor forms the most important source of food. To sustain a healthy population of cassowaries, a rich and well-balance forest of native trees is required and left to their own devices the birds themselves ensure the continued survival of their habitat. In their droppings, they inevitably pass pips and seeds as they wander in search of fruit. This eventually spreads young trees through the forest for the benefit of generations of cassowaries to come.

The One-wattled Cassowary (below left), named for the single wattle of skin that hangs from its throat, inhabits the northern lowlands of New Guinea and some offshore islands. All three members of the family have a horny casque on the forehead that varies in size and shape with the species.

Cassowaries. It is by no means certain that the present range of cassowaries in New Guinea is the natural one. As one would imagine, cassowaries are a source of meat for the native peoples, who catch and keep youngsters for the pot. Once a species becomes used in trade it is inevitable that some will escape, so that some populations may have arrived on nearby islands in this way.

They are large flightless birds, related most closely to the Emu *Dromaius novaehollandiae*, also to be found in Australia. Unlike their relatives, the head of a cassowary is bare with blue skin and a prominent horny casque. Birds in captivity have used this appendage to dig for food, so they may not use it to protect the head whilst pushing through dense vegetation.

When adult the plumage is black and shaggy, an effect caused by the double feathers, illustrating the species' relationship with the Emu. The double feather is a secondary one that offshoots from the main shaft of a body feather. The primaries, or the main flight feathers on flying birds, have evolved to mere quills on the cassowary. This makes the bird a formidable adversary when it uses wings in conjunction

EMU
Order: *Casuariiformes*
Family: *Dromaiidae*
the genus *Dromaius* contains a single species *Dromaius novaehollandiae*.

The Emu *Dromaius novaehollandiae*, the second largest bird in the World after the Ostrich *Struthio camelus*, bears a strong resemblance to that species and to the rheas *Rhea spp.* of South America. However, they are more closely related to the cassowaries *Casuarius spp.* of tropical north-eastern Australia and New Guinea. The lax brown body plumage of the Emu consists of double-shafted feathers, a feature shared with the Cassowary.

Although there is now only one species of Emu, although formerly smaller emus occurred on Tasmania, and on Kangaroo and King Islands off South Australia and the state

Until man arrived in Australia the Emu (above and facing page) had few natural enemies, but with human settlement and the spread of agriculture, conflicts of interests arose. Emus require a regular supply of water, although they can travel great distances without when in search of a fresh food supply. The Emu is the National Bird of Australia.

of Victoria respectively. The Kangaroo Island Black Emu *D. diemenianus* became extinct in 1830. It may never be known if the others were distinct species or merely small insular races of the mainland bird for they were also wiped out by settlers during the early years of the 19th. century.

Emus are widespread over much of Australia from quite arid areas through into tropical woodland, although they are replaced in the tropical rain forests of the north-east by the Southern Cassowary *C. casuarius*. Emus are vegetarian and being fastidious feeders, eat almost exclusively foods that are particularly nutritious such as new growth, flowers, fruits and seeds. In times of abundance, usually after the rains, they are able to store large quantities of body fat and will travel long distances to their next food supply. During these nomadic treks their body weight can be reduced by as much as 50%.

Emus are dependent on a daily water supply and it is the need to search for food and water that has brought the species into direct conflict with farmers and settlers. Farms with permanent water for livestock and irrigation for such crops as cereals make ideal targets for the wandering Emus. In 1932 Emus reached pest proportions in Western Australia to the extent that the authorities detailed soldiers armed with machine guns to deal with the problem. Faced with such opposition Emus broke up in to small groups, thus turning military action into an uneconomical proposition and the 'Emu Wars' ended. Perhaps not the most glorious campaign in the history of military warfare! To prevent Emus invading the important wheat producing areas of south-western Australia a fence, some 600 miles (1000 km.) long, was erected to protect the area.

The preferred habitat of the Emu (this page) varies from arid inland plains to tropical woodlands. The male incubates the eggs and rears the chicks, a pattern typical of the large flightless birds. In spite of the formidable protection afforded by the male, predators, such as dingos and introduced foxes, still manage to catch and eat small chicks. Emus are mainly vegetarian, but they also eat insects and small invertebrates. They continually search for fresh growths of vegetation, as well as flowers, fruit and seeds.

As with the other species of large flightless birds it is the male that incubates the clutch of 5-15 blue eggs. These are laid by the female at about 2-3 day intervals, although incubation, which takes about 8 weeks, does not commence until the clutch is complete. This results in all the eggs hatching over a period of hours rather than days and thereby increases the survival rate of the youngsters. During incubation, and for the first few days after hatching, predators such as the Dingo *Canis dingo*, a species of wild dog, can take their toll of eggs and young.

When hatched the chicks, covered with cryptically striped down, are active and feeding themselves within hours. This, together with the protection afforded by the attendant male, enables them rapidly to become adept at survival, therefore making it harder for any predator, be it animal or bird, to locate them. They stay with their father for up to 6 months, by which time they begin to grow their adult plumage and are about three quarters grown. It takes about 12 months for an Emu to become full grown, by which time it can weigh up to 105 lb.(45 kg.). Sexual maturity is reached in two years.

KIWIS

Order: *Apterygiformes*
Family:*Apterygidae*
the genus *Apteryx* contains three species.

When Man arrived in New Zealand from Polynesia about 1000 years ago, he found an archipelago where mammals were unknown. Extraordinary plants such as the tree ferns grew and the dominant animals were birds. Without natural enemies many had forsaken the power of flight or could only fly weakly and most had no natural fear. Mammals came with Man in the form of cats and dogs together with livestock such as pigs, and inevitably, rats arrived as well. The birds fell easy prey to cats and dogs, whilst the rats and the omnivorous pig took their toll of nests, eggs and youngsters. The native bird species in New Zealand are highly specialised, having evolved

corner of the North Island. The Great Spotted Kiwi is confined to the South Island and in particular to the areas west of the Southern Alps, where recent studies have shown it to be more plentiful than was previously thought. Because of their secretive and nocturnal habits, there is still much to be learned about Kiwis, especially relating to present distribution.

Along with similar flightless birds the male kiwi incubates the eggs and cares for the young. Of all the world's species of birds it is the Little Spotted Kiwi which produces the largest egg in relation to its body weight. The egg weighs 11oz. (310 gm.), which is about 25% of the weight of the female! An ostrich egg from East Africa was found to weigh 4.35 lb. (1.974 kg.), which is 6.35 times heavier than the kiwi eggs, but then an adult Ostrich *Struthio camelus* can be as much as 130 times heavier than a kiwi! Needless to say, an egg of this size takes a long time to hatch and in the case of the kiwi this is up to 12 weeks! Young kiwis are active on hatching and are already fully feathered, however they are not likely to become sexually mature until they are at least two years old.

A male Highland Tinamou photographed in its nest on the forest floor of the Monteverde Cloud Forest, Costa Rica. Again the usual parental roles are reversed: the male incubates the beautiful blue-green eggs and rears the chicks, which leave the nest only one or two days after hatching. When danger threatens they crouch amongst the leaf litter for concealment.

in the unique flora of the islands. When Man brought about habitat changes many species were unable to adapt to the new environment. Such changes to a world where birds were so confiding and vulnerable had a devastating effect on the indigenous population.

Largest of these were the ostrich-like Moas *Anomalopterygidae* and by the time European settlers arrived in the 18th. century several species were already extinct or became so soon after. Nowadays, the moas' nearest surviving relatives are the three species of kiwi.

Kiwis display characteristics found in no other species of living bird. They are nocturnal and about the size of a barnyard fowl with very small eyes, which are unusual as most nocturnal birds have larger than average eyes. However, their poor eyesight is compensated by other effective detection organs. Near the tip of the bill are sensitive nostrils and they have large ears, although these are concealed by bristle-like feathers around the base of the bill. For a bird with no natural enemies this was all that was needed to guide it through the native forests in search of its food, which mainly consists of earth worms, insects and fruit.

Of the three species the Brown Kiwi *Apteryx australis* formerly occurred widely on both the North and South Islands, but is now confined to the remote areas. The Little Spotted Kiwi *A. owenii*, which had a similar distribution, now has a range slightly more extensive than the Great Spotted Kiwi *A. haastii*. In 1913 the Little Spotted Kiwi was successfully introduced to Kapiti Island off the south-west

TINAMOUS

Order: *Tinamiformes*
Family: *Tinamidae*
nine genera containing 46 species.

Tinamous are a primitive family of South American birds found from southern Mexico to Argentina. They occur in a range of habitats from forests to grasslands.

They are elusive birds, more often heard than seen. Tropical rain forests at dusk echo with the haunting whistles of the Great Tinamou *Tinamus major*. Superficially the family resembles small to medium sized game birds, but in spite of being able to fly they are very distantly related to Rheas. Being very weak fliers, they have little control when airborne, so consequently fatal collisions with branches and other obstacles occur. Tinamous' running ability is not much better, for when chased they have poor stamina and frequently trip over in their haste. The secret of survival is concealment, for the camouflaged plumage of a hidden Tinamou is its best protection. On sensing a predator, the bird crouches amongst the surrounding vegetation and only springs from cover at the last moment when discovered. Sudden surprise is sufficient to secure the bird's escape.

Tinamous are mainly vegetarian, searching for food on the ground, but as with many other birds they will eat insects and small vertebrates, given the opportunity.

The domestic arrangements of tinamous might have shocked people in the 19th. century, but perhaps not nowadays. The precise behaviour patterns vary from species to species and sometimes within a single species. In some territories a number of females might lay in the same nest having been mated by the territorial male, and other females will lay in a number of nests in the territories of several different males! The clutch varies between 1-12 eggs, but the nests with the largest numbers have probably involved the labours of more than one female. There is much still to be learned about the breeding biology of tinamous, but in most species the male incubates the eggs and cares for the young when hatched. The eggs are amongst the most beautiful laid by any bird. Some incubating males are so confiding that it is possible to lift them from the nest. Incubation lasts 19-20days and after hatching the young stay with the male for several weeks. The male Tataupa Tinamou *Crypturellus tataupa* feigns injury to lead a predator away from the nest. Other species scratch leaves and other débris over the eggs when they leave to feed.

Some species are very rare and we have little knowledge about their domestic lives or even their specific status. One such species is the Magdalena Tinamou *C. saltuarius*, for it is only known from the type specimen collected from an area of forest in the foothills of the Sierra de Ocaña in Colombia in 1943. Possibly this already rare and local bird has been driven to extinction through the destruction of its habitat. However, recent research suggests that it may be or might have been a subspecies of the Red-legged Tinamou *C. erythropus*. There is still much for scientists to discover.

PENGUINS
Order: *Sphenisciformes*
Family: *Spheniscidae*
six genera containing 18 species.

When the sailors and explorers of the 15th. century ventured from Europe into the southern oceans, they discovered flightless birds that recalled the Great Auk *Alca impennis* of the North Atlantic, which the French called *pingouin*. Not being taxonomists they also called these birds *pingouin* and today we know the family as Penguins.

Penguins are familiar birds, for we can enjoy watching them in the warmth and comfort of our own living rooms through the miracle of television or see them strutting around at a zoo. They look almost comical as they walk in well-regimented lines over the ice, and are so well turned-out, that given a bow-tie they could go anywhere. In reality their life-style and the hardships they have to endure make them amongst the most resilient of birds. The everyday living conditions of some species has caused the death of Great Explorers we look upon as heroes.

Taxonomists disagree over the exact number of species, but the minimum is 16 and the maximum can be 18. Throughout the world there are birds 'split' from closely related species by some experts and 'lumped' by others. In the case of penguins the Royal Penguin *Eudyptes schlegeli*, endemic to the sub-antarctic island of Macquarie, may just be a sub-species or race of Macaroni Penguin *E. chrysolophus*. Likewise the White-flippered Penguin *Eudyptula albosignata* is very closely related to the Little Blue Penguin *E. minor*.

To many people it is the lordly Emperor Penguin *Aptenodytes forsteri* that typifies a penguin. It is the largest species standing nearly 4 ft. (1.2 m.) tall and it can weigh up to 40 lb. (18 kg.) in peak condition.

During the brief austral summer Emperor Penguins live in the ocean around Antarctica feeding on the rich marine life to be found in the cold waters. They eat mainly squid and have been recorded staying below the surface for up to 18 minutes and descending to over 900 ft. (300 m.) in search of prey. The abundant food supply enables these birds to build up the thick layer of blubber necessary to see them through the ordeal of the breeding season during the dark Antarctic winter.

During March and April, as winter sets in and the seas freeze around the coasts of Antarctica, Emperor Penguins begin a long trek south across the ice to their breeding colonies or rookeries, situated on the ice sometimes as far as 60 miles (100 km.) from open water. The rookeries are often close to a cliff that affords some measure of protection from the elements. There is no nest and they do not hold territories like other birds. Pairing and mating throughout the rookery is synchronized, in order that the eggs hatch together and all the females leave for the sea at the same time. The single egg laid on the ice is carefully transferred to the top of the male's feet, where protection is afforded from the severe weather by a fold of feathered lower belly skin. The transfer is not always successful and up to 25% of all eggs can be lost in the process, for in those temperatures an exposed egg will freeze quickly. The male begins a vigil that lasts almost two months.

The nights can be up to 20 hours long, lit by the stars and the dancing curtains of the Southern Aurora, whilst the days are little more than twilight. The male will live off the fat built up in the form of blubber during the summer months at sea. In addition penguins have evolved special feathers, which when described sound like computer jargon – double feathers, high density! Feathers and blubber alone are not sufficient to protect the birds from the winds, blizzards and frosts that

batter the rookeries during the winter. The lack of competition for breeding territories is an asset to the Emperors for it enables the males to huddle together for warmth. With up to 10 birds per square metre the communal central heating thus generated can save up to 50% of body heat!

On returning to the sea the females will not have eaten for up to two months and will have also survived on the blubber stored earlier in the summer. Here the synchronization at the breeding colony plays a significant part in their survival, for off-shore Killer Whales *Orcinus orca* and Leopard Seals *Hydrurga leptonyx* lie in wait. If the females reach the sea individually they make easy pickings for the predators, but by arriving in groups many survive to replenish reserves and collect food.

After six weeks incubation on the feet of the male the eggs hatch during August. Synchronization plays a part once more for hatching occurs shortly before the females return from the sea. The male provides the chick with its first meal in the form of a regurgitated special protein-rich crop-milk. It will sustain the chick for the day or so before the female arrives. The adults reunite with their partners using calls learned during courtship months earlier. Location calls will be an important aspect in the survival of the growing chick over the following weeks. After the chick has been transferred to the feet of the female the male treks back to the sea to end his four month fast.

By September the days are getting longer and are slowly becoming warmer. Along the coast the sea-ice begins to break up, so that as the chicks grow and demand more food the

Above: a group of Adelie Penguins comes ashore, returning to the colony in their Antarctic home. Above left: an adult Chinstrap Penguin attends its down-covered, three-quarters grown youngster. Far left: a Little Blue Penguin at Jervis Bay, Australia, shedding its down to reveal its first waterproof plumage. Left: an adult Macaroni Penguin displays the long, yellow head plumes after which the species is named.

journeys made by the parents to the sea become shorter and more frequent. At about six weeks the young penguins leave the warmth and protection of their mothers' skin-flap to face the bitter cold outside. Temperatures can still drop to -30°C and the frequent blizzards kill those chicks that become lost or are under-nourished. At this age the young birds form crèches, mimicking the huddles that will ensure the survival of their offspring in years to come.

Spring arrives in October in the Antarctic increasing the rate of the break up of the sea-ice. In November the adult Emperors return to the sea to prepare themselves for the next breeding season, whilst the juveniles begin their first moult. Living off fat reserves, built up over the last few weeks with their parents, they shed the down of youth in exchange for

antarctica Penguins. After the Emperor and King, these black and white penguins are the largest and breed exclusively in Antarctica and the surrounding sub-antarctic islands. Standing at 30in. (75cm.) tall, they all weigh about 9lb. (4kg.) or more when in peak condition at the start of the breeding season. Breeding begins in September and October in the rookeries, where all three species usually lay two eggs in rudimentary nests. Incubation lasts 33 days for the Gentoo and 36 days for the other two species. The young Adelie and Gentoo Penguins form crèches as they grow older, but the juvenile Chinstrap stays within the territory declared by its parents.

In and around the rookeries the main threat to eggs and young, apart from the weather, comes mainly from skuas *Catharacta spp.* and sheathbills *Chionis spp.* At sea the ever

Facing page top: two Adelie Penguins approach the camera with curiosity as they come ashore in Antarctica. Adelie Penguins, the most abundant of the penguin species, run the gauntlet of predatory Killer Whales and Leopard Seals whenever they return to the sea from their breeding colonies.

their first feathered plumage. Waterproof and independent they take to the sea for the first time, not returning for up to five years. By that time they will have become sexually mature and will answer the urge to waddle across the empty, frozen wastes of Antarctica to the breeding colony.

Closely related is the King Penguin *A. patagonica* breeding on sub-Antarctic islands, that ring the continent. It is slightly smaller than the Emperor, but unlike that species, its long breeding season takes place during the summer months and therefore cannot breed every year.

Life for the other penguins is more orthodox, but because of the climate so far south, it is none the less arduous. They look quite different from one another and are spilt into five genera or sub-families by taxonomists. For instance, those with yellow ear-tufts are placed in the genus *Eudyptes*, whilst the smaller black and white penguins belong to the *Spheniscus* genus.

The three species that make up the genus *Pygoscelis* are the Adelie *P. adeliae*, Gentoo *P. papua* and Chinstrap *P.*

present Leopard Seal waits off-shore.

Slightly smaller than the *Pygoscelis* genus are the six species of *Eudyptes* penguins, characterised by their yellow ear-tufts. Most species occur in that area of the Southern Ocean encompassing the south of New Zealand, Macquarie Is, to the Antarctic. However, the Macaroni and Rockhopper *E. chrysocome* both breed round as far as the Falklands, whilst the range of the Rockhopper extends north to Tristan da Cunha and Gough Islands. Most of this group also lay two eggs except for the Macaroni, which lays three. Unlike those species discussed so far, the Fiordland Crested *E. pachyrhynchus* nests in caves and under tree roots in the forests that grow along the coasts of the South Island of New Zealand. The species with the most restricted distribution is the Royal Penguin found only on Macquarie Island lying between New Zealand and Antarctica.

The Yellow-eyed Penguin *Megadyptes antipodes* is also endemic to the New Zealand area and is no longer as widespread as formerly due to exploitation by man. It is about the same

Above: with their backs to the wind, catching the evening sun, two Emperor Penguins pass the time whilst their mates return to the sea for fish. After hatching, the Emperor chick is fed a special crop-milk produced by the male.

coasts of South Africa, particularly where the cold Benguela Current flows up the west coast. The braying call has given the bird its name and, where common, it is an important guano producing species. In natural conditions Jackass Penguins breed in burrows excavated in sand or in crevices, although around a construction site by the harbour at Lambert's Bay, Cape Province, birds also nest in discarded pipes! Being a bird of inshore waters, it rarely strays more that a few miles from the coast. This makes it particularly vulnerable along such a busy maritime highway as the route around the Cape of Good Hope. Accidents happen and willing helpers are always on hand to rescue those birds contaminated by oil – sadly not all are in time. Across the Atlantic Ocean, the Jackass is replaced by the Magellanic *S.magellanicus* on the Falkland Islands and on the Argentine coast from 41° S to Cape Horn. North up the west coast from Chile to Peru, the Peruvian Penguin *S. humboldti*, is a very important guano producer on off-shore islands. It occurs along the Humboldt Current and during the *El Niño* years, when the current leaves the coastline, the population of penguins and the other 'guano' birds fails. The remaining species is the smaller Galapagos Penguin *S. mendiculus*, which lives on the Galapagos Islands that straddle the Equator. Only the cold and nutrient rich waters of the Humboldt, sweeping north from much farther south, make it possible for a penguin to survive at such latitudes. It is the rarest of penguins, with a population of only a few thousand birds.

Left: a Common Loon, with a ruby-red eye and immaculate breeding plumage, utters its lonely and haunting call from a remote lake in the northern United States. Undisturbed waters are essential for the breeding success of this species.

size as an Adelie and has rather more yellow on the head than those of the *Eudyptes* genus. Two eggs are laid in the shelter of bushes and forest as much as half a mile (0.8km.) inland. Incubation lasts 40-50 days and the chicks fledge after a further 110-115 days.

The Little Blue and the White-flippered Penguins are the sole members of the genus *Eudyptula*, and as mentioned earlier, may be just one species. The Little Blue occurs in Tasmania, along the southern coast of Australia and in parts of New Zealand, where it overlaps with the White-flippered along the coasts of the South Island. Birds return to the breeding colonies at dusk and in places have become tourist attractions. Two eggs are laid and often both chicks reared. Incubation lasts about 39days with fledging taking place some 55-58 days later.

The final genus *Spheniscus*, comprises four species of black and white penguins that range from South Africa, around South America, north to the Galapagos Islands. The Jackass Penguin *S. demersus* occurs in the seas around the

LOONS or DIVERS
Order: *Gaviiformes*
Family: *Gaviidae*
the genus *Gavia* contains 5 species.

One of the loneliest and most haunting sounds in the Natural World is the wailing cry of the Common Loon *Gavia immer*. It is a call most often heard whilst the birds are on their breeding lakes. During the spring migration period birds will sometimes start to display to one another en route on quiet lakes or on the sea, such as the sea lochs along the west coast of Scotland, where birds breeding in Iceland stop-over during their journey north. Sheer magic!

Loons, or Divers as they are known in Europe, are highly adapted fish-eating birds breeding around oxygen-rich lakes in the higher latitudes of the northern hemisphere. Unlike the

auks *Alcidae* they do not use their wings to 'fly' through the water, but with powerful legs set well back along the body they pursue their prey below the surface of the water. On diving, loons are usually submerged for under 60 seconds during which time the bird usually descends to 10-30ft. (3-10m.). In exceptional cases birds have been discovered trapped in fishing nets set at 230ft. (70 m.) below the surface.

During the fall all species assume a dull grey and white non-breeding plumage and migrate south. Common Loons travel as far south as Florida and Mexico; and in the eastern Atlantic they reach the Channel coasts of Britain and mainland Europe, although in severe winters they may spread farther afield.

There are four or five species of loon *Gaviidae*, the largest being the closely related Common Loon, called the Great Northern Diver in Europe, and the Yellow-billed Loon or White-billed Diver *G. adamsii*. Both species occur around the Arctic Ocean, although most Common Loons breed mainly in North America. It is one of the few Nearctic species with a foot-hold in Europe, where up to some 300 pairs may breed

in Iceland. Each year some birds summer south of the normal breeding range and occasionally this results in breeding, such as in Scotland in 1970. In North America, Common Loons breed throughout most of Canada and as far south as New York State, and occasionally down to Jackson Lake in the Grand Teton National Park, Wyoming.

The similar Yellow-billed Loon breeds on freshwater lakes north of the tree-line in the tundra along the Arctic coast west of Hudson Bay in Canada to northern Europe, where small numbers breed in Arctic Norway. The species does not winter as far south as the Common Loon. Those breeding in North America winter along the coasts of British Columbia and south-eastern Alaska. With a bill recalling half a banana, Yellow-bills always attract the interest of birders wherever they turn up unexpectedly.

The two or three remaining species are Arctic (or Black-throated Diver in Europe) *G. arctica*, Pacific *G. pacifica* and Red-throated *G. stellata*. The Arctic and Pacific Loons are very closely related and could possibly be one species. The Arctic Loon breeds across northern Europe and Siberia, being

The Little Grebe, or Dabchick, is a widespread species that breeds on quiet ponds and lakes throughout much of sub-Saharan Africa and the temperate Old World. Its floating nest, made of aquatic vegetation and secured to a reed, rises and falls with the water levels.

During the breeding season loons suffer disturbance from fishermen walking around the edges of lakes and from boats used on an ever increasing number of remote waters. However some of the most serious threats to loons comes from pollution. Many former breeding lakes in northern Europe and in the north-eastern United States are now silent because Acid Rain has reduced the oxygen in the water and killed the fish on which the loons were dependent. Loons are at the top of their food chain, so that contaminated fish from a polluted environment in wintering grounds, close to industrial sites, can cause a build up of chemicals in the body tissues. Another serious threat to loons in coastal waters are oil slicks, all too often caused by tanker crews illegally washing out their vessels' tanks at sea, or from such dreadful accidents as the grounding of the *Exxon Valdez* off Alaska in March 1989.

GREBES

Order: *Podicipediformes*
Family: *Podicipedida*
five genera containing 21 species.

If the haunting cries of the Common Loon *Gavia immer* stir the emotions, then the sight of a pair of courting Western Grebes *Aechmophorus occidentalis* engaged in their pre-nuptial display on a still lake in spring must be ballet.

The 21 species of grebe are divided between five genera which are scattered across all the continents and hemispheres except for Antarctica. The family evolved in the New World, where of the fifteen species present, twelve are endemic. The other three-Eared *Podiceps nigricollis* (called Black-necked Grebe in Europe), Horned *P. auritus* (Slavonian in Europe) and Red-necked *P. grisegena* Grebes are of Holarctic distribution. Grebes range in size from the Least Grebe *P. dominicus* 8 in. (20 cm.) of Central and South America to the Great Crested Grebe *P. cristatus* 19 in.(48 cm.) of Eurasia, Africa and Australasia.

Like loons *Gaviidae*, grebes are specialised fish-eating predators, sharing the same streamlined appearance with legs placed at the rear of the body, making them ungainly on land. Leading a similar life-style, they also face the same environmental problems of pollution and disturbance. They are more widespread than loons, being birds of marshes, lakes, ponds and quiet rivers.

Amongst the most colourful species are those that belong to the genus Podiceps. Particularly striking are Horned Grebes, which have wonderful golden tufts to the sides of the head during the breeding season. After breeding most species moult into a dull plumage for the winter months.

Grebes have thickly-feathered plumage and in Britain and elsewhere in the mid-19th. century the skins of Great Crested Grebes were in great demand by the millinery trade for fashionable ladies' stoles and muffs. Known as 'Grebe Fur', initially skins were imported into Britain from Europe, but attention soon turned to the native population, which was decimated to such an extent that by 1860 it stood at just 42 pairs. Conservation seems to be one of the 'buzz' words of the late 20th. century, but in 1869 legal protection covering seabirds and grebes was passed by the British Parliament. Subsequently the population slowly increased and a survey in 1965 showed that the population had risen to over 4000 birds. An important aspect has been the spread of abandoned gravel pits in the southern and midland counties of England over the last fifty years. Many pits were allowed to fill with water after the gravel had been extracted for building and other purposes, and became colonised by many forms of wildlife, resulting in ideal breeding sites for grebes and other water birds.

Although some species are resident, in the Northern Hemisphere a number move south or to larger areas of water to avoid the winter freeze. Generally Grebes only have cause to fly when migrating, for when threatened they choose to dive as the main means of escape.

The need to fly is so remote that on isolated lakes in South America some species have become flightless, or nearly so. The Short-winged Grebe *Rollandia micropterum* from Lake Titicaca in Bolivia is flightless, whilst the Atitlan *Podilymbus gigas* and the Junin Grebes *Podiceps taczanowskii*, have not been seen to fly! These two birds occur on Lake Atitlan,

replaced by the Pacific Loon in North America. Both species breed around larger and deeper lakes than the more slightly built Red-throated Loon, often choosing to nest on islets in the lake.

The Red-throated Loon is a bird of smaller lakes, often flying some miles to fish in larger lakes or the sea. Being so well adapted for swimming, Red-throats and the other species of loon are very clumsy on land, so the nest of vegetable matter is built very close to the water's edge. This enables the incubating bird to slip unobtrusively into the water when disturbed. Unfortunately heavy rain in late spring can raise water levels dramatically, resulting in the flooding of nests.

All species of loon usually lay a clutch of two eggs, which may take from 24-30 days to hatch depending on the species. The chicks, covered in a thick black down, can swim and dive soon after hatching. They fledge after 4-6 weeks, again depending on the species, and most youngsters stay with their parents until after the migration south to the winter quarters. Two to three years pass before the offspring are old enough to breed.

Guatemala and on Lake Junin, Peru respectively. The future of these species is precarious, especially the Junin Grebe, currently threatened by pollution from a nearby copper mine. In 1938 the bird was abundant on the lake, but by 1978 the population had crashed to only 300 individuals. Attempts are being undertaken to clean the lake and to translocate grebes to a neighbouring and uncontaminated water. It is possible that another South American grebe is already extinct. The Colombian Grebe *Podiceps andinus*, described as abundant on Lake Tota in the Colombian Andes, in the 1940s, was down to only 300 by 1968 and in 1977 only two or three birds could be found. It is closely related to the more widespread Eared Grebe and considered by some authorities to be a sub-species or race.

There are still secrets hidden in remote parts of South America, for as recently as 1974 a new grebe was discovered on a lake in southern Argentina. The Hooded Grebe *P. gallardoi*, initially found on Laguna Las Escarchadas, has a more extensive range than some of the other grebes of the region. The whole population leaves before the ice arrives, but where do they go? No one knows!

In 1983, the American Ornithologists' Union, in the United States, decided that the form of Western Grebe, with white extending above the eye and known for some time as 'Clark's Grebe' was a full species in its own right *A. clarkii*. It closely resembles its relative, but in addition to the extra white of the head it utters a single call and not the double note of the Western. Careful searching through non-breeding Westerns, during a trip I made with my colleague Lawrence Holloway in the summer of 1989 to Utah and Wyoming, produced a number of Clark's Grebes on several lakes including Jackson Lake in the Grand Teton National Park.

Grebes usually choose the seclusion of reed-beds and waterside vegetation amongst which to nest, although some species such as the Little Grebe *Tachybaptus ruficollis* will nest in the open, concealed among floating water-lily *Nymphaeaceae* leaves. All species construct nests of vegetable matter, secured to growing plants. Being floating structures they are able to rise and fall with water levels, thus usually avoiding the problems of flooding faced by Loons. Two to six whitish eggs are laid, but these become stained by the nesting material. When the incubating bird leaves the nest unattended it covers the eggs with nest debris to conceal them from predators. Incubation is shared equally by both parents and hatching takes place 3-4 weeks after the laying of the first or second eggs. The chicks are covered with a brown and white striped down and although they are active soon after hatching, they are dependent on their parents for protection and warmth. Often they can be seen nestling into the feathers on the backs of the adults. The brood, split between the pair, stay as a loose family group until after the youngsters have fledged. Small

Clark's Grebe (top) shows more extensive white on its head than the Western Grebe. The Australasian Grebe (above left) is a close relative of the Little Grebe. Above: a Wandering Albatross chick sits on its earthen nest.

fry are caught by the parents for the chicks, who beg vigorously to be fed. The size of the prey increases as the youngsters grow. Fledging varies from species to species and lasts for up to 10-12 weeks in the case of the Great Crested Grebe.

ALBATROSSES
Order: *Procellariiformes*
Family: *Diomedeidae*
two genera containing 12 species.

Albatrosses are the great wanderers of the bird world for those species that breed on the sub-antarctic islands, spend their adolescent years circumnavigating the globe around the Roaring Forties. Their flight is effortless; with long narrow wings giving a high aspect ratio, they are masters of their environment. Such aerodynamics, enable them to glide with only the occasional wing beat for days, and hundreds if not

Phoebetria albatrosses. In November the males are the first back at the colony, ready to greet the females with an elaborate display of spreading wings and bill snapping. Albatrosses are usually faithful to a partner until one of the pair dies. Separation only occurs if a pairing has been fruitless over several seasons.

The nest of mud and turf is situated in an exposed position to facilitate take-offs and landings, and after the pair-bond has been reaffirmed, the birds repair the remains of the old nest from their previous breeding season. By the end of December a single egg is laid and the incubation period, shared by both parents, lasts for about 70 days. Clad in a coat of white down the chick grows quickly on a rich supply of regurgitated marine animals, mainly squid, collected by the adults at sea. The young birds are brooded for about the first 35 days, by which time the white coat is replaced by a more subdued grey down. As winter approaches, the chick is large enough to be left alone as both parents collect food at sea. At this age predatory attacks by skuas *Catharacta spp.* are not as likely as they would have been a few weeks earlier.

By the beginning of July the visits of parents become less

Below: master of the air, an adult Wandering Albatross glides effortlessly on outstretched wings. This bird, with its white body plumage, would have started life on a bleak, windswept slope on a remote island.

thousands of miles at a time. Eight of the twelve species that make up the genus *Diomedea* occur in the Southern Hemisphere. The four remaining species inhabit the Pacific Ocean. Three species occur north of the Equator and the fourth, the Waved Albatross *D. irrorata*, breeds on the Galapagos Islands straddling the Equator some 595 miles (960 km.) west of Ecuador. Recently a small population was discovered breeding on the Las Platas Islands off the coast of Ecuador. The remaining two species belong to the genus *Phoebetria*, and occur in southern latitudes.

There are 12 species divided between two genera; three species stand out as being larger than the rest. These, the 'great' albatrosses, are Wandering *D. exulans*, Amsterdam *D. amsterdamensis* and Royal *D. epomophora*.

The Wandering, with a wing-span recorded up to 11ft.11in. (3.63m.) has the longest span of any living bird. Distribution is circumpolar, breeding on sub-antarctic and temperate islands north to Tristan da Cunha in the South Atlantic. Wandering Albatrosses, like most others are colonial breeders, but because their breeding cycle takes 11 months to complete, they only breed in alternate years. This also applies to the other 'great' albatrosses, the Grey-headed *D. chrysostoma* and the

The Gray-headed Albatross (left) breeds on sub-Antarctic islands, where it raises a single chick. Its down-covered nestling will stimulate its parent to regurgitate food that has been collected at sea, and will fly about 18 weeks after hatching!

21

frequent and the chick, now grossly overweight, sits out the rigours of the austral winter with others in the colony. Once abandoned it will slim as it moults into the chocolate brown plumage of a juvenile Wandering. In November the young birds take to the wing for the first time and leave the colony. They are at the mercy of the relentless winds of the Southern Ocean and will not touch land again for at least five years, when they return for their first breeding season. A month or so after the chicks leave, other adult Wandering Albatrosses return to the deserted colony to start another season.

The plumage of juvenile Wandering Albatrosses is chocolate brown with a white face and white under-wing linings. They become progressively whiter with each moult. In July 1967 an immature bird spent two days standing on a cliff-top at San Ranch, California and is one of the few records from the Northern Hemisphere.

Recently it has been discovered that the albatrosses from Amsterdam Island in the southern Indian Ocean are a separate species. Throughout its life the Amsterdam Albatross, which is probably a smaller bird than the Wandering, retains, with slight differences, a dark plumage that recalls a juvenile Wandering Albatross. It is the rarest albatross in the world with a population of only 30-50 birds and is in need of urgent help on an island over run by feral cattle, cats and rats.

The breeding cycle of the Royal, the remaining 'great' albatross, which breeds on the Otago Peninsula in New Zealand and several off-shore islands, follows that of the Wandering. It is about the same size, but not a record breaker! The adults are like Wandering Albatrosses, which undoubtedly leads to confusion when birds appear beyond their usual areas. Outside the breeding season Royals range from Western Australia to the east coast of South America. On occasions they have been recorded off the south western coast of Africa, where an increasing interest is being shown in pelagic birding trips. Juvenile and immature Royals do not display the dark plumages shown by Wandering Albatrosses at the same age.

Sharing the same latitudes as the Wandering and Royals are five smaller species of *Diomedea* Albatross. These are known as 'Mollymauks' – a name given to them by sailors; indeed the German name for the Black-browed Albatross *D. melanophris* is still *Mollymauk*. The species are similar with white bodies and black backs and wings. The Black-browed is one of the commonest and most widely distributed of the species, and is the species most likely to be encountered in the North Atlantic and that is not very often! In the late 1960s an adult Black-browed took up residence during the breeding season in a colony Northern Gannets *Sula bassana* on the Bass Rock in the Firth of Forth, Scotland. It reappeared for three years and then a few years later the same or a different bird was discovered in another gannetry farther north in the Shetland Isles. That bird was a regular visitor to the northern isles for some 15 years.

Over their native southern oceans the *Mollymauks* fly on slender wings with the same skill and majesty as the 'great' albatrosses and have similar life styles, although most breed annually. They feed on squid and fish and have learnt to exploit ships and can be found in large numbers around the fish-processing vessels that operate in southern waters.

In the Pacific Ocean are the four remaining members of the genus *Diomedea*. The Waved Albatross breeds on the Equator, but the other three, Short-tailed *D. albatrus*, Laysan *D. immutabilis*, and Black-footed *D. nigripes*, all breed in the north Pacific.

The Short-tailed is the World's rarest albatross after the Amsterdam, and restricted to Torishima Island, Japan. In its juvenile plumage it is virtually an all-dark albatross, but becomes progressively paler with age. By the time it is mature it is whiter than all the more southerly species other than the Wandering and Royal Albatrosses. At the beginning of 20th. century it was abundant and bred on a number of islands in the region, but plumage hunters reduced the population to such an extent that only a handful remained and they were restricted to Torishima. In historical times the numbers must have been vast, for bones of Short-tailed Albatrosses have been identified in large numbers in the middens of North American Indians along the Pacific coastline. By 1929 the population on Torishima was 1400 birds and in 1939, when a major volcanic eruption took place, it fell to 30-50 birds! The Second World War inevitably took its toll and when, in 1949, the species failed to appear, it was prematurely declared extinct. As has already been seen with the Wandering Albatross, these long-

lived birds take several years to reach maturity, so that in 1950 a pair of Short-tails were back on Torishima and breeding. The population has increased very slowly and a recent estimate has put the population, including non-breeders, at about 250 birds. During the 1985 breeding season 51 young were reared. The species has been the subject of considerable conservation efforts, for living on an active volcanic island, the future is by no means certain. Attempts to clear the island of cats and rats, which are so often associated with human settlements, are being made, and to help increase the number of available breeding sites turf is being laid on the volcanic slopes.

The Laysan and Black-footed Albatrosses breed more widely and both are to be found breeding in the Hawaiian group. The former is the commonest albatross in the northern Pacific and the latter unusual, because it is the only all-dark *Diomedea* species. In 1986 at least six pairs of Laysan Albatrosses were discovered breeding on Guadalupe Island, only 250 miles (400 km.) west of Mexico, and 2,500 miles (4,023 km.) from Hawaii. The close affinity of these Pacific albatrosses to their relatives in the southern hemisphere is illustrated by the fact that they choose to breed during the northern winter, summertime in the southern latitudes. The remaining albatrosses belong to the genus *Phoebetria* and are the Sooty *P. fusca* and Light-mantled Sooty *P. palpebrata*. Both are all-dark birds and agile, with a wedge-shaped tail and very slender wings giving a wing-span of about 7 feet (213 cm.). The Light-mantled Sooty is perhaps the most beautiful of albatrosses, with dark brown head and wings, a greyer body and an incomplete white eye-ring. Both species are found in southern latitudes, where the Light-mantled

The Black-browed Albatross is named for the dark mark across its eye. It is probably the most abundant and widespread of all the albatross species, breeding on the windy slopes of sub-Antarctic islands and eating a diet of squid and fish.

Sooty has a more southerly and circumpolar distribution. The Sooty is absent from the sector between Australia and South America and breeds farther north to Tristan da Cunha and Gough Island. Unlike the *Diomedea* species neither Sooty breeds colonially, but chooses a wind swept cliff ledge.

Unfortunately, with increased fishing and exploitation in the southern seas, even albatrosses can be found with their plumage stained by oil. Waters circulating around the oceans of the world are contaminating the food chains of these superb birds with chemical pollutants.

and refuse to be found at seal and penguin colonies.

Some species recall mini-albatrosses and, in fact, the Northern and Southern Giant Petrels *Macronectes halli* and *M.giganteus*, 34 in. (87 cm.) long, with a wing-span of 76 in. (195 cm.), are almost as large as the smaller *Diomedea* albatrosses. These two are closely related, and have been considered to be a single species in the past, but an increase in awareness of Antarctic birds has shown that two species are involved. Like the albatrosses, the giant petrels and other members of this family have straight hooked bills, but unlike

PETRELS and SHEARWATERS
Order: *Procellariiformes*
Family: *Procellariidae*
11 genera contain 60 species

Petrels and shearwaters are familiar birds to sailors and to those who cross the seas and the oceans of the world by ship; to birders, sea-watching from an exposed headland, they can present a challenge of identification and the possibility of a rare bird. Whilst some species are largely sedentary, others are great travellers; the Great Shearwater *Puffinus gravis* breeds in the South Atlantic, mainly on the islands of the Tristan da Cunha group, and after the breeding season they head north across the Equator and up the eastern seaboard of the United States, to spend the summer off the Grand Banks of Newfoundland. There they moult and become flightless while the new feathers grow. In the fall they head south again; many, presumably adults returning to breed, return along the same route, but others cross the Atlantic and occur in varying numbers off the west coast of Ireland, around the Hebrides of western Scotland and in the Bay of Biscay.

The family appears to have originated in the Southern Hemisphere, probably sharing a common ancestor with the penguins *Spheniciformes*, and have spread throughout the seas and oceans of the World. They feed on such marine life forms as krill, squid and fish; some scavenge around fishing boats, and others, feed on the various animal and bird remains

Above: a Manx Shearwater returns to its nesting burrow on the Welsh island of Skomer, where some 95,000 pairs breed. In 1973, a single pair was discovered breeding on an island off Massachusetts. This species and the Northern Fulmar (left) are known as 'Tubenoses' for their nasal tubes.

their larger relatives, have developed nasal passages that are placed along the top of the upper mandible; hence the familiar name for petrels and shearwaters – 'tubenoses'.

The Northern and Antarctic Fulmars *Fulmarus glacialis* and *F. glacialoides*, 19 in. (48 cm.) long, are very similar birds, found at opposite ends of the globe. They look gull-like to the uninitiated, with a white body and grey wings. However, they have heavier tubenosed bills and a thick bull-neck, and fly effortlessly on stiff straight wings. The Antarctic bird is paler than the Northern Fulmar, which also has a dark grey colour phase known as the 'blue fulmar'. The ratio of dark phase to pale phase Fulmars increases in the higher latitudes of the Atlantic, but along the Pacific coast of North America the ratio is reversed, with the majority of northern birds being of the pale phase.

The twenty-six species of Gad-fly Petrels *Pterodroma* form the larger genus in the family. These are large petrels, some larger than shearwaters, and can be difficult to identify at sea. They come in various shades of brown and grey, with or without white in their plumage. Most of the grey plumaged species have a black zigzag across the wing, recalling the wing pattern of a juvenile Black-legged Kittiwake *Rissa tridactyla*. They occur mainly in the southern oceans, where some species are common and widespread, and others are restricted to perhaps one island during the breeding season.

competition for nesting sites with the more aggressive White-tailed Tropicbirds *Phaethon lepturus*. Two other gad-fly petrels, the Mascarene and Magenta Petrels *P. aterrima* and *P. magentae*, from the Indian and Pacific Oceans respectively, have re-appeared in recent years for the first time this century.

The Prions *Pachyptila* are a family of small grey and white petrels, with a characteristic black 'W' across the wings, like some of the gad-fly petrels. In former times they were known as 'whale-birds', for they could be found in considerable numbers in the presence of the great leviathans. The species are hard to separate and recent studies have reduced the number of species from six to three.

Another large genus in the family comprises the shearwaters; 19 species belong to the genus *Puffinus* and two more belong to *Calonectris*. Many species have white under-parts and black or brown upper-parts, while some species are completely dark all over, perhaps with a paler under-wing. The family comprises a number of long distance migrants, including the Great Shearwater discussed earlier. Some fascinating experiments involving Manx Shearwaters *Puffinus puffinus*, 13 in. (33 cm.) were carried out from the island of Skokholm off the south-west coast of Wales. Two birds that had been air-freighted and released at Boston, Massachusetts, returned to their nesting burrows 3,500 miles (4,900km.) away, 12.5 and 15 days later. Birds from the British Isles

A flock or 'raft' of Cape Pigeon feed from the surface of the sea. The Cape Pigeon is a distinctive pied Petrel of the Southern oceans. It breeds on sub-Antarctic islands and along the coasts of Antarctica.

During the austral winter they wander the oceans, but in many cases the extent of their travels during the rest of the year is a mystery. Only three species breed in the Northern Hemisphere; the Bonin Petrel *P. hypoleuca*, 12 in. (30 cm.) long, occurs in the north-eastern Pacific and some islands of the Hawaiian group. Sadly, the colony on Midway Island, once the third largest in the World, is in grave danger of extinction following the introduction of rats to the island. The Black-capped Petrel *P. hasitata*, 16 in. (41 cm.) long, was formerly widespread and occurred on several Caribbean islands, but now breeds only in the highlands of Hispaniola. The Bermuda Petrel or Cahow *P cahow*, 15 in. (38 cm.) long, was thought to have become extinct in 1661, but in 1951, some 290 years later, a small breeding colony was discovered on the offshore island of Nonsuch. It had been a plentiful bird in the days of early settlement, but had been over-cropped for food. The threat nowadays does not come from man, but from

migrate to winter in the southern Atlantic off the coasts of South America, and a bird banded at the colony on Skokholm was found as a tide-line corpse in South Australia. Some of the largest concentrations of shearwaters are to be found in south-eastern Australia, where in colonies of the Short-tailed Shearwater or Mutton Birds *P. tenuirostris* 16 in. (41 cm.) long, the chicks or squabs have been harvested for many years. Nowadays regulations control over exploitation.

Petrels and shearwaters are usually social breeding birds, ranging from a number of birds sharing the same breeding ledge, such as the Northern Fulmar, or breeding in colonies of tens of thousands, as with some shearwater species. Some species are diurnal and others are nocturnal, thus avoiding the predatory attentions of gulls *Laridae* and so on. A single egg is laid on a ledge, amongst rocks or in a burrow in the soil. Usually such nesting sites are close to the sea, but on the Isle of Rhum, in Scotland's Inner Hebrides, Manx Shearwaters breed up to 2,600 ft. (790 m.) on a mountain side some 1.8 miles (3 km.) inland. The incubation period can last 2 months and the chick may take from 3-5 months to fledge. From hatching it is covered in a warm coat of down and soon builds up a fat reserve within its body. During the last weeks of fledging the parents abandon their grossly overweight youngster; as it grows its first feathered plumage it embarks on a drastic diet – nil by mouth! By the time it leaves the nesting site it is sleek and looking immaculate. It is September when the young Manx Shearwaters leave their burrows high on the mountains of Rhum. While we lived on Mull, about 30 miles (48 km.) south-east, we waited anxiously on stormy nights for the first young shearwaters to arrive at our home. They would come in boxes of all shapes and sizes, for a first flight for any young bird is an adventure, but when it is into the teeth of an Atlantic gale, the first flight is rather more hazardous than that. Our birds were the lucky ones that arrived unexpectedly in folks' backyards and gardens, attracted by the lights of the town. How many were lost in the heather moorland will never be known. Sometimes the last remnants of down would still be showing on their heads and they would love to crawl up an arm and snuggle into an armpit. We would keep them warm overnight and the following day take them to a quieter part of the island and release them once more to the wild. In a matter of weeks the survivors of the storm would be sailing over the waves, thousands of miles south off the coasts of Brazil or Argentina – quite a baptism!

STORM-PETRELS
Order: *Procellariiformes*
Family: *Oceanitidae*
the eight genera contain 20 species.

The name Petrel is a corruption of St. Peter given by sailors who observed these small seabirds pattering over the surface of the sea with fluttering wings as if they too were walking on water.

Storm-petrels, twenty species placed in eight genera, evolved in the Southern Hemisphere, but are now widely distributed over the oceans of the world, except for the Arctic. They appear to be frail and dainty, but in reality they are tough. They have the same tube-noses as the larger petrels and shearwaters *Procellariidae*, but are finely-built birds. Storm-petrels fall into two groups; the birds of the Northern Hemisphere have longer wings and shorter legs than those of their southern relatives. Thirteen species belong to the genera *Hydrobates*, *Halocyptena* and *Oceanodroma*. The remaining seven species that breed in the Southern Hemisphere, fall into five genera, characterised by their shorter, rounded wings and longer legs. All species are a combination of a black or grey body, with or without a white rump or belly. Some have forked tails and others have regular ones. Storm-petrels range in size from the Least *Halocyptena microsoma*, 5 in. (13 cm.) long, breeding on islands off the coast of Baja California; to the White-throated Storm-petrel *Nesofregetta fuliginosa*, 10 in. (26 cm.), which occurs in the tropical western Pacific Ocean. Some species stay comparatively close to the breeding areas throughout the year, whilst others are great travellers. Wilson's Storm Petrel *Oceanites oceanicus* breeds around the shores of the Antarctic continent and on the sub-antarctic islands in such vast numbers that it is the commonest of seabirds. Some authorities have suggested that it might even be the most abundant of all birds. After the breeding season has ended it heads northwards across the Equator and into the North Pacific and North Atlantic Oceans. In the Atlantic, Wilson's Storm-petrels are more frequent along the American seaboard than across on the European side, where it is only in the late 1980s, when birders have headed out on pelagic trips from Cornwall, that Wilson's Storm-petrels have been seen in any numbers.

Storm-petrels in general breed by the sea in burrows, crevices in rocks and beneath large boulders at the top of beaches, but there is an exception – Hornby's Storm-petrel *O. hornbyi*, thought to breed in the desert along the coasts of northern Chile and southern Peru. As a precaution against predators, such as gulls *Laridae*, storm-petrels return under the cover of darkness as do all the other species, except for the

diurnal Wedge-rumped or Galapagos Storm-petrel *Oceanodroma tethys*.

The nest sites of storm-petrels have a distinctive odour and the churring of incubating birds can be heard by day and night. In western Britain, British and Leach's Storm-petrels *O. leucorhoa* are banded at their breeding colonies by scientists and helpers, who catch them in fine-meshed nets called 'mist-nets', strung between stout poles. The birds are lured by playing tape-recordings of their calls; they are banded, weighed and measured and released into the night. This research has provided information on movements between colonies and longevity that would be unobtainable by any other means. To be at a colony at night is a wonderful experience. In their book *Wild America*, Roger Tory Peterson and James Fisher describe their night on the Coronado Islands, south of San Diego, witnessing the nocturnal arrival of the Black Storm-petrel *O. melania* to their only breeding station in the United States. Storm-petrels lay a single egg, incubated by both parents for almost six weeks. Fledging is also a protracted process lasting for up to two months, by which time the chick has grown fat on a diet that includes fish-oil. Some species abandon the chick at this stage as it moults out of a soft down into its first feathered plumage. Others feed the youngster during this period intermittently until it leaves to find its way in the World.

A Wilson's Storm-Petrel incubates its single egg in the seclusion of a rocky crevice, safe from the attentions of predators such as skuas. Wilson's, together with most other storm-petrels, fly to and from their nests at night.

DIVING-PETRELS
Order: *Procellariiformes*
Family: *Pelecanoididae*
the genus *Pelecanoides* contains four species.

Diving Petrels represent a genus of small Tubenoses found in the Southern Hemisphere. Most species breed on sub-antarctic islands, but one, the Peruvian Diving Petrel *Pelecanoides garnoti*, occurs north along the South American coast to Peru, associated with the cold waters of the Humboldt Current.

All species are very similar, having dark upper and white under-parts. The most distinctive is the Magellanic Diving Petrel *P. magellani*, which has a partial white collar, visible at close range. Diving Petrels are very similar to the auks *Alcidae* of the Northern Hemisphere and resemble the Dovekie or Little Auk *Alle alle* in particular. This is a case of convergent evolution, where two completely unrelated families, occupying the same ecological niche in different parts of the World, are governed by the same natural constraints to evolve similar characteristics. Diving Petrels are small seabirds, 7-10 in. (18-25 cm.) long, with short, stubby wings. They fly with a rapid whirring flight like a Dovekie, but unlike that species, enter and leave the water in flight without any hesitation as they break the surface. It must be quite a sight to see a small bird emerging from a wave in full flight! Once below the surface they fly through the water like an auk, or a penguin *Sphenisciformes*.

Diving Petrels are birds that usually stay close to their breeding areas, remaining in coastal waters throughout the year. It used to be thought that birds could be safely separated on distribution, but recent studies have shown that the Common *P. urinatrix* and the Georgian Diving Petrels *P. georgicus* have breeding ranges that overlap on several widely scattered sub-antarctic islands.

A single egg is laid in a burrow or in a cavity beneath a rock, where the parents share the incubation for 29 or more days, depending on the species. The birds take turns incubating for one to three days at a time and once hatched the chick is brooded for several days before both parents leave to collect food at sea. The chicks are fed a regurgitated mixture of crustaceans caught in the seas nearby. To avoid the predatory attacks of skuas *Catharacta spp.*, the adult diving petrels only come ashore at night to feed their young.

Left: an adult Red-billed Tropic Bird rests on a rock on Hood Island in the Galapagos. This seabird breeds in the tropics from the eastern Pacific to the western Indian Ocean, often choosing a site in a recess or beneath rocks.

The future of most species is reasonably secure, barring a major ecological disaster. In South Georgia the population of the Georgian Diving Petrel has been estimated at two million birds! The most vulnerable species is the Peruvian Diving Petrel, occurring on islands off the coasts of Chile and Peru. Several of the few known breeding colonies are on the *guano* islands, where the species has seriously declined through habitat destruction.

TROPIC BIRDS

Order: *Pelecaniformes*
Family: *Phaethontidae*
the genus *Phaethon* contains three species.

As their name suggests Tropic Birds are birds of tropical seas and islands. One could watch them all day as they cruise in pairs or small groups over their oceanic breeding colonies on islands such as Aride and Cousin in the Seychelles. Pure white with black markings, adult White-tailed Tropic Birds *Phaethon lepturus* look immaculate against a back drop of a rich blue sea or over lush green vegetation with their long elegant tails fluttering behind. In parts of the World with a strong nautical tradition they are called 'Bo'sun Birds' as the shrill call is reminiscent of a bo'sun's whistle.

There are three species, of which the White-tailed Tropic Bird is the most widespread and found in the West Indies, the tropical Atlantic, Indian and south-western Pacific Oceans. The Red-billed *P. aethereus* occurs amongst the Galapagos Islands, the West Indies, the tropical Atlantic and north-western corner of the Indian Ocean. The remaining species is the Red-tailed Tropic Bird *P. rubricauda*, which occurs across the Indian and Pacific Oceans. Outside the breeding season tropic birds wander over wide areas of tropical and sub-tropical oceans, far from land.

They are white seabirds with varying amounts of black on the wings depending on the species. All three have a black mark through the eye and long wispy central tail feathers. The Red-tailed is the whitest species with little black in the plumage, whilst the Red-billed Tropic Bird is the darkest with black primaries and black barring across the back and upper wing coverts. The barring recalls the juvenile plumage of all tropic birds. The White-tailed also has black primaries and a strong black bar on each wing. As expected, the Red-tailed has a red tail, but it is only the elongated central feathers that are coloured. The White-tailed has a yellow or an orange bill, whilst the other two have red bills. Of the three species the Red-billed is the largest with a body length of 18-19.5 in. (46-50 cm.) and a tail that adds an additional 18-22 in. (46-56 cm.)! The Red-tailed has a slightly shorter body, but the tail is a mere 11-14 in. (30-35 cm.) long. The smallest is the White-tailed Tropic Bird, which is 15-16 in. (38-40 cm.) long with a tail of a further 13-15 in. (33-40 cm.).

Above: in flight over the Galapagos Islands, the long tail of an adult Red-billed Tropic Bird flutters behind. This is the largest member of the family and, when fully developed, the tail can exceed the body length.

The breeding cycle of tropic birds is complex. The Red-tailed and Red-billed species breed annually and the White-tailed breeds every six to nine months. At some sites all birds breed at the same time and at others, involving the same species, breeding can take place throughout the year. They nest in holes beneath rocks, in cavities amongst rocks, and amongst roots of trees or beneath fallen trees. They usually nest in loose colonies, on islands which do not have introduced predators such as rats or at inaccessible sites on those that do. It is possible that colonial breeding is imposed on the birds by a concentration of suitable breeding sites in a limited area. Tropic Birds are monogamous and a successful pair will breed together for many seasons. Before breeding they engage in superb courtship flights in unison, with their long tails blown by the breeze. There is no proper nest, just a shallow scrape, sometimes with a simple lining, beneath a boulder or tree. A single egg is laid and is incubated by both birds. Incubation lasts 42-44 days for the Red-billed and Red-tailed Tropic Birds and slightly less for the White-tailed. The young birds stay in the nest until they fledge. Initially they are covered with a fine white and black down that has a spikey appearance, making them look like 'punks'! The chick is only a matter of days old when it is left unattended by the adults, who return to sea to collect food and at times only return every two or three days. This results in a protracted fledging period that may last for 11 weeks or more, in spite of the first feathers appearing 10 days or so after hatching. They are fed a regurgitated mixture of marine animals, often flying fish and squid, which the parents have caught by diving into the sea from the air.

The chick is most vulnerable when left alone, perhaps not so much from predators, but from other tropic birds attempting to usurp the rightful occupants from the site.

It will leave the colony to fend for itself as it wanders the ocean alone. Initially it lacks the long tail and coloured bill, but these will appear, together with the adult plumage, over the three or four years before it returns to the colony. It will start breeding after five years.

PELICANS
Order: *Pelecaniformes*
Family: *Pelecanidae*
the genus *Pelecanus* contains
seven or eight species.

The seven or eight species of pelican are found in warm temperate and tropical regions throughout the World, although the least exploited faunal region is the Palearctic. The uncertainty over the number of species arises over the uncertainty of the status of the Peruvian Pelican *Pelecanus thagus*. It is considerably larger than the more familiar Brown Pelican *P. occidentalis* and given specific status by some

Below: on an East African alkaline lake shared with Greater and Lesser Flamingos, Eastern White Pelicans preen themselves – the maintenance of clean feathers is of the utmost importance for all birds. Bottom: in the Everglades, Florida, a Brown Pelican delicately preens wing feathers with its apparently unsuitable bill.

authorities. Pelicans require a reliable and regular supply of fish and in areas such as Africa they will wander to new feeding areas when existing wetlands become unsuitable in the dry season.

Pelicans can be split into two groups within the genus. One contains the four large white species, namely the American White *Pelecanus erythrorhynchos*, the Eastern White *P. onocrotalus*, the Dalmatian *P. crispus* and the Australian Pelican *P. conspicillatus*. They are social birds that feed in groups and nest in large colonies on the ground. The second group consists of the smaller Pink-backed *P. rufescens*, the Spot-billed or Grey *P. philippensis* and finally the Brown Pelican and its very close relative – the Peruvian Pelican.

All species occur on either fresh or brackish water in warm climates, although the American White occurs as far north as Canada during the breeding season; it migrates south to the Gulf of Mexico, the Caribbean and Central America in the Fall. The Eastern White Pelican is also migratory in part of its range, with birds from south-eastern Europe migrating through the Middle East to winter in Egypt and beyond. This species is equally at home on a lake in Greece; on one of the alkaline lakes of Africa's Great Rift Valley, such as Lake Nakuru in Kenya; or along the wind swept Skeleton Coast of Namibia in southern Africa. Only the Brown and its very close relative, the Peruvian Pelican, are essentially coastal birds. In South America the Peruvian Pelican occurs in very large numbers along the coasts of Peru and northern Chile, associated with the cold Humboldt Current. Together with boobies *Sulidae* and cormorants *Phalacrocoracidae*, it is an important *guano* producing species.

Facing page: a Brown Pelican contentedly incubates its eggs. Left: Brown Pelicans nest amongst mangroves in western Florida. When not fishing, Brown Pelicans spend much of their time preening.

The plumage of the four species of White Pelican is similar, although the amount of black on the wings varies. On the American and Eastern White Pelicans it is confined to the primary and secondary flight feathers. The Dalmatian Pelican has a slight greyish cast to the colour of the body plumage and shows less black on the under-wing. The Australian Pelican, which also has a black tail, is the darkest; the whole wing is black except for an area of white between the wing coverts and fore-wing. The Spot-billed and Pink-backed Pelicans are both decidedly grey birds and an adult Pink-backed shows a soft pink back in breeding plumage.

The plumages of the Brown and Peruvian Pelicans are quite unlike any of the other species; each having a dark body and brown neck with a yellow crown in breeding plumage.

Pelicans are fish-eating birds, and prey is often caught by a group of White Pelicans herding a shoal of fish into shallower water and then using their huge bills to catch the fish. Once it has caught a fish inside the bill, the Pelican raises the bill upwards and swallows. The exception to this feeding method is the Brown Pelican that dives from the air to catch fish below the surface of the sea. Flocks involving dozens, if not hundreds of birds, congregate over a large shoal of fish. Birds circle with lazy wing beats and on sighting a fish the Pelican closes its wings and hurtles down towards the prey. To increase streamlining and reduce impact on hitting the water, wings are thrust back along the body at the last moment before entering the sea.

The White Pelican species breed in large colonies in areas that are usually free from predators. The greatest threat come from such predators such as Coyotes *Canis latrans* in North America and Black-backed *C.mesomelas* and Side-striped Jackals *C.adustus* in Africa. Usually Pelicans are to be found

Above left: in a colony of Peruvian Pelicans, a naked chick feeds on a meal of digested fish from its parent. Above: a Spot-billed Pelican comes into land using its huge webbed feet and spread tail as airbrakes.

nesting on islands in the middle of large lakes, but in the dry-season water levels can become low enough for these animals to cross in safety to raid the colonies. In some areas, such as the Danube Delta in Eastern Europe, Eastern White Pelicans nest in reed beds, where substantial nests are constructed by the female with material carried in by the male. Two eggs are usually laid and incubation, shared by the pair, lasts 28 – 37 days, depending on the species. The young are naked for the first two weeks before becoming covered with black down. They are fed a mixture of digested fish, which they retrieve by reaching down into the throats of their parents! They are able to fly in 10 weeks, after which time they become independent. The smaller Pink-backed and Spot-billed Pelicans, nest colonially in trees and the Brown Pelican usually lays three eggs in a platform nest often built in mangroves. The Peruvian Pelicans nest in colonies, scraping a shallow depression in the guano built up on the rocks beneath them during previous breeding seasons.

thrust back along the body. There have been sad reports of Northern Gannets that have died from impaling themselves on planks of driftwood, mistaken for fish! Adult Gannets are gleaming white, with a yellowish-cream crown and black feathers on the wings. On the Northern Gannet this is confined to the outer half of the wing between the carpal joint and the wing tip. On the Cape Gannet the secondaries are also black, as is the tail. The Australasian Gannet is similar except that the black on the tail is reduced to some of the central feathers. All three species have a black stripe leading down on to the throat from the base of the lower mandible; this is shortest on the Northern and longest on the Cape Gannet. Juvenile gannets of all species are dark brown and black, with paler bellies and white speckling on the wings and back. As they grow older they become progressively whiter, so that after about four years they appear in their immaculate adult plumage.

Northern Gannets breed in colonies in the North Atlantic, the Cape Gannet around the coasts of South Africa and

GANNETS and BOOBIES

Order:*Pelecaniformes*
Family: *Sulidae*
the genus *Sula* contains nine species

There can be few more spectacular sights than Gannets or Boobies diving into a shoal of fish. They belong to a genus whose members inhabit the tropical and temperate seas and oceans of the World, except for the north Pacific.

The nine species fall into two groups – three species of Gannet and six of Booby. An increasing number of authorities take the classification of these birds a stage further by placing the Gannets in the genus *Morus*, whilst retaining the Boobies in the genus *Sula*.

The Gannets are the larger members of the genus, the three species being the Northern Gannet *Sula bassana*, the Cape Gannet *S. capensis* and the Australasian Gannet *S.serrator*. All three species are so closely related that some authorities consider them to be conspecific. However, they are full species in their own right, forming a group known as a *superspecies*. They are large birds with solid, yet streamlined bodies, wedge-shaped tails and long wings, giving a span of some 6 ft. (1.8 m).They dive for fish, plummeting down on closed wings from a height of up to 140 ft. (42 m.). At the last minute, to reduce impact on hitting the water, the wings are

Namibia, and the Australasian species breeds on islands in the Bass Strait and around Tasmania in Australia. It also breeds on islands around New Zealand, which also boasts a well-known colony at Cape Kidnappers, south of Napier on the North Island.

An ornithologist, J.H. Gurney, was the first to undertake a complete census of the Northern Gannet, although counts had been made of individual colonies previously. With such a conspicuous seabird, such a census was a practical proposition. Colonies are to be found in Newfoundland and Quebec in Canada, and on the eastern side of the Atlantic around Iceland, the British Isles, the Faroes and Norway. Until and during most of the 19th. century the bulk of the World population of this species bred at colonies along the eastern seaboard of North America. In 1834 100,000 pairs were estimated breeding on Bird Rocks in the Gulf of St. Lawrence, but over the following years the slaughter of this population reduced it to such an extent that by 1889 only 860 pairs remained. The World population dropped to an all-time low of 53,000 pairs in 1894, and of these only 4000 pairs or 7.5% remained in North America. Gurney's 1912 figure was 50,500, revised later upwards to 65,000. Gradually the population recovered, so that by 1939 the total figure was 83,000 pairs, with 16% breeding at the colonies in Canada. Since then the population has soared to about 198,000 estimated during a 1969-71 census, which also showed that the percentage split between North America and Europe had remained unchanged. The human predation at the European colonies

was not as severe as on the other side of the Atlantic, but it still had a detrimental effect on the Gannet population. Seabirds were the main source of protein for the islanders living on Hirta, largest island in the remote St. Kilda group that lies 110 miles (177 km.) west of the Scottish Mainland and 45 miles (72 km.) out into the Atlantic, west of the Outer Hebrides. It was a tough life for the islanders, reaping a harvest of seabirds and eggs, from cliffs and rocks that towered hundreds of feet above the ocean with names such as Stac an Armin and Stac Lee. Sufficient eggs and birds were collected and preserved to feed the islanders through the rigours of a North Atlantic winter. Young Gannets, taken during the annual harvest, were salted down for the winter, but the numbers declined through the 19th. century from 5000 at the beginning, to a mere 300 at its end. The decline almost certainly resulted from over-cropping by the islanders, who not only collected the young birds, but the eggs as well. St. Kilda was evacuated in August 1930 and its inhabitants resettled on the Mainland. Since that time the Gannet population has steadily increased from a figure of 14,750 pairs in 1902 to 52,000 occupied nests counted from aerial photographs in 1969. On a very windy, but sunny day one May I stood on the deck of a fishing boat below the towering cliffs of Stac Lee and gazed up at the Gannets, wheeling like snow flakes high above me; life and men must have been tough in those lonely isles, before the 20th. century caught up with them.

Outside the breeding season gannets disperse from their breeding colonies. The adults tend not to travel as far as the

Above left: Northern Gannets at the famous Bass Rock colony in Scotland. Amongst the birds incubating their eggs, a pair greet one another by bill-knocking. Above: also at Bass Rock, Northern Gannets wheel overhead as an adult returns to its nest site with additional material. The darker-winged birds are nearly adult but too young to breed. Left: a brown-phase adult Red-footed Booby with its down-covered youngster at its nest in a Red Mangrove.

immature birds. Young Northern Gannets disperse southwards, those from the Canadian colonies reaching the Gulf of Mexico, whilst their European counterparts reach West Africa, where they may mingle with immature Cape Gannets which travel north to the Gulf of Guinea. Sometimes birds get muddled and end up in the wrong places, for in 1982 an Australasian Gannet was banded at the Lambert's Bay Cape Gannet colony in South Africa and a Cape Gannet has been resident at Port Phillip Bay, Victoria, Australia. In 1988 a Cape Gannet was seen during a pelagic birding trip off south-west England, but this record has yet to be accepted by the records' committees.

The six species of booby are found mainly in tropical seas, but are not great travellers like the gannets, although they can still appear unexpectedly when driven off course by storms. Adult boobies, with the exception of the Masked Booby *S. dactylatra* and the white phase of the Red-footed Booby *S. sula*, are darker than gannets. The other colour phase of the Red-footed Booby is all brown. The Masked is the largest species, overlapping in size with the Australasian Gannet, but recalling the plumage of a Cape without the yellow-cream head. The Brown Booby *S. leucogaster* is dark brown, contrasting with a white belly and under-wing. The Peruvian *S. variegata* and Abbott's *S. abbotti* Boobies have white bodies and dark wings, although the former has a dark back and less white on the under-wings. The Abbott's Booby has a spotted rump unlike other species. The remaining species is the Blue-footed Booby *S.nebouxii*, similar to the Peruvian, but the head and neck are darkly streaked. Juvenile Boobies are darker than their parents, although the young Abbott's differs by its grey and not yellow bill.

The most widespread species of Booby are the Masked, Red-footed and Brown found throughout the tropics, although the Masked and Red-footed are only vagrants to the west coast of Africa. In the eastern Pacific two other species are found. The Blue-footed Booby occurs south from the Gulf of California to northern Peru and westwards across the Pacific to the Galapagos Islands. Occasionally they are to be found wandering north up the coast of California, but most records from that state are from the inland Salton Sea. Farther south, the Peruvian Booby is an important *guano* producing species occurring along the coasts of southern Peru and Chile. Rarest, with the most restricted range of all is Abbott's Booby, found only on Christmas Island in the north-east Indian Ocean. Formerly it occurred across the Indian Ocean to Rodriguez and the Seychelles. It has a very slow reproduction rate, comparable to some of the albatrosses *Diomedeidae*, for it only breeds in alternate years and takes some five or six years to reach maturity. The population of 2,000 pairs breeds in tall trees in rain forests, but unfortunately the area is being exploited by phosphate mining and although an area covering 30% of the breeding population has been declared a National Park, this may not be sufficient to secure the survival of a viable population.

Gannets and most species of Booby nest on the ground, the exceptions being the Red-footed that nests in shrubs and bushes and Abbott's Booby that nests in tall forest trees. All species, except for Abbott's, are colonial birds, and the nest of seaweed, vegetation and mud is built and often re-used during subsequent breeding seasons. One to four eggs, depending on the species, are laid and incubated for about 44 days by both parents, beneath the broad webs of their feet. At the first signs of chipping as a youngster starts to break out of its shell, the egg is transferred to the top of the feet and there it hatches and the chick brooded for the first two weeks. Both

Left: probably as an indication of imminent departure, an adult Northern Gannet 'sky-points' beside its dark-plumaged youngster at the Bass Rock Colony. Below left: an adult Masked Booby, photographed on Isla Plaza, Galapagos, a tropical relative of the Gannet. Below: on Hood Island, also in the Galapagos, a Blue-footed Booby settles on its nest containing two chicks.

the adults share brooding and collecting food, which the nestling takes directly from its parents' throat. As the result of sibling rivalry only one or two young fledge. Juvenile gannets become independent on fledging after about 15 weeks, but the boobies feed their young for some time afterwards. In the case of Abbott's Booby it can be as long as a year after fledging and this extended breeding cycle explains why they only breed every other year.

CORMORANTS
Order: *Pelecaniformes*
Family: *Phalacrocoracidae*
three genera contain 28 species

Many of the birds used by Man meet a premature death; they are either killed for their meat, for the oil contained in their bodies or for their plumage. Cormorants are amongst the few species that live to tell the tale.

extends much farther south than usual, displacing the nutrient-rich waters of the Humboldt. This natural phenomenon occurs around Christmas time; it is called *El Niño* meaning the 'Christ Child' in Spanish, and spells disaster for those living along the coast. In *El Niño* years there are few plankton in the waters along the coast on which the Anchovetta feed; the fish die in vast numbers and of course so do many of the birds that are dependent on them for their survival. Nature is remarkably resilient when left to its own devices; sooner or later the Humboldt returns to dominate the coastline again, bringing back the life-giving plankton. It is not long before the Anchovetta shoals and the guano birds recover their former numbers.

In China and some other eastern countries, local fishermen still train Great Cormorants *P. carbo*, 35 in. (90 cm.) long, for fishing. Several birds at a time may be deployed around a small dingy, and as soon as a cormorant catches a fish, the bird is hauled aboard. They are prevented from swallowing their prize by a ring placed around the neck; after the daily requirements of the fisherman are satisfied, the ring is removed and the birds allowed to feed themselves.

The family probably evolved in the Southern Hemisphere,

A young Double-crested Cormorant fishes on a pond in Everglades National Park, Florida. A widespread species across North America, it occurs on both salt and fresh water. The adult is black with a greenish sheen to its plumage, has a crest above each eye and an orange gular pouch.

Off the Pacific coast of Peru and Chile, and Namibia's Atlantic coast, cormorants breed in their millions on islets and on artificial platforms, where they deposit vast quantities of excreta. The annual deposit can be as much as 3 in. (8 cm.) and without rain it dries to become one of the richest natural fertilisers, high in nitrogen and phosphate. Known as 'guano', the name given by the Incas, it is extracted from the breeding colonies commercially. One important South American contributor is the Guanay Cormorant *Phalacrocorax bougainvillii*, 30 in. (76 cm.) long; it nests in huge colonies, some estimated to contain over six million nests! The cold Humboldt Current sweeps north up the coasts of Chile and Peru, bringing with it vast quantities of plankton. The plankton supports incredible numbers of a herring-related fish, the Anchovetta *Engraulis ringens*, on which the guano-producing birds and local fishermen depend. Over fishing by man can deplete the fish stocks to the detriment of the 'guano' birds and those extracting the end product. Once every few years, for no apparent reason, impoverished warm equatorial water

where the greatest number of species now occur. They are divided into three genera with the majority, 24 species, being placed in the genus Phalacrocorax; five small species with longer tails and a stubby bill, belong to the Haliëtor genus, whilst the flightless Galapagos Cormorant *Nannopterum harrisi* is the sole member of its genus and endemic to just two islands in the Galapagos group.

Cormorants occur along coasts, rivers and by lakes and wetlands throughout the World, except for the extreme northern and southern latitudes. They are birds of either coastal or freshwater habitats, but few species occur in both. Among the cross-over species are the Double-crested Cormorant *P. auritus*, 29 in. (74 cm.) long, found across North America, and the widespread Great Cormorant. It occurs throughout Europe, Africa, Asia and through Australia to New Zealand. In North America it is confined to the eastern seaboard, where it is increasing in numbers, breeding in north-eastern Canada and wintering south to New Jersey and in smaller numbers, farther south. Cormorants are often scraggy-looking, fish-eating birds belonging to the Order of pelicans and their allies *Pelecaniformes*, and like most other members of the group have all four toes connected by webbing. Their legs are set far back along the body, so that when standing they are upright. Their large feet enable them to swim well beneath the surface of the water in pursuit of fish, squid and crustaceans, their principal food items, but they do not use their wings to 'fly' through the water like penguins *Spheniscidae* and auks *Alcidae*. After spending time in the water fishing, cormorants often stand on rocks with outspread wings, drying their feathers. They have strong hooked bills, with which to hold the fish, and an enlarged throat, although this is of modest proportions, unlike the related pelicans *Pelecanidae*. Most cormorants are black, sometimes with a glossy sheen to the plumage of the adults; many have white under-parts or sometimes just patches somewhere about their person. An exception is the grey and white Red-legged Shag *P. gaimardi*, 30 in. (76 cm.) long. This species, amongst others, has red legs, but the greatest variety in colouration among the species is in the colour of the eye, eye-ring and the bare skin around the base of the bill and

atriceps, and renamed Imperial Shag. The name 'shag' is given to a number of the more slightly built and rangier species. In Africa the race of Great Cormorant has a white throat and breast and is sometimes treated as a full species *P. lucidus*.

Cormorants nest in colonies, sometimes scattered amongst rocks like the Shag; some Double-crested Cormorants, amongst others, nest in trees, whilst the Guanay Cormorant of South America and the Cape Cormorant *P. capensis* of southern Africa, nest in vast colonies on open ground. Cormorants make untidy nests of seaweed, feathers and other débris found along the tide-line, including driftwood, fisherman's rope and netting and even plastic detergent bottles! The female Great Cormorant builds the nest from materials supplied by the male. Other bits and pieces are added throughout the incubation period.

Incubation of the 2-4 eggs lasts about 4 weeks and is usually shared by both parents. The newly hatched chicks are naked, but soon grow a coat of down. They leave the nest after about 28 days, yet may not fledge for another three weeks.

throat; hence the Red-faced Cormorant *P. urile*, 33 in (84 cm.) long, that occurs around the coasts and islands of the North Pacific, from southern Alaska across the Aleutian chain and south to Hokkaido. A few species have crests; one of the most pronounced is the forward-curling crest of the Shag *P. aristotelis*, 25 in. (65 cm.) long, a species found around the coasts of northern and western Europe, throughout the Mediterranean and along the Atlantic coast of North Africa. They often choose to nest beneath boulders and amongst rocks; and the crests, present early in the breeding season, soon wear away.

The taxonomy of some members of the family is complex; recently, several of the island forms around New Zealand have been reduced to subspecific status and lumped together. The King Cormorant *P. albiventor* has also lost its specific status and is now placed with the Blue-eyed Cormorant *P.*

ANHINGA

Order: *Pelecaniformes*
Family: *Anhingidae*
the genus *Anhinga* contains four species

My first Anhinga *Anhinga anhinga*, 35 in. (89 cm.) long, was in Florida, where probably many other birders also have their initial sightings. Soaring over the tall buildings of the John F. Kennedy Space Centre near Merritt Island National Wildlife Refuge, was a black bird with long broad wings, a long ample tail, long thin neck and a ridiculously small head. It was not quite the Anhinga I had expected from the field guides! Besides being an expert swimmer and fisherman, the Anhinga

A young Reed Cormorant attempts to swallow a small catfish on the banks of the Chobe River, Botswana. Cormorants often appear to have 'eyes bigger than their stomachs', but usually manage to swallow the fish eventually.

can fly and soar well, once it has laboriously taken-off from the water; even birds taking to the air from a branch drop several feet before becoming airborne properly.

Anhingas, or Darters as they are called in some parts of the World, resemble extremely slender cormorants *Phalacrocoracidae* with dagger-like bills. Their relationship with other members of their Order, *Pelecaniformes*, is illustrated by the webbing between the toes that extends to all four toes, unlike many unrelated waterbirds that have webbing just between the three longest. Anhingas share with cormorants the habit of sitting for long periods, drying their outstretched wings.

Anhingas are mainly fish-eating birds, although they will take insects. They occur in warm temperate, tropical and equatorial regions of the World, inhabiting slow rivers, lagoons and sometimes brackish pools. They can be found resting in bare trees or on sand-bars when they are not fishing. The Anhinga is sometimes called 'Snake-bird' because of the snake-like appearance given while swimming with just the head and neck showing above the surface of the water. Diving

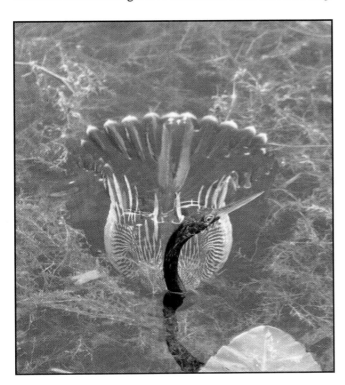

Above left: a male Anhinga fishing in the clear water of Everglades National Park, Florida. With only its head above water the bird has a reptilian appearance – hence its nickname, 'Snakebird'. Above: a young male Anhinga preening – the brown head feathers indicate that this bird is not fully adult.

Left: a group of male African Darters panting to keep cool in the branches of a tree in their breeding colony in Botswana's Okavango Delta.

is very simple, for the Anhinga just submerges its head and disappears with the minimum of fuss and disturbance to the surface of the water. If the hunt is successful the bird will surface with a fish impaled on the end of the bill; once above the surface the fish is tossed into the air with a sharp flick of the head then caught in mid-air, before being swallowed head first – quite a party trick!

There are four species of anhinga; the Anhinga of the Americas, the Indian Darter *A. melanogaster*, the African Darter *A. rufa* and the Australian Darter *A. novaehollandiae*. The taxonomy of anhingas is another either/or situation. Some authorities maintain that there is but one species; others consider that there are four. The Anhinga occurs from the south-eastern United States, south through Central America to northern Argentina. The male is black with a green sheen to his plumage and white feathers across the wing coverts. The distinctive female has a buff head, neck and breast. The other three species are very similar; the males resemble the American species, but have a deep chestnut throat and neck, separated from the back of the head and nape by a thin cream line. The African Darter occurs over much of sub-Saharan Africa and Madagascar. It formerly occurred in Turkey and Israel, but now its range in the Middle East is restricted to a small population in south-western Iran. However, after the recent Iran/Iraq war the outlook for the species in that region is uncertain. The Indian Darter ranges from India east across Asia to the Philippines and Indonesia. To the south it is replaced in New Guinea and Australia by the Australian Darter. There is one record from New Zealand that lacks a satisfactory explanation. In 1874 a skin of a freshly dead Australian Darter was found nailed inside a shed in Hokitika, on the west coast of the South Island; current reference books give no further details or any explanation!

Anhingas breed in colonies, often in the company of other waterbirds. In Botswana's Okavango Delta, the African Darter shares colonies in Water Fig bushes *Ficus verrucolosa* with other water birds such as the Reed Cormorant *Phalacrocorax africanus*. The male anhinga chooses the nest site and provides sticks with which the female constructs the nest. A clutch of four eggs is laid, with both parents sharing incubation which lasts for about 28 days. Unlike most other birds the eggs are incubated on top of the feet until hatched. In such climates the eggs are kept cool by shading, rather than being kept warm. The chicks, naked when hatched, grow a coat of down in two days. After about five weeks the chicks scramble from the nest, to the security of the surrounding bushes. Two weeks later they are able to fly, but remain dependent on their parents for food for some time afterwards, but for how long has yet to be revealed.

FRIGATEBIRDS
Order: *Pelecaniformes*
Family: *Fregatidae*
the genus *Fregata* contains five species

Over coastal Florida, its Keys and around the Gulf of Mexico, the Magnificent Frigatebird *Fregata magnificens* floats effortlessly on long narrow wings as it rides the thermals. This is characteristic of all five species which occur over the tropical seas and oceans of the World. Through evolution they have become the most aerial of all seabirds. Their wings are so long that it is virtually impossible for them to take off from water, so consequently their oil glands are reduced to the extent that the plumage lacks the water-proofing found in other aquatic birds. Likewise their feet have lost most of the webbing between the toes, and their legs and feet are so small that they can do little more than perch. The long bill is hooked at the tip so that the bird can snatch food and nesting material from the ground or the surface of the sea without having to land.

Frigatebirds are large seabirds and, in addition to their slender wings, have long forked tails to aid manoeuvrability. The black plumage is glossed green and purple, with a varying amount of white depending on the age, sex and species. The largest species is the Magnificent Frigatebird, 45 in. (114 cm.) long, with a wing-span of up to 96 in. (2.44 m.). It occurs on both the Atlantic and Pacific coast of Central

America, throughout the Caribbean and the Gulf of Mexico, and more extensively along the Atlantic than the Pacific coast of South America. Outside this nucleus, Magnificent Frigatebirds breed on the Galapagos Islands, west of Ecuador, and the Cape Verde Islands, lying off the west coast of Africa. Vagrants have occurred in the Gulf of Alaska and on Tiree in the Inner Hebrides, Scotland, where the local bank manager discovered a moribund immature in a fishing loch. It died later that day. The smallest species is the Lesser Frigatebird, 32 in. (81 cm.) long, with a wing-span of 76 in. (193 cm.), it occurs across the Indian and Pacific Oceans, with a small population on the islands of Trinidade and Martin Vaz in the Atlantic east of Brazil. The other three species are slightly smaller than the Magnificent Frigate. The Great Frigatebird *F. minor* occurs widely in the Indian and Pacific Oceans, whilst the Ascension Frigatebird *F. aquila* breeds only on the Atlantic isle of Ascension. The Christmas or Andrew's Frigatebird *F. andrewsi* breeds on Christmas and neighbouring islands in the eastern Indian Ocean.

Above: with its wings spread, a preening Anhinga in the Everglades, Florida, demonstrates how the bases of the important primary and secondary flight feathers are protected by the smaller coverts. Left: a male Frigatebird brooding chicks in the nest on a reef in the Coral Sea, Australia. Both Great and Lesser Frigatebirds occur in this part of the world and, although females can usually be identified at rest, identification of males can be more difficult unless they are in flight.

In spite of their size, Frigatebirds are very agile and accomplished fishermen, catching flying fish and squid by plucking them from the water as they pass slowly over the surface of the ocean. They are also pirates and chase boobies *Sula spp.*, terns *Sternidae* and tropicbirds *Phaethon spp.*, forcing them to disgorge the food they had intended to give to their young.

Prior to the breeding season, male frigatebirds inflate a large red gular or throat sac to attract the female. This is the same part of the anatomy that forms the pouch on the lower mandible of a pelican *Pelecanus sp.* Having wooed a female the pair start to build a nest with the male delivering the materials to the female. Some will have been gathered legitimately, whilst other items may have been taken from unattended nests. Birds have even been recorded stealing from their own nests in the absence of their mate! That must take some explaining, or perhaps it helps to explain why frigatebirds usually have a different mate next time round!

A single egg is laid and incubation shared by both parents for about 55 days; after hatching the chick is brooded for two weeks, by which time it has grown a coat of grey down and can be left while both adults search for food. By the time it is 16 to 20 weeks old it is fully feathered, complete with the white or rufous head which characterises all juvenile frigates. The youngster stays with its parents for the next two to six months during which it will learn the skills essential to survival. With the young birds being dependant for so long, frigate birds only breed in alternate years. Many young frigates reared on Aldabra in the western Indian Ocean fly with their parents to Aride, a granitic island in the central Seychelles group, where on the steep northern side of the island they practise flying to their heart's content. One October we passed beneath the hill in a small boat and witnessed an estimated 5000 frigates, mainly Greats, in the air at once!

A male Magnificent Frigatebird (below left) inflates its throat pouch in display on Tower Island, Galapagos. After display, the pouch shrinks and becomes just a small red patch. Below: with legs dangling and white wings raised a Squacco Heron takes off from vegetation at Lake Baringo, Kenya. Only in flight does this straw-coloured heron show the white in its plumage.

HERONS

Order: *Ciconiiformes*
Family: *Ardeidae*
17 genera contain 61 species

One of the best places to see herons in the United States is Florida, where all twelve species found on a regular basis in North America occur. They range from the stately Great Blue Heron *Ardea herodias* 54 in. (137 cm.) tall, to the very secretive Least Bittern *Ixobrychus exilis,* 11 in. (28 cm.). In places such as Merritt Island National Wildlife Refuge, Ding Darling NWR on Sanibel Island and the Everglades National Park superb views can be had of many species within comparatively limited areas.

Herons come in all shapes and sizes. They occur throughout the World, except for the higher latitudes and polar regions and some remote islands. The Great Blue perhaps characterises the family to many people; the patient fisherman quietly standing at the water's edge, waiting for a fish or frog to reveal its presence. Other species stalk through water-side vegetation in the hope of surprising a prey species. At least two species have developed fishing strategies that refute the disparaging statement 'bird-brained'. In Africa, the Black Heron *Egretta ardesiaca*, 20 in. (50 cm.) long, holds its outspread wings forward to spread a shadow over the water in front of the bird. The purpose of this is two-fold; the shadow cuts out extraneous reflections so that the bird can see the fish clearly, yet also offering what appears a shady refuge safe from predators – wrong! The Green-backed Heron *Butorides striatus*, 16 in.

of good photo-optics, it should be no necessary to obtain a bird to establish the first national or state record anywhere in the World. I've met birders who call the practice of shooting birds for science 'Auduboning'; perhaps one day people will associate the name 'Clementine' with the increasing list of extinct species – 'lost and gone forever'! The lone Cattle Egret was just the tip of the iceberg, for during 1952 others turned up in Illinois and Florida, and thankfully they were not treated as harshly as the Massachusetts bird. Since then the expansion of Cattle Egrets throughout the south-eastern United States has been rapid. During a trip to Utah in June 1989, we found that Cattle Egrets were widespread on agricultural land along the eastern side of the Great Salt Lake.

Facing page: a male Little Bittern visiting Sussex, England, from southern Europe. The species is a close relative of the Least Bittern, a species found in the Americas.

(40 cm.) long, has been observed using bread as bait to attract small fish within range of its dagger-like bill. Herons can be divided into four groups within the family; the true herons are the most widespread and conspicuous members; Night Herons are a group of mainly nocturnal species; Bitterns are a group of generally secretive marsh birds, whilst Tiger-herons are a small group of less secretive bittern-like herons. Some species, such as the Purple Heron *A. purpurea* of western Europe, and northern populations of the Great Blue Heron in North America, are migratory.

One of the most famous colonists of the New World, other than the Pilgrim Fathers, has been the Cattle Egret *Bubulcus ibis*, 21 in. (53 cm.) long. They were first recorded in South America in 1880 and probably crossed the Atlantic from West Africa, but it was not until the 1930s that the species expanded out of its bridgehead in the Guianas. By the late 1940s and early 1950s there had been a few records from the United States, but at the time it was thought that they might have escaped from zoos or other collections. Then a bird was found feeding amongst cattle in Massachusetts in April 1952. The following day it was shot to establish the first record for the United States, but what a pitiful end for an unusual bird! Even in those days photographic evidence should have been sufficient to establish the record and now, with an abundance

The true herons include the typical herons, several smaller species and the elegant egrets; a number of the latter are pure white. These include the Great Egret, which is almost cosmopolitan in warm temperate and tropical regions of the World. A very similar bird occurs with the Great Egret in southern Florida; this is the white form of the Great Blue Heron.

Although the night herons are nocturnal birds, they can be seen during the day, often when inadvertently flushed from their day-time roost. The most widespread species, the Black-crowned Night Heron *Nycticorax nycticorax*, 25 in. (64 cm.) long, occurs throughout many of the warm temperate and tropical regions of the world. It is absent from the Australasian region where it is replaced by the Rufous Night Heron *N. caledonicus*, 23 in. (59 cm.) long. In North America a second species of night heron occurs, a heavier-billed bird, the Yellow-crowned Night Heron *Nyctanassa violacea*, 26 in. (66 cm.) long. It specialises in catching and eating crustaceans, particularly crabs and crayfish. One of the most distinctive of all species is the Boat-billed Heron *Cochlearius cochlearius*, 20 in. (50 cm.); found in Central and South America, it has a very broad bill, unlike any other species of heron. Usually a peculiar shaped bill suggests that the species has evolved a special adaptation to enable it to exploit a particular food

Above left: an immature Rufescent Tiger-heron waits for a fish or frog to reveal itself in a weed-clogged pool in Venezuela. This South American species occurs from Honduras to Argentina. The Grey Heron is widespread throughout much of the temperate Old World and sub-Saharan Africa. Above: a young Grey Heron in a lake in East Africa.

supply; the Boat-billed Heron appears to use its bill as a scoop to catch slow moving or sedentary prey amongst leaves or mud.

Bitterns are secretive birds from swamps, marshes and sometimes bushy waterside habitats. Twelve species of bittern are divided into two genera. The four large cryptically-coloured species belong to the genus *Botaurus*, the most widespread of which is the Eurasian Bittern *B. stellaris*, 30 in. (76 cm.) long, found from the British Isles east to Japan. In Africa it occurs discontinuously down the length of the continent. In North America it is replaced by the American Bittern *B. lentiginosus* 26 in. (66 cm.) long, a slightly smaller species that is not quite as secretive as its Old World relative. The other two species occur in South America and Australia. The remaining eight bittern species are much smaller and by comparison are brightly coloured. The male Little Bittern *Ixobrychus minutus*, 12 in. (30 cm.) long, is mainly black and warm-buff; the female is duller and most of the remaining species are variations on the theme, except for the darker African Dwarf Bittern *I. sturmii*, 12 in. (30 cm.) long, and the larger Black Bittern *I. flavicollis*, 23 in. (58 in.) long, of southern Asia and Australasia.

conspicuous bird. Smaller and declining is the Slaty Egret *E. vinaceigula*, 17 in. (43 cm.), found only in northern Botswana and Zambia; it breeds in the swamps, and often occurs at other times of the year at pools on drying flood-plains. The total population may be under 1000 birds.

SHOEBILL
Order: *Ciconiiformes*
Family: *Balaenicipitidae*
the genus *Balaeniceps* contains a single species *Balaeniceps rex*

In the great swamps of Central Africa that occur in parts of the Sudan, Uganda, Zaïre and Zambia lives a strange looking bird with an outrageous bill. This is the Shoebill *Balaeniceps rex* or as it is sometimes called Whale-headed Stork. Records from outside its normal range are most unlikely for Shoebills

The remaining members of the heron family are the tiger-bitterns, a group of six species divided between four genera and found scattered across tropical regions of the World. Four species occur in Central and South America, one in Africa and the final species in New Guinea and neighbouring islands. They resemble the larger bitterns, getting the name from the black barring across chestnut upper-parts of most species.

Herons are often to be found breeding colonially, hence 'heronries', either with their own species or with other herons and egrets. The Grey Heron *A. cinerea*, 36 in. (91 cm.) long, the Old World equivalent of the Great Blue, occurs throughout much of the Palearctic and Africa. In the British Isles and parts of Western Europe it breeds in monospecific colonies in tall deciduous or coniferous trees. Their breeding success in Britain has been monitored by a national survey organised by the British Trust for Ornithology since 1928. The bitterns and tiger-bitterns are mainly solitary nesting species, although some of the smaller species may form loose colonies or breed amongst other herons. The usual clutch size is 3-10 eggs, depending on the species, and incubation lasts from between 16 and 30 days, again depending on the species. Both heron parents share this duty, which is carried solely by female bitterns. A precise fledging period is hard to determine, for after a week the young birds vacate the nest and scramble amongst the surrounding vegetation.

Several members of the heron family are very rare and one, the Imperial or White-bellied Heron *A. imperialis*, 50 in. (127 cm.) long, may be very close to extinction. It occurs from Nepal to Burma; there are few recent records of this large and

are non-migratory and the only wanderings are to fresh feeding areas as the water-levels on the nearby flood-plains change with the seasons. Recently the only Southern African record, which came from the Moremi Wildlife Reserve on the edge of the Okavango Delta in Botswana, was removed from national and regional bird-lists.

It is a long-necked and long-legged wading bird, but is neither stork nor heron, although it may look like both. In fact there is nothing else like it, so scientists have placed the unique Shoebill in a family of its own.

The Shoebill feeds on fish caught while standing silently on the edge of a water channel. The large bill enables it to grab fish amongst aquatic vegetation. By grinding the upper and lower mandibles together it can remove the weeds and retain the fish. In addition to fish the diet includes small crocodiles, frogs, small mammals and water snakes. Shoebills are usually solitary birds and often feed at night, which is probably an advantage to a fisherman standing nearly 4 ft. (1.2 m.) tall! Together with other species of wading birds the Shoebill takes advantage of the rich harvest of fish that become trapped as pools in the flood-plains around the swamps dry out. This rich source of food is an annual event exploited by a great variety of wading birds from the small egrets to the lordly storks. Each has evolved to feed on a particular size of fish and therefore they feed together without undue competition. The huge bill of the Shoebill enables it to catch species, such as catfish, that are too large for other birds.

In the large nest, constructed in the reed-beds, two eggs will be laid, although it is unusual for a Shoebill to rear more

Above left: fish-eating wading birds at a pool in Florida include a Tricoloured Heron, a Wood Ibis and a Great Egret (far left), which is magnificent in flight with its neck withdrawn and long black legs extended. Above: a Tricoloured Heron has just caught a fish amongst mangroves in Florida. The aptly named Boat-billed Heron (left) uses its unique bill to scoop up slow-moving prey. It is a crepuscular, South American relative of the Night Herons.

41

than a single chick to fledging. The surface of the egg shell is flaky, an adaptation to prevent a build up of bacteria and fungi in the humid and damp environment beneath the incubating adult. In the heat the adults carry large amounts of water in their bills to douse the eggs and chicks to help them remain cool.

Shoebills are vulnerable as they live in a fragile ecosystem of waterways and marshes. Such places are easily destroyed by local farmers clearing land to graze cattle, although the presence of the Tsetse Fly *Glossina sp.*, that causes Sleeping Sickness, usually restricts human activity in such areas. Hunters, particularly those after the swamp-haunting Sitatunga *Tragelaphus spekei*, set fire to the drying swamps in order to flush out their prey and to generate fresh new growth. It results in habitat destruction for the Shoebill and other species found only in such areas.

HAMERKOP
Order : *Ciconiiformes*
Family : *Scopidae*
the genus Scopus contains a single species
Scopus umbretta

In Africa the strange looking Hamerkop *Scopus umbretta* is a bird of folk-lore and legends, and because of this is rarely persecuted by Man. It is an odd bird, once thought to be related to the herons *Ardeidae* , but analysis of egg-white proteins have placed it closer to the storks *Ciconiidae* , although it shows only a passing resemblance. The Hamerkop occurs in south-western Arabia, and all over sub-Saharan Africa and in Madagascar, except for those areas that are too arid. Usually found singly or in pairs, Hamerkops will gather at drying pools in flood plains, after the rains. Fish become trapped and provide many water birds, including the Hamerkop, with a feast. The Hamerkop wades, snatching fish, frogs and other aquatic animals from the water, sometimes disturbing prey from the mud with its feet.

The Hamerkop, 22 in. (56 cm.) long, is a sturdy, brown bird with a shaggy crest, which when combined with a stout bill gives it the alternative name of Hammer-headed Stork. The large rounded wings extend beyond the tail when at rest, whilst in flight it flaps its wings with a rather jerky down-beat and glides intermittently. It soars well on parallel-edged wings, and the short tail and 'hammer-head' present a distinctive silhouette.

A pair of Hamerkops spends much of their life together working on the house. The nest, sited in the fork of large branches in a tree, can be up to 65 ft. (20 m.) above the ground; sometimes it will be built on a ledge on a cliff face or rarely on a sandbank. It is constructed by both birds from sticks and mud collected from the margins of a nearby wetland, and

when complete, the oven-shaped chamber, will be up to 6 ft. (2 m.) in diameter. It takes up to six weeks to complete. First the bowl is completed and at this stage the builders are sometimes evicted by a pair of Giant or Verreaux's Eagle Owls *Bubo lacteus*. The sides and the entrance tunnel are finished before the roof, up to 3 ft. (1 m.) wide, is added. The entrance hole faces out and downwards, so that the returning birds fly up and straight into the 2 ft. (60 cm.) long tunnel that leads to the nesting chamber. Up to 7 eggs are laid and incubation is shared by both parents for about 30 days. Fledging takes a further 50 days, but the precise length of time is uncertain because of the difficulties of examining the nest. One of the legends associated with the Hamerkop is that other birds help with the construction of the nest, but this probably arose as a result of several other species using the empty nest after the chicks have flown. Likely candidates for the desirable residence include Barn Owls *Tyto alba* and Egyptian Geese *Alopochen aegyptiacus* .

STORKS
Order: *Ciconiiformes*
Family: *Ciconiidae*
six genera contain 17 species

Spring is the time for renewal, new life, and when the European White Storks *Ciconia ciconia* return to their nests in towns and villages in Europe, from wintering grounds thousands of miles away in Africa. Theirs is a journey of contrasts. In the fall they leave the breeding areas in an increasingly modern rural villages of Western Europe, where they are declining steadily and head towards one of the traditional crossing points into Africa. Most travel via Turkey, where on a thermal of warm air, they spiral upwards with a host of hawks and eagles, to glide across the Bosphorus from Europe into Asia Minor. Their route then takes them south over the trouble-torn Middle East to Africa, where some travel as far as South Africa and Namibia. Others choose a more direct route across the Straits of Gibraltar, from Spain to North Africa, a flight that involves a long and more tiring sea crossing. Thermals do not form over water, so the birds must gain as much height as possible before leaving Europe for North Africa. They commence a long steady glide, but usually the distance is too great and the birds have to flap hard over the sea to complete their passage. These birds will rest and feed, before facing another hazard – the Sahara, where doubtless they will find no shortage of thermals. In Africa, they are just as much at home on the plains and savannahs as on the chimneys and roofs of Europe. After the long journey, the top priority of the birds is to feed well and replenish the lost reserves of body fats for the return flight, now only a few months away. They feed on insects and amphibians, amongst cultivated fields, savannah and in the aftermath of bush fires, where they join opportunist feeding flocks of the intra-African migrant Abdim's Stork *C. abdimii*.

There are 17 species of Storks, divided between six genera. They are tall wading birds, but lack the elegance of the herons *Ardeidae* or the unrelated cranes *Grus*. They are distributed over most of the temperate and tropical regions of the World. Storks have long wings and can fly and soar well. Some species are sedentary, whilst others are long-distance migrants.

There is only one species of stork in North America, the Wood Stork, or Wood Ibis, *Mycteria americana*, 40 in. (117 cm.) long. It is a white bird with black primaries and secondaries, and it has a bare black head with a slightly decurved bill, from which the alternative name originates. It is related to three African and Asiatic members of the genus, that have yellow bills; both the Yellow-billed Stork *M. ibis* and the Painted Stork *M. leucocephala* have pink in their plumage, particularly during the breeding season.

The other close relatives of the European White and Abdim's Storks include the Black Stork *C. nigra*, that ranges from Europe to China, the Woolly-necked Stork *C. episcopus*, found in both Africa and Asia, and the Maguari Stork *C. maguari* of South America, a bird similar in appearance to the European species. This genus includes two Asiatic forms, treated as sub-species by some authorities, and given full

Left: an immature European White Stork rests during its migration flight. White Storks migrate between Europe and Africa, some reaching South Africa. When fully adult this youngster will display the red bill and legs of the breeding bird. Far left: a young male Saddle-billed Stork searches for food in an East African pond. The glossy black of the adult plumage is beginning to replace browner feathers on the neck and wings. Standing nearly 5 ft. high when fully grown, this is the tallest African stork.

Left: Jaribu Storks, with their heavy bills and red neck-bands, tower above Wood Storks and Great and Snowy Egrets, all enjoying a feast of fish at a pool in the Pantanal, Brazil. Far left: the Hamerkop, photographed in Botswana, which builds a huge nest and, as a result, features in many African tribal legends.

specific status by others. Whichever way, the Asiatic White Stork, a race of the European White, and Storm's Stork, a race of the Woolly-necked Stork, are both very rare and endangered. The problems they face are shared by the more widely distributed members of the family – habitat changes, pollution and hunting.

Two striking species are the Saddle-billed Stork *Ephippiorhynchus senegalensis*, from Africa and the Black-necked Stork *E. asiaticus* of Asia. They are both black and white, although when seen at close range the black has a blue and green sheen. The males of both species have dark eyes and the females yellow. Another pair of storks split between Africa and Asia are the open-bills. The black African Open-bill *Anastomus lamelligerus* and the white Asiatic Open-bill *A. oscitans*, they have a gap between the upper and lower mandibles. Their preferred diet is fresh-water snails.

The large Jaribu *Jaribu mycteria* is 55 in. (140 cm.) long, and the only other stork that occurs in South America. It is a white stork with a massive black bill, and a bare black head and neck with a red collar.

The final three members of the family belong to the genus *Leptoptilos* and include the Marabou Stork *L. crumeniferus* 60 in. (152 cm.) long, of Africa. This, and the two Asiatic members of the genus, are repulsive-looking birds and are scavengers, often to be found at a carcass on which vultures *Gyps sp.* are feasting.

Storks eat a variety of vertebrates including frogs, fish and snakes. Some feed in grasslands on grasshoppers and locusts, others are specialised in eating snails, and the large *Leptoptilos* are scavengers.

Food is an important aspect in regulating the breeding success. If water-levels are too low or the weather too cold, then only some of the population in a given area will breed. Some species are colonial, others semi-colonial or solitary. The nest made of sticks can be sited in a variety of locations in trees, on bushy islands and on buildings. Most species lay from 3-5 eggs and incubation, which commences from the first or second egg, is shared by both adults for 26-28 days. The fledging period lasts for 50 days for the smaller species and to up 100 days for the Marabou.

agriculture. These two species are treated as conspecific by some taxonomists, but they appear to breed side by side in Louisiana, without hybridizing, which is a fair indication that the two are full species. These two birds look like dark curlews; they are sometimes erroneously called 'Black Curlews' by country people.

The Sacred Ibis *Threskiornis aethiopicus*, 35 in. (90 cm.) long, is a white bodied species with black tips to the trailing edge of the otherwise white wings. They are found over much of sub-Saharan Africa, except permanently arid areas. The

Facing page top: a flock of superb Scarlet Ibis in Trinidad includes a single brown and white juvenile. The colourful Painted Stork (facing page bottom) of Asia is a bird characteristic of wetland reserves.

IBISES and SPOONBILLS
Order: *Ciconiiformes*
Family: *Threskiornithidae*
17 genera contain 27 species

The Ibises and Spoonbills are distinctive members of the Order of stork-like birds *Ciconiiformes*, found throughout the temperate and tropical regions of the World. Ibises have strongly decurved bills, whilst spoonbills have long, flat bills, with a broader and rounded tip; therefore 'Spoonbill'.

There are 27 species of ibises divided into 17 genera; the greatest variety of species occur in South America, where 11 species are to be found, 9 of which are endemic to that continent. They are ground-feeding birds; most species feed along the margins of a variety of wetlands including shallow lakes, flood-plains and drying pools, or in grasslands.

The most widespread species is the Glossy Ibis *Plegadis falcinellus*, 23 in. (58 cm.) long, occurring where there are suitable habitats from the south-eastern United States and the Caribbean in the New World, and discontinuously from the Mediterranean, across Asia to Australia and over much of Africa. The adult of the species is a rich maroon-chestnut, with a green and purple sheen to the wing feathers. In the western United State occurs the very similar White-faced Ibis, a bird that had benefited from the use of irrigation by

Above: a European White Stork which returns annually to nest on a favoured chimney stack at Rust in Eastern Austria. Of the world's six species of spoonbill, the most colourful is the Roseate Spoonbill (left), which ranges from the southern United States to Argentina.

Sacred Ibis has a bare head and neck, extended in flight. The Ancient Egyptians revered the Sacred Ibis, depicting it on wall-paintings and placing mummified specimens in their tombs. In those times, the species was abundant along the Nile, when suitable habitat in Ancient Egypt extended much farther than it does today. Nowadays the Sacred Ibis only occurs in the area as a rarity. Closely related species occur in Asia and Australasia.

Not all ibis are black or white; one of the most striking wading birds is the Scarlet Ibis *Eudocimus ruber* , found mainly on Trinidad and in northern South America. Birds occasionally wander further afield, occurring from time to time in Florida. Sometimes they interbreed with the locally abundant White Ibis *E. albus* ; the resultant off-spring look pink when mature.

There was no mistaking one I saw a few years ago at Flamingo, in the Everglades National Park – it was an incredible bird, but almost certainly an escape; so the sight of a flock of wild Scarlet Ibis must be breath-taking.

Spoonbill look unlike ibis, although they share membership of the same family. They are taller, slimmer, birds with a long spoon-shaped bill, which may be black, white or yellow, depending on the species. Spoonbills are mainly white birds, except for the one North American representative. This is the Roseate Spoonbill *Ajaia ajaja* , 32 in. (81 cm.) long; a superb combination of white, pink and red. In the United States it occurs in Florida, and around the Gulf of Mexico to Texas. Further afield it occurs in suitable brackish and freshwater

habitats, as far south as central Chile and Argentina. The population of the Roseate Spoonbill in the United States has made a steady recovery under protection after being persecuted by plumage-hunters, earlier this century.

When ibis feed, they prod here and there with their long curved bills, feeling for their prey that includes crustaceans, fish, frogs, insects and molluscs. Spoonbills also feel for food, but by swinging their bills from side to side, as they wade through the water. Most species of ibis and spoonbills nest in colonies, sometimes with other wading birds. A platform nest is constructed, where 2-5 eggs are laid. The incubation period lasts between 21-29 days and is shared by both parents. The fledging period for both ibises and spoonbills can last up to 50 days, depending on the species. Young ibises leave the nest prior to fledging, but the spoonbill chicks remain until they fledge.

Several species of ibis are very rare. Amongst the rare ibis are three Asiatic species. Until the mid-19th. century the Japanese Crested Ibis *Nipponia nippon* was a common bird in eastern China, Japan and eastern Siberia, but then it declined dramatically in the face of hunting pressures and habitat destruction; it is a tree-nesting species. By 1973 the last Japanese birds were in captivity, but the breeding programme failed. It looked as if the species had become extinct, when a small colony of 7 birds was discovered in China in 1981. Under protection this had increased to 17 birds by 1984. Hopefully this early success will continue. Further south, in Indo-China, the White-shouldered and the Giant Ibis *Pseudibis davisoni* and *P. gigantea* , suffered as a result of military activity in the region, and subsequently from hunting pressures to supplement food shortages.

FLAMINGOS
Order: *Ciconiiformes*
Family: *Phoenicopteridae*
three genera contain five species

One of the greatest and most colourful wildlife spectacles on earth are the flamingos around the shores of Lake Nakuru, one of the Great Rift Valley lakes in Kenya. Sometimes there can be more than two million birds, mainly Lesser Flamingos *Phoeniconaias minor*, 35 in. (90 cm.) tall, that form a pink ribbon around the periphery of the alkaline lake. The best general view can be obtained from the top of the Baboon Rocks above the western shore, where one can fully appreciate the incredible numbers. Down by the muddy lake-shore the air is full of their calls as they preen and fly in small flocks to and from other parts of the lake. Standing taller than the multitude, but in considerably smaller numbers, are the paler Greater Flamingos *Phoenicopterus ruber* 55 in. (140 cm.) tall, occasionally lifting their heads to show that their angled bill is largely pink, unlike the dark red of the Lesser. Flamingos move to other areas when the water level is unsuitable, so that it is possible for one to visit the lake and find only a few hundred birds present.

There is nothing quite like a flamingo with its very long legs, long neck and peculiar angled bill used to filter algae,

Far left: the brilliantly coloured Caribbean Greater Flamingo. Left: a Sacred Ibis preens in an East African lake. These birds were once revered by the ancient Egyptians.

An adult Scarlet Ibis (below left) is the most striking member of the ibis family. Below: a group of Lesser Flamingo filter feed along the edge of a Kenyan lake.

shrimps and the other forms of aquatic life that make up the diet. The filter system is unique amongst birds, and in the animal kingdom only the great baleen whales *Mysticeti* have evolved the same feeding method. The relationship between the flamingos and other bird families is not clear. It is generally accepted that they should be placed with the stork-like birds *Ciconiiformes*, but exactly where in the Order is still a matter for debate. They share anatomical similarities with both the ibises *Threskiornithidae* and the storks *Ciconiidae*, but recent studies of the egg-white proteins suggest that they should be placed closer to the herons *Ardeidae*, still within the same Order however. On the other hand, it has been argued from studies of behaviour that flamingos could be linked with the wildfowl *Anseriformes*, and yet another proposition is that there is a tie-up with the shorebirds! One day the confusion will be resolved, but not by an enthusiastic field worker studying under the African sun, but by a white-coated scientist in an air-conditioned laboratory.

The five species of flamingo are divided into three genera, and four species are to be found in South America. The Greater Flamingo occurs from northern South America and the Caribbean to southern Europe, Africa, Central Asia and India. From Peru and Uruguay in South America it is replaced

SCREAMERS
Order: *Anseriformes*
Family: *Anhimidae*
two genera contain three species

Screamers are an endemic family of large South American birds, distantly related to both Flamingos *Phoenicopteridae* and Wildfowl *Anatidae*. The Horned Screamer *Anhima cornuta* is the most widespread ranging from Colombia and Venezuela south to Brazil. It was formerly resident on the West Indian island of Trinidad, where it became increasingly rare from 1910 and probably became extinct as a breeding bird shortly afterwards. Recent records are probably of immatures wandering from the nearby Venezuelan mainland. The Crested Screamer *Chauna torquata* has a more southerly range occurring in southern Brazil, Uruguay and northern Argentina. More localised in its distribution is the Black-necked Screamer *C. chavaria* found only in northern Colombia and north-western Venezuela. Taking all three species together, Screamers are found throughout tropical and sub-tropical

Below: Greater Flamingoes taking off from a shallow lake in Kenya. The Greater Flamingo is the most widespread member of the family, ranging from South America to India and down through Africa. In times of drought the species wanders in search of suitable breeding and feeding areas.

by the Chilean Flamingo *Phoenicopterus chilensis*, which occurs up to 15,000 ft. (4,500 m.) in the Andes. Its breeding colonies were only discovered in 1957, when an expedition visited an area of salt-lakes at 14,000 ft. (4,250 m.) in the Bolivian Andes. All three species endemic to South America were found breeding; the other two being James's *Phoenicoparrus jamesi* and the Andean *P. andinus* Flamingos. The smallest species is the Lesser Flamingo of Africa and north-western India.

Flamingos breed in colonies and are invariably associated with alkaline or salt lakes, where numbers can run into tens of thousands. To minimise the effects of any terrestrial predators, breeding throughout the colony is highly synchronised, so that all eggs are laid and hatched within a matter of days of one another. Both parents construct the nest platform of mud and stones. It may be 1 ft. (30 cm.) above the surrounding water level and a depression is moulded on top, where the single egg is laid. They share the incubation period of 28-30 days, and when the down-covered chick is about 8 days old it leaves the nest and joins other youngsters to form creches. Most species feed the young until the hooked bill is sufficiently well developed for them to feed themselves.

The goose-sized Crested Screamer (left) is a member of a South American family related to both flamingos and wildfowl. This species is characterized by its crest, narrow black collar and grey plumage and it occurs in Brazil and Argentina.

South America and are absent from the western side of the main length of the Andean chain and southern Patagonia.

Screamers are aberrant wildfowl with heavily built bodies similar in shape to that of a goose *Anser sp*. They have short necks, small heads and a small bill recalling that of a chicken. They have strong legs, but the feet have the minimum of webbing. All species have stout spurs on the leading edge of the wings and the Horned Screamer, the only member of the genus *Anhima*, has developed a strong quill of about 3 in. (7.5 cm.) that protrudes from the crown. The plumage is dark glossy green with white mottling to the crown and sides of neck. The belly is white and in flight shows a conspicuous white shoulder patch and under-wing coverts. The Crested and Black-necked Screamers are mainly grey birds with a black neck collar. This is much broader on the Black-necked, which also has a large white chin patch that extends up to the sides of the head. Both species have short crests at the back of the head. Screamers fly strongly on broad wings and soar well. They are noisy birds and the name 'Screamer' comes from the loud, strident, shrill calls. They are vegetarian, eating aquatic plants, roots and seeds.

Breeding takes place in the Spring and a large nest of vegetation is built by both adults close to water. A clutch of 2-6 eggs is laid and incubation, probably shared by both parents, lasts 43-45 days. After hatching the chicks do not stray far for several days and will not move to drier areas until they are strong enough to run from danger.

DUCKS, GEESE and SWANS
Order: *Anseriformes*
Family: *Anatidae*
49 genera contain 151 species

To many people one of the most evocative sights and sounds of the Natural World is that of migrating geese. For me, living in Scotland, it used to be the Pink-footed Geese *Anser brachyrhynchus* flying down from Iceland to winter on the banks and surrounding fields of the Solway Firth. To other people it might be a noisy skein of Canadian 'honkers' *A. canadensis* heading down the Mississippi flyway, or a blizzard of Snow Geese *Chen caerulescens* arriving to winter in California's Central Valley.

Above: a Caribbean Greater Flamingo tends its chick on top of its mud nest. Not all swans are white, for example the Black Swan (far left) from Australia. However, it does have concealed, white primary and secondary wing feathers. This species is often found in ornamental wildfowl collections. The Black-necked Swan (left) from southern South America and the Falkland Islands is also a popular bird for such collections.

Members of this family come in all shapes and sizes – 151 species in all, divided between 49 genera. They are an extremely varied assortment of waterbirds, to be found throughout the World wherever there is a suitable wetland habitat. Some species only occur on freshwater, others mainly on the sea, and yet more breed by freshwater and winter on estuaries or in the sea. Some species are sedentary and others winter south of their normal breeding grounds; some in warmer climates are nomadic, moving from one wetland to another as the waters from the previous rainy season dry-out. In appearance they range from the huge snow-white Trumpeter Swans *Cygnus buccinator* of North America, to the tiny Cotton Pygmy Goose *Nettapus coromandelianus* of tropical Asia.

Names can be confusing at times; the three species of pygmy geese, found in wetlands of tropical Africa, Asia and Australia, are dabbling ducks, and likewise the tall Spur-winged Goose of Africa is a member of an old family of perching ducks.

As man started to domesticate mammals and birds, two species of wildfowl were particularly important. The widespread Mallard *Anas platyrhynchos* of the Northern Hemisphere and the Greylag Goose *Anser anser* from the Palearctic, gave rise to our familiar domestic ducks and geese. Other species to be domesticated have been the Swan Goose *A. cygnoides* of Asia, which in its domestic form has become the Chinese Goose; whilst the Muscovy Duck *Cairina moschata* a South American species, still resembles its wild ancestors in many ways. In the wild, the Muscovy occurs from Mexico to Uruguay and northern Argentina. There is only one other member of the genus and it lives half a world away, the White-winged Wood Duck *C. scutulata*. It is an endangered bird that was formerly fairly common over a large area of south-east Asia from Assam to Java, but the usual three pressures of habitat changes, over-hunting and pollution, have reduced the population to an estimated 200 pairs. Thankfully the Wildfowl and Wetlands Trust at Slimbridge,

The Red-breasted Goose (above left) is an attractive migratory bird that breeds in Siberia and winters in eastern Europe and Asia. The American Wigeon breeds in northern and western North America. Above: an American Wigeon drake in Colorado. The drake Mandarin Duck (left) is one of the most colourful of all wildfowl. In its native China it is now rare, but it has become a successful species in Surrey, England.

England has established a breeding population and is able to send eggs to Thailand in an attempt to increase the wild population.

The ease with which many species of wildfowl can be kept in collections has increased the appeal of these attractive birds. Through lessons learnt at collections with a scientific approach, such as the centres run by the Wildfowl and Wetlands Trust in Great Britain, lies the future of many endangered species. For some, such as the Labrador Duck *Camptorhynchus labradorius*, it is too late. This attractive duck appears never to have been particularly common. It was a sea duck that bred in eastern Canada and wintered south to Chesapeake Bay which borders both Maryland and Virginia. The last bird was recorded in 1878, and is now in an excellent display at the American Museum of Natural History in New York; if only more museums were as good as this one!

In the Northern Hemisphere most ducks can be placed into one of two groups - the dabbling or the diving ducks. Dabbling ducks include the Mallard and the other *Anas* species; the drakes are richly coloured and the females are mottled brown, although when the males molt towards the end of the breeding season, they assume a similar plumage. This is so they are less conspicuous during the period when they are flightless when

As a rule the diving ducks are heavy-bodied birds, frequently needing a runway of clear water for take-off. There is considerable variety in the plumages of both the drakes and ducks of the various genera, but often those species that habitually winter on the sea are the more attractive. The drake also molts into the eclipse plumage during their flightless period. Diving ducks eat mainly forms of animal life that include crustaceans, molluscs and fish, the latter being the principal food of the mergansers *Mergus* with their long, serrated 'saw-bill.'

The separation in the Southern Hemisphere is not as clear as in the north, for several aberrant forms occur. These include the remarkably streamlined Torrent Duck *Merganetta armata*, a species that has evolved along the swift streams and rivers that flow from the Andes in South America. Also from South America are the steamer ducks *Tachyeres*, large sea-ducks that fill the niche occupied in the Holarctic by the eiders *Somateria*. They are unrelated and three of the four species are flightless; the fourth is the Flying Steamer Duck *T. patachonicus*, but in spite of its name often appears reluctant to fly, and some large males may be unable to do so!

A variety of food items appears on the diet of the wildfowl as a whole; some species are solely vegetarian and others eat

Snow Geese in a New Mexican field of corn. They breed in Arctic Canada and Alaska, but each fall they migrate to favoured areas, including New Mexico. Wildlife refuges plant corn and other cereals as winter food for wildfowl, cranes and other species.

new flight feathers are growing. When feeding in water, dabbling ducks take either vegetable or animal matter from the surface or reach the bottom of the pool, lake or river by up-ending - heads down, tail up. This is why dabbling ducks are often to be found in shallow waters. Several species, including the Northern Shoveler *A. clypeata*, have evolved broad, spatulate bills with which they sift material for food. Dabbling ducks lift easily when taking-off, a fact reflected in the English collective name for the Green-winged Teal *A. crecca*: a 'spring' of teal.

entirely animal matter, including invertebrates, crustaceans, molluscs and fish.

Those that are vegetarian may feed on grass, crops on land or on floating or submerged aquatic vegetation. In coastal southern England the Brant *Branta bernicla* was formerly dependent on eel-grass *Zostera*, a plant that grows in tidal waters; however in recent years they have turned inland. In arable fields near the coast winter wheat is grown and the geese have discovered this to be a palatable substitute. During recent winters on the Scottish island of Islay, David Stroud and members of the Greenland White-fronted Goose Study Group have shown that the importance of the wintering areas for migratory wildfowl is vital for a successful migration and subsequent breeding season. The endangered Greenland race of the White-fronted Goose *Anser albifrons* winters in Scotland and Ireland, and undertakes annual migration to western Greenland across the North Atlantic via Iceland. If the birds have had a good winter and ample reserves of fat for the journey, then they arrive on the breeding ground in good condition and the chances of successful breeding is greater.

Breeding behaviour varies considerably amongst wildfowl species. The swans and geese usually pair for life, but ducks only pair for the breeding season and then they only stay together until the duck commences to incubate the eggs. The drake often finds the excuse to join others of their sex and spends the rest of the summer in a molting flock. The nests

The Wood Duck (left) is a tree-nesting species. Each year the Trumpeter Swans (facing page) on the Madison River delight visitors to Yellowstone National Park.
Below: a Mute Swan with her cygnets on an English river. Wintering Greylag Geese (bottom) found in Ranthambhore Reserve, India, migrate there from breeding grounds in U.S.S.R.

vary from one genus to another; swans build large platforms of vegetation, whilst most geese in the Northern Hemisphere line a hollow with vegetation and feathers. Many ducks just line a hollow with down, the most famous being the Common Eider *S. mollissima*, whose soft eider-down has been used by Icelanders for generations. Nesting sites also vary considerably, although many nest amongst waterside vegetation. In north-east Greenland, the Barnacle Goose breeds on cliff-ledges, so that when the goslings hatch there is only one way to go - downwards. Those that survive the fall also have to face the jaws of the Arctic Foxes *Alopex lagopus* waiting below; but enough get through. The shelducks *Tadorna spp.* build in disused mammal burrows, and several species of duck nest in holes in trees. Over recent years the Common Goldeneye has colonised northern Scotland from Scandinavia with the aid of nest-boxes secured to trees around suitable lochs and lochans.

The clutch size varies from 4 – 12 eggs. Swans and the true geese incubate from 24 – 36 days with both adults incubating and tending the youngsters, who leave the nest soon after hatching. The incubation period for ducks is 21 – 28 days and is undertaken by the female, and as a rule she alone rears the ducklings. Fledging is a protracted exercise; ducklings may fly at 6 weeks and cygnets at 9 – 13 weeks.

There is one notable exception to the usual pattern of wildfowl breeding biology. The Black-headed Duck *Heteronetta atricapilla* from South America is parasitic and lays its eggs in the nests of many other birds including wildfowl, coots and ibis. The duckling hatches after about 25 days and only a few days later they leave to make their way in the world alone!

Left: a pair of Snow Geese in flight across the blue sky of California, where large numbers spend the winter in Central Valley.

NEW WORLD VULTURES
Order: *Falconiformes*
Family: *Cathartidae*
five genera contain seven species

There is a birding term that expresses the disappointment of birders missing a good bird; one 'dips out' so that those birders who failed to see a wild Californian Condor *Gymnogyps californianus*, 50 in. (127 cm.) long and with a vast 9 ft. (2.75 m.) wing-span, can consider themselves 'big dippers.' Sadly, with escalating pressures on wildlife in the late 20th. century, the only hope the Condors and an increasing number of other birds and animals have to survive, is a successful captive breeding programme or relocation scheme. Now that young Condors have been reared in captivity and a large area of prime habitat exists in the 13,537 acre (5478 ha.) Bitter Creek National Wildlife Refuge, the future of the California Condor seems to be heading in the right direction – upwards.

The seven species of New World vultures are placed in five genera, which are unrelated to the Old World species. Recent research into the relationships between these birds and other bird families points to a closer link with the storks *Ciconiiformes* than the traditionally assumed relationship with the Raptors *Falconiformes*. Should this prove to be the case, this is one of the most extreme cases of convergent evolution.

Top left: a Eurasian Green-winged Teal drake. The North American type has a vertical chest stripe and no horizontal stripe. Top centre: a Mallard drake upends, and (left) Plumed Whistling Ducks in Queensland, Australia, show the distinctive upright stance of their family. Above: a male Andean Condor in Peru, with under-carriage lowered for landing. Andean Condors are the largest of the world's birds of prey.

Now that there are no longer Californian Condors in the wild, only two species of New World vultures remain in North America. Most widespread is the Turkey Vulture *Cathartes aura*, 27 in. (68 cm.), with a wing-span of nearly seven feet. It occurs from British Columbia to Tierra del Fuego and the Falkland Islands; the northern population contracts southwards for the winter months. This is the 'buzzard' of North America, but more widely in the World the term 'buzzard' usually applies with qualification to various *Buteo* species. The Turkey Vulture has a distinctive silhouette in flight with long parallel wings and long tail. It glides with a steady sideways rocking motion, as it sails along in search for food. The New World Vultures are scavengers, but the Turkey Vulture is unique, for unlike other species it locates much of its food by smell, through highly developed olfactory organs. Research suggests that they can locate a carcass within 24 hours of death. Turkey Vultures frequent a variety of habitats. The two other members of the genus occur in South America; the Greater and Lesser Yellow-headed Vultures, *C. melambrotus* and *C. burrovianus*. The Greater Yellow-headed is larger than the Turkey Vulture and is a bird of tropical lowland forests, whilst the smaller Lesser, 30 in. (76 cm.) long, inhabits savannahs and marshes.

The American Black Vulture (facing page) ranges from the south-eastern United States to Argentina. It searches for food by sight, lacking the well-developed nasal passages of the Turkey Vulture; the red-headed Turkey Vulture (above left), for instance, finds its food mainly by smell. This is a larger bird than the Black Vulture with a wider distribution in North America – its more northerly population is migratory. Black Vultures may associate with Turkey Vultures, knowing they will be led to food. Left: American Black Vultures roosting on Cardon cactus.

The other North American species is the American Black Vulture *Coragyps atratus*, 22 in. (56 cm.) long; it is less widespread than the Turkey Vulture, occurring in the southern United States, Central and South America. It has shorter, broader wings and a shorter more rounded tail than the larger species. The wings are held flatter and the pale on the under-wing is restricted to the primaries; the under-wing of a Turkey Vulture shows paler secondaries and primaries. It finds food by searching, and often takes a short-cut by following the scent-seeking Turkey Vultures when they home-in on a food supply.

South America is home to the two remaining New World Vultures. The American King Vulture *Sarcoramphus papa*, 30 in. (76 cm.) long, is a forest-dwelling, white bodied bird with black and white wings, and a bare red head and wattles. It ranges from Central Mexico and Venezuela south to northern Argentina. Last, but not least is the mighty Andean Condor *Vultur gryphus*; at 42 in. (1.10 m.) long it is shorter than the Californian species, but the wing span of 10 ft. (10 m.) is a foot

wider. It is the largest flying bird, with a greater wing area than the Wandering Albatross *Diomedea exulans*, whose span has been measured at 11 ft. 11 in. (3.63 m.) wide. The Andean Condor occurs from Venezuela, where it was rediscovered in 1977, and down the Andes to Tierra del Fuego. Condors soar endlessly on the up-draughts over the mountains and along suitable coasts, ever watchful for dead and dying animals that may range from the Vicuña *Vicugna vicugna* high on the Puna Desert to the carcasses of seals on the beaches.

Unlike the Old World Vultures, the New World species do not build nests, but lay on a ledge, under a boulder or in a cave. The Lesser Yellow-headed Vulture has been found nesting in tree cavities. The condors and the American King Vulture lay a single egg, the American Black lays two, and the Turkey Vulture may lay 1-2 eggs. Depending on the species, the incubation period lasts 32-58 days. The fledging period also varies considerably from 70 days for the American Black, and an amazing 25 weeks for a young Californian Condor.

OSPREY

Order: *Falconiformes*
Family: *Pandionidae*
the genus Pandion contains a single species
Pandion haliaetus

The Osprey *Pandion haliaetus* is one of the most widespread raptors in the World, breeding on all continents except for Antarctica and South America. Northern populations migrate south in the fall; those that breed in North America winter in Central and South America, leap-frogging resident birds in Florida and the Caribbean. From northern Europe birds travel to Africa, whilst those in the Mediterranean region are resident.

The Osprey is a magnificent predator and it is always worth while taking the time to watch one as it flaps slowly over a lake, peering down for a fish. Once the prey has been sighted the Osprey plunges down, entering the water feet first to grasp the fish with its talons; then, with powerful wing beats, it bursts from the surface in a shower of spray. With the fish held firmly head first in its claws, the bird flies powerfully away to a nearby perch or back to its nest. After the first few wing beats Ospreys always give themselves a good shake and loose some height in the process.

The Osprey is a brown and white fish-eating bird of prey, 22-25 in. (56-64 cm.) long, about as large as one of the medium-sized eagles and is an invaluable barometer of its environment. Ospreys eat solely fish and are therefore at the top of their food chain. Any toxic chemical residues in polluted water build up in aquatic life and ultimately reach the Osprey through the fish it has eaten. During the 1960s the effect of the widespread use of DDT as a pesticide was noticed when the breeding success of species such as Ospreys and Peregrine Falcons *Falco peregrinus* fell dramatically. One colony, on Gardiner's Island, off Long Island New York, held 300 nests at the beginning of this century, but during the 1960s this had crashed to only 20 pairs!

In Britain the Osprey bred in Scotland until the late 1890s, but they were doomed. Ospreys and their eggs were in great demand by the Victorian collectors, so the rarer they became the greater the demand. The end was inevitable and for over 50 years, lochs and glens that had traditionally been home to the birds for centuries were deserted. During the years after World War II, Ospreys occurred more frequently in northern Scotland, until a nest was found in 1954. The young fledged successfully, but it was not until 1959 that another pair raised any young. Thanks to a splendid public relations exercise by the Royal Society for the Protection of Birds, many members of the public were to watch these birds from a specially

The fish-eating Osprey (these pages) is a widespread raptor, a brown and white bird with a distinctive, almost gull-like, kinked wing shape. Osprey populations in the northern latitudes are migratory and, whilst migrating, stop to fish in waters en route. Ospreys return to the same eyrie year after year and often with the same mate. Left: two Ospreys in Everglades National Park, Florida, where the species is common.

constructed blind, equipped with powerful binoculars. Many years later, after alternating periods of disappointment and elation, the Ospreys at Loch Garten in Speyside are still a major tourist attraction. During the 1987 breeding season in Scotland 51 pairs bred, 30 of which were successful and 56 youngsters reared. The Ospreys that originally re-colonised Scotland were from Scandinavia, but now sufficient young are being produced by those established pairs for the population to expand farther afield, and although the robbing of nests by egg-collectors is still a serious threat, the future of Scottish Ospreys looks brighter than for decades.

The first time I visited Florida I was amazed at the numbers of Ospreys to be seen; we had excellent views of them fishing as we drove through the Ding Darling National Wildlife Reserve on Sanibel Island near Fort Myers, and nearby watched a pair mating on a huge nest built on top of the sirens of the fire station. Anyone driving down US1 to Key

Ospreys circle above the water watching for an unsuspecting fish just below the surface. Once a victim is sighted the bird usually hovers before plunging feet first into the water. If successful, it rises from the water in a cloud of spray with a fish struggling in its strong talons. If unsuccessful, the search begins once more.

Largo cannot fail to notice the Ospreys' nests on power poles. Ospreys often use the same nest year after year and in areas where there is little or no damage during the non-breeding season huge structures may accumulate. Two to four eggs are laid and although both parents share the incubation, the female carries out much of the work, including the night shifts. After 37 days the eggs start to hatch, for incubation commences with the first egg. The female broods the young and feeds them fish brought to the nest by the male. The youngsters are flying after about 53 days and become independent some four to eight weeks later. They reach breeding age after three years.

Vulture *Torgos tracheliotus*, 39 in. (100 cm.) long, that breaks through the hide. Once the Lappet-faced has eaten, then the quarrelsome Rüppell's Griffon and African White-backed Vultures *Gyps rüeppellii* and *G. africanus* take over to clear most of the meat, leaving the smaller Hooded and Egyptian Vultures *Necrosyrtes monachus* and *Neophron percnopterus* to clear up the small tit-bits left on the bones and in inaccessible places. The Egyptian Vulture is one of the few bird species to use tools; they throw stones at Ostrich eggs to break the shell and reach the contents. It is also widespread in rural India, where it is an important scavenger of human waste.

Facing page: a young Martial Eagle defends its kill: a Thomson's Gazelle fawn. The Martial is the most powerful of Africa's eagles, as can be seen from its strong legs and bill. The Egyptian Vulture (left), an Old World species, has a comparatively lightweight bill and feeds on scraps or at a carcass after the other vultures have eaten.

HAWKS and EAGLES
Order: *Falconiformes*
Family: *Accipitridae*
61 genera contains 219 species

Most diurnal birds of prey, or raptors as they are called by birders, belong to either the hawks and eagles *Accipitridae* or the falcons and caracaras *Falconidae*.

Hawks and eagles have a world-wide distribution except in the Antarctic and on a number of islands. There are 219 species divided between 61 genera occurring in a great variety of habitats. With a family of such proportions, these birds come in all shapes and sizes, from tiny sparrowhawks to mighty eagles.

Amongst the largest members of the family are the Old World Vultures; 14 species placed in 7 genera, and are unrelated to New World vultures that include the familiar Turkey Vulture *Cathartes aura*. They occur in warm temperate and tropical regions of the Old World, from Spain to Indo-China and throughout much of Africa, where up to five species may feed on the carcass of an animal. They have differing-sized bills that enable them to perform different tasks at a feast. Soaring effortlessly over the plains of Africa, vultures are ever-watchful, constantly scanning the ground for food or watching other soaring vultures. When one starts to descend it is noticed by others, who follow and are in turn seen by yet more vultures; within minutes birds are arriving from all points of the compass. If the dead beast has not been opened by a predator, it is the huge bill of the Lappet-faced

Left: a Kenyan Lappet-faced Vulture – the strongest African vulture. Its leggings and the white stripe along its wing are distinctive features used to identify this bird.

Widespread, but not common, is the magnificent Lammergeier or Bearded Vulture *Gypaetus barbatus*, a bird of mountain ranges, from the Pyrenees to the Himalayas, and in Africa south to the highlands of Ethiopia and Swaziland, where an isolated population occurs. Besides conventional scavenging, the Lammergeier has learned to drop bones and tortoises from the air onto rocks below, breaking them, so enabling it to reach the contents. Aeschylus, an ancient Greek dramatist, is reported to have come to an untimely end, when a passing Lammergeier, carrying a tortoise aloft, mistook his bald pate for a white rock – nasty! Golden Eagles also drop tortoises so there might have been a case of mistaken identity; but either way Aeschylus died.

The Palm-nut Vulture or Vulturine Fish Eagle *Gypohierax angolensis*, of sub-Saharan Africa is not a true vulture in the accepted sense, for besides eating carrion such as dead fish along rivers, it eats palm-nuts. It is probably the link between vultures and the fish eagles.

Above left: an ever watchful adult Golden Eagle in Colorado. This bird is a hunter, feeding on carrion when necessary. The Black-shouldered Kite (above) is frequently found on the African savannah. The African Fish Eagle (left) is related to the Bald Eagle of North America, but lacks its yellow eye and white tail and, unsurprisingly perhaps, feeds principally on fish.

There are many species of eagle; amongst the largest species are the Fish or Sea Eagles *Haliaeetus* and it is to this genus that the Bald Eagle *H. leucocephalus* belongs. It is a noble bird, even if some people feel that its image is tarnished by being a scavenger, for an adult Bald Eagle soaring against a blue sky is superb. It is not the largest member of the genus; that honour goes to the impressive Steller's Sea Eagle *H. pelagicus* of north-eastern Asia. This black and white eagle has a white wedge-shaped tail, shoulder patches and forehead, and a massive yellow bill. Occasionally they occur in the Aleutians, but if one wants to see a Steller's Sea Eagle and does not mind the cold, then Hokkaido in northern Japan is the place to visit during winter. In Scotland, an attempt to reintroduce the White-tailed Eagles *H. albicilla* from Norway looks like being successful, provided the birds are given a chance. They usually rear two chicks and during the reintroduction program fledglings were taken from Norwegian nests, leaving the adults one chick to raise. These fledglings

Left: an African White-backed Vulture coming in to land with its legs lowered. This is the commonest of African vultures and usually forms the majority of the avian scavengers at a carcass in the game parks.

were transported by land. sea and air to the Isle of Rhum, off Scotland's west coast, where they were cared for by John Love of the Nature Conservancy Council, until they were old enough to be released into the wild. During the following winter food dumps were provided for the birds, some of which stayed on the island while others wandered farther afield. In a matter of years these birds were scattered over a wide area of north-western Scotland and as they progressed towards maturity it became apparent that eventually breeding would take place. The last recorded breeding attempt had taken place in 1916. Little did I expect that on a fine day in early April 1983, in a remote glen in western Scotland, I would be the first person since 1916 to find an incubating White-tailed Eagle. That nest failed for natural reasons, but in 1985 the first young White-tailed Eagle to be reared in Scotland for nearly 70 years graced the skies. Another member of the genus is the African Fish Eagle *H. vocifer*; it is slightly

smaller than its more northerly relatives. During our tours to northern Botswana it is one of the most familiar and characteristic raptors of the region.

The other North American eagle is the Golden Eagle *Aquila chrysaetos*; about the same size as a Bald Eagle, it belongs to the group of true eagles *Aquila*. Whilst they are renowned hunters, they are also opportunist feeders, turning to carrion if available. Whilst some species are sedentary, others migrate in large numbers, including the Lesser Spotted Eagle *A. pomarina*, which crosses the Bosphorus, Turkey, in thousands during the fall migration period.

Many other large raptors are also eagles; amongst the largest are the Harpy Eagle *Harpia harpyja* from the forests of South America and the endangered Philippine Eagle *Pithecophaga jefferyi* found in the dwindling forests of its island home. Monkeys feature in the diet of the Harpy Eagle, but although the Philippine Eagle was formerly known as the

Almost symbolic of power and strength, the Bald Eagle (above) was chosen as the national bird of the United States in 1782. It was once widespread but is now uncommon outside Alaska.

Monkey-eating Eagle, this was somewhat of a misnomer, for its principal prey is flying lemurs *Cynocephalus*. In Africa the Martial Eagle *Polemaetus bellicosus* is large enough to take young antelopes.

Another distinct group of 10 species comprise the harriers *Circus*, a genus of long-winged, long-tailed raptors that occur in temperate and tropical grasslands and marshes throughout the World, being absent from the highest latitudes. The most widespread species is the Northern Harrier *C. cyaneus*, which occurs over much of the Northern Hemisphere. It leisurely quarters marshes and fields, on wings held in a shallow 'V' above the line of the body; sometimes it beats into the wind, flying low over the grass searching for small rodents and small birds. Harriers are spectacular birds and it is always worth watching them carrying food to the nest during the breeding season. Several times I have watched the gray male Northern Harrier carrying prey across Willow Flats by Jackson Lake, Grand Teton National Park, Wyoming. As it approached the nesting area, the brown female flew up and passed beneath him; as she did so she flipped over and the male dropped the prey to her waiting talons. The female returned to the nest and the male carried on hunting.

Many other raptors come in the group loosely described as hawks, including the broad-winged hawks *Buteo*, the bird-

Amongst the remaining species worthy of mentioning are two that occur in the south-eastern United States. The American Swallow-tailed Kite *Elanoides forficatus*, is a graceful and elegant raptor with a deeply-forked tail, which migrates south to winter in South America. The Snail Kite *Rostrhamus sociabilis* is a declining bird of the swamps of southern Florida, although it remains more plentiful in Central and South America. It feeds on a diet of Apple Snails *Pomacea caliginosa*; the contents are extracted with its long hooked bill.

Facing page: a Dark Chanting Goshawk feeds on a small bird. One of many African raptors, it can be differentiated from the Pale Chanting Goshawk by its barred, as opposed to white, rump.

The Philippines Eagle (left) is one of the world's rarest raptors. Hunting and destruction of its habitat have led to the decline of this magnificent bird. The Red-shouldered Hawk (far left) is a distinctive North American *buteo*. Cooper's Hawk (below) is one of three North American accipiters.

hawks *Accipiter* and various kites. In North America it is the buteos and accipiters that form the bulk of the hawk passage over Hawk Mountain, Pennsylvania. These two genera are widespread across the globe and account for 25 and 47 species respectively. In other parts of the world the buteo hawks are usually called 'buzzards', a term applied in the Americas to the Turkey Vulture. The common buteo of North America is the Red-tailed Hawk *B. jamaicensis*, but nine other species also breed north of the Mexican border. In Western Europe the Common Buzzard *B. buteo* is the most widespread species, although in winter the Rough-legged Hawk or Buzzard *B. lagopus* appears in varying numbers from the northern latitudes.

The accipiters have evolved many species, some being restricted to isolated islands, especially in the area that includes the East Indies, New Guinea and the Western Pacific. One of the largest species is the Northern Goshawk *A. gentilis*, a powerful bird of Holarctic distribution that takes prey as large as Capercaillie *Tetrao urogallus* and hares *Lepus spp.*. Two other members of the genus occur in North America, Cooper's and the Sharp-shinned Hawk *A. cooperii* and *A. striatus*. These, like most other members of the genus, hunt birds with a dashing flight and the element of surprise in their favour. Both migrate south in the fall.

All members of the family spend varying lengths of time on the wing, but it is doubtful if any are more aerial than the Bateleur *Terathopius ecaudatus* of sub-Saharan Africa. The name comes from the French meaning 'tumbler', a reflection of the aerobatic display flight performed by the male. This is one of Africa's most characteristic birds of prey. Bateleurs seem to fly for the sheer joy of being in the air, constantly tilting their wings this way and that to compensate for the virtual lack of tail.

The diet of members of the family covers all forms of carrion, mammals as large as small antelopes, birds of all sizes, fish, reptiles, including poisonous snakes, insects, crustaceans, snails and other invertebrates. The Palm-nut Vultures is partially vegetarian.

Some members of the family build their own nests, whilst others take over the old nests of other birds. Nest sites vary from cliffs to trees; some nest on the ground. Large eagles may have two or more eyries, and choose the one best suited to the weather conditions prevailing at the time. The nest is constructed from sticks and other strong vegetable material, and often lined with softer materials such as wool. The clutch size may vary depending on the species from 1 – 7 eggs. Incubation, longest in the larger species, usually commences with the first egg and it is often only the first or strongest chick that survives; sibling rivalry causes the death of many raptor chicks. The success of breeding also depends on the availability of food, typified by the Rough-legged Hawk whose breeding performance is linked to the abundance of lemmings *Lemmus spp.* and other small rodents; in a good year as many as seven chicks may be reared, but only two in a poor one. Young raptors may stay with their parents for several months after fledging, it can be very entertaining to watch as they are taught hunting skills.

Sadly the numbers of birds of prey have declined through persecution and pollution. They are vulnerable to both, and being at the top of their food chain are an important barometer of our own environment, a fact we should not ignore.

Above: two Bateleurs survey their territory in Kenya's Masai Mara Game Reserve. These birds spend much of their time on the wing, but even at rest their comparative lack of tail is obvious. The Ferruginous Hawk is the largest of North America's *buteos* and occurs in the dry Western States. Left: a pale-phased Ferruginous Hawk with chestnut feathered leggings.

SECRETARY BIRD
Order: *Falconiformes*
Family: *Sagittariidae*
the genus Sagittarius contains a single
species *Sagittarius serpentarius*

Across the plains of Africa the Secretary Bird *Sagittarius serpentarius*, standing 4 ft. (1.2 m.) tall, wanders alone or with its mate, patiently searching and probing the grass with its long legs for food. It is an unlikely-looking raptor, with its elegant grey and white plumage offsetting the black wings and leggings. The two long central tail feathers give the impression of coat-tails and the lax crest feathers perhaps recall a 19th. century Dickensian clerk with a quill pen behind his ear. It is popularly supposed that this is where the name Secretary Bird came from, but recently it has been suggested

The Secretary Bird strides across the plains of Africa displaying the distinctive head feathers that may have given the species its name. Its diet includes snakes, eggs and mammals.

that the name is a corruption of the Arabic *saqr et-tair* meaning 'hunter-bird'. It must be born in mind that Arab dhows were trading down the coasts of Africa long before Europeans opened up the Dark Continent for settlers.

Traditionally Secretary Birds have been considered to be aberrant birds of prey or raptors, but recent analysis of egg-white proteins show that there is a possible relationship to the crane-related birds – *Gruiformes*. The only birds in the World that look anything like the Secretary Birds are the Seriemas *Cariamidae* of South America and they are classed as *Gruiformes*. Further detailed studies into behaviour and so on are necessary to establish the relationships fully. For the time being the status quo must prevail.

Secretary Birds are birds of the open savannah and plains, where the seasonal grass hides a multitude of prey species. They have excellent eyesight and usually walk quickly or run before any threat comes anywhere near them. When pressed they will fly with slow wing beats far enough to feel secure once more. They are thought of as snake-eating birds, but snakes make up only a small part of the diet. Grasshoppers, beetles and small rodents are the main food items, but it will take prey as large as a hare *Lepus sp.*, as deadly as Puff Adder

Bitis arietans and Cobra *Naja sp.*, and as unlikely as a clutch of eggs from a ground- nesting bird.

During a game drive in Kenya's Samburu Game Reserve the minibus in which I was travelling disturbed a Secretary Bird beside the track. It flew a few hundred yards across a dry gully, where a few minutes later we were able to watch it successfully catch and eat a young Cape Hare *Lepus capensis*. The prey was small enough to be swallowed whole, but a full-grown animal would have been dismembered and eaten. The bird, with a swollen crop, carried on probing and poking around clumps of grass and small bushes, and within 50 yd. (45 m.) it caught a snake about 18 in. (45 cm.) long. The Secretary Bird kept its distance, jabbing repeatedly at the writhing reptile with its long legs until eventually it proceeded to swallow the lifeless snake head first.

There is an amusing tale related in Peter Steyn's excellent book *Birds of Prey of Southern Africa*. A Secretary Bird, much to the dismay of the player, picked up a golf ball that had just been driven. Obviously the bird mistook the ball for an egg and left the golfer wondering if he could mark that hole down as a 'birdie'! I cannot help feel sorry for the Secretary Bird, who no doubt felt egg-bound.

Snakes are attacked and rendered harmless by the Secretary Bird's long legs and strong feet before being eaten. The fleshy upper legs are protected by thick feathers.

The nest is often sited in the crown of a flat-topped Acacia *Acacia sp.* where the three eggs are mainly incubated by the female for about 45 days. She is fed by the male at the nest, but he takes a turn if she leaves the nest to feed for herself. Usually only two eggs hatch and brooding is undertaken by both parents during the first weeks after hatching, although food is mainly brought in by the male, which he regurgitates at the nest. Prey at this time of the year can also include the eggs of ground nesting birds such as francolins *Francolinus sp..* After about a month the female joins the male in the hunt for food for the growing brood. Unlike many raptor broods there is no sibling rivalry between the chicks, so there is a good chance that both will survive. Food is no longer regurgitated, but delivered whole. Although they are unable to fly properly, the youngsters leave the nest after about 75 days and can fly a week or so later.

manoeuvrability at slow speeds is more important than power. South America is home to two other genera that are not typical falcons. The forest-falcons *Micrastur spp.* are forest birds as their name suggests, and resemble the goshawks *Accipiter spp.* The Laughing Falcon *Herpetotheres cachinnans* is a little more falcon-like, but is sluggish and includes snakes in its diet. The typical falcons consist of four genera found in a variety of open habitats from forest margins to the Arctic tundra. The largest genus contains the true falcons *Falco*. The other three contain the pygmy falcons or falconets, found in warm temperate or tropical regions of South America, Africa and Asia. These are tiny raptors; the Black-legged Falconet *Microhierax fringillarius* from south-east Asia and Indonesia is only 6 in. (15 cm.) long.

The true falcons range from the magnificent Gyr Falcon *F. rusticolus*, 25 in. (64 cm.) long, of the Arctic to the tiny

The Striated or Forster's Caracara (below) occurs in southern South America and in the Falkland Islands, where they scavenge at seabird colonies. Although hawk-like in appearance, caracaras are related to falcons.

FALCONS

Order: *Falconiformes*
Family: *Falconidae*
10 genera contain of 62 species

Some of the most exciting avian predators are the falcons, especially the Peregrine Falcon *Falco peregrinus*, that hunts with such flair. It circles, apparently idly, watching for prey, then, with a few strong wing-beats, it closes its long pointed wings and stoops at breath-taking speed of up to 112 mph. (180 km/h.) onto its target.

Falcons are a widespread family that occurs throughout much of the World, except Antarctica and some remote oceanic islands. Most are diurnal raptors, although the Bat Falcon *F. rufigularis*, from South America, is partially crepuscular, for bats make up part of its diet.

The family comprises 62 species divided into 10 genera, most resembling typical falcons, but the caracaras *Daptriinae* of the southern United States, Central and South America, comprise four genera totalling nine species. Caracaras are more hawk-like than other members of the family, for unlike the falcons they are omnivorous and scavengers; therefore

Seychelles Kestrel *F. araea*, marginally larger than the falconets. Nearby, also in the Indian Ocean, the Mauritius Kestrel *F. punctatus*, is one of the rarest birds in the World. A captive breeding programme has met with only limited success and the total population of captive and wild birds is under 20 individuals.

Whilst many species are sedentary, some wander during the winter months; others are long distance migrants. Northern Hobbies and Western Red-footed Falcons *F. subbuteo* and *F. verpertinus* both breed in the western Palearctic, but winter in southern Africa; yet, neither matches the migration of the Eastern Red-footed Falcon *F. amurensis*. It breeds in the Far East and winters thousands of miles away in Botswana, Zimbabwe and South Africa, but the route is unclear. The paucity of records between Assam and southern Africa suggest that perhaps it undertakes the long sea crossing.

Not all species hunt with the same panache as the Peregrine, others dash with fast rapid wing beats like the Merlin *F. columbarius* or hover like the kestrels. Many take small prey, including small birds, rodents and a variety of insects. A number have become specialists and are worthy of mention. Several, including the Western Red-footed Falcon, catch and eat bees and beetles on the wing. The Taita Falcon *F. fasciinucha*, an uncommon African species, is fast and agile enough to catch swifts *Apodidae* in flight; whilst the Gyr

Facing page: (top left) the Lanner – a large falcon found mainly in Africa and the Near East, and (top right) the Common Kestrel, which occurs over much of the Old World. Facing page: (bottom left) the American Kestrel – the smallest North American raptor, and (bottom right) the Crested Caracara, a South American species, found in the south-western states and Florida.

Falcon *F. rusticolus* kills birds as large as a Barnacle Goose *Branta leucopsis* and mammals including the Arctic Hare *Lepus timidus*. During the fall Eleaonora's and Sooty Falcons *F. eleonorae* and *F. concolor* breed on cliffs around the Mediterranean and the Middle East. They coincide their breeding season with the southward migration of small land birds through the region. In South America are a number of interesting specialists. The Laughing and Bat Falcons have already been mentioned; the Barred Forest-Falcon *Micrastur ruficollis* sometimes preys on the small birds that follow the swarms of army ants *Ecitoninae*.

Caracaras build their own nests, but most other species use the old or abandoned nests of other birds. Sites might be in cracks in trees, in the canopy of trees or on cliff ledges. The African Pygmy Falcon *Polihierax semitorquatus* breeds in the huge colonial nests of the Sociable Weaver *Philetairus*

socius in southern Africa, and in the smaller condominiums of buffalo-weavers *Bubalornis spp.* in East Africa. The clutch size, length of the incubation and fledging periods vary considerably within the family; the extremes are 2 – 6 eggs, incubated from 25 – 32 days and the young fledge some 40 – 49 days. Young African Pygmy Falcons may fledge after 27 – 0 days in the nest, both parents having shared the domestic duties. In other species the female incubates and broods the young, while the male brings food to the nest.

Falcons are at the top of their respective food chains, and are therefore particularly vulnerable to the build up of toxic chemicals. Chemicals, often from agricultural pesticides, are absorbed by the body tissue of prey species, sometimes several links down the food-chain from the falcons. They do not break down, but are passed on up the chain, until they reach the top. DDT was widely used in North America and Europe until it was realised the effect it was having on the environment. Birds of prey, and in particular the populations of Peregrines and Ospreys *Pandion haliaetus*, went into decline due to breeding failure resulting from thin egg shells. It is disturbing to note that DDT is currently being used in some African countries to control Tsetse Fly *Glossina morsitans*. How long before the birds of prey are effected and DDT is carried back to Europe by the migratory species?

in. (60 cm.) long, and the Brush Turkey, *Alectura lathami* 28 in. (71 cm.) long. Megapodes spend much of their time on the ground and only fly when forced to escape danger. They are usually birds of the tropical rain forests, but in northern and eastern Australia, the largest species, the Brush Turkey also inhabits drier scrub. They are omnivorous, with a diet that includes fruit, seeds and other vegetable matter, as well as insects and small animals such as lizards.

The nesting behaviour of this family is unique amongst birds and the term 'incubator bird' is most appropriate. The different species employ a variety of methods to incubate their eggs; the common denominator is that none of the species hatch their eggs in the conventional manner. The simplest method is that used in Sulawesi by the Maleo Fowl *Macrocephalon maleo*, and the Common Scrub Hen *Megapodius freycinet* in some parts of its range. At a site in sandy soil or at the top of a beach a mound some ten feet (3 m.) high and 15 ft. (4.5 m.) across is constructed in which the eggs are laid and covered with sand; the sun does the rest! On hatching, the well developed chicks struggle through to the surface and are off into the world, with no parental guidance. On the islands of the New Britain group and the Solomons, megapodes bury their eggs in volcanic soil where they are incubated by the heat from the earth. Other members of the

MEGAPODES
Order: *Galliformes*
Family: *Megapodiidae*
seven genera contain twelve species.

The Megapodes *Megapodiidae* are terrestrial birds occurring from the Nicobar Islands in the north-east Indian Ocean to the Philippines, and down through a mosaic of islands large and small to New Guinea and Australia. The name Megapode means 'great foot'.

They are large birds varying from 19in.(50cm.) to 28 in. (71 cm.) long, depending on the species. Being fowl-like birds they vaguely resemble others of their kind; some recall gamebirds, in particular the Mallee Fowl *Leipoa ocellata* 24

family, such as the Brush Turkey, construct a mound of soil and vegetable debris, so that the eggs are incubated by a combination of heat from the sun and from the decomposing vegetation. Some species supervise the process by adding or removing material to maintain the correct temperature. Brush Turkeys will vigorously defend the nest against predation by large goanna lizards, using the same method that they employ to construct the mound in the first place. They face away from the threat and, using strong legs and feet, kick a continuous barrage of leaves and twigs over the predator, forcing it to withdraw. The clutch can be laid over a period of several months, depending on the species. The Mallee Fowl can lay up to 33 eggs at intervals of a week. Each egg weighs one tenth of the weight of the female, so that in the course of a breeding season the eggs produced weigh three times her own weight! Each egg starts to develop as soon as it is laid, but takes up to eight weeks or so to hatch. Once the well-developed chick has

The Brush Turkey is a member of the Megapode family that occurs in eastern Australia. Its eggs are buried in a huge mound nest constructed using their strong feet.

broken out of the shell it can take several hours to emerge from the mound. After a few hours it can run quite quickly and within 24 hours can fly well enough to escape from danger. Extraordinary!

Throughout much of their range the large eggs of the megapodes are collected from the conspicuous nests; these represent an important food supply for the native populations. In some tribes the collection of eggs has become part of their rituals and has afforded some measure of conservation, for living in harmony with their environment they only take sufficient for their needs. With the spread of western civilization a cash economy has emerged and consequently more megapodes and their eggs are being taken than are necessary for the needs of a family or a village. The profit factor, when combined with increasing destruction of the forest habitats, indicates that there must be a serious decline in the population of megapodes in some areas as losses exceed regeneration.

CURASSOWS and GUANS
Order: *Galliformes*
Family: *Cracidae*
nine genera contain 44 species

The family of Curassows is split into three groups – there are nine species of Chachalacas, 21 of Guan and 14 species of Curassows. They occur from south-eastern Texas through Central America, into South America as far south as northern Argentina.

Most species are to be found in humid lowlands forests, although some inhabit drier, less densely wooded habitats. They are largely arboreal, birds with short rounded wings and long ample tails. Many have a bare throat patch that becomes more brightly coloured in the male during the breeding season. They have strong legs and feet to enable them to run and jump between branches up in the trees, using their wings for balance, as they search for food. They are omnivorous, with a diet consisting of young leaves, insects and frogs. Such items as flowers and fruit are collected from the forest floor.

The smallest are the nine species of Chachalacas *Ortalis*. They are to be found throughout the range of the family *Cracidae*, although the greatest variety of species stretch from Mexico through Central America to Colombia, where seven of the nine species occur. One species widespread in northern South America is the Rufous-vented Chachalaca *O. ruficauda*, 22 in. (56 cm.) long, which is also found on the island of Tobago, as well as on two islands in the Grenadines to the north where it is becoming increasingly rare. The most northerly species is the Plain or Common Chachalaca *O. vetula* 20 in. (50 cm.), a brown bird that occurs from southern Texas to Nicaragua. Unfortunately, along with the rest of the family, they make very good eating and are regarded as a gamebird in many places.

The Guans consist of 21 species divided into five genera, most of which, 14 species, are placed in the genus *Penelope*. Guans tend to be larger than Chachalacas and have a more varied plumage. Some species are brown, with scaled or streaked feathers on the head, neck and upper-breast. Others are black and may have white wing patches and a white head, like the Common Piping Guan *Aburria pipile*, 27 in. (69 cm.) long, which is widespread and ranges from Trinidad to Paraguay. The very rare Horned Guan *Oreophasis derbianus*, 34 in. (86 cm.) long, has a red casque protruding from the forehead. It is a black bird, found in evergreen forests on a few volcanoes between 7,000-10,000 ft. (2,100-3,000 m.) in south-eastern Mexico and southern Guatemala; there have been few recent sightings.

The largest members of the family are the Curassows, 14 species, of which 13 belong to the genus *Crax*. The other bird, the Nocturnal Curassow *Nothocrax urumutum*, 26 in. (66 cm.) long, is a brown species found in a small region of Amazonian forests from south-western Venezuela to eastern Peru and western Brazil. All members of the family are vocal, but this is the only species to sing at night. The largest species is the Great Curassow *Crax rubra*, 38 in. (96 cm.) long, which occurs from Mexico to Ecuador. It is a large black bird with a white belly, has a tight forward curling crest on the forehead

and a yellow wattle at the base of the bill. These features are shared by several species, but some, such as the Razor-billed Curassow *C. tuberosa*, lack the crest and wattle, but have an enlarged bill and chestnut belly. The closely related Alagoas Curassow *C. mitu* has recently been rediscovered after it was thought to have been extinct for 300 years! It occurs only in a very small area of the forests of Alagoas, Brazil. This species is so rare that unless conservation methods, such as a captive breeding program can be effective, it will certainly disappear for good.

Knowledge of the breeding biology for a number of species is either non-existent or at best poorly known. It is highly likely that the domestic life of most species is similar. Most make a small nest in trees, although some, including the small chachalaca-like Highland Guan *Penelopina nigra*, 21 in. (53 cm.), that occurs from southern Mexico to northern Nicaragua, breeds on the ground. Two to three eggs are laid and incubation lasts between 22 and 34 days, depending on the species. The chicks leave the nest shortly after hatching, already having well-developed flight feathers. They hide amongst foliage, but are able to fly sufficiently well within three or four days to cross from one tree to another. The adults and young stay together for some time after fledging and join up with others of their kind to form flocks of up to 20 birds.

The future for many species in the family looks bleak, for not only are they suffering from over hunting, but in places serious habitat destruction is taking place. The Curassows themselves are particularly susceptible to disturbance, let alone persecution and deforestation. Six species have sufficiently low populations that they are endangered; the population levels of a further nine species are seriously threatened, so that it is possible that in the next decade or so some species may become extinct.

A beautiful male Common Peafowl, a noisy bird familiar through collections and zoological gardens throughout the world. In the wild it occurs in India and Sri Lanka. Further east it is superseded by the closely related Green Peafowl, which has a green head and neck.

PHEASANTS and GROUSE
Order: *Galliformes*
Family: *Phasianidae*
62 genera contain 211 species

The family of pheasants and grouse *Phasianidae* is almost global in its distribution, absent only from various islands, southern South America, the Saharan region of Africa, the Greenland icecap and the polar regions. The only species to occur in New Zealand are introduced, for the endemic New Zealand Quail *Coturnix novaezelandiae* became extinct during the late 19th. century.

The diverse family contains 211 species placed in 62 genera; a varied group, they range from the tiny quails to the

Wild Turkey *Meleagris gallopavo* of North America. The latter, of course, is a familiar domesticated bird, as is the chicken, the domestic descendant of the Red Junglefowl *Gallus gallus* or one of its close relatives. Junglefowl are Asiatic in origin, but in which country the initial domestication occurred is uncertain, although contemporary records reveal that there were domestic birds in India over 5,000 years ago, in 3200 B.C. Another domesticated species is the Helmeted Guineafowl *Numida meleagris*, one of a number of similar African species and excellent when served with a white wine sauce!

Members of the family come in a host of shapes, sizes and colours. The smallest species are the thrush-sized Old World

quails *Coturnix spp.*, a cryptically-coloured genus of grassland gamebirds, unlike the larger New World species. By comparison the quails of western North America and Mexico, such as the California Quail *Callipepla californica* 10 in. (25 cm.) long with its striking head plume, are well-marked. A little larger are the partridges and francolins of the Old World; 20 genera that contain 93 species, and the largest group in the family. The largest genus is the 41 species of francolins *Francolinus*. The giants of the group are the grouse-like snowcocks *Tetraogallus* of Central Asia. The Himalayan

Snowcock *T. himalayensis* 28 in. (71 cm.) long, appears to have been successfully introduced in Nevada. The grouse are among the traditional gamebirds, and occur in a variety of habitats from the prairies of the Mid-West, to the northern coniferous forests and tundra. The males of many species have developed elaborate head patterns used in conjunction with spread tails during display; a number perform to females at communal 'leks'. The ptarmigan *Lagopus spp.* live in the highest latitudes and altitudes, and molt from a cryptic breeding plumage to an all-white winter garb in the fall. The largest

Below: a male Red Grouse on a Scottish moor. It is a member of the British Willow Ptarmigan family, but lacks the characteristic white wings.

grouse or grouse-like bird is the Wild Turkey, which needs no introduction. Yet in northern Central America there is a less well-known relative of similar proportions, the Ocellated Turkey *Agriocharis ocellata*.

Most colourful members of the family are the pheasants, a group of 49 species placed in 16 genera that include the Red Junglefowl. The plumages of these birds are spectacular as well as colourful, but as with many other families the females are dull. To describe all the variations would take a book in itself. Amongst the most outstanding are Temminck's Tragopan *Tragopan temminckii*, the Himalayan Monal Pheasant *Lophophorus impeyanus* and the Common Peafowl *Pavo cristatus* with its wonderful tail.

Most members of the family are sedentary, although the Common Quail *C. coturnix* of Europe winters in Africa. A close relative, the Harlequin Quail *C. delegorguei* moves

Above far left: a male Blue Grouse of the forests of western North America in display, and (above left) a male Wild Turkey in all his finery, now less widespread in the United States than formerly. Far left: also displaying, a Greater Prairie-chicken, a bird of the North American prairies. The Ring-necked Pheasant (centre left) is native to Asia, but was introduced for sport elsewhere. Left: a male White-tailed Ptarmigan, one of three North American grouse that turn white in winter.

73

seasonally as the rains stimulate the grown of new grass. On Savuti Marsh in Botswana it is particularly common in such conditions, but six months later, when the grass is impoverished prior to the next rains, it can be a difficult bird to find. In Asia some species are altitudinal migrants, others wander in search of favourite foods. Most species are largely vegetarian, with a diet of seeds, fruit, leaves, roots and new shoots. This may be supplemented with earthworms and insects. The Common Peafowl has been recorded eating lizards and snakes, and on the Isle of Mull in Scotland, I watched a Ring-necked Pheasant *Phasianus colchicus* attempt to eat a Common Frog *Rana temporaria*. Grit and small stones are swallowed to aid digestion as food passes through the gizzard.

The nest is often a grass-lined scrape on the ground, sometimes on the sheltered side of a rock or a shrub. The Marbled Wood-quail *Odontophorus gujanensis* builds a covered nest with a side entrance, but the breeding biology of some species is so poorly known that it is unclear if this is typical of closely related species. Tragopans are the only members of the family to nest in trees. The number of eggs varies within this diverse family, tropical species laying

fewer than their northern relatives. Up to 20 eggs have been recorded in the nest of the Grey Partridge *Perdix perdix*; in other species such large clutches may be the result of more than one female laying in the same nest. Incubation is usually by the female alone, but the Red-legged Partridge *Alectoris rufa* and closely related species sometimes lay two clutches in different nests, each being incubated by one adult. The incubation period lasts 16 – 28 days depending on the species and the youngsters leave the nest shortly after hatching; they are capable of short flights to escape danger within a week.

Because of habitat destruction and the demands made by collections, many species of pheasants are endangered and are sufficiently rare to give cause for concern.

HOATZIN

Order: *Galliformes*
Family: *Opisthocomidae*
the genera *Opisthocomus* contains a single species *Opisthocomus hoatzin*

There are few birds that present more of a problem to taxonomists than the Hoatzin *Opisthocomus hoatzin* of South America. It occurs along river systems and the margins of swamps, where it inhabits trees and bushes overhanging the

The male Capercaillie (top) is the largest European grouse and occurs in pine forests east into Asia. Above: a male Swainson's Francolin, an African member of the pheasant and grouse family, proclaims his territory in Namibia's Etosha National Park.

water. Over the years it has been placed with at least eight different Orders. In 1973 it was re-assigned to the cuckoo-like birds *Cuculiformes*, from the fowl-like birds *Galliformes*, after researchers analysing egg-white proteins discovered that it appeared to be related to the anis *Crotophaga sp.*, a relative of the cuckoos. Then, in 1979, just when everything looked settled, someone studying immunological data came along and tossed the poor Hoatzin back amongst the chickens again!

Whatever relationship the Hoatzin has with other birds, it is an extraordinary creature in its own right. Much of its 25 in. (64 cm.) length consists of a long ample tail and a long scraggy neck; it almost looks permanently dishevelled in a suit of feathers too big for the body. The head, with a punk-like spiky crest, and under-parts are chestnut-orange, whilst the back and wings are bronze-olive with buff markings. It clambers through the branches in search of its diet that consists mainly of the leaves of aquatic plants, especially arums *Montrichardia* and White Mangrove *Avicennia*. Unlike other vegetarian birds, which use the gizzard to digest the plant matter, the Hoatzin has evolved a particularly muscular crop, to break up the food before it passes to the stomach. This may seem a good idea, but it raises and brings forward the bird's centre of gravity to such an extent, that after the Hoatzin has eaten it is in danger of tipping base over apex! To compensate for this natural imbalance, the skin covering the sternum is thicker and more callous than usual, and is used after feeding as a third foot, supporting the front part of the body as the Hoatzin works its way through the branches. Hoatzins scramble through the bushes and trees, using strong legs and feet with wings held out for balance. They are very poor fliers, often doing little more than gliding across to lower branches.

Hoatzins are social birds found in flocks of 10-20 birds and breed colonially at any time of the year. The clutch of two to four eggs is laid on a platform of twigs in a tree or bush 6-20 ft. (2-6 m.) above the water. Incubation lasts for about four weeks, but it is uncertain how long the adventurous youngsters take to fledge, for they are soon off, exploring their environment under the watchful gaze of their parents. Unlike any other young bird, it has claws on the first and second digits of the wings which it uses to help itself to clamber around branches. This behaviour prompted early scientists to suggest that it was a link with the prehistoric Archaeopteryx. Not only can the young Hoatzin climb, but if threatened by a predator it drops into the water for safety, for it also dives and swims well, useful attributes to escape from danger when living in branches over water. After two weeks it loses its claws and aquatic talents. Before it fledges, the young bird goes through two coats of down before it finally assumes its first proper feathers. Both parents feed the chicks and sometime additional adults are present, leading some authorities to suspect polygamy.

MESITES
Order: *Gruiformes*
Family: *Mesitornithidae*
two genera contain three species

Mesites are members of the crane-like birds *Gruiformes*, and have evolved in isolation on the island of Madagascar off the east coast of Africa. There are three species, poorly known, but all considered to be rare mainly because of the destruction of forests on their island home. Only 10% of Madagascar remains forested.

Mesites are terrestrial birds, about 12 in. (30 cm.) in length with long, ample tails and short wings. They feed on insects and fruit and run rather than fly to escape danger. Even the nest, a few feet above the ground in a bush, is situated so that the adults can reach it by climbing!

The genera *Mesitornis* contains two species that occur in forests. The Brown Mesite *M. unicolor* inhabits moist evergreen forests on the eastern side of Madagascar. It is perhaps the most widely distributed, but details of its precise range, population and breeding biology are still largely unknown. It is reddish brown above and paler below with a white stripe on the side of the head. The bill is short and

slender. The sexes are similar as they are with the other member of the genus, the White-breasted Mesite *M. variegata*. This species inhabits the dry forests of north-eastern Madagascar that have little or no under-scrub. Until recently it was known only from two areas in that part of the island, but recent studies have found it present at other sites on the west coast. It has a longer bill, but shorter legs and is well marked with white, rufous and black streaks on the sides of the head and black spots on the white breast and throat.

The remaining species and the only one belonging to the genus Monias is Bensch's Monia *M. benschi* found in arid brush woodland in the south-western part of Madagascar. Unlike the other two species it has a long decurved bill and the plumage of the sexes differs with the female being the more brightly coloured. The bird is greyish brown with a white superciliary and the male has a white throat and black spots to the white chest. On the female the throat and chest are densely covered with chestnut markings. In most birds a brightly coloured female suggests that it is the male who incubates the eggs and tends the chicks, but not necessarily in the case of the Monia. Details of the breeding biology of this and the other two species tends to be rather sketchy.

The nest in a bush is a platform of twigs lined with grass and usually a single egg is laid. A nest of Bensch's Monia was found that contained two eggs. The second egg had been laid by another female mated by the same male as the first. It is uncertain if the male shared incubation duties with one or both of the females.

BUTTONQUAILS
Order: *Gruiformes*
Family: *Turnicidae*
two genera contain 14 species

Buttonquails are small birds most frequently found in open grasslands, although some species occur in more wooded habitats and the Black-breasted Buttonquail *Turnix melanogaster* inhabits tropical rainforests of north-eastern Australia. Buttonquails and the true quails *Coturnix* resemble one another because, although unrelated, they have through evolution converged to meet the needs of the same habitat. They are both terrestrial birds that run rather than fly from danger; however, unlike the true quails, they have three and not four toes. Their sex life is rather muddled as well, for they are one of the few families where the female is more brightly coloured than her mate. She lays the eggs and leaves him to get on with the job.

Thirteen species of buttonquail range from Europe and Africa to Asia and Australia, where no less than seven species occur. They are not easy birds to see and of those I have seen in Africa, only on two or three occasions has the view been good enough to identify them specifically as Kurrichane Buttonquails *T. sylvatica*, 5.5 in. (14 cm.) long. At other times it has been a process of elimination, something that birders often practice. Sometimes when a bird is poorly seen and its range does not overlap with any similar or closely related bird, the birder often assumes the bird to be that particular species. In the case of these buttonquail, no other species occurred in the areas concerned. The Kurrichane Buttonquail is the most widespread species; in south-western Europe it has the unfortunate name of Andalusian Hemipode, whilst in parts of Africa the name Little Buttonquail is used; yet in India another variation is Little Bustard-quail. The name Little Buttonquail is given to a different species in Australia – *T. velox*.

Buttonquails are well camouflaged, being stone coloured with black, brown and grey markings on the upper-parts. The females are slightly larger and more brightly coloured than the males, who are left to incubate the eggs and rear the young, while she goes in search of another male. The diet of buttonquails consists of invertebrates such as ants, insects, termites and vegetable matter, including new shoots and seeds.

The nest is usually a shallow cup of grasses and leaves, hidden in a tuft of grass or beneath a bush. Both birds build the nest and occasionally the female is motivated to help incubate the clutch of four eggs during the first few days. After that she leaves to find and seduce another mate, while the male completes the short incubation period of 12-13 days. On hatching, the chicks are remarkably well developed and can feed themselves after two or three days, although during the first week the male also provides them with food. A week later they can fly and after a further seven to fourteen days the family will split up. By the time the youngsters are six or seven weeks old they are fully grown. Between three to five months, depending on the species, they are mature enough to breed for the first time. Life is short and sweet for buttonquails, who are thought to live for only two years.

The Quail Plover *Ortyxelos meiffrenii*, 4.5 in. (12 cm.) long, is a very small terrestrial bird, closely related to the buttonquails and endemic to Africa. It occurs along a narrow belt of semi-arid country along the southern margins of the Sahara and also in a few localities in East Africa. Its plumage is similar to a buttonquail, except that when it flies it has long narrow wings that are conspicuously black and white. Two eggs are laid and there is no evidence to suggest that the parents have anything other than a conventional home life.

Left: a Siberian Crane, one of the world's rarer cranes, wintering at Bharatpur in India.

PLAINS WANDERER
Order: *Gruiformes*
Family: *Pedionomidae*
the genus *Pedionomus* contains of a single species *Pedionomus torquatus*

The Plains Wanderer *Pedionomus torquatus* is a rare bird found on native plains and grasslands in south-eastern Australia. It is a bird that might never have been common, but it has undoubtedly become rarer through an inability to adapt to habitats changed by Man through the introduction of sheep farming and other forms of agriculture.

The female Plains Wanderer, 6.75 in. (17 cm.) long, is larger and more brightly coloured than the male 6.25 in. (16 cm.) long. They are related to and resemble the Button Quails *Turnicidae*, being small terrestrial birds recalling gamebirds. Female Plains Wanderers are cryptically coloured sandy-brown birds with black marked feathers on the upper-parts, chestnut breast and a black and white patterned collar. The male is paler with a less distinct collar. Plains Wanderers only have short rounded wings and are reluctant to fly; when escaping from danger they prefer to run in a crouching position through the grass or 'freeze' motionless relying on camouflage for protection. Unfortunately this has made them vulnerable to the introduced Foxes *Vulpes vulpes* and Feral Cats *Felix sylvestris catus*, for Plains Wanderers have a distinctive odour that defeats any successful attempt at camouflage.

The breeding season lasts from September to January and four eggs are laid in a shallow grass-lined nest on the ground. As with most species where the female is more conspicuously coloured than the male, the roles of the sexes are reversed after the eggs are laid. It is left to the male to incubate the eggs for about 23 days and to rear the young single-handed; the chicks leave the nest as soon as they are dry after hatching. Plains Wanderers of all ages feed on small seeds and insects.

Below: a pair of Sarus Cranes at Bharatpur tower above a wintering sandpiper. This crane is a widespread Asiatic species occurring from India to northern Australia.

CRANES
Order: *Gruiformes*
Family: *Gruidae*
four genera contain 15 species

There are few birds as tall and elegant as the cranes The sight of a migrating skein passing overhead calling, or a pair trumpeting as they perform a pre-nuptial dance, instill memories. They are birds of wide open spaces and to many people represent the disappearing wilderness.

Cranes form two groups; the *Gruinae*, 13 species, are divided into three genera, whilst the *Balearicinae* are the two species of the genus *Balearica*. They occur in temperate and tropical parts of the world, but are absent from South America, although crane-like birds *Gruiformes* belonging to six other families occur on that continent.

The greatest variety of cranes occurs in the Far East and of the eight species recorded from China no less than five are endangered! Most species belong to one genera; the 10 species of true cranes *Grus* include all those endangered Asiatic species, but the crane most at risk is not from Asia, but from North America. The Whooping Crane *Grus americana*, 52 in. (132 cm.) long, is pure white with black primaries and has a red and black head pattern shared, with several other species.

Wildlife Service and the United States Fish and Wildlife Service have been collecting a number of 'spare' eggs each year. Some have gone to a captive breeding program at the Patuxent Wildlife Research Station, Laurel, Maryland, and others to an ambitious attempt to establish Whooping Cranes at Grays Lake NWR, Idaho. Scientists have introduced eggs into the nests of the smaller Sandhill Crane *G. canadensis*, 41 in. (104 cm.) long, a common bird at the Refuge, in the hope of establishing a second flock. These Sandhills winter at Bosque del Apache NWR in New Mexico, but unfortunately the project has met with only limited success, due in part to low water levels at Grays Lake and the failure of sub-adults

Most northern cranes have suffered as a result of hunting and habitat changes along their migration routes and at their wintering grounds, and the Whooper is no exception. It was probably never a common bird after the climate became drier following the last Ice Age, but no other crane has a population as low as the Whooper. That this species has not become extinct, is a tribute to the efforts of those researchers and conservationists who have put many thousands of man-hours into its future. Although the Whooping Crane is far from secure, the knowledge gained over recent years will benefit not only the Whooper, but also those endangered Asiatic species. The story of the Whooping Crane is well documented; being large and white they made an easy target for hunters. The population stood at about 1300 in the 1890s, declining to under 200 birds by the turn of the century. By 1946 this was down to just 20 birds and of these, 17 wintered along the coastal marshes at Aransas, Texas. The last nest had been found in 1922, so the breeding area of these birds was unknown. However, during an aerial survey of the vast Wood Buffalo National Park in Canada in 1954, a pair with a chick was sighted. This was the beginning; a campaign was mounted to increase public awareness and to reduce the numbers killed along the 2,200 mile (3,250 km.) migration route. The population has slowly increased and now over 140 birds make the journey down from Canada to what is now the Aransas National Wildlife Refuge.

Whooping Cranes lay two eggs, but usually rear only one chick. Over recent years, in a joint operation, the Canadian

to reach maturity. To date only 13 birds survive from over 200 translocated eggs and so far no breeding attempt has taken place. In 1989, my colleague, Lawrence Holloway and I took the first organised party of British birdwatchers to Grays Lake; it was a great thrill to look out over the marsh in front of the visitor centre at distant Whoopers, feeding with Sandhills. The staff were very informative, and one could share their sense of disappointment in the lack of success so far. Recently a second captive flock has been set up at the headquarters of the International Crane Foundation at Baraboo, Wisconsin.

Another very rare member of the family is the Siberian Crane *G. leucogeranus*, 53 in. (135 cm.) long. It is slightly larger than the Whooping Crane, a white crane with black primaries, red bill and face. It breeds in two widely separated areas in the Soviet Union and winters in India and China. They travel a dangerous route through Afghanistan to reach India to winter at the wonderful bird sanctuary at Bharatpur. Formerly they were more widespread in India and Pakistan, although there may still be a small wintering population in northern Iran. The Indian birds have declined steadily, so that during the winter of 1988/89 their numbers at Bharatpur were down to under 30 birds and in December 1989 only 13 birds had returned. The numbers of birds that wintered in China were also very low, until the discovery in 1985 of over 1,400 wintering at the Po-yang Lakes. If the lakes can be preserved and if the measures being undertaken in the Soviet Union and China, with help from the International Crane Foundation,

The Grey Crowned Crane of Africa is a spectacular bird with its golden crown and red-throat wattle. The numbers of this species in the wild are declining as a result of the demand for this attractive crane by zoos and bird garden collections.

are successful, then perhaps the future of the Siberian Crane will be assured.

The other rare and endangered Asiatic cranes are the Black-necked *G. nigricollis*, Hooded *G. monacha*, Japanese *G. japonensis*, and White-naped *G. vipio*. The other purely Asiatic species, the Sarus Crane *G antigone*, 61 in. (156 cm.) long, ranges from India to Indo-China. It is a large grey crane with red head and neck. The discovery in 1966 of Sarus Cranes in northern Australia amongst the very similar Brolga *G. rubicunda*, 55 in. (140 cm.) long, came as a surprise. Because of the similarity between the two species, they had probably been overlooked previously. The Brolga is the only member of the genus to occur south of the Equator. The only significant difference between the two birds is that the Brolga has less red on the head.

Most widespread of this genus is the Common Crane *G. grus*, 50 in. (130 cm.) long; a grey bird with black primaries and a white stripe on the side of the head and neck. This provides a stark contrast with the black head and throat. The Common Crane breeds east into Siberia from Scandinavia and migrates to winter farther south in Europe, in north-east Africa, northern India and China. Vagrants have occurred in North America, most frequently in flocks of Sandhill Cranes. The Sandhill Crane is the most familiar of the North American cranes, with a resident population in Florida, and birds breed in marshes in several western States. During the winter months Sandhills migrate from Alaska, Canada and Siberia to winter in such southern states as New Mexico and Texas. Sandhills breeding in Siberia migrate east across the Bering Strait to Alaska and then south to winter in the lower states. This suggests that perhaps the Siberian breeders colonised from Alaska in the not so distant past and have retained their traditional migration routes. As they collect prior to the fall migration, an occasional Common Crane joins the flocks and thus explains the birds recorded from New Mexico and other places that at first glance appear unlikely. In Japan the reverse happens when vagrant Sandhills arrive in the flocks of other crane species. Elsewhere in its range the Common Crane rubs shoulders with the smaller Demoiselle Crane *Anthropoides virgo*, 38 in. (96 cm.) long. Although Demoiselles are smaller, they have a similar plumage pattern that makes the two species difficult to separate at long range. With elongated tertials it lacks the bushy stern of its larger cousin. Demoiselles breed mainly across Soviet Central Asia and winter in north-east Africa, India and Pakistan. Until recently a small population bred in North Africa, but it appears to have become extinct over the last few years. The only other member of its genus is the Blue Crane *A. paradisea*, 42 in. (107 cm.) long. This is a beautiful soft blue-grey crane, with longer tertials giving it a particularly elegant appearance. It occurs in South Africa and in northern Namibia where a small population inhabits the margins of Etosha Pan.

Africa is home to the three remaining cranes. Largest is the Wattled Crane *Bugeranus carunculatus*, 47 in. (120 cm.) long, and has two distinct populations; a small population is resident in Ethiopia, but its status there is uncertain. In central and southern Africa it occurs mainly in southern Tanzania, Zambia, northern Botswana and Zimbabwe; but throughout this huge area there could be as few as 4000 birds. Threats to the environment come from reclamation of wetlands and flooding from hydro-electric schemes.

The other African cranes are the Black *Balearica pavonina* and Grey *B. regulorum* Crowned Cranes. These two are closely related, the most obvious difference being the body colour; the Black ranges discontinuously from West Africa to Ethiopia, and is replaced by the Grey Crowned Crane from Kenya to South Africa. Crowned cranes are frequently kept in zoological gardens and are very distinct with their stiff yellow tufted crowns, white and red head pattern and large white wing patches. Perhaps the biggest threat to the species comes from the demands made by collections.

Cranes mate for the life of one partner and the pair-bond is established during the adolescent years. Birds remain in pairs throughout the year and on returning to the breeding areas a large nest is built, often on marshy ground. Usually two eggs are laid and although both may hatch, most species only rear a single chick successfully. Both birds share the incubation that lasts for 30-40 days, depending on the species. After hatching, the young are fed by their parents. The fledging period varies from 55 days for the Grus cranes to 105 days for the Wattled Crane.

The Sarus Crane (left) has now been identified in Australia, where it had previously occurred undistinguished from the native Brolga. These two stately birds both have red heads, but on the Brolga the red colouring is less extensive on its neck. Facing page: a Grey Crowned Crane at a pool in the Masai Mara Game Reserve in Kenya.

LIMPKIN
Order: *Gruiformes*
Family: *Aramidae*
the genus *Aramus* contains a single species
Aramus guarauna

The Limpkin *Aramus guarauna* is an unusual bird of shady swamps and marshes in the New World. In the United States it occurs in southern Georgia and Florida and in the Caribbean on the islands of Cuba, Hispaniola, Jamaica and Puerto Rico. Elsewhere on the mainland its range extends from Mexico to Argentina, although it does not occur west of the Andes. It is a bird with anatomical affinities with cranes *Gruidae*, but it has a digestive system that shows a relationship with Rails *Rallidae*.

The Limpkin (above), although widespread in Central and South America, is restricted to the south-eastern states in North America. It is a relative of the crane family and is found in wetlands where its main food item, the Apple Snail, also occurs.

The Limpkin is a large brown bird, 24-28 in. (61-71 cm.), with white streaking on the head, neck, breast and back. It has a long decurved bill and when it flies it does so on broad, rounded wings with legs and neck extended. The result looks more like an ibis *Threskiornithinae*, with which it has no relationship.

Limpkins haunt shady, wooded areas of swamps and marshes, where its weird wailing cries are a familiar sound of the night. It is dependant on a good, natural habitat where its main source of food, the Apple Snail *Pomacea caliginosa*, occurs. If marshes and swamps are drained, the snail disappears as the water levels fall and although Limpkins also eat earthworms, frogs and lizards, they appear to be unable to survive without the bulk of their food in the form of snails. The snail is also preyed upon by the Snail or Everglades Kite *Rostrhamus sociabilis*, which lives in more open areas of the swamps. The Limpkin collects the snail from the water and carries it ashore. Holding the mollusc securely with its toes it manages to remove the hard protective plate or operculum from the entrance of the shell. Unprotected, the snail is plucked from the shell and eaten. Discarded shells litter favoured areas of a feeding territory.

The nest of sticks and vegetation is situated either in shade on the ground or in a tree or bush. Four to eight eggs are laid and incubated by both parents, but surprisingly little is known about the incubation and fledging periods.

TRUMPETERS

Order: *Gruiformes*
Family: *Psophiidae*
the genus *Psophia* contains three species

The name 'Trumpeter' comes from the loud trumpeting calls made by the males of all three species belonging to the genus *Psophia*. They are sedentary birds found in the dense lowland rain forests of the Amazon and Orinoco river drainage systems in South America.

The three species look similar, large, mainly black birds with a humpbacked appearance and the main difference between the species is the colour of the secondaries, inner wing coverts and the lower back. Little explanation is necessary when the birds have names like the Grey-winged or Common *Psophia crepitans*, the White-winged *P. leucoptera* and the Green-winged Trumpeter *P. viridis*! They are about the size of a Barnyard Fowl *Gallus gallus* some 17-20 in. (43-52 cm.) long. They have a fowl-like bill and a disproportionately small head with large eyes that give the bird a 'kind' face. Perhaps not scientific terminology, but accurate nevertheless! The black feathers on the head and neck are soft and velvety similar to those found on the forehead and crown of the Plushcap *Catamblyrhynchus diadema* and may have evolved for the same reason. Both Trumpeters and Plushcaps inhabit wet forests, where through feeding the plumage of the head could be permanently dishevelled, these plush-like feathers can withstand the conditions better than conventional ones. They usually run from danger, but when necessary fly heavily on rounded wings into the middle or upper branches of a tall forest tree. They can only fly short distances and swim rivers that present too wide an obstacle.

Trumpeters are gregarious birds and flocks up to 100 or more birds can be found on the forest floor, sometimes alone

Pukeko (left) is the local name given to the New Zealand Purple Swamphen, a large gallinule of the Old World and Australasia. However, it is even smaller than the other New Zealand gallinule, the almost Turkey-sized, flightless Takahe. The American Purple Gallinule (below) is a smaller, yet more colourful relative, found from the south-eastern United States to Argentina.

or in the company of the Black Curassow *Crax alector*, which shares the same habitat and range as the Grey-winged Trumpeter in the Guianas and northern Brazil. Flocks of trumpeters are also to be found feeding on the ground below troops of monkeys *Cebidae*, who carelessly drop fruit from the trees above. Besides fruit, trumpeters eat invertebrates and other vegetable matter. Amongst food items recorded are amphibians and reptiles and one of the reasons that the local people catch and keep trumpeters as pets on their property is their ability to deal with snakes. Being noisy birds they give an alarm call at any disturbance, day or night, all making the Trumpeter a useful addition to the household. Unfortunately these birds fall easy prey to hunters, who have exterminated them in less remote parts of their range.

Trumpeters nest in holes and hollows in trees, laying six to ten eggs incubated by the female. The young leave the nest soon after hatching and are supposedly carried to the ground in their mother's bill. Much of the breeding biology is still to be unravelled.

RAILS and their allies
Order: *Gruiformes*
Family: *Rallidae*
41 genera contain 124 species

When the Japanese occupied Wake Island in the Pacific, during World War II, one of the island's natives was the flightless Wake Island Rail *Rallus wakensis*. Sadly the bird's days were numbered, for with food scarce the occupying forces turned to the Rail and by 1945 it was extinct.

In the past, more species of rail and coots have become extinct than in any other bird family, for many have evolved in isolation on oceanic islands free from mammalian predators. There were few if any dangers, so they had little or no reason to fly and lacked natural fear. For terrestrial species this proved to be disastrous; Man discovered and settled in such places, bringing with him dogs, cats, and pigs. Inevitably rats arrived simultaneously and quickly the whole ecosystem that had evolved over hundreds of generations was shattered.

The Corncrake *Crex crex*, a grassland species of the western and central Palearctic, has declined dramatically during the 20th. century. The reason for this is twofold; changes in farming practice and increased industrialisation. The Corncrake breeds in fields and meadows, but with increased mechanisation and more efficient farming methods, this species has been unable to adapt. When hay was cut by hand the farm worker would flush the Corncrake from its nest and leave the nest and eggs untouched, but when machines took over many incubating birds perished beneath the blades of the equipment. Corncrakes winter in Africa and breed in the Palearctic; they are low-flying nocturnal migrants. However, with the proliferation of power and telegraph lines across Western Europe since World War I, untold numbers of these birds have struck cables and been killed. The population in the British Isles is now confined to remote northern and western areas, but the numbers have deceased markedly within living memory in spite of agriculture being somewhat 'old-fashioned' in these areas.

There are 124 species divided between 41 genera; members of the family occur throughout the World except for the polar regions and the higher latitudes of the Northern Hemisphere. The rail family comprises two main groups; the rails including the crakes, and the gallinules which include the coots. One of the smallest species is the Black Rail *Laterallus jamaicensis* 6 in. (15 cm.) in length; it is a shy and elusive bird that occurs from the United States to Chile. By comparison, the gallinule-like and flightless Takahe *Notornis mantelli* is a massive bird, 25 in. (63 cm.) long, and found in a remote area on the South Island of New Zealand. It was known from only four specimens, the last collected in 1898, and presumed to have become extinct until the discovery of a population near Lake Te Anau in the south-western corner of the island in 1948.

Rails and crakes are usually secretive birds of rank vegetation in marshes and grasslands, although many species that have evolved in isolation show no reservations. They have short rounded wings and short erect tails. These birds have long legs and toes, the bills of some are long and slightly

decurved, whilst others are stubby and conical in shape. Most species with long bills are called rails, but in the Americas so are those with short ones; elsewhere these are usually known as crakes. Several species occur in North America. One of the most widespread is the Sora Rail *Porzana carolina*, a gray and brown bird with barred flanks, a black face with a short yellow bill. In the northern part of its range it is migratory and has even occurred in the British Isles on a number of occasions. Soras are to be found in many small wet areas where there is sufficient cover; these are not always in the most salubrious situations! During a recent tour, just north of Salt Lake City, we watched a pair feeding around the margins of a reedy pool that was in danger of being smothered by an expanding car-dump. Such small wetlands are important, and it is a tragic waste when they are filled in by the garbage of the 20th. century.

The other half of the family tends to be more conspicuous birds and are mostly blue or black. In North America one of the most colourful members of the family occurs in the south-eastern United States. This is the American Purple Gallinule *Porphyrula martinica*, which can be watched easily from the Anhinga Trail at Royal Palm Hammock in the Everglades as it picks its way across lily pads. Nearby there will probably be a Common Moorhen *Gallinula chloropus*, a species that

Below: a Common Moorhen in England, distinguished by its smaller, red, frontal shield from the North American family. It is widespread throughout much of the world except for Australasia, where it is superseded by the Dusky Moorhen.

occurs throughout much of the World except Australia and New Zealand. In the Australasian region it is replaced by the closely related Dusky Moorhen *G. tenebrosa*, that may be merely a subspecies of the more familiar bird. Another North American member of the family and one with a more widespread distribution in the continent is the American Coot *Fulica americana*. The coots are more aquatic than most other members of the family, with lobbed toes to help them swim and dive. Perhaps the most striking feature of these otherwise all-black birds, is the white frontal shield above the bill. This appears to vary between individuals, so one should be very wary when attempting to identify a Caribbean Coot *F. caribaea* in the United States. During a tour to Jamaica, where both the American and Caribbean species occur side by side, they were not easy to separate, and one was left wondering if perhaps they are conspecific. Throughout the Old World there are only two species of coot, but in the Americas there are a total of eight, six of which are South American endemics.

The diet of the family consists mainly of animal life, including insects, earthworms, leeches, molluscs, small fish and frogs. Vegetable matter is also eaten by many species and some are almost completely vegetarian. The Purple Swamphen *Porphyrio porphyrio*, a widespread species of warm temperate and tropical wetlands of the Old World and Australia, eats mainly plant material, but also eats the eggs and young of swamp-breeding herons *Ardeidae*.

The nest is often well hidden, but some species, the coots for instance, build obvious nests amongst floating vegetation; the male either helps the female with the construction or just supplies her with materials. The clutch size varies between 1 – 15 eggs; the larger clutches may result from more than one

one of three closely related species of Finfoots, which have each been placed in their own genus by taxonomists. English being the language it is, the plural is not Finfeet!

Finfoots are found along quiet stretches of tropical rivers, generally slipping unobtrusively beneath the branches of overhanging bushes and trees. They feed quietly pecking at insects and invertebrates among branches and debris along the sides and banks of the river. One bird I watched recently at Victoria Falls caught and ate a small crab. Unlike similar sized water birds such as Grebes and Cormorants *Phalacrocorax* the legs of the Finfoot are placed about midway along the body enabling it to walk easily on the river banks in search of food. Diving is not an essential part of life as it is with the Grebes and Cormorants, who need their legs at the rear of the body to provide the propulsion needed to pursue prey beneath the water. Finfoots appear reluctant to fly, preferring to slip unobtrusively away through water beneath the trees, bushes and other vegetation that line the river banks. If caught out on open water it will patter along the surface with wings flapping like a Common Murre *Uria aalge* attempting to get airborne, but the Finfoot usually reaches cover before taking-off.

The African Finfoot occurs from West Africa and Kenya

female laying in the same nest. Incubation is usually shared by both adults and lasts from 14 – 28 days, again depending on the species. The down-covered young are tended by their parents, who are sometimes be helped by the offspring of a previous brood. The fledging period is difficult to gauge, but some chicks remain dependent for 8 weeks after hatching.

FINFOOTS
Order: *Gruiformes*
Family: *Heliornithidae*
three genera each containing a single species

If one rises before the Sun and stands quietly on the banks of the mighty Zambezi as it flows east towards Victoria Falls in Zimbabwe, there is magic on the river! The water slowly gathers pace as it heads towards the Falls, and wildlife stirs in anticipation of the new day. It is probably the best time to glimpse the shy and elusive African Finfoot *Podica senegalensis* as it crosses the river to feed along the opposite bank. Long and low in the water it looks like a Grebe *Podicipedidae*, but as it swims the head is often jerked forward and back like a Moorhen *Gallinula chloropus*. It is

south to the eastern part of South Africa. Similarly across south-east Asia from north-east India to Malaysia and Sumatra, the Masked Finfoot *Heliopais personata* occurs. In the New World, the American Finfoot or Sungrebe *Heliornis fulica* is found from southern Mexico south to north-eastern Argentina. The alternative name Sungrebe comes from the Grebe-like lobes along the toes instead of webbing between them as on most other water birds. The African and American species are sedentary, whilst the Masked Finfoot may be a partial migrant with birds extending farther south during the winter months.

The largest species is the African Finfoot at 23 in. (60 cm.) long. The upper-parts of the male are olive-brown with white spotting on the back. The chin, throat, upper breast and sides of head and neck are grey, separated from the olive brown by a white line. The female is similar, but has paler chin, throat and under-parts, with more pronounced white strip down the side of the head. Both sexes have red bill and legs. Slightly smaller is the Masked Finfoot, 21 in. (53 cm.), recalling the African species except that the bill is bright yellow and the grey replaced by black, hence the name 'Masked'. Smallest of the three species is the American Finfoot at only 12 in. (30 cm.) long. The most striking aspect of the birds' plumage is the black and white striped head pattern of the male.

Finfoots build a nest of sticks, lined with reeds and grass, on a branch or in a fallen tree about three feet (90 cm.) above the river, often amongst the flotsam deposited by the last

Members of the rail family (left) are well represented in Florida's Everglades. Above left: an American Coot – a species widespread from North America to Chile. The Common Moorhen (far left) is a member of the North American family. Above: with elongated toes, the American Purple Gallinule walks on water lilies. Left: a well-camouflaged Clapper Rail at Eco Pond, Flamingo, Florida – true rails rarely offer more than a glimpse of themselves.

flood. The African Finfoot lays 1-3 three eggs which are incubated for about 14 days, although full details of this and fledging remain unknown. This applies to the Masked Finfoot that lays as many as seven eggs, although five is the usual sized clutch. The nest of the American Finfoot was not discovered until 1969, and since then birds in Mexico have been studied. Two eggs are laid, but incubation only lasts for 11 days, an unusually short period for a bird of this size.

The chicks, naked when hatched, leave the nest deposited in pouches of skin on the flanks of the male. Probably this fascinating aspect of parental care has enabled the American Finfoot to evolve such a short incubation period. With the chicks in the pouches the male is able to swim and even fly! The nearest thing to a marsupial bird! This interesting aspect of upbringing, first reported in 1830, was not confirmed until the early 1970s.

KAGU

Order: *Gruiformes*
Family: *Rhynochetidae*
the genus *Rhynochetos* contains a single
species *Rhynochetos jubatus*

In a few remote valleys, amongst the wet montane forests on the eastern side of New Caledonia, lives a strange flightless bird, endemic to the island and quite unlike anything else in the region. It is the Kagu *Rhynochetos jubatus*, classed by some as an aberrant species of Heron *Ardeidae*, but generally accepted as being one of the families of birds making up the Order *Gruiformes*. It bears some resemblance to herons, but is distantly related to the Sun-Bittern *Eurypyga helias* of South America The Kagu is a very rare and endangered bird. Its habitat has come under pressure from timber extraction and despoliation from nickel mining. The bird has been persecuted by Man and is still kept as pets by locals. With Man came pigs, cats, dogs and rats, all threats to any terrestrial species, even more so to one that was flightless. Its habit of running from danger and then stopping has not helped it survive.

This flightless species is a rather nondescript grey bird with a stout red bill and legs and upright stance. However, in display it raises a lax crest and spreads spectacular rufous, black and white wings. It is 24in. (60cm.) long and although flightless, relies on gravity to help it glide down hillsides.

The Kagu is a ground nesting species, but little is known about the breeding biology of the species in the wild, so that much of our knowledge has come from studies made of captive birds. A large nest of sticks and leaves is constructed by the pair and a single egg is laid. Incubation, shared by both parents, lasts about 36 days and on hatching, the chick, covered in down, leaves the nest after three days. Initially it is dependent on the parents, but after about 70 days, it becomes progressively independent. Full independence is gained after three and a half months, although the family stays together until the youngster is at least six months old.

SUN-BITTERN

Order: *Gruiformes*
Family: *Eurypygidae*
the genus *Eurypyga* consists of a single
species *Eurypyga helias*

In tropical Central and South America, from southern Mexico south to Peru and Brazil, lives the Sun-Bittern *Eurypyga helias*, an unusual bird of the forested margins of ponds and streams. The name suggests a bittern *Botaurinae*, but there is no relationship, for bitterns are members of the heron family *Ardeidae*. During the days of discovery, when people were finding birds and animals that had not previously been described, a scientific and a popular name was given to the species. The popular name was often based on some other species that the discoverer was familiar with elsewhere. Birds

in many parts of the world have red breasts and are called Robin after the familiar Robin *Erithacus rubecula* of Europe. This is why the American Robin *Turdus migratorius*, although it is a thrush, is called a Robin.

The Sun-Bittern has no close relative on the continent, but across the Pacific on the island of New Caledonia, the Kagu *Rhynochetos jubatus*, is perhaps more closely related than any other member of the family *Gruiformes*.

Sun-Bitterns eat small fish and other invertebrates caught in the water or found amongst waterside herbage. They have broad wings, a long ample tail, a long thin neck and legs – it looks like a combination of several species. It has the long body and centrally placed legs of a finfoot *Heliornithidae*; the neck and bill of a heron and rufous, black and white wings that exhibit the distant relationship with the Kagu *Rhynochetos jubatus*. The back is finely barred grey, brown and black; the head is black with white superciliary and moustachial stripes and when in display the bird leans forward and spreads the patterned wings and tail, showing the rufous-orange patches in the wings that add the 'sun' to the bird's name. As part of the display and cementing the pair bond the male offers a small item of food. It may be a fish, butterfly or some other morsel. She accepts, although not always the first time and then eats the gift.

The nest, located in a tree or bush close to the water, is a large globular structure made of vegetation and mud with a depression on top where the two eggs are laid. Incubation lasts for about 27 days and duties are shared by both birds. The nestlings, covered in down, stay within the confines of the nest for about three weeks, by which time the feathers develop.

Below: in a Costa Rican riverine forest, a juvenile Sun-bittern shows its wonderfully patterned wings in a 'startle' display. The 'sun-bursts' on the wings give the species it name. Denham's or Jackson's Bustard (facing page bottom) is one of the larger members of its family found on the plains of Africa.

SERIEMAS

Order: *Gruiformes*
Family: *Cariamidae*
the genera *Cariama* and *Chunga* each
contain a single species

There are two species of Seriema that make up the family *Cariamidae* occurring only in South America. The more widespread species, the Crested or Red-legged Seriema *Cariama cristata*, occurs in pampas and savannah from central and eastern Brazil, south to northern Argentina and Uruguay. The second species, with a greatly reduced distribution, is the Burmeister's or Black-legged Seriema *Chunga burmeisteri*, found only in Argentina and western Paraguay inhabiting open woodland and scrub.

Seriemas, long legged and long necked birds, occupy a similar ecological niche to the Secretary Bird *Sagittarius serpentarius* from the plains of Africa. The Secretary Bird is

considered to be an aberrant bird of prey, but recent analysis of the egg-white protein shows that there is a possible relationship with the crane-like birds *Gruiformes*. Further studies in behaviour etc. are necessary to establish any ties between seriemas and Secretary Birds.

They are terrestrial birds that are reluctant to fly and when escaping from danger they run with their heads held low. They feed on small snakes, but are not immune to poison if bitten. Insects and fruit are also on the diet of Seriemas.

The Crested Seriema is the better known of the two species, standing some 30in. (76cm.) tall; it is grey brown above with fine black barring and paler under-parts and has a banded black and white tail and long bare red legs and red bill. The forehead sports a crest, which is not as pronounced on the smaller Burmeister's Seriema, which is 22 in. (57cm.) long with black legs and bill.

The nest of sticks is constructed in a tree up to 10 ft. (3m.) above the ground where the clutch of two eggs is incubated for about 27 days before hatching. Both parents look after the down covered chicks, who stay in the nest until they are well developed. In some areas, young are taken from nests and kept with fowls to act as noisy watch-dogs.

BUSTARDS
Order: *Gruiformes*
Family: *Otidae*
the 11 genera contain 24 species.

Throughout the grasslands and semi-arid areas of the Old World and Australia occurs a family of plump, long-legged birds that belong to the Order of crane-like birds, *Gruiformes*. These are the Bustards *Otidae*, which include in their number the heaviest flying bird; a large male Great Bustard *Otis tarda*, 39in. (100cm.) long, has weighed up to 46.3 lb. (21 kg.).

In many parts of the World, bustards have declined as they have been forced to retreat, their habitats being taken over for cultivation; or hunters have increasingly invaded their territories. For successful breeding, bustards require wide open spaces with no disturbance. In Europe the Great and Little Bustards *Tetrax tetrax*, 17in. (43cm.) long, have adapted to changes to a certain extent and moved into the open cereal fields, but have further declined as a result of the use of chemical insecticides and weed-killers, in spite of legal protection afforded to them in some areas. The Great Bustard is now a rare bird in western Europe, and one of the best places to witness the spectacular display of the male in spring is in eastern Austria. Close to the Hungarian border is an area known as the Hansag, where the World Wildlife Fund for Nature supervises a reserve large enough for the birds to live and survive successfully without interference. In the Middle East and North Africa. hunting is a particularly serious problem where bustards, formerly hunted with falcons, are now chased by men in four-wheeled drive vehicles, brandishing high-powered rifles. In these areas, the Houbara Bustard *Chlamydotis undulata* is particularly threatened.

The greatest variety of Bustard species is to be found in Africa, where all but four of the World's species occur. Three species, the Great, Houbara and Little Bustards now only have a precarious foothold in North Africa. Without enforced

Above: amongst the trees of a riverine forest in Costa Rica, an adult Sun-bittern feeds a frog to one of its two chicks in a nest of mud and vegetation built on a horizontal branch. The Sun-bittern, a member of the crane family, is a native of tropical Central and South America, but its nearest relative is perhaps the flightless Kagu of New Caledonia in the western Pacific.

protection, the Great and Little will probably become extinct within a few years, because of hunting pressures. The more northerly Eurasian populations of these three species move south in the fall; most others are sedentary birds.

Bustards give the appearance of being long-legged gamebirds, their cryptically-coloured plumage blending superbly with the background of their habitat. The males are usually larger and more boldly marked than the females, and some species such as the Black Korhaan *Eupodotis atra*, 20in. (51cm.) long, a species found mainly in south-western Africa, is strongly dimorphic.

Bustards are omnivorous, feeding on a variety of seeds and other vegetable matter, insects and invertebrates such as molluscs, whilst the list of recorded vertebrate species includes frogs, reptiles, rodents and other small mammals, also the eggs and chicks of other birds.

The female bustard makes a simple scrape in the ground, and in most species she alone incubates the eggs and looks after the rearing of the chicks. The clutch size varies between 1 – 6, although most African species lay only 1 – 2 eggs. Incubation lasts from 21-28 days and once dry, the chicks are mobile and during the first few days are fed by their mother. The fledging period lasts up to 40 days.

The Comb-crested Jacana (above) lives up to the name 'lily-trotter' on still ponds, lakes and swamps of the East Indies, New Guinea and Australia. Its comb is a fleshy wattle that protrudes from its forehead. The Black Korhaan is a small species of bustard endemic to south-western Africa. Left: a male Black Korhaan in Etosha National Park, Namibia.

Left: an adult male Kori Bustard, one of the heaviest flying birds, struts around in display with his neck inflated and tail spread. This species is common on the plains of east and southern Africa, and is often to be seen feeding amongst game.

JACANAS
Order: *Charadriiformes*
Family: *Jacanidae*
six genera contain eight species

In the warmer regions of the World occurs an aberrant family of shorebirds that has evolved to exploit an environment, where few other birds dare to tread. These are the Jacanas, or Lily-trotters as they are sometimes called. They have developed very long toes, to distribute their weight evenly as they walk on water-lily leaves, a feature shared with few other birds. Common to all members of the family, but rarely seen for they are covered in feathers, are spurs on the carpal joints of the wings.

Jacanas inhabit wetlands on the larger islands in the Caribbean, and are also found in Central and South America, in sub-Saharan Africa, India to south-east Asia and south to Northern Australia. They are sedentary, but move locally to take advantage of ponds as other areas dry out.

The eight species are divided between six genera; there is comparatively little overlap between the various species. Both the Lesser Jacana *Microparra capensis*, 6in. (15cm.) long, and the larger and more colourful African Jacana *Actophilornis africana*, occur in the same areas, but have different habitat preferences; the Lesser Jacana inhabits less open areas and is often a more secretive bird besides being the smallest member of the family. At wetlands in India, where I have seen two species side by side, there appeared to be little or no intra-specific competition between the Pheasant-tailed Jacana *Hydrophasianus chirurgus*, and the Bronze-winged Jacana *Metopidius indicus*. With the exception of the Lesser Jacana, the old world species are 12 in. (30 cm.) long; the tail of the Pheasant-tailed Jacana doubles its length, whereas the American species, the Northern and Wattled Jacanas , are 9.5 in. (24 cm.) and 12 in. (25 cm.) respectively.

In the Americas, the Northern Jacana *Jacana spinosa* occurs from southern Mexico to Panama, and on the larger Caribbean islands of Cuba, Jamaica and Hispaniola. It is a striking member of the family, with brimstone yellow secondary and primary wing feathers. The rest of the wing and body is deep chestnut and green. On the carpal joint of the wing is a sharp spur, also to be found on the wings of the Wattled Jacana *J.jacana*, a closely related species found from

Above: an African Jacana in the Okavango Delta, Botswana, pauses on a patch of floating vegetation, revealing its incredibly long toes. This species is widespread in suitable habitats over much of sub-Saharan Africa. Polyandry – the female mating with more than one male – is practised by African Jacanas, and the male incubates the eggs and rears the chicks, which he sometimes carries to safety tucked beneath his wings.

southern Panama to northern Peru. The two species form an allopatric pair, considered by some authorities to be conspecific with its northern cousin.

The African Jacana occurs over much of sub-Saharan Africa, where ever there is suitable habitat. It is absent from permanently arid areas, such as the Namib Desert and the Skeleton Coast in Namibia, and scarce or absent, in areas of equatorial rain-forest. The general impression is of a chestnut-coloured bird, white on the throat and with a yellow breast; it has a powder-blue bill and frontal shield. It is a bird found around the margins of lakes and swamps, where there are areas of floating vegetation. In flight they have rounded wings and trail their long legs behind. They can swim well, but this is not always to their advantage. During one of our Botswana tours several party members witnessed an incident that was over in a split second. We were watching birds in Moremi on the eastern edge of the Okavango Delta; in front of us was a pool, which still had a fair amount of water left in it from the last rains, some six month previously. Feeding amongst the aquatic vegetation around the pool's margins, were two or three African Jacanas. All was at peace with the World, when one bird foolishly decided to swim 10 ft. (3 m.) across the narrowest part of the pool, to the far side. Half way across it suddenly disappeared, in a swirl of ripples; it had been snatched from below by a Crocodile *Crocodilus niloticus*, before most of us had realised what had happened!

The Lesser Jacana is a much smaller bird, with a continuous range from Tanzania, Zambia and Angola south-east to South Africa; north of this area there are scattered pockets of distribution, south of the Sahara. It is a paler bird and with its striped head can be mistaken for a juvenile African Jacana. The Lesser Jacana is found in areas of mixed water-lilies and reeds; only the size of a sparrow, this can be a difficult bird to see well.

If the Northern Jacana is the most striking member of the family, then the Pheasant-tailed Jacana in breeding plumage is the most elegant. It is a brown-bodied bird with white wings, face and throat; the crown and nape are golden-yellow and at the stern is a long tail, resembling that of a pheasant *Phasianinae*. It occurs from India to Java, sharing much of its range with the Bronze-winged Jacana. It overlaps with the Comb-crested Jacana Irediparra gallinacea in Indonesia. The latter ranges from the Philippines and Borneo to north and eastern Australia.

Jacanas search areas of floating vegetation and the margins of pools, for their diet of insects, other invertebrates, small frogs and fishes.

At least four species of jacana are polyandrous; female Northern Jacanas establish territories that include up to four resident males. The domestic arrangements for the other four species are insufficiently known, and cannot be confirmed either way. The nest is often placed amongst floating vegetation and in all known instances it is the male that incubates the 4 eggs for about 28 days. The known exception is the Lesser Jacana; both parents share the incubation and the rearing of the young. The males of some other species protect their chicks between their wings and their bodies, but so far only the African and Comb-crested Jacanas have been seen to carry their young in this position. Female jacanas guard the territory when the male feeds, leaving the chicks unattended. If he fails to return, the chicks will starve, the female playing no part in their welfare.

PAINTED-SNIPES
Order: *Charadriiformes*
Family: *Rostratulidae*
two genera *Rostratula* and *Nycticryphes*
each contain a single species

In tropical areas in the New and Old Worlds live two colourful shorebirds that are secretive birds of marshes and other freshwater wetlands. The two species of Painted-Snipe feed mainly at dawn and dusk, but sometimes can be seen feeding in the open later in the day, or when flushed from cover. Mostly Painted-Snipes pass the day in the shade of a clump of rushes or small bush in the marsh, where they sleep and preen. When flushed they fly slowly short distances with broad rounded wings and dangling legs. Neither species is migratory, but both move locally as suitable feeding areas, such as marshes and flood plains, dry out after the wet season. One extralimital bird was seen by Simon Boyes and an Ornitholidays' birding tour to Morocco in 1986. This constituted the first record for the Western Palearctic outside Egypt and Israel.

In the Old World, the Greater Painted-Snipe *Rostratula benghalensis* occurs from West and South Africa, through India, Japan and south-east Asia south down to Australia. It is the larger of the two species, 9.5 in. (24 cm.) long, and the sexes show greater plumage differences than the South American Painted-Snipe *Nycticryphes semicollaris*. The female Greater Painted-Snipe has a striking white patch through the eye and sides of the dark head. The neck, throat and upper breast are dark chestnut, whilst the upper parts are dark bottle green, finely barred with black. The bird has a buff-coloured crown stripe and buff 'braces' up the back that become white as they extend down the sides of the body to join the white lower breast and belly. The male is a duller bird, with grey and buff mottled upper parts and a less conspicuous head pattern. The South American species is a smaller and drabber bird, 8in. (20cm.) long, that does not show such a marked difference between the plumages of male and female; the tail is more wedge-shaped. Both species have a long bill, decurved at the tip with which they probe the mud for invertebrates.

The nest of the Greater Painted-Snipe is a platform of vegetation hidden in an area of thick cover and built by the male, although sometime the female has been present. The usual clutch is four cryptically marked eggs, incubated for about 20 days by the male alone. The female pays no further part in the well-being of that nest and its subsequent brood, but instead leaves to attract and seduce another male and starts all over again. She defends the territory against any intruding female. The second male will be sitting on his clutch before the first brood has hatched. The nests of a female can be up to 30ft. (10m.) apart forming a loose colony and in Japan a female has been found to lay two to four clutches.

The breeding biology of the South American Painted-Snipe is less well known. The female helps with the incubation of the eggs, but appears not to play any part in the rearing of the chicks. The fact that it is the male that tends the young suggests that polyandry may also be part of the life style of this species, although perhaps to a lesser extent.

CRAB PLOVER
Order: *Charadriiformes*
Family: *Dromadidae*
the genus *Dromas* contains a single species *Dromas ardeola*

The Crab Plover *Dromas ardeola* is one of the most elegant and spectacular of all shorebirds. It only breeds around the Arabian Gulf, the coasts of Arabia and north-east Africa. Unlike all other shorebirds Crab Plovers are colonial breeders

Facing page: a female Greater Painted Snipe in a marsh in the Masai Mara, Kenya. This is usually a shy and retiring species that few people are able to see so clearly, let alone photograph. Its large eye shows that this is a bird of crepuscular and nocturnal habits.

Left: an immature Crab Plover on the Seychelles island of Praslin; only a few months earlier it was raised in a burrow near the shores of the north-eastern Indian Ocean. Its long legs resemble those of a stilt and its stout bill enables it to crush crabs.

and even more peculiarly nest in burrows! The adult looks immaculate with crisp black and white plumage and standing on long blue-grey legs it appears to tower above most other shorebirds. It is 16 in. (41 cm.) long, although much of the length comes from the legs and a particularly stout bill evolved to crack the hard shells of crabs, which form its main source of food. The juvenile, immediately recognisable as a Crab Plover, is mainly black and white with a pale grey back.

Breeding begins in April, but this seems to vary within the breeding range. The species breeds in colonies that can contain several hundred birds. The colonies, on sandy ground or in sand dunes can be up to half a mile (0.8km.) from the sea and cover several acres. The ground is honeycombed with tunnels, excavated by one or both birds, each some four to six feet (1.2-1.8 m.) long with the nest chamber at the end. A single white egg is laid, but little is known about the breeding biology of Crab Plovers. Such information as, does one parent incubate, or do they share the task, and for how long etc., waits to be revealed.

By nesting at the end of burrows Crab Plovers are able to incubate their eggs away from the heat of the merciless sun. This adaptation has led to yet another deviation from the usual characteristics of shorebirds. In most species of shorebird the chicks are active and leave the nest shortly after hatching, however Crab Plover chicks are helpless and are dependent on their parents until after fledging. I have seen juvenile birds that have arrived with their parents in the Seychelles for the winter still begging for food several months after being hatched further north. After the breeding season is over most birds disperse to tidal sand and mud flats around the western side of the Indian Ocean, although some birds travel around India and Sri Lanka to the Andaman Islands. The majority are found to the south and west, but information is so fragmented it is still not clear if the species is migratory or only partially so. Birds winter along the East African coast and are especially numerous on the tidal flats of Kenya and Tanzania. Small numbers reach Mozambique and Natal and others winter around Madagascar and Indian Ocean islands such as Aldabra and the Seychelles. In Kenya individual flocks of 400 or more are unusual, but in 1968 tidal flats in south-east Tanzania held at least 3000 birds; quite a sight! The distinctive immature birds can still be found with their parents until at least October and November.

The big attraction of tropical flats are crabs numbering thousands. It is not just the Crab Plovers that feed well, for other shorebirds such as Black-bellied Plover *Pluvialis squatarola* are very adept at stalking and catching crabs. At high tide this valuable food source retreats to the safety of submerged burrows, and shorebirds, including the Crab Plover, roost. As the tide falls and the mud becomes exposed once more the Crab Plovers start to feed again. They have large eyes, no doubt an asset when low tide occurs after dark, and they can feed while the temperatures are cooler.

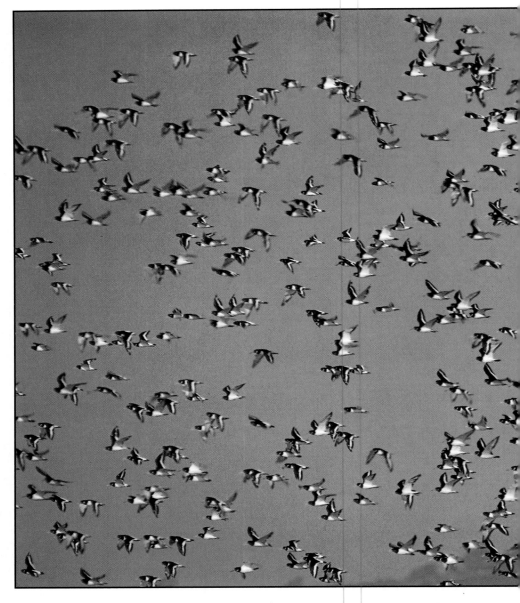

OYSTERCATCHERS
Order: *Charadriiformes*
Family: *Haematopodidae*
the genus *Haematopus* contains ten species

Oystercatchers are large shorebirds found throughout much of the World except the Polar regions. They are distinctive, noisy birds most frequently found along rocky shores and tidal estuaries, although three species regularly breed inland. Five species are pied, four are black and the tenth species has three colour phases – pied, black, and intermediate.

Oystercatchers get their name from eating oysters *Ostreidae*, although this represents only a small percentage of the diet; other bivalves such as Cockles *Cardium edule* and Mussels *Mytilus edulis* are eaten in far greater quantities by the Eurasian Oystercatcher *Haematopus ostralegus*. All oystercatchers have evolved long red bills that effectively break into the shells of bivalves or chisel and lever limpets *Patella* from rocks. Inland, birds use the bill to probe the soil for earthworms. They are wading birds, but swim well if the need arises. Sometimes they swim the short distance from one mussel bed to another, rather than fly; it would appear to be out of laziness rather than for any other reason. I once watched

one swimming in about a foot (30cm.) of water and some 5 ft. (1.5m) from the shore. Quite unexpectedly it upended like a duck and surfaced with a mussel that it took ashore and dealt with in the usual manner.

There are five species of pied oystercatcher found in North and South America; from western Europe to Australia and New Zealand.

The most widespread species is the Eurasian Oystercatcher, although a case is argued to call this bird the Northern Pied Oystercatcher to distinguish it from the Australian species. The term 'Northern' does not necessarily exclude the American Oystercatcher. The Eurasian Oystercatcher occurs from Iceland east to the eastern shores of the Bering Sea. However,

Above: an American Oystercatcher adult and a young adult with a darker-tipped bill, on the edge of a saltmarsh. This species ranges from the United States to Argentina and Chile.

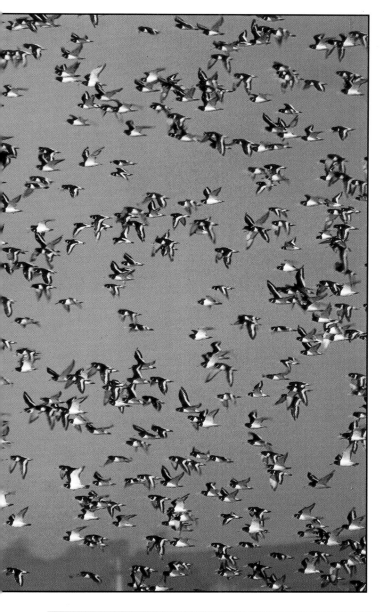

distribution east of the Yenisey River in Siberia is confined to the Kamchatka Peninsular and an area of north-eastern China. Over much of its range it is a bird of gravel, shingle and stone shores of lakes, rivers and surrounding farmland. In some areas such as north-western Europe and Iceland, it is a familiar bird of the coasts and estuaries. It is the most migratory species of all the oystercatchers, for in winter most inland breeding areas are deserted as the birds move to the coast or migrate southwards. Birds from the inland populations of Europe and Asia move to the coasts of western Europe, the Middle East, Africa and Asia in the Fall. In East Africa it occurs mainly on offshore islands, rarely on the mainland and only as a vagrant inland. It is also a vagrant in South Africa and Namibia.

The American Oystercatcher *H.palliatus* is a more sedentary and a less gregarious species than the Eurasian bird. Unlike that bird, the back and wings are dark brown and not black, it lacks the white lower back and the white wing-bar is less extensive. It is a bird of the coasts, found from New England south to northern Argentina on the Atlantic side, and from Baja California to northern Chile, including a population on the Galapagos Islands, on the Pacific coast. The only significant movements are those of the New England breeders, who head south in the Fall.

In southern parts of Chile and Argentina, also on Tierra del Fuego and the Falkland Islands to the east, the Magellanic Oystercatcher *H.leucopodus* replaces the American species. It is also one of three species that largely breeds inland, although it moves to the coast in winter. Otherwise it is mainly sedentary, although Tierra del Fuego is only occupied during the breeding season.

Around the coasts of Australia the Australian Pied Oystercatcher *H.longirostris*, occurs; a bird that looks very like the Eurasian species; in fact some taxonomists even treat them as the same species. Unlike most other species it is not a bird of rocky shores. It is also to be found breeding in New Zealand, where the population is classed as yet another species in some books! In New Zealand it breeds on the South Island, although there has been a recent breeding record from the North Island, where it is a common wintering species. On the South Island birds breed inland on shingle banks in rivers and in fields. At other times of the year they occur on coasts and estuaries.

Above left: a flock of wintering Eurasian Oystercatchers in flight over the Solway Firth on the English/Scottish border. In this part of the British Isles, many oystercatchers breed inland in agricultural areas and along shingle river beds, moving to the coast in the fall.
Left: a Eurasian Oystercatcher nesting on coastal shingle in Norfolk, England, has just hatched the first of its three eggs.

The fifth and final species of pied oystercatcher occurs on the Chatham Islands, lying to the east of New Zealand. The Chatham Islands Oystercatcher *H.chathamensis* is the rarest oystercatcher; assuming that the Canarian Black Oystercatcher *H.meadewaldoi*, last recorded in 1913, is extinct. The population stands at about 70 birds, having risen from a low point of 50 individuals. It is a bird of the coasts and is non-migratory, although marked birds have wandered from island to island. It shows the least amount of white on the upper-parts of any pied oystercatcher.

There are four species of black oystercatcher scattered around the globe. They are widely separated and are all almost identical in appearance.

Down the Pacific coast of North America from the Aleutian Islands to Baja California is the American Black Oystercatcher *H.bachmani*; to the south, the Blackish Oystercatcher *H.ater* occurs from Peru south to Tierra del Fuego and the Falklands, and north up the Atlantic coast to Uruguay. Across the Atlantic in Africa, one finds the African Black Oystercatcher around the coastlines of South Africa and Namibia, but what of the records of black oystercatchers from Senegal during the 1970s? Could they have been vagrants from southern Africa or perhaps birds from a hitherto unknown relict population of the Canarian Black Oystercatcher, presumed to be extinct since 1913? Black oystercatchers of unknown origin were seen in Tenerife in the Canary Islands in 1968 and 1981. The fourth black species is the Sooty Oystercatcher of Australia. This species occurs around all the coasts, but is less common than the Australian Pied Oystercatcher, but unlike that species it inhabits rocky shores.

The last oystercatcher is the Variable Oystercatcher *H.unicolor* and unlike all the other species it comes in three colour forms – pied, black and intermediate. During the breeding season it is a coastal bird, so does not come into conflict with the Australian Pied Oystercatcher; timing its breeding season a little later in the year. The pied form differs from the Australian Pied by having more extensive black on the breast, the edge of which is also less clearly defined. The intermediate form is similar, but has darker upper-tail coverts and the black form, well – it is black!

Oystercatchers usually lay two to four eggs, well camouflaged in a shallow scrape in shingle, sand or grass. Incubation is by both parents, who vigourously and noisily defend the site against all comers. On the Scottish island of Mull I once watched a Eurasian Oystercatcher take on a sheep and its lamb that got too close to the nest. The incubating bird started piping noisily when the ewe came to within 5ft. (1.5m.) and this was sufficient to turn the ewe aside, but the lamb did not react. The Oystercatcher tried injury-feigning to lure the lamb away, but when this failed it flew at the lamb, striking it with its wings and legs. This was enough to drive it back to its mother. Later when I looked at the nest more closely I realised that the lamb had come to within 20in. (50cm.) of treading on the eggs.

Young Eurasian Oystercatchers hatch after the eggs have been incubated by their parents for 25 – 26 days; other species take about the same length of time. They are active as soon as they are dry, but unlike other wader chicks are fed by the adults throughout the five week fledging period and for about a week afterward. During the early days one parent broods, while the other searches for food that it brings to the chicks. As they get older both parents collect food, and the chicks, often hiding amongst large stones or vegetation, will run to greet the adult. The final stage before independence covers the period shortly before and after fledging. The chicks, now almost the size of an adult but with shorter dark bills, follow close behind their parents, noisily begging for food. During our time in Scotland I used to band the chicks of shorebirds and am especially fond of baby oystercatchers. One day, by a river that flowed into a large sealoch, I found two chicks that were about three weeks old. I approached hoping that they would crouch by some rocks, but these two were too big for children's games like hide and seek; they decided to make a run for it. I almost reached one chick as it scrambled on to some rocks by the river and dived in! From above I could see it in the clear water, swimming upstream about 20in. (50cm.) below the surface and flapping its wings to propel itself along. It broke the surface after about 12ft. (4m.) and in a very bedraggled state, with several strands of seaweed draped over it. It swam ashore, gave a good shake and ran off. All this time the adults were keeping a close eye on events, so perhaps the

bird on the opposite river bank was equally horrified to see the second chick, who decided to swim the river, being swept down stream by the current. The U.S. cavalry appeared in the form of a female Red-breasted Merganser *Mergus serrator*, and saved the day! She was swimming along the opposite shore and, seeing the chick, swam quickly across the river and apparently shepherded it across the fastest stretch of river. It swam with the chick for at least 23 ft. (7m.) and was never more than 18 in. (45cm.) away. As soon as they were in quieter water, the Merganser swam away and the young Oystercatcher reached the shore, where one of its parents was waiting. Nature never fails to take one by surprise.

IBISBILL
Order: *Charadriiformes*
Family: *Ibidorhynchidae*
the genus *Ibidorhyncha* contains a single
species *Ibidorhyncha struthersii*

Along the rivers of central Asia where the water flows milky with the melt-water from the mighty Himalayas above, lives a very distinctive shorebird. In the past the Ibisbill *Ibidorhyncha struthersii* has been placed with the Avocets and Stilts *Recurvirostridae*, but it is now considered to justify a distinct family in its own right.

The Ibisbill occurs along the shingle beds of rivers from Turkestan east to Kashmir and north into Tibet and China. It can be found from 5600 ft. (1700 m.) above sea level to as high at 14450 ft. (4400 m.) during the breeding season. Ibisbills migrate altitudinally, so that those birds from the highest elevations descend to winter at more hospitable altitudes.

It is a striking bird, and at 17 in. (43 cm.) long is slightly larger than a Whimbrel *Numenius phaeopus*. Like that bird, the Ibisbill has a long decurved bill from which it gets its name, but unlike the Whimbrel, the Ibisbill has a red bill. Most of the body plumage is grey-brown. The nape, crown, forehead and throat is a striking mask of black and across the upper breast is a black band. The lower breast and belly is white. The legs are slightly out of proportion and look a little too short for the body size. The long bill of the Ibisbill is ideally adapted to finding food amongst the stones and rocks that line the beds of the rivers that are its home. Sometimes they wade up to the breast in water and in such conditions have to probe between stones for prey with their heads below the surface. Their diet consists of worms, molluscs, crustaceans and other invertebrates.

The breeding season takes place between late March and the end of May or early June, but the timing depends to a certain extent on the level of the river. The female Ibisbill lays four eggs in a shallow scrape on the exposed shingle banks and incubation is undertaken by both parents, although details of incubation and fledging are still largely unknown.

AVOCETS and STILTS
Order: *Charadriiformes*
Family: *Recurvirostridae*
three genera contain seven species

The first time I visited the Bear River Refuge near Brigham, Utah in July 1987, I was amazed at the numbers of Black-necked Stilts *Himantopus mexicanus* and American Avocets *Recurvirostra americana* that abounded around the edge of the Great Salt Lake. Many of the young birds reared that season were flying and helped swell the numbers, so that the memory of these black and white shorebirds will last for ever.

Both Avocets and Stilts are elegant, long-legged shorebirds, found mainly in the warm temperate and tropical regions of the World.

There are four species of avocet scattered across the continents, but there is no overlap of distribution. They are immaculate pied birds with long, grey-blue legs and a long, thin recurved bill. They feed on small aquatic creatures,

Right: a Pied Avocet scraping a nest. This bird is the emblem of the Royal Society for the Protection of Birds, Britain's foremost bird conservation body. The Avocet ceased breeding regularly in Britain in 1842 and, although intermittent breeding took place subsequently, East Anglia was not recolonised permanently until 1947.

caught with sideways sweeps of the bill. They swim readily and 'upend' like ducks to feed in deeper water. All species are about 17in. (43cm.) long.

The American Avocet breeds in the United States and Canada. Along the Eastern seaboard it is a coastal bird, breeding as far north as North Carolina, with migrants reaching Massachusetts in the fall. In winter it ranges from Florida, through the West Indies to Central, but does not reach South, America. In the western part of its range it is a bird of the coast and interior, where it reaches Saskatchewan during the breeding season. In winter it occurs from California and western Mexico, but only rarely south to Costa Rica. The American Avocet has an orange-brown head, neck and breast during the breeding season, which become grey in Winter. In flight it shows more black on the wings than the Pied *R.avosetta* and the Red-necked *R.novaehollandiae* Avocets. All three species show black 'braces' down the back. The Red-necked Avocet of Australia is the only other species to show a colour other than black and white. It has a deep chestnut head and neck forming a hood. Unlike the American species the adult

Above: an American Avocet in breeding plumage feeds in still, shallow water. In winter plumage the rufous colouring of the head and neck becomes white. It breeds in North America, mainly in the western states and Canadian provinces, and winters south in the Caribbean and Central America.

Red-necked Avocet retains this plumage throughout the year. It is sedentary, although in particularly dry seasons inland breeders withdraw to the coast. The most widespread species is the Pied Avocet that occurs across the Old World from England to China and south throughout Africa, where seasonal movements take place to take advantage of rains filling dried pans. Birds in the northern part of the range move south and west for the Winter. This species is the emblem of the Royal Society for the Protection of Birds, the foremost conservation body, based in England. After the Second World War and through protection measures taken by the RSPB, Pied Avocets bred in England for the first time since 1842 and are now well established in East Anglia. The Andean Avocet *R. andina* has the most restricted range of the four species, occurring mainly above 11,500ft. (3,500m.) in southern Peru, western Bolivia, northern Chile and north-western Argentina. Little is known about the movements of this species, although some appear to move to lower altitudes for the austral winter. The Andean Avocet lacks the striking flight pattern of the other species,

for the wings, back and tail are black, contrasting with the white head, under-parts, rump and lower back.

The Stilts are a complex groups of birds whose plumages vary across the globe. They are slim shorebirds with long coral pink legs and a long fine bill. The most widespread species is the Black-winged Stilt *H. himatopus*, 15in. (38cm.) long, found across the Old World to New Zealand. It is mainly a white bodied bird with black back and wings, although races differ slightly and often have different local names; the Black-winged Stilt of Europe is the same species as the Pied Stilt of New Zealand. Many authorities include the Black-necked Stilt of North and South America with this species, but the American Ornithologists' Union still considers it to be *H.mexicanus* in the 1983 Checklist. It shares a similar distribution with the American Avocet in the United States, but unlike the Avocet, occurs throughout much of South America except for the extreme southern latitudes. In New Zealand the Black Stilt *H.novaezelandiae* is an endemic species, perhaps the rarest shorebird in the World, whose population has suffered a natural decline. It has a very restricted range centred on a valley threatened by a hydro-electric scheme, but the decline has been the result of hybridizing with the Pied Stilt. Until European farming

methods provided the species with an increase in breeding sites, the Pied Stilt was a rare bird in the islands. The population expanded, bringing it into contact with the native Black Stilt, thereby creating opportunities for the two species to hybridize. This has taken place on such a scale that there are probably no pure Pied Stilts left in New Zealand and only about 15 pairs of pure Black Stilts remain.

The Banded Stilt *Cladorhynchus leucocephalus*, 16in. (40cm.) long, is the only member of its genus and occurs only in south-western and south-eastern Australia and in Tasmania. It is a whiter bird in flight than the other stilts, with a white body, including the back, and white secondaries. Unlike the other stilts the adult Banded Stilt has a chestnut breast band, extending down to the legs, where it becomes darker. The juvenile has white under-parts.

Avocets and stilts breed in open areas, often by alkaline lagoons and lakes and form scattered colonies. Usually four eggs are laid in a scrape, sometimes lined or rimmed with dry grass or other vegetable matter. Incubation is shared by both parents for about 24 days. The chicks are active as soon as they are dry, but often brooded to shade them as much as to keep them warm. Avocet youngsters fledge in five to six weeks, whilst young stilts are flying in about four.

Top: a flock of Black-winged Stilts in Tanzania. Above: an anxious Bush Thick-knee on its nest in open woodland, Australia. Facing page: (top left) a Black-winged Stilt, and (top right) a Double-banded Thick-knee in Costa Rica. The latter are found in Central and northern South America where they inhabit areas of open grassland. Facing page bottom: an immature Pied Avocet feeds with two Black-winged Stilts at a pool in the Masai Mara Game Reserve, Kenya.

THICK-KNEES
Order: *Charadriiformes*
Family: *Burhinidae*
two genera contain nine species

The only major land mass not to be colonised by a species of thick-knee is North America, for although the Double-striped Thick-knee *Burhinus bistriatus* occurs from southern Mexico to northern Brazil, it is a sedentary species and not likely to occur other than as a very rare vagrant. The only record from the United States is of one shot in Texas in December 1961.

The seven species of Thick-knees are also known as Stone-curlews in some parts of the World, and in Africa the name Dikkop is applied. They are large, cryptically coloured shorebirds, recalling large plovers *Charadriidae* and found in dry open habitats. Some species such as the Spotted Dikkop

B.capensis prefer bushes in their territory, where they find shade during the heat of the day; others, including the Water Dikkop *B.vermiculatus*, choose to live along sandy river banks. The largest species is the Bush Thick-knee *B.magnirostris* of Australia, 22in. (55cm.) long, and the smallest is the Senegal Thick-knee *B. senegalensis* 14in. (45cm.). This species occurs in Africa from Egypt south to north-western Kenya and across to West Africa; a confiding bird of river banks and adjacent open areas, which may or may not be cultivated.

Thick-knees are buff-coloured birds, and except for the Peruvian Thick-knee *B. superciliaris*, are heavily streaked or spotted with black, brown or grey. In flight all species show white patches in the primaries and some have a pale wing panel. The Double-striped and Peruvian species have bold head patterns. The name 'Thick-knee' comes from the enlarged leg joint; erroneously often called the 'knee', it is actually the ankle, the knee is at the thick end of the 'drumstick' and usually hidden by feathers. Thick-knees are largely crepuscular and nocturnal birds; birds seen during the day are often just standing in the open or in the shade of a bush, staring back at the observer with large yellow eyes. As the sun sets, they become active and search for food that includes invertebrates such as earthworms and insects, and larger items including

The nest is a shallow scrape, sometimes lined with small stones or shells, where most species lay two eggs. The Senegal Thick-knee sometimes forms small colonies such as the 21 nests discovered earlier this century on a flat-roofed house in Cairo, Egypt! Both parents share the incubation period that lasts for 25-27days, and the chicks leave the nest as soon as they are dry and wander with their parents in search of food until they can fly some six weeks later.

COURSERS and PRATINCOLES
Order: *Charadriiformes*
Family: *Glareolidae*
five genera contain 17 species.

This family of shorebirds occurs in the warmer regions of the Palearctic, Africa and Australasia. It is split into two halves; nine species of coursers and eight pratincoles.

The coursers are birds of arid country and some are nocturnal, although the Egyptian Plover *Pluvianus aegyptius*, 7.75 in.(20cm.) long, an aberrant member of the family,

frogs and lizards. Most thick-knees are sedentary, although some seasonal movements as a result of rain, or perhaps the lack of it, occur locally. The only exception is the European Stone-curlew *B. oedicnemus*, whose northern populations migrate south to the Mediterranean, North Africa and India in the fall.

The remaining species belonging to the genus *Esacus* are the Great Thick-knee *E.recurvirostris* and the Beach Thick-knee *E.magnirostris*. They are larger than most thick-knees, about the size of a Bush Thick-knee, but lack the striated plumage. They both have stronger markings on the head and a much heavier bill than the *Burhinus* thick-knees. The two species closely related are considered by some authorities to be conspecific. The Great Thick-knee occurs both inland and on the coast from Iran east to Sri Lanka and Indo-China. The Beach Thick-knee is a coastal bird from Malaysia and the Philippines, south through islands large and small to Australia, where it occurs on the north and east coasts.

occurs on sandbars along large rivers in Africa, mainly between the Tropic of Cancer and the Equator. It is a beautiful combination of blue-grey, black and white with apricot-buff under-parts. It has long been associated with crocodiles for both share the same habitat, but its supposed habit of cleaning food and parasites from the teeth and gums of crocodiles has yet to be substantiated. The Egyptian Plover lays two to three eggs in a deep scrape on a sandbar; incubation is shared equally by both male and female for 28–31 days. During this period the eggs are partially or completely covered by a thin layer of sand to prevent them over-cooking in the heat and as an additional precaution to help keep the eggs cool the parents frequently soak their belly feathers in the river before settling over the nest. In the early days after hatching, the parents use the same method to cool the chicks, who drink moisture from the damp breast feathers.

The Coursers are divided into two genera. Those species belonging to the genus *Cursorius* are sandy-brown shorebirds

Above: a Heuglin's or Three-banded Courser on its nest in East Africa. The species ranges from Sudan to northern South Africa, yet it is not commonly seen, being active mainly at dusk and during the night.

that occur, often far from water, in deserts and dry grasslands of Africa, and from the Middle East to India. They have short decurved bills and long legs. They run well, often fleeing from danger by running in a slightly crouched position, intermittently stopping, standing erect and looking around, before running on again. The four species are very similar and all are about 8.5 in.(22cm.) long. Widespread in India is the richly coloured Indian Courser *C.coromandelicus*, the only courser to have white upper tail-coverts. Replacing this species over most of sub-Saharan Africa is the closely related Temminck's Courser *C.temminckii*. The Cream-coloured *C.cursor* and Burchell's Courser *C.rufus* are paler birds; the former ranges across North Africa to the Middle East and into western India, whilst Burchell's was considered to be endemic to southern Africa until recently. Current thinking suggests that two races of courser that occur in north-east Africa and formerly assigned to the Cream-coloured Courser should be placed with Burchell's; further investigations are necessary. Although mainly sedentary, the Cream-coloured Courser occasionally occurs as a vagrant to north-western Europe from its home in North Africa. The remaining coursers are four species of nocturnal birds found in Africa and India. They are more cryptically-coloured birds with well patterned heads and necks, often inhabiting less open areas than the previous genus, although we frequently find the Double-banded Courser *Rhinoptilus africanus*, 8.5 in. (22cm.) long, sharing the same habitat with Temminck's Coursers during the day at Savuti in Botswana's vast Chobe National Park. Great interest was generated in 1986 by the rediscovery in India of Jerdon's Courser *R.bitorquatus*, 10.5 in.(27cm.) long. It had not been seen since 1900 when it was last recorded in eastern India and was thought to be extinct. Previous attempts to find this bird had failed, but perhaps those who had searched earlier had not realised that it was nocturnal. The problems faced by nocturnal birds were illustrated recently at the end of a tour to Namibia. Along a stretch of fast metaled highway we discovered four or five dead Violet-tipped Coursers *R.chalcopterus*, on the road. They appear to have been feeding at night and dazzled by the lights of oncoming vehicles.

Coursers lay 1 – 3eggs that are incubated for about 26 days, although it is uncertain if incubation is shared by both parents. When hatched the chicks are fed by the adults until they fledge some 40days later.

Pratincoles are the most aerial members of the family, looking like large swallows as they hawk insects. They are brown, slender-winged birds, and except for the Australian Pratincole *Stiltia isabella* 9in.(23cm.) long, have forked tails and short legs. That species has a short, slightly rounded tail and long legs recalling the coursers and although it is also an aerial feeder, it spends more time feeding on the ground than the members of the genus *Glareola*, to which the remaining pratincoles belong.

Pratincoles are birds of open areas such as salt marshes, flood plains and pans, where the most widespread species is the Common Pratincole *G.pratincola*, 9.75 in.(24cm.) long. This species ranges from the Mediterranean to western Asia and down through Africa, where the local breeders are joined by wintering birds from the northern parts of its range. This bird is also called Collared or Red-winged Pratincole, but both the closely related Black-winged *G.nordmanni* and Oriental *G.maldivarum* Pratincoles have collars and the latter also has a red under-wing. Both of the last-named species lack the white trailing edge to the wing found on the Common Pratincoles. Both the Black-winged and the Oriental Pratincoles are Asiatic species, the former wintering in western and southern Africa from its Central Asian breeding grounds, whereas the Oriental Pratincole occurs from India to the Far East and winters through Indonesia to northern Australia. All three species occur as vagrants outside their normal range during migration times. In 1988, whilst leading a tour to the Seychelles, we discovered both Common and Oriental Pratincoles together on the island of Praslin.

The Rock Pratincole *G.nuchalis*, is 7.5 in.(19cm.) long; it breeds on rocky outcrops in large rivers and tends to move from area to area as dictated by water levels. It has a distinctive white collar extending from the eyes to the back of the head. It does not have as long a forked tail as its larger relative; neither does the closely related Madagascar Pratincole *G.ocularis*, 9.5 in.(24cm.) long, a bird of similar appearance that breeds along rocky rivers in Madagascar and spends the

non-breeding season along the East African coast. The most distinctive of all is the Grey Pratincole *G.cinerea*, 7.5 in. (19cm.) long, a West African species found on sandbanks of large rivers, where its pale grey and white plumage makes excellent camouflage. It has a pale chestnut nape and breast and in flight shows more white than the closely related Little Pratincole *G.lactea*, 6.75 in. (17cm.) long, of India.

Pratincoles lay one to four eggs, depending on the species, and often form loose colonies. Incubation lasts 17 – 22days and is undertaken equally by both parents. The young leave the nest soon after hatching and fly 25 – 30 days later.

PLOVERS
Order: *Charadriiformes*
Family: *Charadriidae*
the 10 genera contain 66 species

Compared with many species of shorebirds, the plovers *Charadriidae* are plumpish birds with round heads, large eyes and an often, stout bill. When feeding they run, stop, peck or run some more, and on again – a distinctive feeding pattern. They occur throughout the World, except in the Sahara and the extreme polar regions.

There are 66 species divided into 10 genera, but this can simplified by considering the family in three groups. The largest number of species belong the genus *Charadrius*, which consists of the ringed and sand plovers, and includes the familiar Killdeer *C. vociferus*. Many members of the

Below: an incubating Double-banded Courser pants in the sun. It is not providing body heat to hatch the eggs, but shade to prevent them cooking! This African species inhabits open, arid areas and has an erratic distribution from the Horn of Africa to the extreme south-west.

Left: a Northern Lapwing in Scotland. The family ranges across the Palaearctic. During the fall, northern populations move south, but they will also migrate further afield to escape very severe weather, occasionally reaching North America.

winters along the coasts of the southern United States, the Caribbean, Central and most of South America. Vagrants have been found as far apart as Tierra del Fuego and the Isles of Scilly, off the tip off south-west England. One of the largest members of this group is the Killdeer, a common and widespread species in the United States and Canada; it occurs in a variety of habitats from lawns, plowed fields and prairies to tidal mudflats. Further south it ranges through Central and northern South America to Peru. Killdeers are often noisy and conspicuous birds during the breeding season, during which time of the year they are past-masters in the art of injury-feigning. If a predator approaches too closely to the nest or chicks, the distraught adult leads the danger away by fluttering along in front of it, trailing an apparently broken wing. Invariably this achieves its objective, and the predator follows the 'injured' bird until it has been lured sufficiently far away, to no longer be a threat.

The Wattled Plover (facing page) is a large African plover that breeds in much of sub-Saharan Africa except for the dry south-west and the equatorial rain-forests. This and several other species have spurs on their carpal joint, but these are often concealed by their breast feathers. Above left: a male Dotterel incubating eggs in a nest in the Cairngorms, Scotland. With this species the parenting roles are reversed. Left: a female Common Ringed Plover patiently incubates her eggs on a beach in England. This bird is a long-distance migrant: its Arctic populations winter in southern Africa.

genus have distinctive head and chest patterns, and range in size from 5 – 10.5 in. (13 – 27 cm.) long, although most species are between 6 – 8 in. (15 – 20 cm.) in length. For the purposes of this survey six monotypic genera of small plovers are also being considered together. The largest members of the family include the lapwings and belong to the genus *Vanellus*; they are bulkier birds and include several well-marked, striking species. The third group includes the three golden plover species and the Black-bellied Plover *Pluvialis squatarola*.

The ringed plover group, comprises usually smaller plovers that frequent sandy beaches and the shores of lakes and ponds; many are great travellers, including the Common Ringed Plover *C. hiaticula*. This wader is a common bird, breeding on undisturbed sandy beaches and gravel-beds in western Europe. A slightly smaller and darker race breeds farther north in the Arctic regions of the Palearctic, Alaska and islands in north-eastern Canada. These remote populations migrate to winter in the Old World, mainly in Africa, where they reach as far as South Africa during the austral summer. It has its New World equivalent in the Semipalmated Plover *C. semipalmatus*; this breeds in north-western Canada and Alaska, where it is found in similar habitats to the Common Ringed Plover. The two species are considered by some authorities to be conspecific, but although it shares the same black and white collared neck and head pattern, it has a shorter bill, and obvious webbing between the inner and middle toes. The Semipalmated Plover

Other members of this group are to be found almost wherever plovers occur, including areas where they can be the only representatives. Several species have evolved to be distinct island endemics, such as the St. Helena Plover *C. sanctaehelenae*; this bird is larger, but not as well-marked as its near relative, Kittlitz's Plover *C. pecuarius*, a widespread species found in sub-Saharan Africa.

Some members of the six monotypic genera of small plovers are also interesting. They include the Wrybill *Anarhynchus frontalis*, a species endemic to New Zealand, where it breeds along the stony rivers of South Island and winters on North Island. It is a grey and white plover with a black pectoral band during the breeding season. Its most unusual feature is the bill, one of the few in the bird world with a lateral curve. The bill, curved to the right, has evolved to find food, in the form of small invertebrates, clinging to the undersides of stones in the rivers. Another endemic plover that formerly occurred in New Zealand is the Shore Plover *Thinornis novaeseelandiae*, now confined to a single island in the Chatham group, lying nearly 400 miles (640 km.) to the east, out in the Pacific. This is a brown and white plover with a black mask, topped with a white edge and brown crown. In 1937 the population was only 70 pairs and since then has fluctuated between 40 pairs in 1982 to 80 pairs in 1987, in spite of the island being declared a reserve in 1954. An unusual aspect of the Shore Plover's breeding biology may have contributed to the end of the New Zealand population.

It is the only plover to nest in a burrow, often choosing old burrows of petrels, or in a tunnel in thick vegetation. Such ground nesting birds are particularly vulnerable to predation by rats, often associated with the arrival of man. The decline of the Shore Plover appears to have coincided with the arrival of European settlers. The rare grey and white Magellanic Plover *Pluvianellus socialis*, 8 in. (20 cm.) long, resembles a plover, but behaves like a Ruddy Turnstone *Arenaria interpres*, and may be a sandpiper – time, and science, will tell.

The largest plovers are the lapwings and other members of the genus *Vanellus*. Some species have extensive distributions across continents and others have a restricted range, such as the Spot-breasted Plover *V. melanocephalus* which is endemic to the Ethiopian Highlands. The most widespread member of the genus is the Northern Lapwing *V. vanellus*, a bird that is black and white when seen in the distance, but at close range it has a long crest, glossy bottle-green upper-parts and chestnut under-tail coverts. It ranges across the temperate Palearctic from Ireland to China; during the fall northern populations migrate south. It is a species that suffers badly during periods of intense cold and frost, which force already weakened birds into cold-weather movements to take them further south and west, than normal. In such winters large numbers arrive in the British Isles from continental Europe and occasionally, those heading for Ireland miss, and carry on over the Atlantic to the Eastern Seaboard. Vagrants have been recorded, sometimes singly or in small flocks, from Baffin Island south to the Carolinas, but mainly from Newfoundland. It is a bird of cultivated fields, rough pastures and wet meadowland during the breeding season. One of the first signs in March of birds taking note of the changing season, is when male Lapwings return to their breeding territories and begin a dramatic twisting and towering display flight, over the fields.

The plumage of most other members of this genus is a combination of brown, black and white. They range in size from 9 – 14 in. (23 – 35 cm.) in length. Only two other species have crests, the Southern Lapwing *V. chilensis*, found over much of South America and the Black-headed Plover *V. tectus*, of sub-Saharan Africa, north of the Equator. Other members of the family have long, drooping yellow wattles, hanging from the base of the bill like over-cooked fried egg; others have spurs on the carpal joints of the wing, some species have both.

The remaining species are the four members of the genus *Pluvialis*, 10 – 12 in. (25 – 30 cm.) long, whose principal breeding areas are in the Arctic. The Black-bellied Plover is a holarctic breeding species, absent only from Greenland and Scandinavia. In immaculate breeding dress it is one of the most stunning waders. The face and under-parts are jet-black, outlined with a broad white band. The crown, nape and upper-parts are white and black giving a spangled silvery-grey effect. In the dull non-breeding plumage it retains black axillaries beneath the wing. In the winter it occurs around many coasts of the world, except in the higher latitudes of the northern hemisphere, parts of the Mediterranean, the Far East and southern South America. The American Golden Plover *P. dominica* and the Pacific Golden Plover *P. fulva* have been split by taxonomists into distinct species. The American species vies with the Black-bellied, for top position in the league of handsome waders – spangled golden where its relative is silver. The winter border to the black face and under-parts is more prominent than on the Pacific species. Both of these are long-distance travellers; the American species winters in South America, and vagrants to the British Isles have occurred annually in recent years. More unusual, was one we found at Swakopmund in Namibia in March 1988. This was the first for that country and only the second to be seen in southern Africa. The first had been reported from South Africa a few months earlier. The Pacific Golden Plover heads for islands in the Pacific, the coasts of Australia and south-east Asia. It is a regular visitor in the fall to the Seychelles, in the Indian Ocean. The other member of the genus is the European Golden Plover *P. apricaria*, a similar bird, but not such a great traveller, with white, not grey, axillaries.

Most plovers in the Arctic and Temperate regions lay 4 eggs in a clutch, whilst tropical species only lay 2 eggs. Most species are monogamous, but dotterels, with their brighter females practice polyandry. The nest is a scrape in the ground, sometimes lined with grass. Some species, such as Kittlitz's Plover, lay in a deep scrape that is easily covered with sand

when the nest is left unattended. This is one of the species which, like the Egyptian Plover *Pluvianus aegyptius*, a courser not a plover, soaks its belly in water before settling over the eggs, to prevent them from becoming over-heated.

Many forms of wildlife are under increasing pressure from the activities of man in the form of developing agriculture and expanding industrial and urban areas. One threat to several species of plover, including the Piping Plover *C. melodus* of North America and the Common Ringed Plover, is the use of beaches for leisure. The cooperation of holiday-makers when they come across a pair of anxious plovers on a beach, may ensure successful breeding.

SANDPIPERS

Order: *Charadriiformes*
Family: *Scolopacidae*
23 genera contain 87 species

The family *Scolopacidae* contains the typical shorebirds, a widespread and diverse group that has evolved to fill an ecological niche not fully exploited by other birds. Most species breed in, or by, wetlands in the Northern Hemisphere, and move away either locally or migrate vast distances, after the breeding season.

Within the family are a number of clearly distinguished genera; godwits *Limosa* are large shorebirds, with straight or slightly recurved bills; curlews *Numenius* include the largest

Below: a Common Redshank incubating its eggs in a damp meadow. As soon as the chicks are dry they leave the nest, under the watchful eyes of their parents. This sandpiper, which breeds across the Palaearctic, is a relative of the yellowshanks of North America.

members of the family, with long decurved bills; sandpipers are represented by several genera of miscellaneous shorebirds, with shorter bills and legs, often to be found in areas of mud; phalaropes *Phalaropus* habitually swim; whilst woodcock *Scolopax* and snipe *Gallinago*, are cryptically-coloured shorebirds that occur in woods and marshes.

Shorebirds, or waders as they are often called in Britain and elsewhere, are a family that fascinate birders, perhaps not so much for aspects of behaviour, but because there is always the chance of finding a rarity. In 1989 whilst in the Seychelles, I discovered a Pectoral Sandpiper *Calidris melanotos*, on the island of Praslin. It was feeding at a shallow tidal pool amongst mangroves, with the commoner Curlew Sandpipers *C. ferruginea*, and had probably arrived with them from north-eastern Siberia. Pectoral Sandpipers may be comparatively recent colonists from North America, for they retain part of their traditional migration route; after crossing to Alaska they join other sandpipers for the long flight to the wintering grounds in South America. Our bird just took a right, when he should have taken a left turn! An even more unlikely sandpiper was discovered in September 1987 at Duxbury Beach, Plymouth County, Massachusetts; an immature Cox's Sandpiper *C. paramelanotos*, the World's least known sandpiper. The bird was caught in a mist-net and detailed examination of the plumage in the hand, and subsequently in the field, confirmed the identity. Cox's Sandpiper was first discovered in Australia, where wintering birds have occurred in the company of other shorebirds that breed in Siberia. The breeding grounds have yet to be located, although it is not beyond the bounds of possibility, that this bird may be a well-defined hybrid between the Curlew Sandpiper and either the Pectoral or the closely related Sharp-tailed Sandpipers *C. acuminata*. Until the questions raised by the relationship problem have been resolved, this bird is not being admitted to the checklist of North American birds by the American Ornithologists' Union. After the Massachusetts' bird had been studied in the field for several days, it was decided to try to recapture it and take some blood for DNA analysis. This might have resolved all the queries, but the Cox's Sandpiper had other ideas, and left with a large number of migrant shorebirds earlier that day!

Many species have richly-coloured plumage during the breeding season, which can transform the species markedly from the plain grey-brown and white plumage, worn during the winter months. Prior to breeding, the male Ruff *Philomachus pugnax*, of the northern Palearctic, exhibits an elaborate head dress, varying in colour from individual to

Above: with a surprised expression, a Masked Lapwing from Australia settles on a clutch of eggs and shows the spurs on the wings. Above left: a Willet, a North American sandpiper, in its breeding plumage. In winter it is a plainer bird. Left: a Common Snipe in Scotland 'freezes' as the photographer approaches, trusting to the effectiveness of its cryptic coloration.

individual; these are often black, chestnut or white, sometimes in combination. Display to attract a mate takes place at a communal display ground known as a 'lek'. Similar communal display is performed by the Great Snipe. *Gallinago media* and several species of grouse *Tetraoninae*. The female Ruff is known as a 'Reeve'. She is smaller than her mate, 9 in. (22 cm.) long compared with his 11.5 in. (29 cm.). The breeding plumage of the female is brighter than in winter, but lacks the ornate feathering of the male. Those shorebirds that are cryptically-coloured, such as snipe and woodcock, show little or no seasonal variation in their plumages. A number of the New World shorebirds have Old World equivalents; for example the Long-billed Curlew *Numenius americanus*, the Marbled Godwit *Limosa fedoa*, and the Greater and Lesser Yellowlegs *Tringa melanoleuca* and *T. flavipes* have very

Phalarope *P. fulicarius*, 8.25 in. (21 cm.) long, is called the Grey Phalarope in Britain, where it usually occurs in its grey winter plumage. It also breeds in the high latitudes of the Northern Hemisphere, but not as extensively as the Red-necked. During migration it travels entirely at sea, to wintering grounds off the Pacific coast of South America, and in the Atlantic Ocean, off west and southern Africa. It reaches more southerly latitudes than the Red-necked, for birds have been recorded from the Falkland Islands and off the coast of the Antarctic Peninsula. The third species is the larger, but more elegant Wilson's Phalarope *P. tricolor*, 9 in. (23 cm.) long, a widespread bird of pools and sloughs in mid- and western North America. The female leaves the breeding areas before the eggs hatch, which explains the huge numbers of Wilson's Phalaropes we found at the Bear River Refuge by the Great

similar counterparts in the Eurasian Curlew *N. arquata*, the Bar-tailed Godwit *L. lapponica*, and the Green- and Redshanks *T. nebularia* and *T. totanus*. All four New World species lack the long white wedge up the back of their European relatives.

One of the interesting aspects of shorebirds' lives is their differing feeding requirements; sometimes one can find a great variety of species in a limited area, showing few signs of intra-specific competition. The reason becomes clear when the physical characteristics are examined; each species is after a slightly different food item in the area. In North America the smallest species of sandpipers, nicknamed 'peeps', have the shortest bills and legs, and are found along the water's edge or at a shallow pool left by the receding tide. Among the North American species, a longer-billed and longer-legged shorebird, the Long-billed Dowitcher *Limnodromus scolopaceus*, thrusts its bill deep into the mud with a very rapid sewing-machine like action. Probing deeper into the mud nearby might be the Marbled Godwit *Limosa fedoa*, with an even longer bill that reaches food items untouched by most other shorebirds. The longest bill belongs to the Long-billed Curlew *Numenius americanus* 22.5 in. (57 cm.) in length, and has a bill 8.5 in. (21 cm.) long! This way, a variety of species can feed together without competing.

Phalaropes, three very distinctive members of the family, are by far the most aquatic. In breeding plumage they are a superb combination of red and grey, mixed with black, buff, chestnut and white. The females are brighter than the males, for once she has presented him with a clutch of four eggs, she leaves and plays no further part the rearing of her offspring. By contrast, the winter plumage is strikingly grey and white, showing dark on the wing in flight. The most widespread is the circumpolar Red-necked Phalarope *Phalaropus lobatus*, 7.5 in. (19 cm.) long, formerly known as the Northern Phalarope. This species winters at sea off the Pacific coast of South America, in the north-east Indian Ocean off Arabia and amongst the East Indies. Certain areas are reached by migrating directly overland; some birds pass the winter inland on some of the alkaline lakes of Africa's Great Rift Valley. The Red-

Salt Lake, Utah in early July. Unlike the other species, Wilson's does not winter at sea, but on ponds and alkaline lakes in South America.

Most members of the Sandpiper family lay up to 4 eggs in a cup-shaped nest on the ground, often concealed in a tuft of long grass, or placed out in open tundra. Three species, the Solitary Sandpiper *Tringa solitaria* breeding across northern Canada and Alaska, and the Wood and Green Sandpipers *Tringa glareola* and *T. ochropus* of the northern Palearctic, have been recorded nesting in trees in disused thrushes' nests. Both birds share the incubation, but in parts of the range of the Sanderling *Calidris alba*, and Temminck's Stint *C. temminckii*, the female lays two clutches of eggs that are brooded simultaneously by both birds – his and her nests! Incubation lasts 19 – 30 days, depending on the species; when hatched, the chicks, covered with cryptically-patterned down, are mobile when they are dry and fledge 4 – 6 weeks later.

Whilst shorebirds form an abundant family of birds, some species are very rare. The Eskimo Curlew *N. borealis*, 14 in. (36 cm.) long, that once was so abundant, still makes the annual journey to Patagonia. Now in such small numbers, they are only seen occasionally, by a lucky few. No other rare shorebird, so low in numbers, faces such a long annual migration route.

SEEDSNIPES

Order: *Charadriiformes*
Family: *Thinocoridae*
two genera each containing two species

Along the Andes from Ecuador south to Tierra del Fuego and across Patagonia, there lives a family of aberrant shorebirds called Seedsnipes *Thinocoridae*. The name comes from their diet and a snipe-like zigzag flight. Seedsnipes feed on the

Above left: on a North Wales shore a Ruddy Turnstone in its dull winter plumage searches for small invertebrates on a barnacle-encrusted rock, and (above) Willets, also in winter plumage, rest on the high-tide line of a sandy beach along Florida's Gulf coast. The slightly smaller and darker shorebirds with them are Short-billed Dowitchers.

ground recalling a small gamebird such as a Bobwhite *Colinus virginianus*, but in flight display the long wings of a shorebird. They might be described as the South American equivalent of the Old World family of sandgrouse *Pteroclididae*, but do not have that family's specialized water-carrying ability, for in fact under natural conditions they appear to obtain all the moisture they require through their food!

The four species are split into two genera, *Attagis* and *Thinocorus*. The two species of the *Attagis* Seedsnipes are the larger species in the family and of these two the Rufous-bellied Seedsnipe *A. gayi*, 12 in. (30 cm.) long, is the largest. It occurs southwards down the Andes from Ecuador through Peru and Bolivia to Chile and Argentina. It is a beautiful bird, with a scaly rufous plumage, more richly coloured in the northern populations. The Rufous-bellied is the hardiest of all four species, inhabiting mountain grasslands and rocky areas up to 13000 ft. (4000 m.) above sea level in the northern part of its range and up to 6500 ft. (2000 m.) in the south. Unlike many other mountain birds it is resident at these altitudes throughout the year. The diet of this and other seedsnipes is mainly seeds and other vegetable matter, from which they also obtain sufficient moisture for their needs. The slightly smaller White-bellied Seedsnipe *A. malouinus*, confined to southern Chile, southern Argentina and Tierra del Fuego, is 11 in. (29 cm.) long and also has a beautiful scaled plumage, but is a greyer bird with distinctive white belly and under-wing coverts. If the larger species resemble gamebirds, then the two smaller birds recall a ground-feeding passerine, but are typical seedsnipes with scaly plumage, shorebird-like wings and a seed-eating bill. The Grey-breasted Seedsnipe *T. orbignyianus*, 9 in. (23 cm.) long, is an upland bird living in the same habitat as its larger relative, the Rufous-bellied Seedsnipe. Unlike that species, which is sedentary, those populations breeding in the highest areas descend to lower altitudes in winter and those at the southern end of the range in Tierra del Fuego move north to mainland South America. Only 7 in. (18 cm.) long, the Least Seedsnipe resembles a lark *Alaudidae* as it searches for food amongst sparse vegetation on plains and in poorly cultivated fields at lower altitudes than its congeners. It occurs from south-western Ecuador south to Chile and Argentina.

All seedsnipes breed during the austral summer, and lay four eggs in a grass lined scrape on the ground. The incubation period of the Least Seedsnipe is 26 days and undertaken solely by the female, while the male keeps a look out for danger. When the female leaves the nest, she scuffs soil over the eggs to conceal them, although they are already well camouflaged to suit their environment. If, when danger approaches, she does not have time to cover the eggs, she performs a distraction display, either by flying weakly away or by feigning injury to lure the predator away. The chicks leave the nest as soon as they are dry after hatching, and during the fledging period, which lasts about seven weeks, both parents protect them from danger by using distraction displays. Family groups join to form larger migratory or nomadic flocks during the rest of the year.

SHEATHBILLS
Order: *Charadriiformes*
Family: *Chionididae*
the genus *Chionis* contains two species

Amongst the great seal colonies and penguin rookeries of the Antarctic and the adjacent sub-antarctic islands lives a dumpy pure white bird that looks like a pigeon, but with longer legs. This is the American Sheathbill *Chionis alba*, an aberrant shorebird, 16 in. (40 cm.) long, that lives by scavenging on animal debris in the form of the after-birth, dead pups or chicks, abandoned eggs or any other refuse to be found. In this environment, the Skuas *Catharacta sp.* are the only serious competitors.

There are two species forming an allopatric pair, the American and the Lesser Sheathbill *C. minor*, which is only marginally smaller. The distribution of the American species takes it along the Antarctic Peninsular to the island groups of South Orkney, South Sandwich and South Georgia. Immatures wander farther afield during the austral winter to the coasts of

the Falkland Is., Tierra del Fuego and to the Patagonian coast of Argentina. The Lesser Sheathbill is a sedentary species and restricted to the sub-antarctic islands of Marion, Prince Edward, Crozet, Kerguelen and Heard that lie in the southern Indian Ocean.

Both species have pure white plumages and have a horny sheath that protects the nasal passages from becoming blocked by blood or other material found while scavenging. Both species also have wattles around the eyes and the base of the bill, less prominent on immature birds, and rudimentary spurs on the carpal joint of the wing that are used in fighting. Both sexes are similar, except in size, where the male tends to be the larger. The American Sheathbill has a yellowish bill and sheath and grey legs, whilst in the Lesser the bill and sheath are black and the leg colour varies between pale pink and

black, depending upon which island the bird occurs.

The nest is made of feathers, bones, seaweed, and limpet shells, and on the sub-antarctic islands vegetation is also used. It is usually hidden in crevices or amongst boulders, often in the vicinity of a penguin colony. The clutch is two eggs, yet on occasions as many as four may be laid, although it is unusual for more than a single chick to survive to fledging. Incubation is by both parents and lasts for 29 days. The chick is covered in down until after seven or eight weeks it is replaced by white juvenile feathers.

Sheathbills are voracious and opportunist feeders that do not always wait for a helpless injured mammal or bird to die before starting to gorge themselves! They bully young penguins out of the way as the parent is regurgitating krill collected at sea. Some inevitably is spilled and the Sheathbill eats it without a moment's hesitation. They have even learned that after a seal pup finishes a meal of its mother's milk, some milk oozes from the nipple and once again the Sheathbill is there before it can drain away or dry!

Above: an American Sheathbill casts its eye over an Antarctic seal colony and penguin rookery, looking for refuse. The horny sheath covering its nasal passages is just visible on the top of the bill.

SKUAS
Order: *Charadriiformes*
Family: *Stercorariidae*
two genera contain seven species

Skuas are the pirates of the bird world and are great fun to watch. A few years ago, with the help of local boatmen John and Alistair Bartholomew, I used to take small parties of birders out to the Treshnish Isles that lie west of Mull in Scotland's Inner Hebrides. One of the highlights during the short breeding season was to sit on a clifftop and watch the Common Murres or Guillemot *Uria aalge* returning with fish to their chicks on the ledges below. In the air, waiting in ambush off-shore, could be up to half a dozen Parasitic Jaegers, or Arctic Skuas as they are called in Britain and elsewhere, *Stercorarius parasiticus*, 19 in. (48 cm.) long. Patrolling with a light bouyant flight, they would switch to overdrive as soon as an unsuspecting Murre came within range; the acceleration and agility of the Jaeger never failed to impress as it raced after the auk, which would turn and twist this way and that in a vain attempt to escape. The majority of attacks ended with the murre dropping the fish to the sea below, but invariably the culmination of the performance would be the final display of aerobics as the Jaeger caught the fish moments before it struck the water.

In North America the term Skua is applied to the larger members of the family which belong to the genus *Catharacta*. The taxonomy of the genus is complex, although most modern books accept that there are four species. Unlike the bouyant jaegers, Skuas are heavily-built powerful seabirds, 23 in. (58 cm.) long. Most species are dark and resemble one of the large immature gulls. Their piratical attacks on other seabirds lack the finesse of the jaegers as they pressurise birds as large as Northern Gannets *Sula bassana* into regurgitating their stomach contents. The only species to breed in the northern hemisphere is the Great Skua *C. skua*, which breeds mainly in Scotland, the Faroes, and Iceland. An expansion in these countries as a result of protection has lead to a population increase and the recent breeding in Norway and Spitzbergen. During the non-breeding season they range widely over the North Atlantic. In the southern hemisphere, where three species occur, the situation is more complicated. The species found breeding on sub-antarctic islands and in southern Argentina is the Antarctic Skua *C. antarctica*, a bird virtually identical to the Great Skua. Outside the breeding season birds range into the Atlantic and Indian Oceans, north of the Tropic of Capricorn. Around the southern coasts of Argentina and Chile occurs the Chilean Skua *C. chilensis*, differing from the Antarctic Skua by a more cinnamon coloured body; the two species hybridize in parts of their mutual range. Most distinctive of the southern skuas is the smaller South Polar Skua *C. maccormicki*, 21 in. long. There are two colour phases; a dark phase resembling the other skuas, but with an indistinct pale collar and a light phase that has a pale grey head and under-parts.

The Great Skua (this page) is the largest and most gull-like of the four species of skua and jaeger that breed in the Northern Hemisphere. In its breeding grounds it is a noisy bird that does not hesitate to attack intruders that approach its nest.

The three species of jaegers belong to the genus *Stercorarius*; elsewhere the name 'skua' is used instead of 'jaeger'. They are more lightly-built birds and parasitise smaller sea birds such as auks *Alcidae* and terns *Sterninae*. All breed in the higher latitudes of the northern hemisphere and the majority migrate to southern hemisphere for the austral summer. Smallest is the Long-tailed Jaeger, *Stercorarius longicaudus*, 23 in. (58 cm.) long, which includes a 10 in. (25 cm.) long tail. The elongated central tail feathers are so flexible that they undulate behind the flying bird. The Long-tailed Jaeger is a more lightly built bird than its congeners and is smart with a black cap, grey-brown back and wings and yellowish under-parts. A dark brown colour phase is extremely rare. This species breeds on the tundra and numbers fluctuate with the available food supply. They feed largely on small rodents and nestling birds. In a good lemming year, which occurs, on average, every four years, the jaegers and other predators will have a good breeding season provided the weather is kind. Although they are not directly involved with the population dynamics of lemmings, many species benefit

The Parasitic Jaeger breeds around the shores of the Arctic Ocean, as well as along the Aleutian Islands off Alaska and the Inner Hebrides west of the Scottish Mainland. Size-wise they fall between the Long-tailed and Pomarine Jaegers, and although the central tail feathers are attenuated, they are not as flexible as those of its smaller relation. During the breeding season they harry other seabirds and take a higher percentage of small birds in their diet. There are two colour phases, dark and light, plus a multitude of intergrades between. Parasitic Jaegers migrate quite close in-shore and are often recorded during sea-watches at migration times. A similar pattern emerges with the largest member of the genus, the Pomarine Jaeger *S. pomarinus*, 29 in. (74 cm.). This includes a tail that can be 8 in. (20 cm.) long, but although the Pomarine Jaeger has elongated central tail feathers they are unlike the other two species; these are ample with a single twist and resemble broad handled spoons. The range of the Pomarine Jaeger is not as extensive as the other members of the genus, yet it occurs during sea-watches as it migrates along coasts. They reach the southern hemisphere for the austral summer, but

Below: a Great Skua chick, only a few days old, has yet to lose from the tip of its bill the white egg-tooth that enabled it to break out of the egg.

from a good lemming year, except for perhaps the lemmings after they have finished making whoopee! The abundance of this small rodent will ensure that there is more than enough food for all. With predators such as the jaegers and Arctic Foxes *Alopex lagopus* concentrating their efforts on the easily caught lemmings, the infant mortality rate is lower than usual for the sandpipers, longspurs and other species. Long-tailed Jaegers usually migrate farther off-shore than the other two species, but during the 1980s an increasing number have been recorded passing north off the Outer Hebrides, Scotland.

apparently do not occur off the Pacific coast of South America as frequently as the other jaegers, for it prefers the open ocean. However, off southern Africa in March we have found it to be the commonest skua or jaeger off Swakopmund on Namibia's Atlantic coast.

Skuas and jaegers usually lay two eggs, often in a hollow in grass or moss; they are incubated by both parents for 25 – 30 days, but often only one chick is reared to the flying stage. The fledging period for jaegers lasts approximately the same length of time, but the skuas average 44 days.

GULLS and TERNS
Order: *Charadriiformes*
Family: *Laridae*
14 genera contain 89 species

When the Mormon settlers arrived by the Great Salt Lake, their impoverished crops were plagued by crickets, until the appearance of flocks of seagulls. That was in 1848 and the California Gulls *Larus californicus* are still there, both in the wild and commemorated in bronze by the Seagull Monument in Temple Square, Salt Lake City.

In some ways this typifies the relationship between several gull species and modern society; for they are opportunist feeders, taking advantage of any food supply, no matter how unpredictable it may appear. It seems only a few years ago that in Britain the appearance of gulls inland was an indication of rough weather along the coasts; but those pioneers discovered municipal garbage dumps and reservoirs! They were ideal places to feed on the trash from society and then

The Laughing Gull (left) is the largest of the North American 'black-headed' gulls and occurs mainly along the Eastern Seaboard and around the Gulf of Mexico. Facing page: Inca Terns on the cliffs of Isla Ballestas off the Pacific coast of South America.

bathe in the clean water intended for human consumption. No wonder diseases are sometimes associated with gulls!

Members of the family *Laridae* fall into one of two groups – gulls and terns. Of the 89 species, 49 belong to 7 genera of gulls and 44 belong to 10 genera of terns.

Gulls are more heavily-built birds than the terns and are usually less oceanic in their wanderings. They are also less plentiful or absent from tropical seas, where the most abundant seabirds are often terns. Gulls vary in size from the tiny Little Gull *Larus minutus*, 11 in. (28 cm.) long, to the huge Great Black-backed Gull *L. marinus*, 30 in. (76 cm.) long. The Little Gull, found across the Palearctic, first bred in North America at Oshawa on the northern shore of Lake Ontario and has since increased its range around the Great Lakes. The Great Black-backed Gull is essentially a North Atlantic seabird, breeding from Hudson Bay to the Kanin Peninsular in the U.S.S.R. In

western Europe it only breeds as far south as Brittany, France, whilst along the Eastern Seaboard of the United States it has extended its breeding range down to North Carolina.

Most gulls belong to the genus *Larus*, but within the genus are several distinct groupings; the 'hooded', white-winged, grey-winged and the black-backed gulls. The 'hooded' gulls include several North American species such as the Laughing and Franklin's Gulls, *L. atricilla* and *L. pipixcan*. The 'white-winged' gulls breed in the higher latitudes, the most widespread being the circumpolar Glaucous Gull *L. hyperboreus*. The 'grey-winged' species include the familiar Herring and Ring-billed Gulls, *L. argentatus* and *L. delawarensis*, which have black and white wing-tips, known as 'mirrors'. Finally, there are the 'black-backed' gulls, including the Greater Black-backed, found along the Eastern Seaboard, and the Western Gull *L. occidentalis* of the Pacific coast of North America.

The Silver Gull (above) is the most widespread species of gull in Australia and New Zealand, occurring over both fresh and coastal waters.

There have been various changes in the taxonomy of some larger species. The yellow-legged race of the Western Gull that breeds in the Gulf of California, has recently been given full specific treatment *L. livens*. In western Europe, it is possible that the yellow-legged races of the familiar Herring Gull might also be 'officially' split in the future.

The gulls belonging to the other genera include the Black- and Red-legged Kittiwakes *Rissa tridactyla* and *R. brevirostris*. The Black-legged has an almost circumpolar distribution, whilst the Red-legged species occurs only in the North Pacific and the Bering Sea. The high Arctic is also home to three other species: the Ivory Gull *Pagophila eburnea*, Ross's Gull *Rhodostethia rosea* and Sabine's Gull *Xema sabini*. The Ivory and Ross's Gulls are vagrants south of the high latitudes, whilst Sabine's Gulls winter south to Chile and South Africa.

Unique amongst the gulls is the Swallow-tailed Gull *Creagrus furcatus*, an endemic species to the Galapagos Islands, for it is the only truly nocturnal-feeding species. In fishing-ports gulls often feed around vessels that are unloading their catch at night, but these are purely opportunists.

Terns are amongst the most graceful seabirds; with their long wings and often a deeply forked tail, they catch small fish by diving from the air. Most species are grey and white with a black cap, and range in size from the gull-sized Caspian Tern *Sterna caspia* to the dainty Least Tern *S. antillarum*. Both species breed in North America. The Caspian Tern is a

widely distributed species, usually found in the warmer regions of the World and surprisingly absent from most of South America. The Least Tern is one of several small, closely related species that are widely distributed, some of which are considered to be conspecific by some authorities. One of the most widespread species of tern is the Arctic *S. paradisaea*, a bird that sees more daylight than any other form of life. It is circumpolar in distribution, with much of its breeding range north of the Arctic Circle. In the fall, the whole population migrates to the southern hemisphere and the seas around Antarctica. It is a record-holder, but the figures can only be estimated. The one-way journey can be 7,995 miles (12,800 km.), and one long-lived bird was at least 26 years old, when recovered, and therefore could have travelled 415,740 miles (669,050 km.) solely on migration, provided it did not deviate from the straight and narrow. Another bird, banded as a chick in North Wales, U.K., in June 1966, was recovered in New South Wales, Australia the following December. Another off-course traveller was an Aleutian Tern *S. aleutica*, that breeds in the northern Pacific around the coasts of Alaska and north-eastern Siberia. In May 1979 one appeared at an Arctic Tern colony on the Farne Islands off the north-east coast of England. The wintering area of this species

is unknown, but it is assumed that this individual joined a flock of Arctic Terns sometime during the non-breeding season, and was led astray northwards, up the 'wrong' side of Cape Horn.

The so-called 'marsh terns' are three species of small dark terns that are associated with fresh-water marshes and sloughs during the breeding season. The Black Tern *Chlidonias niger* is a widespread breeding species in North America, in suitable habitats across the northern half of the United States and across the southern Canadian provinces. Although a fresh-water breeding species, it winters at sea, but there is still much to be discovered. In March 1989, during a tour to Namibia, we found tens of thousands of Black Terns feeding in the Atlantic surf along beaches from Hentiesbaai, south to Walvis Bay; an estimate would be in the order of 30 – 50,000 birds.

Gulls feed on fish and other forms of small marine animals, as well as invertebrates such as marine and earth worms. Some species are scavengers around seabird and seal colonies. The Herring Gull, amongst others, drops shellfish onto rocks to reach the contents. Larger species also take the eggs and young of other birds, and now they have discovered garbage dumps. Terns feed mainly on fish, squid and small crustaceans.

The Black-headed Gull (top left), together with other related species, loses its dark hood in winter, and the Arctic Tern (above left) sees more daylight in a year than any other living creature. The Fairy Tern (above and far left) is a delicate tropical species that lays its single egg on a bare branch. The South American Inca Tern (left) is the only species to have developed plumes on the side of the head.

Many members of the family are colonial breeding species, and in particular the large tropical tern colonies are a sight to behold. On Cousin and Aride, two granitic islands in the central Seychelles, colonies of the tree-nesting Lesser Noddy *Anoüs minutus*, a tropical tern, exceed 100,000 pairs. Nearby, on the flat, sandy Bird Island, the Sooty Tern *S. fuscata* colony is in excess of 350,000 pairs. In the Gulf of Mexico, the Dry Tortugas, 70 miles (112 km.) west of Key West, hold vast numbers of breeding Sooties. Most gulls and terns have an annual breeding cycle, but several tropical species may breed earlier if local conditions are suitable. Many species are ground or cliff nesters; the noddies make platforms of vegetation in trees, the pure-white Fairy Tern *Gygis alba* lays its single egg in a slight depression on a horizontal branch and the Inca Tern *Larosterna inca* breeds in burrows.

The clutch size is 1 – 4 eggs, although usually 2 – 3 are laid. Incubation, shared by both parents, lasts 3 – 4 weeks, and the down-covered youngsters are active when they are dry. They are fed by both parents throughout the 4 – 8 week fledging period. The young of many species are dependent on their parents for several weeks afterward.

Whilst many species are thriving, some have declined seriously due to human pressures. In some areas, terns have suffered as a direct result of fish-stocks depleted by over fishing. Along the coast of West Africa, small boys, using hooks and lines, catch large numbers of wintering terns from western Europe, as much for 'sport' as necessity. Hopefully current programmes initiated by conservation bodies such as the R.S.P.B., will reach the minds of these youths.

The Swallow-tailed Gull (above left), endemic to the Galapagos Islands off Ecuador, is the world's only nocturnal gull. Above: a pair of Western Gulls stand guard over their breeding territory. This species breeds from British Columbia to Southern California, its pink legs distinguishing it from the Yellow-footed Gull of Baja California. Left: Crested Terns in non-breeding plumage, found in Brunei. These birds range from Namibia across the Indian Ocean to the western Pacific.

SKIMMERS
Order: *Charadriiformes*
Family: *Rynchopidae*
the genus *Rynchops* contains three species

The first time I saw a Black Skimmer *Rynchops niger* was one December in southern Florida; distant birds at first, but as we drove through the Ding Darling National Wildlife Refuge one flew across a lagoon close to the road. The immaculate black and white bird flew with slow deliberate wing beats only inches above the water, slicing the surface with its red knife-like lower mandible. Since then I have been fortunate to show many people their first Skimmers; the African species *R. flavirostris* this time, on the Zambezi, upstream from Victoria Falls in Zimbabwe or along its tributary, the Chobe, in Botswana. There is a great sense of satisfaction, as they too, get the same buzz of excitement when they see their first Skimmers skimming.

There are three species of Skimmer found in the World. The Black Skimmer occurs in North and South America, from Massachusetts in the east and San Diego in the west, southwards to Argentina and Ecuador, although northern birds winter south to Chile. The plumage of this and the other Skimmers is similar – black above, and white under-parts, forehead and face and trailing edge to the wing. In non-breeding plumage it has a white collar. The Black Skimmer is the largest species,

over smooth water with the bill wide open and the lower mandible slicing the surface like a knife. As soon as a fish is detected the head jerks downwards as the mandibles close to secure the prey. The bird raises its head once more, swallows the fish and carries on skimming. The action is instantaneous and does not interrupt the level flight path. Skimmers often feed early in the morning or late in the afternoon, times of the day when the fish are rising and the water is usually calmer than during the middle in the day. They also fish on clear moonlit nights. Having cut one track through the water, Skimmers sometimes repeat the exercise along the same track in an attempt to catch any fish attracted by the disturbance caused by the first pass over the area.

Neither the African nor Indian Skimmers are particularly associated with salt or brackish water, instead they occur along rivers and lakes, where they breed on sand bars exposed as the water levels fall before the next rains. They are not migratory to the extent of their American counterparts; their movements tend to be more of a nomadic nature. They move to another area of water when the present becomes unsuitable; either it has dried out too much, or the area has become flooded.

The African Skimmer is found from Senegal and the Sudan south to southern Africa, where although it has bred in Zululand, it is a rare bird south of the Okavango, Zambezi and Lundi river systems. Birds migrate within Africa, being absent from rivers in flood only to reappear as water levels fall, exposing the sand bars on which they breed. In the north, non-breeding birds reach the Nile Valley in Egypt. Smaller

Below: a White-eyed Gull, found in Egypt. These birds breed in the Red Sea area but wander further afield at other times of the year.

18 in. (46 cm.) in length, with long slender wings and a shallow forked tail. The juvenile is mottled brown, where the adult is black. Black Skimmers are coastal birds, breeding on beaches and salt marshes and feeding in bays, tidal waters and lagoons. In South America they range along the mighty river systems, such as the Amazon, where they sometimes feed in association with the fresh water Amazon Dolphin or Boutu *Inia geoffrensis*.

Skimmers have very short legs and an amazing bill. The lower half of the dark tipped red bill is longer than the upper half and has evolved to accommodate the unusual method of feeding adopted by Skimmers. They fly low and deliberately

than the Black Skimmer, 16 in. (40 cm.) long, it has an orange-red bill with a yellow tip and the upper-parts are blackish-brown rather than the intense black of the larger species.

The Indian Skimmer occurs along rivers and lakes across India to Indo-China, moving as water levels dictate. It is the same size as the African Skimmer, but unlike the other two species it retains its white collar throughout the year.

A Skimmer's nest is an unlined shallow scrape in the sand or along a tide line, where a number of pairs form loose colonies. During the breeding season adults engage in formation flying in small groups, flying in perfect unison, matching wing beat for wing beat. Two to four eggs are laid and incubation by both parents lasts for about three weeks. Sometimes the adults wet their under-parts before sitting on the eggs or brooding the chicks, in an attempt to keep them cool. Skimmers are awkward feeding chicks with small fish because of their bills, but the chicks have conventionally shaped bills and no problems. In five weeks the youngsters are flying and at the same time the lower mandible begins to grow to the characteristic shape associated with Skimmers.

AUKS

Order: *Charadriiformes*
Family: *Alcidae*
12 genera contain 22 species

In bygone seafaring days the old sailors called the Puffin 'sea parrot' because of its unusual shaped bill. The Atlantic Puffin *Fratercula arctica*, 11 in. (28 cm.) long, together with its slightly larger Pacific relatives the Horned *F. corniculata* and the Tufted Puffin *Lunda cirrhata*, are members of the Auk family *Alcidae*, with large triangular-shaped bills; they are no relations of the parrots *Psittacidae*.

The auk family is the Northern Hemisphere's equivalent of the penguins *Sphenisciformes*, found in the Southern Hemisphere. The similarity is the result of convergent evolution. This takes place when a particular habitat or

feeding requirement imposes certain constraints on the evolution of a species or family. The living species are much smaller than penguins, but until 1844 a larger and flightless auk bred on remote islands in the North Atlantic. This, the Great Auk *Alca impennis*, 32 in. (81 cm.) long, was, until it became extinct, an important source of fresh meat for fishermen and sailors. Until its demise it was the only flightless bird to occur in Europe and North America!

There are 22 species belonging to the family, divided into 12 genera. Auks are dumpy seabirds with short wings; they spend much of their lives at sea. They come ashore only to breed or in a distressed condition, covered in oil from some vessel or other; another pathetic victim of the disrespect man has for the environment. The family can be divided in to four groups: the larger auks, puffins, auklets and murrelets. Auks are expert fishermen that dive and swim well, with legs set well back along the body to aid propulsion; additionally wings are used to help them 'fly' through the water in pursuit of fish, their staple diet. The diet of several species including the auklets and the Dovekie consists mainly of plankton. Black, brown and grey combined with white, are the plumage colours of most auks; the Tufted Puffin has long yellow head plumes during the breeding season. Several species of auklet have plumes on their heads, but theirs are less spectacular and are also lost during the months when the birds assume their non-breeding plumages. The enlarged and colourful bills of the three species of puffin become smaller and duller during the winter.

Auks occur in the northern Atlantic and Pacific Oceans, but it is in the latter that auks probably evolved. No less than 16 species are endemic to the coasts of the North Pacific, compared with only three species endemic to the North Atlantic. The Common Murre *Uria aalge*, 17 in. (43 cm.) long, the Thick-billed Murre *U. lomvia*, 19 in. (48 cm.) long, and the Black Guillemot *Cepphus grylle*, 13 in. (33 cm.) long, are to be found in both oceans. In Britain the two species of murres are known as the Common and Brünnich's Guillemot. The two murres and the Razorbill or Razor-billed Auk *Alca torda* are the largest members of the family. The Razorbill is one of the three North Atlantic endemic auks and is about the same size a Common Murre. It has a laterally compressed bill and looks like a miniature edition of the Great Auk. The remaining North Atlantic species is the Dovekie or Little Auk *Alle alle*, 8 in. (20 cm.) long, that breeds in countless thousands on islands in the Arctic Ocean. The breeding population around the coasts of Greenland runs into millions! There is evidence that due to climatic changes, the northern colonies are increasing at the expense of the southerly ones, indicating a northward drift of the population. During the winter months Dovekies and several other species are highly pelagic and are usually only seen hundreds of miles from land. Occasionally great winter storms blow Dovekies towards the coasts and sometimes 'wreck' them inland, many miles from the sea. Unfortunately many are so weak that they rarely survive. T. A. Coward, the English ornithologist, writing in 1920, simply states 'The Little Auk comes to us to die.' It is probable that a few pairs may now breed with auklets at colonies in the

Facing page: an Atlantic Puffin returns to feed its chick with a meal of Sand Eels, fish on which puffins and other seabirds in the North Atlantic depend for their survival.

The Razorbill (below left) is one of two auks endemic to the North Atlantic; the other is the Atlantic Puffin. Below: in the Pribilof Islands of Alaska a group of five Crested Auklets share the rocks with an isolated Least Auklet.

Bering Strait. All 12 species of auklet and murrelet are to be found around the coasts of the North Pacific where most occur around the Gulf of Alaska, the Bering Sea and the Siberian coast south to the Kamchatka Peninsular. The closely related Xantus' and Craveri's Murrelets *Synthliboramphus hypoleucus* and *S. craveri*, 8.5 in. (21 cm.) long, are considered by some to be conspecific. They breed on islands off Baja California, farther south than any other auk species.

Most members of the Auk family breed colonially along the coasts, where they are to be found during the summer months. The murres nest in tight rows along ledges, where their single egg is laid. The egg, rounded at one end and pointed at the other, spins rather than rolls, so that it can be safely incubated on a narrow ledge without fear of it falling into the sea below. Razorbills also lay their eggs on ledges, but they prefer to be tucked away amongst rocks. Black Guillemots and the closely related Pigeon Guillemot *C. columba*, lay their eggs amongst rock piles and crevices and unlike their larger relatives produce two eggs. The puffins excavate burrows in the soil along cliff-tops or on grassy slopes, where they lay a single egg. Atlantic Puffins also take over the burrows of Manx Shearwaters *Puffinus puffinus* and Rabbits *Oryctolagus cuniculus*. Auklets nest amongst boulders on scree slopes and in rock piles, where they also lay a single egg. Two species, Cassin's Auklet *Ptcyhoramphus aleuticus*, 9 in. (23 cm.) long, and the strange-looking Rhinoceros Auklet *Cerorhinca monocerata*, 15 in. (38 cm.) long, nest in burrows; the latter with its enlarged bill is more closely related to the

Brachyramphus marmoratus, 9.5 in. (24 cm.) long, remained undiscovered until 1974, this in spite of it being a common bird along the north-western coast of North America during the summer months. A logger working in forests south of San Francisco, California discovered a nest with a down-covered chick 130 ft. (39 m.) above the ground in a Douglas Fir *Pseudotsuga menziesii*. Since then other nests have been found, some on the ground recalling the nesting habits of the similar Kittlitz's Murrelet *B. brevirostris*, 9 in. (23 cm.) long. These non-colonial auks rely on their mottled brown breeding plumage for camouflage, and perhaps because neither species

puffins than to the auklets. Cassin's Auklet is unusual, for birds from the southern part of the breeding range in California and Baja California rear two broods per year and is the only auk to do so. A warmer climate than Alaska enables them to start earlier in the year and have the time for a second brood. Double brooding is known from only two other seabirds; the Little Penguin *Eudyptula minor* and the Silver Gull *Larus novaehollandiae* both of which occur in Australia. The murrelets still pose a number of unanswered questions about their breeding biology. The nest of the Marbled Murrelet

nests under the cover of rocks or in burrows, both have become nocturnal. Unlike the auklets, murrelets lay two eggs.

Incubation of the clutch lasts for 28 – 40 days, depending on the species, but the fledging period remains a mystery in several instances. One of the most studied species, the Ancient Murrelet *S. antiquus*, 10 in. (25 cm.) long, takes its two downy chicks to sea 2 – 4 days after hatching. The young murres and razorbills leave with their parents when they are half grown, jumping from their ledges on open wings to the sea below. This usually takes place at dusk to avoid the predatory

Top: a group of African Skimmers flies in formation over a sandbar in Zimbabwe, and (above) Black Guillemots rest on a ledge in Orkney, Scotland.

attentions of gulls, jaegers and skuas. It was once thought that young puffins were, like young shearwaters *Puffinus*, over-fed by their parents and then abandoned to slim down before making their own way to sea. Recent research indicates that young puffins are fed by their parents normally until they leave the burrow on a moonless night; they shuffle to the edge of the cliff and over they go. During our years living on the Isle of Mull, Scotland, Atlantic Puffins bred on several islands off the west coast. During pelagic trips to see seabirds west of the breeding colonies in late July and throughout August, few young Puffins were noted, so presumably they travel as far as out into the Atlantic as they can during the hours of darkness, an important survival strategy.

Auks are a vulnerable family and no doubt their numbers are lower now than at any other time in their history. Man has long exploited a number of species as a source of food. This led to the extinction of the Great Auk, and serious decreases in the population of other species. However, nowadays fewer people are dependent on auks for food. The greatest threats come from pollution, mainly oil spillages, and from the decline in fish stocks in areas of over fishing.

Above left: Thick-billed Murres, or Brünnich's Guillemots, line a cliff ledge in the Pribilofs, an area where the Tufted Puffin (above) also occurs. Its spectacular head plumes are the most ornate of any member of the auk family. Left: an immature Black Skimmer in Florida, with a Ring-billed Gull in the background.

SANDGROUSE
Order: *Pterocylidiformes*
Family: *Pteroclididae*
two genera contain 16 species

Although they may resemble gamebirds when feeding or shorebirds whilst on the wing, the sandgrouse were formerly placed in the Order *Columbiformes* with the doves and pigeons. However recent studies of egg-white protein indicate their taxonomic place lies between the shorebirds and their allies *Charadriiformes* and the doves.

Sandgrouse inhabit arid and semi-arid parts of the Old World from south-western Europe to Central Asia and south to India, and in Africa they occur throughout the continent, except in areas of forest and woodland. The most restricted distribution is that of the Madagascar Sandgrouse *Pterocles personatus*, found only in western Madagascar. Most species are sedentary, or perhaps move to suit local conditions. A few species are migratory, although may not move vast distances. For example, the Yellow-throated Sandgrouse *P. gutturalis* has two populations; the one in East Africa is sedentary, but the other in southern Zambia and northern Botswana migrates south and east into western Zimbabwe, south-eastern Botswana and South Africa during the rainy season. The greatest movements are performed irregularly by Pallas's Sandgrouse *Syrrhaptes paradoxus*, when the population irrupts westwards out of Central Asia into western Europe. The greatest eruptions occurred in the springs of 1863, 1888 and 1908; during the 19th. century birds reached as far west as Northern Ireland and Scotland's Outer Hebrides. They are plump, terrestrial birds with small heads and short legs, and are cryptically coloured, especially the dimorphic females who lack the patterned head and breast of their mates. Some species have elongated central tail feathers which increase the length of the bird considerably. The length of Pallas's Sandgrouse, 16 in. (40 cm.), includes central feathers, extending some 3.5 in. (8.8 cm.) beyond the rest of the tail. Sandgrouse fly swiftly with rapid wing beats, recalling a European Golden Plover *Pluvialis apricaria*.

Sandgrouse are well known for their dawn and dusk flights to drink at water holes. During the dry season they will fly up to 18 miles (30 km.) or more to drink. At Savuti in

Above: Yellow-throated Sandgrouse flock to a waterhole in the Serengeti National Park, Tanzania. Sandgrouse may fly up to 18 miles or more to drink during the dry season. Left: a member of another species from East Africa, a male Black-faced Sandgrouse found in Kenya. Male sandgrouse have evolved special water-retentive breast feathers to enable them to carry water to their offspring.

Botswana's Chobe National Park, the Double-banded Sandgrouse arrive to drink at sunset; the first hesitant flocks land on the banks of the water hole when there is still sufficient light to see the black and white foreheads of the males. They are restless and wary, for it only takes a sudden noise, such as an Elephant *Loxodonta africana* flapping its ears, to unsettle them. The sandgrouse run to the water's edge and drink before taking off with rapid wing beats, and soon all that can be seen are the whirring shapes of birds against the deepening velvet sky. Amazingly they find their way back home across several miles of bush to where chicks await their arrival in complete darkness. Sandgrouse have evolved special belly feathers that retain water during the flight back to the chicks and from which they drink. The only exception to this is the Tibetan Sandgrouse, found in mountainous areas of northern India and Central Asia, where it is never far from water, so that the need to hold moisture in the plumage does not arise.

The nest of sandgrouse is a shallow scrape in open ground, lined with a few small stones or some dried grass. The three eggs are incubated by the female during the day and the male at night, when his less well camouflaged plumage is of little consequence. The incubation period lasts 21 – 31 days, depending on the species, and the young leave the nest as soon

Below: a pair of Yellow-throated Sandgrouse. The male is distinguished by his yellow throat patch edged with black trim, whilst the female is more cryptically coloured.

Left: trusting to its camouflage, a Chestnut-bellied or Indian Sandgrouse chick crouches motionless on the sands of India's Little Rann of Kutch.

117

as they are all dry. They are not fed by their parents, who only point out small seeds with their bills. Usually it is only the male who carries water in his belly feathers, but the female does so if the male is killed or if he is unable to meet the demands of the chicks as they approach fledging. The fledging period lasts 4 – 5 weeks.

DOVES and PIGEONS
Order: *Columbiformes*
Family: *Columbidae*
40 genera contain 294 species

Throughout the World many species of doves and pigeons *Columbidae* are rare and endangered; the sin of most is that they make good eating, and perhaps live in an area where there has been significant habitat change since the arrival of Man. Since 1835 only seven species have become extinct, though current lists show 49 species endangered or threatened around the World, many occurring on the islands off southeast Asia or in the Pacific.

The most dramatic of all extinctions was that of the Passenger Pigeon *Ectopistes migratorius* in North America. This must have been one of the World's most abundant birds in its day, with migrating flocks described as 'darkening the sun.' The vast numbers of these birds posed such problems of crop devastation to struggling farmers that steps were taken to destroy the forests and woods where the bird bred, and wherever they roosted, outside the breeding season. So effective were the measures that by 1914 the only survivor was a single female in Cincinnati Zoo; she died on the first of September of that year. The last wild bird was recorded in 1900.

One of the most ornate head dresses of any dove or pigeon is that of the Victoria Crowned Pigeon (top left) of northern New Guinea. Left: this Cape Turtle Dove drinking at a waterhole at Savuti in Botswana is a prolific member of the family in eastern and southern Africa.

Doves and pigeons are familiar in one form or another to all; this is a large family of 294 species divided into 40 genera. They range in size from the tiny Plain-breasted Ground-Dove *Columbina minuta* 6 in. (15 cm.) long, a diminutive species from Central and South America, to the Southern Crowned Pigeon *Goura scheepmakeri* 29.5 in. (75 cm.) in length, a New Guinea endemic. The difference between doves and pigeons should be straightforward: the smaller ones are doves, and the larger species are pigeons, but there is some overlap in size and nomenclature where the two meet.

Doves and pigeons are a widespread family that occurs throughout the World, except for the polar regions and the higher latitudes of the Northern Hemisphere. They reside in a range of habitats, from tropical rain forests to semi-arid areas of scrub and to storm-swept sea cliffs. It is from the cliffs and mountains of the Old World that the wild ancestor of the town or city pigeon came. This is the Rock Dove *Columba livia*, that is still found in wild places, but the numbers of pure bred birds are being diluted, as more feral pigeons take to the remoter areas. Many species are sedentary. In North America the Mourning Dove *Zenaida macroura* is a migrant in the northern part of its range; elsewhere other species such as the Namaqua Dove *Oena capensis* of Africa is nomadic when not breeding.

The fruit-eating Seychelles Blue Pigeon (above) is endemic to the Seychelles in the Indian Ocean; the Nicobar Pigeon (far left) ranges from the Nicobar Islands in the eastern Indian Ocean to the Solomons in the western Pacific, and the Squatter Pigeon (left), or Partridge Bronzewing, is found in north-eastern Australia.

One of the most interesting changes in distribution is that of the Collared Dove *S. decaocto*. Until about 1930 it did not occur west of the Balkans, but then, and the reasons are unclear, it broke out and headed north-west across Europe, breeding in France for the first time in 1952, and crossing to breed in the British Isles in 1955. A pair bred in Iceland in 1971, but do not appear to have colonised. In recent years a feral population has become established in southern Florida, leaving one wondering if it will consolidate its position, and then head north and west.

Members of the family have large, rounded heads with a prominent eye. The crowned pigeons of the tropical Australasian region have ornate fan-shaped crests. The bill size varies, depending on the type of food eaten by the species. Fruit eating species often have slightly larger bills than those of the seed or grain eating species; the only species to differ significantly from the theme is the Tooth-billed Pigeon *Didunculus strigirostris* from Western Samoa, with a parrot-like hooked bill.

The breeding biology is well-known for those species that inhabit the developed world, but poorly known for those in the remote areas. Most species build a shallow platform of woven twigs, sometimes so thin that one can see the eggs from below. Construction is usually by the female, from material supplied by the male. Two eggs are laid and the adults share the incubation of 14 – 18 days until they hatch. Both parents produce 'pigeon's milk' in their crops, which is fed to the nestlings during the first days of life. Besides all the doves and pigeons, the only other species known to feed their young crop-milk are the Greater Flamingo *Phoenicopterus ruber* and the male Emperor Penguin *Aptenodytes forsteri*. After fledging, which may take up to 35 days, or as long as 90 days as reported for the Nicobar Pigeon *Caloenas nicobarica*, the young birds remain dependent on their parents until they are strong enough to fly well.

LORIES

Order: *Psittaciformes*
Family: *Loriidae*
12 genera contains 55 species

Lories *Loriidae* are colourful members of the Order of parrots *Psittaciformes*; they occur on the islands of the East Indies, and in the Australasian region from New Guinea and Australia, east across a myriad of Pacific islands to Henderson Island in the Pitcairn group, where Stephen's Lorikeet *Vini stepheni* is endemic. Many other species have also evolved in isolation

The Western Black-capped Lory (left and above left) of New Guinea is one of several closely related species found in an area that includes the East Indies and New Guinea. The Rainbow Lory (above) is a widespread and colourful member of its genus. It ranges from the East Indies to Australia.

Preening is an essential part of a bird's daily routine and is undertaken with great care. Facing page: a Collared Lory, endemic to Fiji, cleaning its feathers.

and are restricted to a single island, where some have become endangered or even exterminated because of habitat changes wrought by settlers and the effect of introduced predators.

There are 55 species of lory, divided between 12 closely related genera. They are slim, long-tailed birds with typical parrot-like hooked bills. All members of the family are brightly coloured, although some Australian species of lorikeet are predominantly green. The Australian species range in size from the Little Lorikeet *Glossopsitta pusilla* 6.25 in. (16 cm.) long, to the Rainbow Lorikeet *Trichoglossus haematodus* 12

Cockatoos occur on some islands in the Philippines, but mainly in New Guinea and Australia, where 11 species are to be found. To the east, Ducorp's Cockatoo *C. ducorpsi* is restricted to the Solomon Islands. Most species of cockatoo are sedentary or nomadic birds, but some, including the Red-tailed Black Cockatoo *Calyptorhynchus magnificus*, 26 in. (66 cm.) long, and the Gang-gang Cockatoo *Callocephalon fimbriatum*, 13 in. (33 cm.) long, are partially migratory. There are populations of the Sulphur-crested Cockatoo on the west coast of New Zealand that probably originated as cage-

The Sulphur-crested Cockatoo (facing page top left) from Australia and New Guinea is a familiar cage-bird. The Palm Cockatoo (facing page top right) inhabits tropical forests and savannah woodland in New Guinea and north-eastern Australia, where it is the only cockatoo with all black plumage – its red cheeks are actually bare patches of skin. Facing page bottom: a Galah, the most widespread cockatoo in Australia, where it is endemic.

Left: a flock of Galahs in Australian open country. The green and red male Eclectus Parrot (below) from Australia and New Guinea, is so unlike the red and blue female that, when initially collected, they were regarded as different species.

in. (30 cm.) long. Being so beautiful and small to medium sized birds, several species have become endangered as a result of the demands made by the pet-trade. In particular, the Red and Blue Lory *Eos histrio* and other species that inhabit islands south of the Philippines, are threatened.

Lories occur in wooded habitats including forests, woodlands, scrub, plantations, tree-lined water courses and urban areas. Certain species such as the Rainbow Lorikeet can become a familiar garden bird.

Lories specialise in eating nectar; they have evolved a narrow bill and a long brush-tipped tongue to extract nectar from blossoms, doubtless aiding the pollination process. Some species travel in noisy, nomadic flocks, in search of flowering trees and bushes, and time their breeding cycle to an abundance of food. Lories tend to be aggressive birds, which becomes apparent when they share a food supply with other nectar-feeders. Also included in the diet are seeds and insects. Several insular species do not flock, but are found in pairs and small groups.

Lories are monogamous birds and pairs probably stay together for the life of a partner. They nest in natural holes in trees, where up to 5 eggs may be laid, depending on the species. Incubation is probably by the female alone and can last up to 21 days, and the chicks take up to 28 days to fledge. They become independent two to three weeks later.

COCKATOOS
Order: *Psittaciformes*
Family: *Cacatuidae*
five genera contain 18 species.

One of the most familiar of the parrot-like birds is the Sulphur-crested or White Cockatoo *Cacatua galerita*, 20 in. (50 cm.) long. It is often to be found as a pet, or perhaps trained as a performing bird.

birds. However, the discovery in 1959, of an exhausted bird on a headland after a period of prolonged westerly winds, raised the faint possibility that the birds had arrived of their own accord. It is unlikely that this could be proved, for the 1959 bird could so easily have been a pet that escaped from a passing vessel, and headed for the nearest landfall.

Cockatoos inhabit a variety of wooded habitats, from tropical rain forests to open woodland and wooded water courses. This preference satisfies the need for suitable nesting sites.

They are parrot-like birds, ranging in size from the Galah Cockatoo *Cacatua roseicapilla*, 14 in. (36 cm.) long, to the Yellow-tailed Black Cockatoo *Calyptorhynchus funereus*, 26 in. (66 cm.) long. The pink and grey Galah is the most widespread species, occurring over much of Australia. Cockatoos have crests that are erected in display; some, such as the black Palm Cockatoo *Probosciger aterrimus*, 24 in. (60 cm.), have spikey, punk-like crests. The Gang-gang Cockatoo is a grey-bodied bird with an up-curling crest on the nape. The crests of several other members of the family are inconspicuous, unless the birds are excited. Plumage colours are black, white, pink, and grey, with various patches of red, white and yellow.

Cockatoos feed on a diet that mainly comprises seeds, nuts, fruit and berries and other vegetable material, but they also take insects, including wood-boring species.

They nest in holes in trees. Some larger species, such as the Red-tailed Black Cockatoo lay a single egg, whilst the closely related White-tailed Black Cockatoo *Calyptorhynchus baudinii*, 22 in. (56 cm.) lays two, about one week apart. Incubation starts from the laying of the first egg, and although both eggs may hatch, sibling rivalry ensures that only the stronger, usually the elder, survives. During incubation the female leaves the nest to be fed by the male. After hatching, the chick is fed by both parents, morning and evening for about three months, before fledging. Sulphur-crested Cockatoos share the incubation of their 2 – 3 eggs during the 30-day incubation period, followed by a 60-day fledging period.

Due to demands by the caged-bird trade, several species that occur north of New Guinea are considered to be sufficiently rare to cause concern.

123

PARROTS
Order: *Psittaciformes*
Family: *Psittacidae*
59 genera contain 260 species

One expects parrots to be brightly coloured and even gaudy birds, but the first that my wife saw, was the rare and endangered Seychelles Black Parrot *Coracopsis nigra*, a subspecies of the Lesser Vasa Parrot, found elsewhere on Madagascar and the Comoro Islands. It is a dull sepia-coloured parrot and a definite anti-climax for non-birders.

Parrots need little introduction, for various species are popular cage-birds. One of the most popular species is the Budgerigar *Melopsittacus undulatus*, found in the wild in Australia, and now successfully established as a feral species in Florida, where several other species are also living in the wild. Budgerigars breed well in captivity, so there are not the demands on the wild population from the pet-trade, that threaten many colourful South American Amazonian parrots and macaws.

Parrots occur in tropical and temperate regions, mainly in the Southern Hemisphere, where the Austral Parakeet *Enicognathus ferrugineus* occurs as far south as Tierra del Fuego. The farthest north that wild parrots occur is Afghanistan,

the tiny Buff-faced Pygmy Parrot *Micropsitta pusio*, only 3.5 in. (8.5 cm.) long, found in New Guinea and New Britain. Most species that occur in the Neotropical, Oriental and Australian regions are brightly coloured, whilst some African species are black or dark brown, with coloured patches. The Eclectus Parrot *Eclectus roratus*, found in New Guinea, its surrounding islands and north-eastern Australia, caused problems when first discovered. The male is mainly green with an orange bill, whilst the female is red with a blue belly and a black bill.

New Zealand is home to many unusual birds that have evolved in an environment free of mammalian predators. One of the most exceptional is the Kakapo 25 in. (63 cm.) long, a heavily-built terrestrial parrot. It is the only flightless parrot and one of the few nocturnal species. Another is the small Night Parrot, a poorly known species from Australia, unrecorded between 1912 and 1979. Both species are green with black barring, but the Kakapo has an almost owl-like facial disc. It has short, but strong legs and powerful feet. The Kakapo has declined dramatically from the effect of the cats, rats and Stoats *Mustela erminea* introduced by the European settlers, although even when the white man arrived it was already a rare bird. Now it is one of the rarest parrots in the World, in fact until additional birds were discovered on Stewart Island, off the southern tip of South Island, all 12 known individuals were males. Their demise seemed inevitable, until in 1979 a colony of 100 birds was found on

The Brown-throated Parakeet (facing page) is found in a variety of habitats from Panama to Brazil. These birds belong to a subspecies endemic to the island of Bonaire, Lesser Antilles.

The Masked Shining Parrot (below left) is endemic to Viti Levu, Fiji, whilst the Crimson Rosella (below) is an Australian species.

where the Slaty-headed Parakeet *Psittacula himalayana* breeds. In the Himalayas it is found at 8,200 ft. (2,500 m.) during the breeding season, migrating to lower altitudes for the winter. The greatest numbers of species inhabit tropical lowland forests in South America and temperate Australia. They occur in various woodland habitats including forests, woodland, plantations, wooded water courses and open tree savannah. The Rock Parakeet *Neophema petrophila* occurs amongst sand dunes, on salt-marshes and on rocky islands along the southern and western coasts of Australia. Three species are entirely terrestrial: the Ground and Night Parrots *Pezoporus wallicus* and *P. occidentalis* of Australia, and the Kakapo *Strigops habroptilus* of New Zealand.

The family of true Parrots *Psittacidae* comprises 260 species divided into 59 genera, They range from the blue Hyacinth Macaw *Anodorhynchus hyacinthinus*, 39 in. (100 cm.) long including tail, of the threatened forests of Brazil, to

there. In 1982, 21 birds were translocated to Little Barrier Island for safety, for when a count took place on Stewart in 1985, one third of the remaining population had been killed by feral cats. An eradication programme has removed that particular problem. Since then, males have been heard in the north-west part of South Island, where it occurred formerly.

The diet of parrots includes fruits, nuts and seeds. The Kakapo eats vegetable matter including fungi, and will also take lizards. Another New Zealand parrot, the Kea *Nestor notabilis*, which occurs in mountainous habitats on South

Island, has adapted to become a scavenger on the carcasses of sheep within parts of its range. Elsewhere its diet includes buds, fruits, insects and leaves.

Most species of parrots, with few exceptions, breed in holes in trees. The Rock Parakeet breeds on the ground or amongst rocks or tussocks, the Ground Parakeet also nests in grassy tussocks, the Kakapo breeds in hollows under the roots of trees, and a few other species nest in termite hills. Details of the breeding biology vary considerably from genus to genus. Most parrots pair for the life of one partner, except for

The Red Shining Parrot (above) occurs on Fiji and Tonga, whilst the Scarlet Macaw (right) inhabits the dwindling forests of South America.

Left: a Ring-necked or Rose-ringed Parakeet in Bharatpur – a member of a familiar Indian species.

the polygamous Kea. The clutch of up to 6 eggs is incubated by the female for 16 – 32 days, and the nestlings take 21 – 70 days to fledge. The young of some species are dependent on their parents for a month or more afterward.

TURACOS
Order: *Musophagiformes*
Family: *Musophagidae*
five genera contain 22 species

In the forests of Africa lives a family of beautiful green and purple birds with red wings. These are turacos *Tauraco*, members of the family *Musophagidae*. Other species are predominantly grey, with or without white in the plumage.

There are 22 species divided between five genera and all occur south of the Sahara; most are richly-coloured forest dwelling birds, but the remainder are mainly grey, and inhabit acacia savannah. Turacos are long tailed birds with short, broad wings, and strong legs and feet. They have strong bills and feed on a diet that consists principally of fruit, but blossoms, buds and leaves are also consumed. When first discovered, they were called plantain-eaters following an erroneous assumption that plantains featured on their menu; certain species are still known by this name.

The White-bellied Go-
away-Bird (above), a
species of Turaco from
East Africa, feeds on
acacia flowers.

Largest member of the family is the Great Blue Turaco *Corythaeola cristata*, 30 in. (76 cm.) long, a forest species that lives in the tree canopy of west and central equatorial Africa. It has blue upper-parts, with a yellow-green breast, and chestnut under-tail coverts. One unusual aspect of the domestic life of the Great Blue Turaco is that the male is present at the nest while the female is laying the eggs.

The remaining species can be divided roughly into two groups, the red-winged turacos and a group comprising go-away-birds and plantain-eaters. They range in length from the widespread Green Turaco *Turaco persa* 16 in. (41 cm.) long, to Lady Ross's Turaco *Musophaga rossae* 20 in. (51 cm.) long, one of the most beautiful species, a purple-bodied bird with crimson wings and crest, and a yellow bill and bare facial patch. It occurs in equatorial and central Africa, occasionally being recorded as far south as the Okavango Delta in Botswana.

The Turacos are the most colourful members of the family, but the taxonomic classification of some species differs from one authority to another. In particular, some sub-species of the Green Turaco are treated as such by some, and given full specific status by others. They are birds of forests, where they search for fruit amongst the canopy of large trees. They scramble and hop amongst the branches, generally only flying from one tree to the next, intermittently flapping and gliding, revealing the crimson wings otherwise concealed. Members of the genus range from West Africa to Ethiopia southwards. Two species, Bannerman's and Prince Ruspoli's Turaco *T. bannermani* and *T. ruspolii*, have very small distributions in the Cameroon and Ethiopia respectively, where both are threatened by habitat destruction.

The genus *Corythaixoides* comprises three species that inhabit acacia savannah. Plainest is the Go-away-bird or Grey Lourie *C. concolor*, a bird found in central and southern Africa. Its call is a characteristic sound of the bush – a nasal 'g'-waaay'. This species is completely grey, with a crest that becomes erect when the bird is excited. Occurring farther north, in the east and north-east, are the larger Bare-faced and White-bellied Go-away Birds, *C. personata* and *C. leucogaster*.

The plantain-eaters are grey birds with striated white under-parts; they form a sympatric pair. The Western Grey Plantain-eater *Crinifer piscator* occurs in West and equatorial Africa; it is replaced by the Eastern Grey Plantain-eater *C. zonorus* farther east and north. They are both birds of wooded and open savannah.

Turacos construct pigeon-like platform nests in trees or bushes; the nest may be up to 65 ft. (20 m.) above the ground, where 2 – 3 eggs are laid. Incubation, shared by both parents, lasts 18 – 23 days. After hatching, the chicks leave the nest after about three weeks, but do not fly for a further two or three weeks. Some youngsters are dependent on their parents for a total of 16 weeks.

CUCKOOS

Order: *Cuculiformes*
Family: *Cuculidae*
39 genera contain 132 species

The European Cuckoo *Cuculus canorus* is a widespread parasitic breeding species in Europe, consequently many people think that all cuckoos lay their eggs in other birds' nests. This is not so, for about two thirds of the 132 species of cuckoos rear their youngsters in the conventional manner.

The cuckoos are divided into 39 genera, and occur in the temperate and tropical regions of the World, in habitats from dry savannah and deserts, to swamps and forests. They range in length from 6 – 35 in. (15 – 90 cm.), the smallest being the glossy cuckoos *Chrysococcyx* that occur in sub-Saharan Africa. Similar species belong to the genus *Chalcites*,

Far left: a Greater Roadrunner at Tuscon, Arizona. This is a bird common in the dry, south-western United States and Mexico. Left: a White-browed Coucal at Samburu, Kenya, member of a family widespread over eastern and southern Africa. Some cuckoos leave their young to be reared by smaller birds. Below left: a European Cuckoo begs for food from its Tree Pipit foster parent. All three of these birds are contrasting members of the cuckoo family.

inhabiting the Oriental and Australasian regions. At the other end of the scale are the coucals *Centropus spp.*, a group of long-tailed, loose-plumaged birds that spend much of their time in thick vegetation or feeding on the ground. Some species overlap cuckoos in size, but others are larger. The European Cuckoo, which has occurred as a vagrant in Alaska, is a grey bird with barred under-parts. Beyond these basic types there is considerable variation in the plumages Old World and Australasian cuckoos. The New World species have a smoother looking plumage, with brown being the dominant colour; most have paler under-parts. In North America the Yellow-billed and Black-billed Cuckoos

Coccyzus minor and *C. erythropthalmus* are summer visitors from South America; both have been recorded as vagrants to the British Isles, but few have survived for more than a day or two after discovery. Other American cuckoos include the anis *Crotophaga spp.*, and the most unlikely-looking cuckoo – the Greater Roadrunner. This is an extraordinary brown and buff bird, with a crest, long tail and legs, that runs swiftly rather than flies, and lives on a diet of lizards, snakes and insects. Cuckoos and coucals feed on a diet of insects, grasshoppers and other invertebrates, and are amongst the few birds to regularly eat hairy caterpillars. The larger species also feed on more substantial prey, including lizards and snakes.

The parasitic species lay their eggs in other birds' nests, but it is not quite as simple as that. European Cuckoos parasitise many small birds, but they are faithful to the species that had reared them. The eggs match those of the host in shape and size. Sometimes the cuckoo finds that there is not a suitable nest of the correct species. The female cuckoo will disrupt the breeding of the intended hosts, by either destroying the eggs or young, resulting in them laying again. The cuckoo then lays another clutch and this time the cuckoo is ready to lay its own egg in place of one of the host's eggs, which it removes. On hatching, the interloper ejects the eggs or hatched young of the host from the nest, and grows rapidly to two or three times the size of its foster-parents.

The other cuckoos build a platform nest of twigs in a tree or bush or amongst thick vegetation and lay a clutch of 2 – 6 eggs. The largest number often is laid by the Black-billed Cuckoo at two day intervals. Incubation starts with the first egg, so that there is already a chick in the nest when the last egg is laid. Incubation may last only 10 days, whilst the fledging period may take up to 20 days, the chick sometimes leaving the nest prematurely.

BARN OWLS
Order: *Strigiformes*
Family: *Tytonidae*
two genera contain 12 species

Barn Owls are a cosmopolitan family of owls which differ from the true owls by their smaller eyes and distinctive heart-shaped facial disk. The twelve species are divided into two genera; ten barn owls *Tyto* and two bay owls *Phodilus*. They occur throughout the World except for the higher latitudes of North America and the Palearctic; the greatest diversity of species occurs in the warmer latitudes of the Oriental and Australasian regions.

The most widespread of the family is the Common Barn Owl *Tyto alba*, 15.5 in. (34 cm.) long, but it is declining in many areas as a result of pesticides and loss of breeding sites. It occurs from southern British Columbia and southern Ontario through most of the United States, Central and South America to Tierra del Fuego and the Falkland Islands, with a subspecies out in the eastern Pacific Ocean amongst the Galapagos Islands. On the other side of the Atlantic, it ranges across Europe, throughout Africa and Arabia, and from India and south-east Asia, down through Indonesia to Australia and out into the western Pacific as far east as Samoa.

Barn Owls are pale in colour, having orange-buff upper-parts, mottled with grey and white, and white under-parts, although some races are darker than others. The facial disk of this and other members of the genus is heart-shaped and encompasses the dark eyes and partially concealed bill. The plumage is incredibly soft, ensuring a silent bouyant flight on long rounded wings, tilting this way and that, as it systematically quarters fields and grasslands for food. The mainstay of a Barn Owl's diet is rodents, but frogs, insects and some birds are also included. They are most active at dusk and during the night, but during the short days of winter in northern latitudes and whilst feeding young in the breeding season, they also hunt by day. A tragic mistake was made in

Klaas' Cuckoo (top) is a small, glossy cuckoo found mainly in Africa. The Common Barn Owl (above left) is the most cosmopolitan, or widely distributed, owl. Above: a Sooty Owl, an Australian species, feeding on a small rodent.

the Seychelles involving the introduction of Barn Owls; initial attempts were unsuccessful, but eventually it became established and the hope was that it would combat the local rat population. Only when the Owls started to decimate the Fairy Tern *Gygis alba* on the main island of Mahé, was the mistake realised. Fairy Terns are pure white and are easily seen as they roost at night; no wonder few, if any, rat remains were found at Barn Owl nests, and a bounty was placed on its head in an attempt to reverse the situation. Although the measures proved to be successful, they came too late for many terns.

Barn Owls usually nest in hollow trees, old farm buildings and ruins, where 4 – 7 eggs are laid. Incubation lasts for 32 – 34 days and is carried out entirely by the female, who only leaves the nest for a few minutes at a time to receive the prey caught for her by the male. The young are fed by both parents during the 7 – 8 week fledging period. Afterwards they enjoy the protection from their parents' territory, before being evicted to fend for themselves.

The other members of the *Tyto* genus occur in the warmer regions of the range; 6 are regular barn owls and the remaining three are known as grass owls. Two of these other barn owl species occur in Australia, where the Common Barn Owl is also to be found. The Masked Owl *T. novaehollandiae*, 19 in. (48 cm.) long, is the largest member of the genus and it is hardly surprising that the Sooty Owl *T. tenebricosa*, 17 in. (43 cm.) long, is one of the darkest. The other four species have evolved in isolation on islands to the north, between Celebes, where two species occur, and New Britain, an island group lying to the east of New Guinea.

The three species of grass owl are darker birds than the Common Barn Owl and roost and nest in long grass. The African Grass Owl *T. capensis*, 14.5 in. (37 cm.) long, occurs in suitable grassland habitats near water, in much of sub-Saharan Africa. It is replaced by a similar species on the island of Madagascar, the Madagascar Grass Owl *T. soumagnei*, and from India to Indo-China by the Eastern Grass Owl *T. longimembris*, 14 in. (36 cm.) long. This species is also found south to Australia, and in the 1860s specimens were obtained on the Fijian island of Viti Levu; but there have been no recent records.

The other two members of the family are the bay owls, belonging to the genus Phodilus. The Asian Bay Owl *P.*

Below: a 12-week-old Common Barn Owl adopts a defensive pose.

131

badius 11.5 in. (29 cm.) long, is similar in colour and general appearance to the barn owls, but the facial disc is almost divided by the forehead which slopes down to the bill from a flatter crown. It ranges from Nepal to south-east Asia and the East Indies. Thousands of miles to the west in eastern Zaïre, an unknown owl was shot as it slept in long grass during daytime in 1951. It was found in an area of montane forest at 7,970 ft. (2,430 m.) This species was new to science and named the Congo Bay Owl *P. prigoginei*, when found to be related to the Asiatic species. Since then the only hint that one of the least known owls in the World still exists, has been unsubstantiated reports from Burundi during the 1970s. Perhaps one day this elusive relict from the days when bay owls were more widespread, will reappear for an intrepid ornithologist in darkest Africa.

OWLS

Order: *Strigiformes*
Family: *Strigidae*
28 genera contain 124 species

Owls are amongst the most popular of birds, judging by the huge variety of genera and species that have evolved in toystores and on commercial logos. With heads set into their bodies and large faces, owls can look particularly endearing.

In the wild there are 124 species of owls; divided between 28 genera, they occur throughout the World except in the Antarctic and much of Greenland. Several species have evolved in isolation within well-defined areas and habitats. Typical of these are the Sokoke Scops Owl *Otus ireneae*, 6.5

Facing page: a rufous-phase Eastern Screech Owl peers from a cleft in a tree in the United States. The huge Brown Fishing Owl (left) ranges from the Middle East to south-east Asia.

The Great Horned Owl, a large owl that ranges from Alaska to Tierra del Fuego, is found in a wide variety of habitats, including rocky areas. Left: Great Horned Owl youngsters.

in. (16.5 cm.) in length, and the Seychelles Scops Owl *O. insularis*. The Sokoke Scops, first discovered in 1965, is confined to the Sokoke Forest, a lowland forest near Kenya's Indian Ocean coast. The Seychelles Scops is another small owl, found only in the montane forests of Mahé, largest island in the Seychelles archipelago. This species, thought to have vanished into extinction in 1906, was rediscovered in 1959, but not seen regularly until the call was captured on tape during the 1970s. The bird responds to tape, but is still a difficult species to see and remains one of the rarest of the World's owls.

Perhaps because of the availability of suitable nest sites, most species occur in forests and woodlands, from sea-level to the top of the tree line. Others are birds of tundra and prairies, whilst Miami Airport is one place to see the long-legged Burrowing Owl *Speotyto cunicularia*, 9.5 in. (24 cm.) long, which ranges from the United States to Tierra del Fuego.

With their hooked bills and sharp claws, they have evolved as nocturnal predators, filling a niche occupied during the day by birds of prey. This is another case of convergent evolution, for they are unrelated families that share several common features through necessity. Owls share a common ancestor

with the nightjars *Caprimulgidae*, the other large family of nocturnal hunters. The largest *Strigidae* are the twelve species of eagle owl *Bubo*, represented in North America by the Great Horned Owl *B. virginianus*, 22 in. (56 cm.) long. Not the largest member of the genus, but one of the most widespread, the Great Horned Owl occurs throughout much of North and South America from Alaska to Tierra del Fuego. It is absent from the high arctic areas of tundra, where it is replaced by the aptly named holarctic Snowy Owl *Nyctea scandiaca*, a ground nesting owl that matches the Great Horned in size and strength. In both these and all other owls, the female is larger than the male. Another group of large owls is the fishing owls; some resemble the eagle owls and others are unlike any other members of the family. It is to this group that my favourite owl belongs. Imagine a ginger owl, larger than a Great Horned

Owl, staring down from a tall tree, with big black eyes that look like lumps of coal; this is the elusive Pel's Fishing Owl *Scotopelia peli*, 26 in. (65 cm.) long, found in African riverine woodland. Until I started visiting the Okavango Delta in Botswana, this bird was one of those species that I hoped, but did not expect to see. They are wonderful birds, with a loose orange-brown plumage, barred with black, and appearing larger that life. One year, when my family and I arrived at the Delta camp, Jedibe, we were met by the camp manager Hennie Rawlinson. Very excitedly, he pointed into the tree above the small jetty and there, only a few feet above us, was a young Pel's. 'Baby' was covered in down, but the feathers that were emerging were looking very dishevelled. He had arrived a few days earlier with some native boatmen. Apparently they had discovered the youngster after it had left the nest prematurely. Usually in such instances, the parents know the whereabouts of any straying youngster, and will tend it until independence is achieved. Hennie and his fiancée,

and calling on old friends for the occasional fish supper. The owl will normally emerge from its roost at dusk and fly to a prominent perch, there to watch and listen for the movements of fish. As the African night settles over the swamps and islands of the Delta, somewhere in the darkness a sudden splash announces that the fishing has been successful.

Fishing Owls do not occur in the Americas, but many other owls can be found in a variety of habitats. Some are resident and others move south for the winter; often they show up unexpectedly. During our first visit to the United States, we paid tribute to the Statue of Liberty shortly after Christmas. The weather was bitterly cold and looking across to Ellis Island, we watched a Short-eared Owl *Asio flammeus*, 15 in. (38 cm.) long, quartering an area of rough ground on the island in search of rodents. The appearance of a Snowy Owl, or perhaps a Hawk Owl *Surnia ulula* 16 in. (41 cm.) long, outside their normal winter quarters is usually a good indication that severe weather has forced them to move.

Angie, were feeding the owl its natural food, fish, but unlike the proper parents they had omitted to include bones in the diet. Many predators need calcium in their diet, and this is what 'Baby' had been lacking, for the new feathers were breaking off as they grew, accounting for the bird's dishevelled appearance. Elizabeth, my wife and I had come across the same problem with a Common Buzzard, *Buteo buteo*, that we had looked after for several months in Scotland. But how does one obtain calcium in the middle of prime wilderness? The answer was ridiculously simple; a short radio call to Maun, at the southern end of the Delta, and the following day a pilot arriving at the nearest airstrip made a delivery.

From then on the young owl went from strength to strength, helped by Hennie and his successor Tony. Now the bird is independent, although still living in the neighbourhood

Some of the smallest species of owls belong to the genus *Otus*; it is one of the most widespread groups and includes the two scops owls mentioned earlier. Two related North American species are the more familiar Eastern and Western Screech Owls *O. asio* and *O. kennicotti*, 8.5 in. (22 cm.) long, an allopatric pair, found in a variety of habitats throughout most of the United States and southern Canada; these closely related species were, until recently, treated as one. Owls of the genus *Glaucidium* are diurnal birds found widely in the Old and New Worlds, where the Least Pygmy Owl *G. minutissimum*, 5.5 in. (14 cm.) long, and found in Central America, is the smallest of the World's owls. In the western United States and Canada resides a larger relative, the Northern Pygmy Owl *G. gnoma*, 6.75 in. (17 cm.) long; it inhabits montane woodland and forest. Like all members of the genus

Above: in Botswana's Okavango Delta, a young Pel's Fishing Owl eats its prey head first. This elusive species is one of Africa's largest owls and is found in riverine forests.

it has a fast, dipping flight. The undulations, are caused by the wings held against the body, between bursts of rapid wing beats. This owl, together with several other closely related species has two black patches on the nape, giving the distinct impression of 'having eyes in the back of its head.' During our tours to Botswana and nearby Zimbabwe, the slightly larger Pearl-spotted Owl *G. perlatum* is a great entertainer. Being a diurnal species, it is often mobbed by birds during the day and its call can be easily mimicked, sometimes so effectively that the caller can draw an owl into nearby bushes.

One has to be very careful with owls, especially in the vicinity of nests and when using tape-recorders. Eric Hosking, the father of modern bird photography, lost an eye when he was photographing at the nest of a Tawny Owl *Strix aluco* 15

tapes for locating shy and elusive species, but thankfully the majority are sufficiently responsible to appreciate the possible implications of their actions.

Owls hunt silently, their soft, well-feathered plumage serving to muffle the slightest sound they might make as they drop on some unsuspecting mouse. To help them in their quest, owls have excellent hearing and low-light vision. Some species, including the spectre of the northern forests, the Great Grey Owl *Strix nebulosa* 27 in. (69 cm.) long, appears to be almost all head. They feed on a wide variety of prey species, ranging from young monkeys and Warthogs *Phacochoerus aethiopicus*, taken in Africa by the Giant Eagle Owl *Bubo lacteus*, to the frogs, insects and rodents taken by smaller species. Birds also feature on the diet of owls, caught

in. (38 cm.) long; a tragic accident, but when many years later he wrote his autobiography it gave him the title *An Eye for a Bird*. Playing tape-recordings can sometimes have such a disturbing influence on breeding owls, that they can behave unpredictably. Recently someone was playing the call of the Barred Owl *Strix varia*, 21 in. (53 cm.) long, in the Everglades was attacked by the owl. This person attempted to take legal action against the National Park authorities, for permitting dangerous creatures to live so close to a board-walk! Since then, the use of tape-recorders and other devices has been banned in the Park.

Recently I heard of another thoughtless incident that had occurred at one camp in Botswana several years previously; the camp was home to a pair of African Wood Owls *Strix woodfordii* (14 in. 36 cm.) long. A client played the recording, but not satisfied with seeing the birds, persisted, and the male became so agitated, that he thought that his mate, not the tape, was the intruder and killed her! Many serious birders now use

while they roost at night, or during the day by diurnal species; even other owls are taken.

Few owls make their own nests, but generally lay their eggs in holes and crevices in trees, rocks or just on the ground. Several species use the old nests of birds of prey and crows *Corvidae*; the Giant Eagle Owl may take over the nest of the Hamerkop *Scopus umbretta*. Usually the clutch size can range from 2–7 eggs, depending on the species, and incubation, undertaken mainly by the female, varies from 26–36 days for the same reason. Incubation begins with the first egg, so that chicks hatch over a period of days. In times of abundant food availability, more will survive than during a lean year. An extreme example of breeding fluctuation is the Snowy Owl, which in a good Lemming *Lemmini* year can lay up to 14 eggs. In some years however, when there are few Lemmings, Snowies may fail to breed entirely.

The greatest threat to many rarer owls of the World comes from habitat destruction, either for timber or clearance for

Above: a Little Owl stands at the entrance to its nest hole with its well-developed chicks. It ranges from Western Europe and North Africa to the Far East.

subsistence agriculture or plantation. The fears of some native peoples that owls are a symbol of evil, cause them to persecute them. In general many rare owls are poorly known and might not be as rare as current information suggests. Some species such as the Flores Scops *O. alfredi* and the Mindoro Scops Owl *O. mindorensis*, from Indonesia and the Philippines have not been seen this century.

OILBIRD
Order: *Caprimulgiformes*
Family: *Steatornithidae*
the genus Steatornis contains a single
species Steatornis caripensis

The Oilbird *Steatornis caripensis* is a strange bird endemic to South America. It is very local in its distribution for it breeds and roosts colonially from eastern Panama and Trinidad, south down the Andes to Peru.

It is a large brown bird 19 in. (48 cm.) long that looks like a nightjar *Caprimulgiformes* crossed with a raptor, with long wings and tail. It has no close living relatives and displays

some characteristics shared with nightjars and others found in owls *Strigiformes*, such as a sharp, hooked beak. Like nightjars and owls, Oilbirds are also nocturnal, but there the similarities end for they are the only nocturnal fruit-eating birds in the world. At night the birds will travel up to 15 miles (25 km.) from their caves. The fruiting trees are usually located by smell, for Oilbirds have very well developed olfactory organs, and the fruit is collected from the trees by the birds in flight. Trees such as palms, whose fruits have no smell, are found by sight. They are noisy birds making a variety of noises, include clicks used by the bird for echo location in the darkness of the cave.

The bulky nest, situated on a ledge high on the side of the cave, is a mixture of regurgitated fruit and seeds and the birds' own droppings. Nests used on successive years build up into substantial structures. The clutch of two to four eggs is laid over a period of several days and incubation by both parents lasts for 33 days. After hatching, the youngsters stay in the

The Tawny Owl (above), related to the Barred Owl of North America, is the common woodland owl of Europe and ranges east to China. The Collared Scops Owl (far left) is a widespread Asiatic species. Left: normally a bird of the Arctic, this two-month-old Snowy Owl chick was reared in a wildlife park in Britain.

137

nest for up to 120 days, longer than any other species apart from some seabirds and raptors. Forty days after hatching the young weigh as much as the adults and by 70 days, weigh half as much again! They grow two coats of down and then slim as they grow their adult plumage. Fat, young Oilbirds were formerly, and to a lesser extent nowadays, collected by the native Indians and boiled down to produce an odourless oil – hence the name Oilbird.

FROGMOUTHS
Order: *Caprimulgiformes*
Family: *Podargidae*
two genera contain 13 species

Frogmouths are a family of nightjar-like birds found in Asia and Australasia. The genus *Podargus* contains three species that occur exclusively in New Guinea, Australia and the Solomon Islands in the western Pacific. The remaining ten species belong to the genus *Batrachostomus* and range from India to Malaysia.

Like other members of the nightjar Order *Caprimulgiformes*, they are nocturnal and cryptically coloured. Their wide mouths gave rise to the earlier assumption that they caught insects in flight, but they are not manoeuvrable on the wing as are nightjars *Caprimulgidae*, and as discovered later, they fly from a perch to catch a beetle or other prey, either on the ground or on a nearby branch. Their diet also includes centipedes, frogs, fruit, scorpions, snails and sometimes small birds.

The largest species is the Papuan Frogmouth *P. papuensis* 21 in. (54 cm.) long, which occurs on the island of New Guinea and on the Cape York Peninsular in northern Queensland, Australia. Of the other two members of this genus, the Tawny Frogmouth *P. strigoides* is widely distributed in woodlands across Australia and Tasmania. The range of the Marbled Frogmouth *P. ocellatus* also includes Cape York and a small area of southern Queensland and northern New South Wales, as well as New Guinea and the islands across to the Solomons. The frogmouths of this genus are particularly well camouflaged and recall the Potoos *Nyctibiidae* of Central and South America, for they, too, become just like the broken end of a branch during the day. This genus makes an insubstantial nest of twigs on a horizontal branch, where two eggs are laid. The Tawny Frogmouth occasionally uses the old nests of the White-winged Chough *Corcorax melanorhamphos* and the Australian Magpie *Gymnorhina tibicen*. It would appear that only the female incubates the clutch, but both share in the feeding of the brood.

The frogmouths of Asia differ from their plain Australasian relatives by having white spots on the back and neck and to a lesser extent on the breast, yet they are also past masters in the art of concealment in their forest and woodland habitat. The Large Frogmouth *B. auritus*, 16 in. (40 cm.) long, is almost twice the length of other members of the genus and because of this is the easiest to identify. These nocturnal birds are hard to separate in the field unless one is very lucky and as a result little is known about their breeding biology. A single egg is laid on a platform made of down from the breasts of the parents, and bound by spider-web and lichen. It has been discovered that the male Hodgson's Frogmouth *B. hodgsoni* usually incubates by day. Presumably the female works the night-shift!

POTOOS
Order: *Caprimulgiformes*
Family: *Nyctibiidae*
the genus *Nyctibius* contains five species

One day, during a tour I was leading for Ornitholidays to Jamaica, our local guide, Robert Sutton, found a roosting Common Potoo *Nyctibius griseus*, 14 – 16 in. (36 – 41 cm.) long, on his farm near Mandeville. A regular site, but perhaps not one that everyone would find, for the cryptically coloured

The Tawny Frogmouth (this page) is a Nightjar-related bird found throughout Australia.

nightjar-like bird blended with its perch so well that it appeared to the unpracticed eye, to be merely an extension of the branch.

Potoos are found from Central through into South America. They are quite poorly known birds, although the Common Potoo, the most widespread species, occurs from Mexico and the West Indies south to Argentina. Further studies are required, for those birds inhabiting the West Indies and Central America south to the Pacific slopes of Costa Rica are larger and have a different call to those birds found farther south. It is possible that there is a north/south split in the populations of the less well known Long-tailed Potoo *N. aethereus*, 20 in. (51 cm.) long, although half of this length is tail. There have only been scattered records from Venezuela south to Brazil. Once again, further studies are required, for it seems that those birds occurring in south east Brazil and Paraguay may warrant specific status. Two other species are very rare; the smallest species, the Rufous *N. bracteatus*, 12

During the day the Common Potoo, a nocturnal bird related to the night-hawks and nightjars, usually roosts motionless at the end of a branch, where its cryptically-coloured plumage blends perfectly with its surroundings. Facing page: a Common Potoo roosting in the Panatel, Brazil.

in. (30 cm.) long, and the larger White-winged Potoo *N. leucopterus*, 15 in. (38 cm.) long; both occur in northern South America. The White-winged Potoo has only been seen a handful of times in a vast area from Venezuela to Ecuador, in parts of Peru and the east coast of Brazil. The few records of the Rufous Potoo come from Ecuador, Peru and once from Guyana. With records from such a huge region, where considerable habitat destruction is taking place, both species are almost certainly endangered. The fifth and largest species is the Great Potoo *N. grandis*, 20 in. (51 cm.) long, and found from south eastern Mexico through to southern Brazil. It is better known than the three preceding species, but much has still to be discovered.

Potoos are nocturnal birds of forests, woodland and plantations, often being found where clearings allow space to enable them to hunt insects on the wing. During the daytime they rely on their superb camouflage to remain undetected, a characteristic that does not help research. Some species, such as the Great Potoo, only call on moonlit nights, and the Common Potoo is more vocal on such nights.

Little is known in detail about the breeding biology of the three rarest species, whilst some details of the domestic life of the Common and Great await discovery. There is no nest, instead, the single egg is laid at the top of a stump or in a depression, such as a knot-hole, along a branch. Both parents incubate the single egg and records from Costa Rica show that the Common Potoo has a 33 day incubation period, after which the down-covered chick takes 47 days to fledge.

OWLET-NIGHTJARS

Order:*Caprimulgiformes*
Family: *Aegothelidae*
the genus *Aegotheles* contains eight species.

The eight species of Owlet-Nightjars, or Owlet-Frogmouths as they are sometimes called, are almost entirely confined to the Australasian region encompassing New Guinea and Australia. The only two species found outside this area are the Halmahera Owlet-Nightjar *Aegotheles crinifrons*, occurring on two nearby islands in the Moluccan group and the New Caledonian Owlet-Nightjar *A. savesi* from the islands of New Caledonia lying in the Pacific Ocean east of Australia. All the remaining species inhabit Papua New Guinea and one, the Australian Owlet-Nightjar, is also widely distributed in Australia and Tasmania. They are birds of forest and more open areas of scrub; the Australian species occurs in more arid country.

Owlet-Nightjars, cryptically coloured mottled brown birds, are closely related to Nightjars *Caprimulgidae* and Frogmouths *Podargidae*. For their size, about 8 – 9.5 in. (20.5 – 24 cm.) long, they have long tails and wide beaks partially concealed by longer feathers above and below the bill, a feature not shared by closely related species.

Many features of Owlet-Nightjar behaviour are poorly known. They catch insects on the wing, but are birds with strong legs. Scientists have discovered invertebrates such as millipedes and spiders in stomach contents, which suggests that they are probably effective ground feeding insectivores.

Breeding takes place from September – December. The nest, sited in a hollow tree and often lined with dry leaves and mammal fur, contains between two and five white eggs. Most details of breeding biology remained to be discovered.

NIGHTJARS

Order: *Caprimulgiformes*
Family: *Caprimulgidae*
19 genera contain 75 species

Of the nocturnal insectivores that belong to the Order *Caprimulgiformes*, the most numerous are the Nightjars *Caprimulgidae*. Members of the family occur throughout the warm temperate and tropical regions of the World. They are absent from New Zealand and most oceanic islands.

Most of the 75 species of nightjars are crepuscular or nocturnal, but in North America, the Common Nighthawk *Chordeiles minor* can be seen hawking insects during the day; larger numbers are active towards dusk. Some species are sedentary, but those with northerly populations, such as the Common Nighthawk and the European Nightjar *Caprimulgus europaeus*, migrate south in the fall, to return the following spring. A constant food supply of moths and other night-flying insects is essential, but in the northern latitudes and mountainous areas these are absent or only occur in reduced numbers during the colder months. One species, the Poorwill *Phalaenoptlis nuttallii* hibernates; some other species of birds slow down their metabolic rate in cold weather, but scientists banded the first hibernating Poorwill to be discovered, and found that it returned to the same site in

The Long-tailed Nightjar (above), with its distinctive bristles around the base of its bill, ranges from India to Australia.

Colorado in subsequent winters. To what extent this applies to all Poorwills is not known.

Members of the nightjar family are cryptically-coloured and pass the day roosting on the ground or on a branch, relying on camouflage for concealment. They are birds of open woodland and scrub. Most species are dark brown, mottled or barred with black, shades of buff and rufous. Some species including the Egyptian Nightjar *C. aegyptius* found in North Africa, the Middle East and western Asia, inhabit deserts, and are sandy-coloured with appropriate mottling. Often the only way to identify a nightjar flushed during the day, is to note the position and extent of the white or buff patches on the wings and tail. Easier said than done when a bird flying up from the path only feet away startles you! Nightjars have longish wings and tails; those belonging to the nighthawk element of the family have narrower and more hawk-like wings. Members of the family range from 6.25 – 16 in. (16 – 41 cm.) long and

Above left: a European Nightjar with its chick in coniferous woodland in Wiltshire, England. Above: a Poorwill, a North American nightjar, in the Mojave Desert, California. It has been recorded hibernating in Colorado. The Roraiman Nightjar (left) is such a rare and poorly known bird from Venezuela and Guyana that it is not even illustrated in the Venezuelan field guide.

this does not take into account the incredible elongated feathers of some species. The male Pennant-winged Nightjar *Macrodipteryx vexillaria*, from equatorial and central Africa, has evolved a single primary feather on each wing that is an amazing 28 in. (73 cm.) long. These feathers are grown for the beginning of the breeding season and break with wear; successive feathers grow longer as the bird ages. The male Lyre-tailed Nightjar *Uropsalis lyra*, of north-western South America, has elongated tail feathers that account for nearly three-quarters the bird's length of 30 in. (76 cm.). Nightjars have short legs and very wide mouths for catching insects in flight; the nightjar family is the most aerial of all the members of the Order of nightjar-related birds.

There is no nest, the clutch of 1 – 2 eggs being laid on the bare ground, where both parents share the 16 – 19 day incubation period. The nestlings, covered with down, fledge in 16 – 20 days.

Several members of the family are endangered; often they are species with restricted ranges and threatened by habitat destruction. A number of nocturnal birds are poorly known; this is illustrated by the rediscovery in 1961 of the Puerto Rican Nightjar *C. noctitherus*, a bird thought to be extinct since 1911. What are the chances of keen birders relocating the Jamaican Pauraque *Siphonorhis americanus*, last recorded in 1859?

SWIFTS
Order: *Apodiformes*
Family: *Apodidae*
18 genera contain 85 species

Swifts, the most aerial of birds, are supremely well adapted to their environment, for they feed, drink, mate and even sleep on the wing. They resemble swallows *Hirundinidae* with their forked tails, but are members of the Order *Apodiformes* to which the hummingbirds *Trochilidae* belong. This might seem an unlikely relation, but both families evolved from a common ancestor way back in time. They have retained the ability to rotate their wings, thus producing lift on the up-beat as well as on the conventional down-beat.

There are 85 species of swifts divided into 18 genera, members of the family occurring throughout the temperate and tropical regions of the world. The greatest variety inhabits the tropical areas, although they are absent as breeding species from much of the Australasian region. In the north of that area they are replaced by the closely related crested or tree swifts *Hemiprocnidae*, a family that is also widespread in southern and south-eastern Asia. A number of species are migrants, especially those that breed in the northern latitudes, for they are dependent on an abundant supply of flying insects. North America is home to four species, the most widespread being the Chimney Swift *Chaetura pelagica*; two other species have occurred as vagrants.

Swifts range in length from 5 – 10 in. (12.5 – 25 cm.) and in flight have characteristic sickle-shaped wings. Nearly all have forked tails of varying depth, but a few have square-ended tails, notably the widespread Little or House Swift *Apus affinis* and the spine-tailed swifts *Telacanthura spp.*, of the Old World. Swifts are not colourful birds, most are black or shades of brown or grey, a number having white rumps, collars, throats or under-parts. They have short legs, but strong claws to enable them to cling to rock faces and tree trunks. Should they land on the ground they are doomed, for their wings are too long to enable them to become airborne again. An African Palm Swift *Cypsiurus parvus* that I discovered on an islet in the middle of the Zambezi in Zimbabwe, was one such bird. How it had become grounded I do not know, but it felt lively when I picked it up and launched it into the air. However it must have been down for sometime, for it flew away rather weakly. The unfortunate bird had only flown a short distance, when an African Goshawk *Accipiter tachiro* flashed past, grasped the swift with one foot and headed off across the river. It was all over in an instant; the poor swift had no idea what happened, as the Goshawk took it from behind. If death was inevitable, it did not suffer the lingering end that faced it on the island.

Swifts breed in a variety of sites; naturally these are in caves, cracks in rock faces and in trees, but over the last few centuries suitable sites have been found under the eaves of houses and in chimneys. Along the Chobe River in Botswana, we have found Horus Swifts *A. horus* nesting in holes in the river bank, amongst a colony of White-fronted Bee-eaters *Merops bullockoides*. In the British Isles most Common Swifts *Apus apus* breed in buildings. Some species are solitary, but many others form large colonies. The nesting materials used are collected on the wing and then bound with saliva.

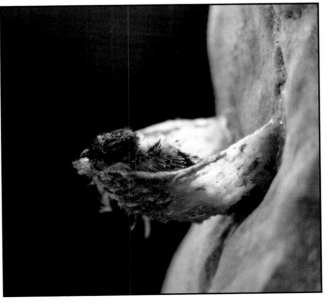

The Little Swift is a widespread species, ranging from Africa to the East Indies. Facing page: a pair of Little Swifts on their nest inside a building in Kenya. Above: White-rumped Swiftlets at their nests. This species is found from the East Indies to Samoa, including north-eastern Australia. Left: the paper-thin nest of a Black Nest Swift in Sabah is nonetheless strong enough to support the weight of a growing chick.

The most well-known nests are those of the Edible-nest Swiftlet *Collocalia fuciphaga*. This south-east Asian species nests high on the walls of caves and there constructs a nest from its own saliva; the nests are collected and form the basis of 'bird's-nest soup.' The cave-nesting species use echo-location to find their way around the depths of the caves. Swifts lay 1 – 6 eggs, which, depending on the species, are incubated for 19–26 days. Swifts have a long fledging period, which ranges from 35 – 56 days. The greatest influence is the availability of food; the nestlings of the Common Swift can starve without undue adverse effects for several days in cold unseasonable weather. Once the young birds leave the nest, they will not land again until they return to breed two years later. Estimates suggest a possible non-stop inaugural flight of over 310,000 miles (500,000 km.)!

TREE SWIFTS
Order: *Apodiformes*
Family: *Hemiprocnidae*
the genus *Hemiprocne* contains four species

Tree or Crested Swifts differ from regular swifts *Apodiformes* on two counts; they are more colourful and habitually perch in trees. The alternative name of Crested Swift comes from the crested forehead displayed by two species, but as all four species perch in trees the name Tree Swift is the more appropriate.

The four species can be split into two groups of two. The Crested Tree Swift *Hemiprocne longipennis* and the Indian Tree Swift *H. coronata* form one pair that some authorities place together in a single species. The other pair consists of the Whiskered Tree Swift *H. comata* and the Moustached Tree Swift *H. mystacea*. Sometimes if one travels abroad bird-watching it is a good idea to double check the scientific names of the birds under consideration if more than one book is being consulted. Whilst researching Tree Swifts I found four different popular names used for *H. longipennis*: Crested Tree Swift, Grey-rumped Tree Swift, Common Crested Swift and Indian Crested Swift! Of these, Crested Tree Swift and Indian Crested Swift were also given to *H. coronata*! The Whiskered Tree Swift *H. comata* fares no better, for the Moustached Tree Swift *H. mystacea* is also called Whiskered in some books. Thank goodness there are only four species!

Tree Swifts are birds of forest margins, clearings and wooded hillsides, where they find perches on branches from which to hawk insects. They are gregarious birds and fly quickly on slender wings, with a long slim tail that recalls that of the Asiatic Palm Swift *Cypsiurus batasiensis*.

The Crested Tree Swift *longipennis* occurs from southern Burma and across south-east Asia through Malaysia to Indonesia. It is 8 in. (20 cm.) long and when at rest the wings extend beyond the tail. It has darker upper-parts than the closely related Indian Crested Swift that contrast with the paler grey rump. The male differs from the female by having chestnut ear coverts.

The allopatric and closely related Indian Crested Swift *coronata* ranges from India eastwards to south central China. It is a larger bird, 9 in. (23 cm.) long, with a noticeably longer tail than the Crested Tree Swift that extends beyond the folded wings at rest. The male has chestnut ear coverts which are more extensive than those of the Crested.

The Whiskered Tree Swift *comata* shares much of the range of the Crested, but occurs over a wider area, extending into Borneo and the Philippines. It is the smallest member of the family, 6 in. (15 cm.) long, and darker than the two previous species, with a glossy blue-black head, wings and tail and a bronzy-brown body. The tertials show some white, and on the head two striking white stripes above and below the eye almost meet on the nape. The range of its close relative, the Moustached Tree Swift *mystacea*, lies amongst the islands to the south and east from the Moluccas and through Papua New Guinea to the Solomon Islands in the western Pacific. It is the largest species in the genus, with a similar plumage to the Whiskered, except for a more conspicuous white patch on the wings.

Tree Swifts make a minute nest of small feathers and moss, held together by hardened saliva. It is secured to the side of a thin horizontal branch and contains a single egg. The nest is so fragile that it is unable to support the incubating bird who sits on the branch and not the nest! Both birds share the tasks of nest building, incubation and feeding the nestling, which, covered with down, sits camouflaged and motionless in the nest, looking like an irregularity along the twig. As it outgrows the nest, so it moves out and takes up a similar position on the branch.

HUMMINGBIRDS
Order: *Apodiformes*
Family: *Trochilidae*
112 genera contain 320 species
Food: ¼c. sugar to 1c. water

Hummingbirds are the gems of the bird world, with the iridescent plumages of the males in particular, sparkling in the sun. The family is markedly sexually dimorphic. Their nearest relatives are the swifts, although it might not be immediately apparent; they shared a common ancestor and both have the ability to gain lift from the air as their wings beat up and down. Other birds only obtain lift on the down beat.

Below: a female Broad-tailed Hummingbird, a summer visitor to the western United States, feeds its young.

Hummingbirds come in many colours, yet those with green upper-parts predominate. They are a New World family, found essentially in the warm temperate and tropical areas of Central and South America. They range in length from 2.3 in. (6 cm.), to the Giant Hummingbird *Patagona gigas* at 9 in. (23 cm.) in length, of which 1.5 in. (3.8 cm.) is bill. The Sword-billed Hummingbird *Ensifera ensifera* is 9.75 in. (25 cm.) long, half of which is a bill that enables the bird to reach inside the hanging trumpet-shaped flowers of the *Datura*. Hummingbirds are to be found as high as 13,100 ft. (4,000 m.) above the tree-line in the Andes down to the tropical rain forests of the Amazon. Their principal requirement is an abundance of flowers from which they can obtain nectar.

There are 112 genera that contain 320 species , but it is possible that there may yet be more undiscovered; but more importantly are the numbers that are threatened by habitat destruction in areas where some hummingbirds have very restricted ranges. The United States has 16 breeding species, although most are confined to the south-west; others have occurred irregularly as vagrants. Of the breeding species, the Ruby-throated Hummingbird *Archilochus colubris* is the most widespread, ranging from the Gulf of Mexico to Canada. It is a migrant, only 3.25 in. (8 cm.) long, and winters from Mexico to Costa Rica. By comparison, Mexico has at least 48 species; Costa Rica over 50; Panama 55, Venezuela 97, and Colombia, an amazing 143 species. South of the Equator the numbers fall away, so that Argentina and Uruguay only list 28 between them.

The names always strike me as so evocative: brilliants, comets, coronets, emeralds, firecrowns, hillstars, Incas, lancebills, metaltails, sabrewings, sapphires, starthroats, sunbeams, topaz, trainbearers, violetears, woodnymphs, and woodstars. The name 'Clay-coloured Sparrow' *Spizella pallida*, does not stimulate my imagination as much as the thought of an 'Amethyst-throated Sunangel' *Heliangelus amethysticollis*!

Hummingbirds do not sing well, the males relying on a display flight that reveals their dazzling colours to defend

their territory, which is often more than a breeding territory. They use energy at such a high rate, that flowering plants within the territory are vital for the bird's survival. They must feed every 10 minutes or more frequently in the case of the smaller species; the Little Hermit *Phaethornis longuemareus* must feed every 3 – 5 minutes. Many plants have evolved just to meet the needs of the hummingbirds; high in the Andes over half the flowering species are dependent on the hummingbirds to pollinate them. Some species have evolved so that only one species of hummingbird can drink its life-giving nectar. The plants are canny, for only a limited quantity is available and thus forces the bird to visit another plant for its next meal. Plants have found that hummingbirds are more

reliable as pollinators than insects, for being warm-blooded, the birds start earlier in the mornings; they can also feed during rain. In the higher altitudes the hummingbirds become torpid when roosting, reducing their heart rate from 1200 beats per minute when flying, to a mere 36 beats per minute while sleeping. In the United States hummingbirds regularly come to special feeders provided by many people in their gardens. Hummingbirds are also insectivorous, mainly flies and spiders. Although important to nestlings, this is of secondary significance to the adults.

Female hummingbirds construct the nest, which, depending on the genus, is either a neat cup made from fluffy vegetation, moss and cobwebs, built on a twig or other

Top: a female Long-tailed Hermit feeds at and pollinates a passion flower in Costa Rica. Above: a female Rufous Hummingbird in Mexico feeding on Salvia flowers.

vegetation, or a hanging nest, fastened to the underside of a leaf or to the wall of a cave. The male plays no part in the incubation of the eggs, or the rearing of the youngsters. Two eggs are usually laid and incubated for 14 – 19 days. Fledging takes place from 18 – 28 days depending on the species.

MOUSEBIRDS
Order: *Coliiformes*
Family: *Coliidae*
two genera contain six species

Mousebirds are the only Order of birds that is endemic to Africa, where the six species inhabit woodland, scrub, and have moved into such cultivated areas as gardens and orchards. Characterised by a soft mouse-brown plumage and often displaying a crest at the back of the head, Mousebirds have a long tail that accounts for two-thirds of their total length of 12 – 14 in. (30 – 36 cm.). Mousebirds, or Colies as they are sometimes called, are very agile when gathering food, and to help in this have four forward-pointing toes, the outer of which can be reversed as required. A stout conical bill is used for eating and tearing the fruit and leaves that make up most of the diet.

They are social birds, often to be found in parties of up to 10–15, which probably include sub-adult birds from previous broods. In flight they travel fast and direct on short wings with a rapid flight that is interspersed with short glides. In southern Africa the Red-faced Mousebird *Urocolius indicus* has been clocked flying at 43 mph. (70 km/h)! Usually all members of a group follow one another from bush to bush, often disappearing right into the middle where they may be found preening one another. Roosting in cold weather they slow their metabolic rate by as much as 90% and huddle up against each other for warmth.

Mousebirds are sedentary and wander locally in search of food, although in South Africa the Red-faced Mousebird moves from inland Natal to the coast during the austral winter. This species ranges widely in southern Africa and north to south-eastern Tanzania. Farther north, from East to West Africa, it is replaced by the Blue-naped Mousebird *U. macrourus*. The two are closely related, both having bare red skin around the base of bill and the eye, but the latter also has a patch of pale blue feathers at the back of the head. One of the most plentiful mousebirds within its range from East to southern Africa is the Speckled Mousebird *Colius striatus*.

Anyone who has visited the Ark, a lodge in Kenya's Aberdare Mountains, will have noticed these as being one of the commonest birds at the bird table along the board walk, where they jostle for fruit and other scraps. The three remaining species are restricted in their distribution. The White-backed *C. colius* occurs in South Africa and Namibia, whilst in a small part of western Angola to the north lives the Red-backed Mousebird *C. castanotus*. Farther north and east in parts of north-eastern Tanzania, Kenya and Somalia lives the beautiful White-headed Mousebird *C. leucocephalus*. This species has a whitish head and delicate dark brown barring on the sides of neck, chin and throat.

Both birds from a pair of mousebirds build the nest of twigs and vegetation, lined with softer material, with one often suppling the other with material. One to seven eggs are laid, depending on the species, and incubation is usually shared by the pair, sometimes aided by a 'helper'. The larger clutches are the result of two females laying in the same nest, a behaviour pattern recalling some of the families of Australian passerines. Incubation lasts for 11 – 15 days, according to the species, and fledging takes place some 20 days later.

Top: a male Resplendent Quetzal, the National Bird of Guatemala, has problems accommodating its long tail in the confined space of its nest hole in the Monteverde Cloud Forests of Costa Rica. The Speckled Mousebird (above left) and the Blue-naped Mousebird (above) are members of an order of fruit-eating birds found only in Africa.

TROGONS

Order: *Trogoniformes*
Family: *Trogonidae*
eight genera contain 39 species

Trogons are some of the most beautiful birds in the World, especially those species found in the Americas, where the males sport wonderful lustrous plumages. The Americas account for more than half of the 39 species, only three reside in Africa and the remaining 11 occur in Asia.

Trogons are arboreal birds of open woodland, clearings and humid forests, from lowland to montane forests as high as 11,800 ft. (3,600 m.), where the Masked Trogon *Trogon personatus* can be found in the western Andes. In the eastern Himalayas, Ward's Trogon *Harpactes wardi*, reaches 9,800 ft. (3,000 m.). All trogons feed by catching insects in flight, or by plucking fruit or caterpillars from branches and leaves whilst on the wing. Trogons can be notoriously difficult to see, often sitting motionless amongst the branches of tall forest trees for long periods.

Although the family comprises eight genera, they fall into two groups; the Quetzals *Pharomachrus* are five species belonging to a single genus and the Trogons, whose 34 species are divided between the remaining seven genera. Perhaps most beautiful of all is the male Resplendent Quetzal *P. moncinno* which occurs from southern Mexico to western Panama. He has a red lower-breast and belly, whilst the remainder of the body is a metallic green that glistens and shimmers as it catches the light. The bird's crowning glory is not on the head, but rather the elongated central feathers of the upper tail-coverts that can more than triple the bird's body length of 15 in. (38 cm.). One of the most wonderful sights must surely be a Resplendent Quetzal with a full tail. The species is afforded protection in many parts of its range, but unfortunately the demand for captive specimens and plumes is such that any measures are ineffective in remote areas, and in Guatemala, where it has been declared the National Bird, the publicity has only served to increase the demand. It is also declining as a result of deforestation throughout much of its range. The Resplendent Quetzal is a bird of legend and was held sacred by the Aztecs and Mayas, whose folklore explains that the red breast comes from the blood of Mayan Indians slaughtered in battle by the Spanish Conquistadores. Unlike the other trogons, the Resplendent Quetzal performs a display flight above its forest home, and perhaps as a result of this the Aztecs and the Mayan civilizations worshipped the bird as the God of the Air. The plumes were used on ceremonial garments and could only be worn by the nobility. Unlike the murderous present day plumage hunters, the Indians simply cut the tails from the birds, who would live to grow another. The other Quetzals are similar, but lack the superb tail.

The remaining species are all true trogons and apart from considerable colour differences, one from Central America looks very similar to one from south-east Asia. They are all sturdy birds with longish tails, ranging in size from the Black-throated Trogon, *Trogon rufus* 9 in. (23 cm.) long, of Honduras and areas south to north-eastern Argentina, to Ward's Trogon, 16 in. (40 cm.) long, found from the eastern Himalayas to north-eastern Vietnam.

Twenty-five members of the family range from the southern United States to northern Argentina; however the greatest concentration of species is to be found in an area encompassing Costa Rica, Panama and Colombia. Here, 20 species occur compared with only three species found in Africa. Males of all the American and African species have iridescent plumages; most have green backs, heads and upper-breasts with scarlet lower breasts and bellies. In some species the green and red are separated by a pale pectoral band. In some the red is replaced by orange or yellow and the head colour may be black or blue depending on the species. The only exceptions to this format are the Cuban *Priotelus temnurus* and the Hispaniolan *Temnotrogon roseigaster* Trogons; they are the only members of their respective genera. They are endemic to those islands; the Cuban species has a white throat and upper-breast and the Hispaniolan bird is grey in those parts. Some of the mainland species are often hard to separate, especially the females, and sometimes a good view of the under-tail pattern is necessary to clinch the identification. On the whole, females

are duller birds, where the green of the male is replaced by brown or slate. In Asia trogons range from India to China and south to Indonesia and the Philippines. They belong to a single genus *Harpactes*, and lack the glossy plumage of all other species, being mainly red, pink and brown, some having black heads.

Trogons nest in a hole in a tree or rotting stump; some species use old woodpecker sites and some may excavate a nest site in active tree nests of termites or wasps. Up to four eggs may be laid and the incubation, which lasts 17 – 19 days, is carried out by both parents. They also share the brooding and feeding of the chicks.

KINGFISHERS

Order: *Coraciiformes*
Family: *Alecdinidae*
14 genera contain 91 species

Birders in the United States suffer with their European counterparts from a shortage of kingfisher species. Only by visiting the lower Rio Grande Valley is there a chance of seeing anything other than the widespread Belted Kingfisher *Ceryle alcyon*. In Europe the only species is the Common

The Buff-breasted Paradise Kingfisher (below) occurs in north-eastern Australia, New Guinea and neighbouring islands.

147

Kingfisher *Alcedo atthis*, and one has to go to the Middle East or beyond to discover further species. The 91 species of kingfishers are divided between 14 genera; the greatest variety inhabit the warm temperate and tropical areas of Asia, and the Australasian region with its adjacent islands.

Many people expect all kingfishers to fish, but this is not so, for although most fish along the margins of many watery habitats, several species, including the Woodland Kingfisher *Halcyon senegalensis*, occur away from water where they feed on insects. Woodland Kingfishers sit on perches like the aquatic members of the family, but drop to the ground to catch their prey. It is an African species, and one of a number that migrate.

Kingfishers are chunky birds that appear somewhat neckless, with large heads and stout bills. They range in length from the Dwarf Kingfisher *Myioceyx lecontei*, only 4 in. (10 cm.) long from Equatorial Africa, to the Laughing Kookaburra *Dacelo novaeguineae* an 18 in. (46 cm.) long species from Australia. Most species show areas of turquoise or ultramarine in the plumage, but not all. Three Central and South American species are among those that lack the typical Kingfisher colours; they are green, chestnut and white. The widespread Lesser Pied Kingfisher *Ceryle rudis* of Africa and Asia is as its name suggests, as is the female Banded Kingfisher *Lacedo pulchella*. This species from south-east Asia is one of the few members of the family that is sexually dimorphic. The female has brown upper-parts barred with black, and white underparts banded black across the chest. Some of the most beautiful are the paradise-kingfishers *Tanysiptera spp.*, mainly found on New Guinea and the neighbouring islands.

The White-tailed or Australian Paradise-Kingfisher *T. sylvia*, the only species that breeds in Australia is 1.75 in. (35 cm.) long, nearly two-thirds being tail. These kingfishers are readily identified by their two elongated central tail feathers that are blue or white, with white rackets.

The food of Kingfishers is primarily fish, although the larger species and dry country inhabitants also eat reptiles. For some, insects form an important part of the diet; others eat crustaceans including crabs and scorpions, whilst the kookaburras take larger prey that includes small birds and

One of the world's smallest kingfishers is the Pygmy Kingfisher (facing page), which occurs across tropical and equatorial Africa.

This page: a Common Kingfisher takes the plunge and explodes from the water with a small fish. Its nictitating membrane, the membrane that enables it to blink, is closed over the eye while the bird is below the water's surface.

snakes. Most species sit, watch and wait for prey, and others that occur along open areas of water, such as the Belted Kingfisher, hover. Kingfishers nest in holes, many excavating their own burrow in an earthen bank that may be as long as 5 ft. (1.5 m.) including the nesting chamber. Others nest in holes in trees, or in holes in termite nests on the ground or in trees. Temperate species lay 6 – 7 eggs and those in the tropics 3 – 4 eggs. Incubation and feeding of the young is shared by both adults, but the length of time taken for both incubation and fledging is unknown is many cases. Where known, incubation lasts 14 – 20 days, and fledging takes place 23 – 27 days later. Some young become independent within days of leaving home, and others stay with their parents for several months.

The Gray-headed Kingfisher (left) occurs from the Yemen to South Africa, feeding on lizards and insects.

TODIES

Order: *Coraciiformes*
Family: *Todidae*
the genus Todus contains of five species

Todies are a group of small colourful birds found only on some of the islands that make up the Greater Antilles in the West Indies. All five species look very similar and form a 'superspecies' as taxonomists call such groupings. They are stubby little birds only 4.25 ins. (10.8 cms.) long and much smaller than the Motmots *Motmotidae* of Central and South America, to which they are closely related.

Each species is iridescent emerald green with a ruby red throat, whitish under-parts, yellow under-tail coverts and pink flanks. They are woodland birds often to be found on the edge of clearings and along streams, where they wait on exposed branches for passing insects. They dash after flying insects, like a jewel, catching the prey and returning in flycatcher fashion.

Todies have evolved on the larger islands in the Antilles and only Hispaniola has more than one species – Narrow-billed *Todus angustirostris* and Broad-billed *T. subulatus* Todies. The former is a mountain bird in Haiti and in the Dominican Republic, where it also occurs at lower elevations alongside the Broad-billed Tody. The latter is more a bird of dry lowland habitats throughout Hispaniola and on Gonâve Island.

Hardly surprisingly, Cuban *T. multicolor*, Puerto Rican *T. mexicanus* and Jamaican *T. todus* Todies, are all endemic to their respective islands. The most studied species in the group is the Puerto Rican Tody, which has been extensively studied by A. K. Kepler.

The nest is in a chamber at the end of a tunnel, 30 ins. (80 cms.) deep and excavated by the adults in the side of a low earthen bank by a stream, track or the roots of a tree. 2 – 5 white eggs are laid and incubated by both parents for 21 – 22 days. The yolk of the egg is unusually large and the egg, in the case of the Puerto Rican Tody, amounts to 39% of the female's body weight! During incubation the adults can be described as being 'laid back', but all changes after the eggs hatch. Each chick can be fed up to 140 times a day, more frequently than any other species. The adults are busy catching insects all day, sometimes helped by nearby birds whose breeding attempt has failed. The chicks fledge after 19 – 20 days and about 6 weeks later are indistinguishable from the adults.

MOTMOTS

Order: *Coraciiformes*
Family: *Momotidae*
the six genera contain nine species

In the forests and jungles of Central and South America live the Motmots, a family of colourful birds endemic to that part of the World. They are related to the kingfishers *Alecdinidae* and to the todies *Todidae*, although more closely to the latter, a family endemic to the Caribbean.

The family is non-migratory and centred on Central America and Mexico, where four species not found south of

Costa Rica occur. The most widely distributed species is the Blue-crowned Motmot *Momotus momota*; it ranges south from Mexico and Trinidad and Tobago, south to Argentina and Paraguay.

Motmots are beautiful birds, resembling the Old World bee-eaters *Meropidae* in appearance, but with a more subtle green, blue, brown and black plumage. Some species have a black patch on the chest, some black ear coverts and some racket shaped tails. The tail is interesting, because it occurs as a result of a weakness in the vanes of two long feathers. There is some uncertainty over the formation of the rackets at the end of about an inch (2.5 cm.) of bare feather shaft. The vanes on this part of the feather are weak and loose and some observers have seen Motmots removing them whilst preening. Other claim that they break off naturally. No doubt it is a combination of both, for the rackets used in display are an essential part of the bird's equipment. The only species not to have the rackets are the Blue-throated *Aspatha gularis* and the Tody Motmot *Hylomanes momotula*. The latter is the smallest

In many African and Asiatic countries the Pied Kingfisher (above) is a bird common beside waterways and in wetlands.

species, being 7 in. (18 cm.) long compared with the largest, the Rufous Motmot *Baryhthengus ruficapillus* 18 in. (46 cm.) long.

Motmots are mainly insectivorous birds found in forests and woodland from sea level to 10,000 ft. (3,100 m.). They perch in a prominent position, keenly watching for any movement that suggests food and dash out and back like a flycatcher. The diet of Motmots ranges from spiders and butterflies to lizards and small snakes; these larger items are crushed between the strong mandibles and beaten into submission before being eaten.

Motmots excavate burrows in the earthen banks of streams and rivers, or beside a track or road. The Blue-crowned Motmot occasionally nests in the entrance wall of a mammal's burrow, a habit shared with the Little Bee-eater *Merops pusillus* of Africa which sometimes chooses to dig its nesting hole in the large entrance to a burrow dug by an Antbear or Aardvark *Orycteropus afer*. In those species of Motmot studied in detail, it has been discovered that most birds share in the excavation of the tunnel, digging with their bills and kicking the debris out with their feet. In the case of the Turquoise-browed Motmot *Eumomota superciliosa*, it appears

stages of fledging the adults feed the chicks an increasing amount of fruit. No nest sanitation takes place, so by the time the chicks fledge the tunnel and nesting chamber must be revolting. No wonder they excavate a new burrow!

BEE-EATERS
Order: *Coraciiformes*
Family: *Meropidae*
three genera contain 24 species

The Bee-eaters *Meropidae* are an Old World and Australasian family belonging to the Order *Coraciiformes*, to which the New World family of motmots *Motmotidae* belongs. Although separated by an ocean in either direction, the two families look similar, but most bee-eaters are more aerial than motmots and some are long distance migrants.

The 24 species are divided between three genera. They are beautiful birds found in warm temperate and tropical regions,

that the female does most of the digging, whilst the male feeds her the occasional insect. Whether this is a token of his appreciation or merely to prevent her from stopping for lunch has yet to be determined! The tunnel can be as long as 14 ft. (4.3 m.), although most are shorter and often have a kink or curve along the passage to the nesting chamber. Blue-throated Motmots start to excavate their next nesting burrow soon after the young birds leave the last one and the Blue-crowned begin work in the Fall. Both species use the tunnels as a place to roost during the colder nights of winter, and after breeding continue to do so until completion of the next tunnel. Lowland species do not roost in their burrows.

Usually two eggs, but occasionally up to four, are laid in the nesting chamber at the end of the tunnel. Incubation is carried out by both birds, each sitting for periods of several hours at a time. The incubation period lasts from 15 – 22 days depending on the species and the youngsters stay in the nest for between 24 and 38 days, again depending on the species. The nestlings are fed mainly insects, but during the latter

ranging between 6 – 13 in. (15 – 33 cm.) in length. Blues, greens, reds and yellows in a host of shades predominate in the colours of bee-eaters, birds that can never be described as dull, either in colour or behaviour. If I had a bird 'Top Ten', bee-eaters would be near the top.

The largest number of species, 21 in total, belongs to the genus *Merops*, and are distributed throughout the range of the family. Members of the two other genera are Asiatic species. The Blue-bearded Bee-eater *Nyctyornis athertoni*, 13 in. (33 cm.) long, is the largest bee-eater and occurs from India to south-east Asia.

On Sulawesi lives the Celebes Bee-eater *Meropogon forsteri*, the only member of its genus, and a bird restricted to the north-eastern part of the island. The central tail-feathers add over 2 in. (5 cm.) to the total length.

Twenty-one species belong to the genus *Merops* and of those 14 are endemic to Africa. Three more breed in Africa and Eurasia; Asia has three endemic species and Australia one. Most species are sedentary or only move comparatively

The Woodland Kingfisher (above) is an intra-African migrant. It feeds on insects, reptiles and amphibians, but rarely fish.

locally within continents. Two particularly long distance migrants are the European and Blue-cheeked Bee-eaters *M. apiaster* and *M. persicus*. Breeding in Europe and Asia, they winter as far south as Namibia and South Africa. European Bee-eaters have also bred regularly in Southern Africa since at least 1886.

They are often restless birds; ever watchful for a passing insect, they chase after it and either eat on the wing or return to their perch to deal with the item. Over 50% of the diet of the *Merops* bee-eaters are bees, wasps and similar stinging insects; from analysis of regurgitated pellets they appear to prefer worker bees rather than drones. They rub their prey against a perch, to force out the poison before eating it or flying to the nest. The Carmine Bee-eater *M. nubicus* manages to perform this feat on the wing. This species is noted for its habit of riding on the backs of antelopes, domestic livestock and Kori Bustards *Ardeotis kori*, which it uses as mobile flight-decks from which to pursue grasshoppers and other insects disturbed by the carrier, as it wanders through the grass. Along the waterways of the Okavango Delta in Botswana, Blue-cheeked Bee-eaters perch on the heads of Papyrus *Cyperus papyrus*, waiting for passing dragonflies, which are pursued and caught.

Bee-eaters nest in burrows that they excavate in sand or dry soil. Some species nest colonially, whilst others are solitary. The Little Bee-eater often excavates its nest-hole in the entrance-wall of a hole, dug in the soil by an Antbear or Aardvak *Orycteropus afer*. Other species nest in sand, or soil cliffs, and the Carmine Bee-eater, so often a cliff-nesting species, can be found breeding in colonies dug down into the Kalahari sand on islands in the Okavango. Most species breed before or at the onset of the rains, except for the Red-throated Bee-eater *Merops bullocki*, which excavates its burrow towards the end of the rains, while the soil is still damp, in anticipation of breeding some six months later.

The clutch size can be from 2 – 6 eggs, and duties during the 18 – 21 day incubation period are shared by the parents. The young take 27 – 32 days to fledge, and during that time the parents may be helped by the off-spring of their previous brood.

The White-fronted Bee-eater (left) is a colourful African species that feeds on insects and breeds colonially. The Little Bee-eater (facing page) is another exquisite African bird. It sometimes excavates its nest hole in the entrance of Antbear burrows.

ROLLERS
Order: *Coraciiformes*
Family: *Coraciidae*
two genera contain 11 species

The name 'Roller' comes from the rolling display flight of these birds, some of the most colourful birds in the Old World. They are split into two genera: the true Rollers *Coracias* and the Broad-billed Rollers *Eurystomus*.

The true Rollers occur from Europe and Africa across Asia to Sulawesi and inhabit open savannah and areas with scattered trees. They fall into two groups. The larger and more thick-set species are the Indian Roller *Coracias benghalensis*, that occurs from India to south-east Asia; the Rufous-crowned or Purple Roller *C. naevia* from Africa, north and south of the equatorial forests; and the Temminck's or Celebes Roller *C. temminckii* that only occurs on the island of Sulawesi, formerly known as Celebes, in Indonesia. To people from cooler climes, who may be unfamiliar with the family, they are the most Jay-like of the rollers and have square tails. In flight they display turquoise and ultramarine wings. It seems likely that the Rufous-crowned and Temminck's Rollers are descendants of the Indian Species. The remaining five species are slightly lighter in build and all have elongated outer tail feathers, although this is least developed in the European Roller *C. garrulous*. The European Roller is the most migratory species, for the whole of the population breeding in southern and eastern Europe, north Africa and western Asia withdraws to Africa south to Namibia and South Africa for the winter. With the exception of the Blue-bellied Roller *C. cyanogaster*, all in this group have turquoise bodies and chestnut backs, and bar the European species they are indigenous to Africa. The odd-ball of this group is the Blue-bellied Roller, found in savannah across Africa south of the Sahara, but most abundant in the western part of its range. Unlike its close relatives, the Blue-bellied Roller has a buff head and breast combined with deep blue under-parts, and the turquoise, such a feature of the others in this group is restricted to the wings. The most

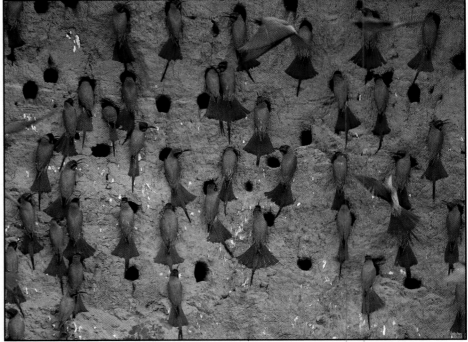

beautiful is the widely distributed Lilac-breasted Roller *C. caudata*, for it also has a lilac breast and the nape is an iridescent green. In some areas of savannah and bush, where there is an abundance of dead trees in which to nest, it seems a shame to reduce such a fabulous bird to 'just another LBR!' Like so many beautiful birds, the Lilac-breasted Roller, along with its congeners, spoils the effect by having a call that is nothing more than a harsh rattle.

Broad-billed rollers are longer winged than rollers and catch their insect prey in flight, often giving the appearance of a falcon-like bird as they dash in pursuit of their next meal. Their vocal abilities are no better than their relatives. The three species of broad-billed rollers are darker than the other species, being birds of forests and woodlands, where they frequent margins and clearings. Two species occur in Africa and are the African Broad-billed *E. glaucurus* and the Blue-throated Roller *E. gularis*, birds with very similar rich cinnamon upper-parts and lilac below. In flight both have blue wings and as expected the latter species has a blue throat. The African Broad-billed is a widespread intra-African migrant found over much of sub-Saharan Africa and Madagascar, and on occasions has turned up as a vagrant on the Seychelles in the Indian Ocean. The Blue-throated Roller is sedentary with a limited distribution in the equatorial rain forests. The Dollar-bird or Eastern Broad-billed Roller *E. orientalis* ranges from India to China and south through the East Indies to

Carmine Bee-eaters (above) form large colonies, often nesting in sand cliffs and riverbanks in Northern Cameroon.

northern and western Australia, reaching the Solomon Islands in the eastern Pacific. Populations in the higher latitudes migrate to warmer climates after the breeding season.

Rollers eat a wide variety of insects including many beetles, although in Africa ants and termites appear high on the menu. Sometimes items as large as frogs, lizards and small birds are taken by rollers, who drop to the ground from a prominent perch at the end of a branch or from a termite mound to catch their prey. Broad-billed rollers are aerial feeders, but on occasions they also drop on terrestrial prey from a perch.

Rollers nest in holes, often in a branch or trunk of a tree or in a wall or earthen cliff. They defend their territory vigourously, taking on all comers, from others of their kind to mighty eagles *Aquila sp.* The breeding biology of many hole-nesting species in general remains largely unknown and rollers are no exception. Both birds incubate the clutch of two to four eggs for about 19 days, with the young birds fledging some 20 or so days later.

GROUND ROLLERS
Order: *Coraciiformes*
Family: *Brachypteraciidae*
three genera contain five species

The Ground Rollers *Brachypteraciidae* are one of a number of unusual bird families that are endemic to the large island of Madagascar, lying in the Indian Ocean to the east of Africa. They are descendants of rollers *Coraciidae* from Africa, but not from the same colonisation from which the Courol or Cuckoo-roller *Leptosomus discolor* evolved.

As their name suggests Ground Rollers are terrestrial birds where they search for their food that largely consists of insects. Detailed stomach analysis of the Short-legged Ground Roller *Brachypteracias leptosomus* has revealed that snake, snail and chameleon also feature on the menu.

Ground Rollers have short wings and longer legs than the true Rollers. Four of the five species belong to two genera that occur in the dense forests of eastern Madagascar and its central plateau. These are poorly known birds, for not only do they inhabit thick dark forests, a notoriously difficult habitat in which to study birds at the best of times, but they are only active at dawn and dusk. There are even suggestions that some might be nocturnal! The forest dwelling species are the Short-legged and Scaly Ground Rollers *B. squamigera*, and

the more slightly built Blue-headed Ground Roller *Atelornis pittoides* and Crossley's Ground Roller *A. crossleyi*. They are the most colourful species reflecting their ancestral relationship; hardly surprisingly, little is known about their breeding biology. Natives who have found the nest of the Short-legged Ground Roller describe it as being in a hole in the trunk of a tree a few feet above the ground. The remaining species, the Long-tailed Ground Roller *Uratelornis chimaera*, which including the tail is 18 in. (45 cm.) long, occurs amongst scrub in the drier south-western part of Madagascar. Because it occurs in a more open habitat more is known about the Long-tailed Ground Roller than its forest relatives. It has cryptically coloured upper-parts, pale blue wing coverts and white under-parts relieved by a black breast band joined to a dark malar stripe. When disturbed it runs for cover beneath a bush, where it stands with long tail erect watching for danger. During the breeding season, both the male and female excavate the four foot (1.2 m.) long tunnel that leads to the nesting chamber where the female will lay 3 – 4 eggs. Only the female incubates the eggs, but the male is in attendance bringing her food throughout the period.

Sadly, four of the five species described above are endangered. The Long-tailed, because of its very restricted range in a part of the island where there is no habitat protection, and the Short-legged, Scaly and Crossley's Ground Rollers are all threatened because of the continuing destruction of the native forests in which they live.

COUROL
Order: *Leptosomatidae*
Family: *Leptosomus*
the genus *Leptosomus* contains a single
species *Leptosomus discolor*

The Courol or Cuckoo-roller *Leptosomus discolor* is another of the unusual birds to have evolved in the isolation of the Malagasy region, where three distinct subspecies or races occur. The nominate form is found on Madagascar and on islands in the nearby Comoro group, which lie to the north-east in the Indian Ocean. On these islands two endemic races occur on Grand Comoro and Anjouan Is. respectively.

The Courol resembles rollers *Coraciidae* of Eurasia and Africa with similar proportions, although it is a larger bird,

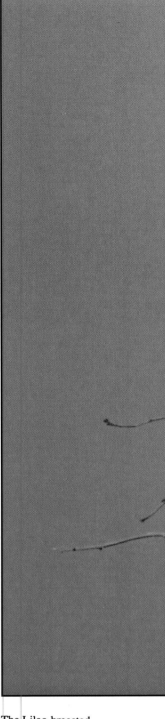

The Lilac-breasted Roller (above far left) of sub-Saharan Africa is one of the most colourful members of its family. Above left: young Hoopoes in the nesting chamber beg for food as an adult (right) returns to the nest.

It is a solitary bird, found either singly or in pairs. The nest is located in a natural cavity in a tree with little or no nest material. Incubation of the two eggs is entirely by the female, who is fed by the male until after the young have hatched. On leaving the nest the juveniles resemble the duller female and it is only later that any males reared will assume the colours of their father. The male is blue-grey on the head and underparts with purple and green iridescence to the black wings, back and tail.

Above: a European Roller in East Africa – a winter visitor to the savannahs from the temperate Palearctic.

HOOPOES
Order: *Coraciiformes*
Family: *Upupidae*
the genus *Upupa* contains a single
species *Upupa epops*

being more the size of an American Crow *Corvus brachyrhynchos*. Unlike the true rollers, it does not catch insects in flight or swoop down on prey from a vantage point, but searches amongst the leaves of trees and bushes for chameleons *Chamaeleonidae*, which together with large insects constitute its main food supply.

The Courol is a mainly forest bird, although on Madagascar it is also found in drier areas. Such birds are always vulnerable to habitat destruction and with a steady increase in tourism over recent years and proposed for the future on the Comoros, populations might be at risk.

The Hoopoe *Upupa epops* occurs widely in temperate and tropical areas from western Europe to China, south to India and Borneo, and throughout most of Africa, except for the Sahara and the dense forests of equatorial Africa. Birds from the Western Palearctic migrate south into Africa as far Tanzania and northern Malawi in the Fall, where they can be found with the darker African race. In Spring, migrants from the Mediterranean often overshoot and arrive in north-western,

Europe including southern England, where they occasionally stay to breed.

Hoopoes are striking birds and in the British Isles vagrants are most frequently seen by non-birders, who on a morning in May might awake to find a strange bird feeding on their neatly mown lawn or perhaps searching for earthworms on the greens of the golf course. To holiday makers to Mediterranean destinations, Hoopoes flop across the roads looking so distinctive that they draw the attention of even avid sun-worshippers. Hoopoes are about 11 in. (28 cm.), the same length as a Blue Jay *Cyanocitta cristata*, but slimmer. Their body plumage is cinnamon, duller in juveniles; they have long curved bills and quite short legs. In flight the bird leaves an indelible impression, for the broad blunt wings are, like the tail, barred black and white. The flight is slow, floppy and slightly undulating, making it hard to imagine that this bird can migrate from Europe to central Africa. On landing, a crest, usually kept flat, is erected and like the body plumage is orange. These feathers have black tips and the general effect is of a Red Indian head dress that has slipped sideways! The crest is also displayed when the bird is excited.

Hoopoes find most of their food by searching on the ground for insects, especially larvae and pupae, discovered by probing the curved bill into the soil. The diet also includes such invertebrates as centipedes and scorpions, as well as frogs and lizards. Hoopoes also find food by turning over animal dung and from amongst decaying garbage and timber. Hoopoes are hole-nesting birds, usually choosing holes in trees, occasionally in old walls, crevices in rock faces or even disused termite mounds in Africa. The nesting chamber, cleaned out by the male, is not always lined. The female lays between four and eight eggs, which she incubates for about 16 days. During this time the male feeds her regularly, and only occasionally she leaves the nest. Both parents feed the young during the 28 – 32 day fledging period and continue to do so for sometime after fledging. Nest sanitation is minimal.

WOOD-HOOPOES
Order: *Coraciiformes*
Family: *Phoeniculidae*
the genus *Phoeniculus* contains
nine species

Wood-Hoopoes *Phoeniculus* belong to a family of slim, long-tailed birds, endemic to sub-Saharan Africa. They are black birds with rounded wings and graduated tails. Some species have white bars or spots on wings and tails, on others they are absent or present on just the wings. Some species have green, purple, violet or blue iridescent feathers in their plumage, and as the name suggests, the White-headed Wood-Hoopoe *P. bollei*, a forest dwelling species occurring from Ghana to Kenya, has a white head; but so do some Forest Wood-Hoopoes *P. castaneiceps*. The head of the latter species also can be buff or brown. The seven species of wood-hoopoes have curved red or black bills, longer and less severely hooked than the two scimitarbills.

The most widespread species is the Red-billed or Green Wood-Hoopoe *P. purpureus*, ranging from Senegal in the west across to Ethiopia and south to South Africa. It is a common species found in a wide variety of wooded habitats except for the tropical forests of equatorial Africa. It is the largest species, 16 in. (41 cm.) long and is very closely related to the Black-billed Wood-Hoopoe *P. somaliensis*, which replaces it in north-east Africa. Some authorities consider the two to be conspecific. Another pair that suffers the same problem are the Violet Wood-Hoopoe *P. damarensis* and Grant's Wood-Hoopoe *P. granti*. The former inhabits a small area of Angola and Namibia, whilst half a continent away, Grant's Wood-Hoopoe occurs in a comparatively small area

Left: an Eastern Yellow-billed Hornbill – a familiar bird in East Africa – found at Samburu, Kenya.

156

of Kenya. Smallest of the wood-hoopoes is the Black or Lesser *P. aterrimus*, 9 in. (23 cm.) long, which occurs from West Africa to Ethiopia, south to Zaïre and Angola. Related to the scimitarbills, it is distinguished from them by a straighter bill. The Abyssinian Scimitarbill *P. minor* is the same size and restricted to Ethiopia, Kenya and northern Tanzania. The Scimitarbill, *P. cyanomelas* 11 in. (28 cm.) long, is the more widely distributed of the two species, ranging from Somalia to South Africa.

The larger wood-hoopoes are often found in small flocks, foraging for insects and invertebrates on the trunks and branches of trees, where agility and long curved bills are well adapted to finding prey items, which may sometimes include lizards, in cracks and crannies in the timber and bark. They are often noisy birds and when one flies on to the next tree the remainder are not far behind. The Black Wood-Hoopoe and the scimitarbills tend to be more solitary birds, found in pairs or smaller family parties.

All species nest in trees, either in a natural hole or perhaps a disused woodpecker nesting hole. The female Red-billed Wood-Hoopoe incubates the eggs and is fed in or near the nest by the non-breeding members of the flock. Later, after 18 days when the young have hatched, the male and helpers bring food to the female who distributes it to the nestlings. After fledging, the youngsters stay with the group from between one and five years before they leave to breed.

HORNBILLS
Order: *Coraciiformes*
Family: *Bucerotidae*
12 genera contain 47 species

Anyone visiting Africa for the first time is invariably amused by the appearance and antics of hornbills, a family of birds that occurs over much of sub-Saharan Africa and from western India to south-east Asia and Indonesia. At one of the camps we use on the Ornitholidays' tours to Botswana, Lloyd's Camp at Savuti, both the Southern Yellow-billed *Tockus leucomelas*, 23 in. (58 cm.) long, and the smaller Red-billed Hornbills *T. erythrorhynchus*, 19 in. (48 cm.) long, frequently come around the dining area after biscuits and other tit-bits. They are quite endearing as they sit on the back of a chair, fluttering their long eyelashes.

Hornbills come in a variety of sizes, from the Black Dwarf Hornbill *T. hartlaubi*, 14 in. (36 cm.) long, of equatorial Africa to the massive Great Pied Hornbill *Buceros bicornis*, 51 in. (130 cm.) long, that occurs from western India to south-east Asia. With the exception of the Southern Ground Hornbill *Bucorvus leadbeateri*, 45 in. (115 cm.) and the very similar Abyssinian Ground Hornbill *B. abyssinicus*, hornbills in flight show about as much projecting in front of the wings as behind. They have long tails and necks, and most species have decurved bills; several have red or blue bare skin around the face and throat. The plumage is usually a combination of black or brown and white; the ground hornbills are entirely black except for white primaries that are only revealed in display or in flight. Some species have a casque on top of the bill, from which the name 'hornbill' is derived. This protuberance is particularly prominent on the larger species and in most cases is hollow, covered by a layer of keratin over a framework of boney supports, and with the notable exception of the Helmeted Hornbill *Rhinoplax vigil* adds little to the overall weight of the bill. There is considerable variation in shape and size, and some almost double the depth and bulk of the bill. The development and colouration is generally bigger and brighter in male birds and only the larger forest species have particularly large casques. That of the Rhinoceros Hornbill *Buceros rhinoceros*, found in south-east Asia, Java and Borneo, has an upturned tip giving it a characteristic shape. The Helmeted Hornbill occurs in Malaya, Sumatra and Borneo, where it has long been prized by the native tribesmen for its horny casque, for unlike the other species, its casque is solid keratin and can be carved like ivory. In former times it was an important commodity in trade between Brunei and China, where during the Ming Dynasty, 14th-17th. century, important government officials wore buckles on their belts made from the casques of the Helmeted Hornbill. It is still

used by the locals for ornamental ear-rings and belt fastenings. Most hornbills, and especially the larger species are forest birds and it is in areas where hunting is still permitted or where indigenous forests are being cleared that the hornbills are under greatest threat. Other species occur along forest margins and riverine forest, whilst many of the smaller *Tockus* species from Africa, and the two Ground Hornbills, inhabit dry bush and savannah. Some tribes wear the stuffed heads of Ground Hornbills as camouflage when in pursuit of game.

Hornbills are omnivorous, eating items as varied as fruit, seeds, reptiles and small mammals as well as a large number of insects. Some of the savannah species pick over elephant droppings which contain large amounts of undigested material. The Ground Hornbills, walking sedately over the plains of Africa are almost entirely carnivorous; they are large and strong enough to deal effectively with poisonous snakes and they are one of the few species that can extract tortoises from their shells without too much difficulty. In addition they devour the chicks of ground nesting birds, and unearth frogs and toads that had hoped to be dormant until the next rains released them from their tombs! At Savuti the hornbills in camp are especially fond of muesli and cheese.

The nesting activity of all but the ground hornbills is particularly fascinating. The nest site is in a cavity in a tree or occasionally in a rock-face. The entrance is partially sealed with mud by the female, who enters and takes lining in the form of bark and leaves from the male, before sealing herself inside, with just a slit for an entrance. Egg laying does not commence until the nest is secure, and during incubation she is fed by the male. During this time some species complete a

An Asiatic species, the Rhinoceros Hornbill (above) occurs from Malaysia to Borneo and has one of the most elaborate casques of any species.

157

moult and can be flightless for a while. After hatching and when the chicks are about half-grown the females of some species break out from the confines of their prisons to help their mates supply the ever-growing brood. After their mother's departure it is the natural reaction of the nestlings to re-seal the entrance with their own droppings, the only chance they will have to practice before they breed themselves in years to come. To protect the feathers from harm they remain within the quills until quite late in the young bird's development. Unlike their relatives, the hoopoes *Upupidae* and *Phoeniculidae*, hornbills practice nest sanitation.

The clutch varies from 1 – 7 eggs, depending on the species and incubation ranges from 25 days with the smaller species and up to 40 days for the ground hornbills. The length of fledging period varies by about the same proportions, 45 to 86 days. Depending on the species the young hornbills become sexually mature in 1 – 6 years.

JACAMARS

Order: *Piciformes*

Family: *Galbulidae*

five genera contain 17 species

In the tropical forests of Central and South America lives a family of small, colourful and active birds called Jacamars; systematically they are close to the puffbirds *Bucconidae*, in the Order of *Piciformes* that includes woodpeckers *Picidae*. Recent studies suggest that they may be more closely related to kingfishers *Alcedinidae*, in fact the two species belonging to the genus *Galbulidae* look more kingfisher-like than other members of the family.

The 17 species are divided into 5 genera, and typically jacamars are slim birds with longish tails and dagger-like bills. Most have iridescent green upper-parts and rufous under-parts, some having a white throat patch; some representatives are duller with brown heads, a colour that may extend to the chest, although the belly may be white. The major exceptions to these colours are the chestnut plumaged Chestnut *Galbalcyrhynchus purusianus* and White-eared Jacamars *G. leucotis*, 8 in. (20 cm.). These mainly chestnut coloured birds have short tails and stronger bills that give a chunky appearance which emphasises the resemblance to kingfishers. The feet of Jacamars are similar to those of woodpeckers, with two toes facing forwards and two backwards; the obvious exception is the Three-toed Jacamar *Jacamaralcyon tridactyla*.

The largest and bulkiest species is the Great Jacamar *Jacamerops aurea*, 12 in. (30 cm.) long, a green and red species with a heavier bill than most, that occurs from southern Mexico to western Brazil. The Paradise Jacamar *Galbula dea* from Venezuela to Brazil, is the same length, but is slimmer and has long elegant tail feathers. The smallest species are the duller birds belonging to the genus *Brachygalba*; they include the widespread Black-billed Jacamar *B. lugubris*, 7 in. (18 cm.) long, that ranges from Colombia to Venezuela and south to Bolivia and Brazil.

Jacamars are insectivorous birds that catch their prey in flight. They perch on an exposed branch, constantly looking this way and that for a suitable target, and dash out to catch the insect in their long bills. They often catch the large forest butterflies, and on returning to the perch proceed to remove the wings by beating them against the branch.

Jacamars nest in burrows excavated by both birds in an earthen bank by a track, stream or on a steep hillside. They dig with their bills and remove the soil by kicking it from the burrow with their feet. The burrow can be as deep as 30 in. (76 cm.), depending on the species, terminating in an enlarged nesting chamber, sometimes used for several years. Some species including the Paradise Jacamar 12 in. (30 cm.) long, excavate their nests in that of arboreal termites. Information about the breeding biology for a number of species is either non-existent or at best poorly known, although it can be expected to be similar for most species. The widespread Rufous-tailed Jacamar *G. ruficauda*, 9 in. (23 cm.) long, occurs from southern Mexico to northern Argentina and lays two to four eggs. During the day incubation is shared by both parents, but the female alone works the night-shift. No nest

sanitation takes place, even the incubating birds regurgitate indigestible insect remains in the nesting chamber. The incubation period lasts 20 – 23 days and when hatched the chicks are covered with down, unlike the naked chicks of puffbirds and other members of the Order. During the fledging period both parents feed the chicks for 19 days or more, depending on weather and the availability of food. Some species return to the burrow to roost after fledging.

As much as any other South American forest species, the greatest threat to jacamars is habitat destruction. Perhaps most at risk is the Three-toed Jacamar with a distribution restricted to south-eastern Brazil.

PUFFBIRDS

Order: *Piciformes*

Family: *Bucconidae*

nine genera contain 32 species

Puffbirds are another family of birds found exclusively in Central and South America and related to the woodpeckers. They are birds of tropical lowland forest and woodland. Puffbirds are thick-set birds with large heads, often to be found sitting for long periods upright on a prominent perch waiting for insects.

The 32 species are divided into 10 genera, but to make life interesting only some are called Puffbirds. These belong to five genera: *Bucco* (8), *Nystalus* (4), *Hypnelus* (1) and *Malacoptila* (7). The others are a single Monklet, the Lanceolated Monklet *Micromonacha lanceolata*; five species of Nunlet all belong to *Nonnula*; the Nunbirds are *Hapaloptila* (1) and *Monasa* (4) and last, but not least, the Swallow-wing *Chelidoptera tenebrosa*.

Puffbirds have a soft plumage that often conceals their short legs while perched. The bill is stout with a hooked tip, although the bill of the Nunlets is slender by comparison. Members of the family vary in size and colour, but are not a brightly-coloured group. The *Bucco* puffbirds now include the black and white species that formed the genus *Notharchus*, one of which is the White-necked Puffbird *B. macrorhynchus*, 10 in. (25 cm.) long. This is the most widespread species and ranges from southern Mexico to northern Argentina. A number of puffbirds are a mixture of brown, black, grey and white, and those belonging to the genus *Malacoptila* have a conspicuous tuft of short white feathers at the base of the bill. The Nunbirds *Monasa*, mainly black, include the largest member of the family, the Black-fronted Nunbird *M. nigrifrons*, 11 in. (28 cm.) long, that occurs in Colombia, Bolivia and Brazil. The four members of this genus are black, with white wing patches, and three are red-billed, the exception being the smaller Yellow-billed Nunbird *M. flavirostris*, 9.5 in. (24 cm.) long, from Brazil, Colombia and Peru. The Nunlets and the White-faced Nunbird *Hapaloptila castanea* are a subtle blend of chestnut browns, cream and grey.

With the exception of the gregarious nunbirds, most puffbirds occur singly or in pairs. They sit for long spells on a prominent perch waiting for food. Their excellent eyesight enables them to see distant prey thus reducing the amount of effort required to find food, unfortunately giving the impression that puffbirds are lethargic in the process! Their diet consists mainly of insects, but in addition some also eat berries, frogs, lizards and spiders. Some species follow the armies of ants and troops of monkeys to feed on the creatures that they disturb as they pass through an area. Most food items, stationary or otherwise, are taken while the bird is in flight.

With several species the breeding biology is very poorly known, but when faced with a bird that nests in a termite nest high in a forest tree how does one discover how many eggs are laid, or how long is the incubation period and with species where the sexes are similar, who is doing the work? It is not easy, so in such cases it is often assumed that the behaviour patterns of the more familiar members are duplicated by most of the other species. Puffbirds either excavate their own holes in the ground, in nests of arboreal termites or they use a hole that might have belonged to a woodpecker or small mammal. Others have been recorded using the old nests of ovenbirds *Furnariidae*. The burrow of the White-whiskered Puffbird *Malacoptila panamensis* is dug into an earthen hillside and may be up to 20 in. (50 cm.) long. Twigs and other vegetable material placed around the entrance attempt to disguise its existence. The Black Nunbird takes this a stage further by excavating a sloping burrow in level ground and constructing a pile of twigs over the entrance. Through this, another tunnel leads to the outside world. Most species appear to lay two or three eggs in a nesting chamber at the end of the tunnel; incubation is by both parents, and when hatched the young are naked, unlike the down-covered jacamar *Galbulidae* chicks. During fledging period, which lasts for 20 – 21 days in most species, the chicks receive a diet that consists of beaten insects, with variety in the form of spiders and small lizards. No nest sanitation takes place and my wife points out that as it is the male White-whiskered Puffbird that broods the chicks, this is only to be expected! The rearing of the young White-fronted Nunbird differs from the other well-known species considerably. The fledging period lasts up to 30 days and during this time the parents are assisted by two or three helpers. On leaving the nest the youngsters are to be found high in the trees, where they collect food in flight from the bills of perched adults. This must be thorough training for the day when they become independent and skillfully take stationary food whilst they are on the wing.

BARBETS
Order: *Piciformes*
Family: *Capitonidae*
13 genera contain 81 species

The Barbets *Capitonidae* comprise a family of 81 species divided into 13 genera, and are related to the familiar woodpeckers *Picidae*. They inhabit much of sub-Saharan Africa, southern and south-eastern Asia, the East Indies and north-western South America, occurring in a variety of tropical woodlands.

They are stout birds, ranging in length from 3.5 – 13 in. (9 – 33 cm.), and may appear heavy-headed and neckless with strong bills. They vary considerably in colour; a handful of species are plain, but most are well-marked. The African species are a combination of patterns and colours, usually black, white, red and yellow. Over half the family occurs in Africa, but in comparison only 12 species occur in South America. Some have similar plumages to their African relatives, whilst others, including the Red-headed Barbet *Eubucco bourcierii* and other members of its genus, are predominantly green, resembling many Asiatic barbets.

The diet of barbets is mainly fruit and berries, supplemented during the breeding season by insects, in many species. Some larger members of the family occasionally take lizards, rodents and young birds.

Barbets nest in holes, excavated by most species in a tree trunk or along the underside of a rotten branch; others excavate burrows in the ground, in earthen banks or in termite

Top: a Small Green Barbet at its nest hole in India, one of the Asiatic barbets characterised by their green plumage. D'Arnaud's Barbet (above) is an African species which nests in a burrow.

mounds. There is no nesting chamber, making conditions cramped inside. The clutch varies with the species from 2 – 5 eggs, and the incubation period lasts from 12 – 19 days. However, as with many hole-nesting species the length of the fledging period is unknown in many instances, although an African species, the Black-collared Barbet *Lybius torquatus*, has a fledging period that averages 34 days. Both parents share the domestic duties, and some are helped by their previous offspring to feed the present brood.

HONEYGUIDES
Order: *Piciformes*
Family: *Indicatoridae*
four genera contain 17 species

During a tour to Botswana's Okavango Delta, our attention was drawn to the guiding call of a Greater Honeyguide *Indicator indicator* in the trees above us. Knowing that this was one of the species that led man to wild bees nests, I asked our local guides if we could follow the bird to see what happened. They readily agreed and after several hundred yards walking through woodland with scattered bushes we found ourselves by a tall tree. At the base of the tree was a large opening that extended up inside the trunk, where the bees had made their nest. We stood back to watch as the locals gathered grass and twigs for a fire which they started at the base of the tree; the smoke was then fanned into the entrance to the nest. It was not long before the bees departed and our guides were able to reach up inside and extract the honey comb. Of course we all tried some, it was not as smooth as the heather honey from Exmoor, in my native Devonshire, but delicious nevertheless. We were not the only ones in for a treat as the guides placed some comb on a nearby branch for the birds. Soon a pair of honeyguides were enjoying the rewards of their efforts and we watched the culmination of a local superstition, for they believe that if a honeyguide takes you to a bee's nest, but no comb is left as a reward, then next time you will be lured to a poisonous snake!

All but two species of honeyguide occur in Africa, and only the Greater and the Scaly-throated Honeyguide *I. variegatus* appear to lead man to the bees' nests. They also guide the Honey Badger or Ratel *Mellivora capensis*; this, a powerfully built member of the weasel family, is very partial to raiding nests, but its extraction methods are probably not as thorough as those of man, so it will not be necessary to make the special effort to leave some for the bird!

Honeyguides are mainly grey, brown and olive coloured birds, some having black markings on the head, but all have white on the outer tail feathers which are flashed as the bird flies away; some species also have a patch of white on the rump. The Lyre-tailed Honeyguide *Melichneutes robustus* has an elaborate tail, which when fanned during a display flight above the forest canopy, makes a snipe-like drumming noise. The largest and most widespread species in Africa is the Greater Honeyguide, 7.75 in. (20 cm.) long; like most other species it has a stout bill and strong legs. The smallest species is the Dwarf Honeyguide *I. pumilio* 4 in. (10 cm.) long, a rare and localised bird known only from montane forests in eastern Zaïre and from the Impenetrable Forest in western Uganda.

Honeyguides are the only birds in the world known to eat honeycomb. Some species have been observed to eat comb, whilst in others it has been found in stomach analysis. They also eat ants, bee larvae and other insects. The more slightly built honeybirds *Prodotiscus* eat mainly insects, caught by foraging like a warbler or on the wing flycatcher fashion.

Honeyguides are parasites, laying their eggs in the nests of hole-nesting species; the honeybirds take advantage of cup or domed-nest species such as warblers *Cisticola sp.* and sunbirds *Nectarinia sp.* The honeyguides most frequently parasitise barbets *Capitonidae*, bee-eaters *Meropidae*, hoopoes *Upupidae*, kingfishers *Alcedinidae* and woodpeckers *Picidae*. The hosts for some of the more obscure honeyguides are unknown and in some instances it is not known for certain if they are parasitic. One of the two Asiatic species, the Indian Honeyguide *I. xanthonotus*, found in the Himalayas, is the only species known to rear its own young conventionally. A

single egg is laid in the nest of the host species, but details of incubation and fledging periods are virtually non-existent. The Lesser Honeyguide's egg hatches in 12 days, but the chick takes some 38 days to fledge. The nestlings of some species have a sharp hook at the tip of the upper mandible with which they eject or kill any other nestlings that may be present in the nest. This hook breaks off naturally after a few days. On fledging, some species are independent immediately and others stay with, and are fed by, their foster parents for several days.

TOUCANS
Order: *Piciformes*
Family: *Ramphastidae*
six genera contain 42 species

Toucans form a New World family that occurs throughout much of Central and tropical South America, in rain forests and woodlands. Most species are lowland birds, but the smaller toucanets *Aulacorhynchus* occur up to 9,800 ft. (3,000 m.) and the Mountain-Toucans *Andigena*, up to 11,150 ft. (3,400 m.). With their large and bulky bills, which in some species are almost as long as the body, toucans bear more than a passing resemblance to the unrelated hornbills *Bucerotidae* of the Old World.

There are 42 species of toucans, divided between 6 closely

related genera; they are colourful birds, but the colours are not just confined to the plumage, for in most species the large bills are usually of more than one colour. The bill, which although bulky is very light, does not hamper the bird's manoeuvrability. The light-weight bill is strengthened internally by a complex of fine boney fibres. The purpose of such a bill is unknown, but it has probably evolved to enable the birds to reach and gather berries and fruit, their principal diet, that would be otherwise inaccessible. Fruit held in the tip of the bill is tossed to the back of the throat by a flick of the head. Besides berries and fruits, other food items include insects, small lizards and snakes; some species take the eggs and nestlings of other birds.

Toucans occur in a wide range of forest types, from sea-level to montane cloud forest; fruit-bearing trees are required both as a food supply and for the provision of nest holes. Toucans rarely descend to the ground and are most frequently seen in small scattered flocks, foraging through the middle

The Toucan Barbet (far left) is a member of the Barbet family and is found in Colombia and Ecuador. The Toco Toucan (left) occurs from the Guianas to northern Argentina. Although bulky, the bills of toucans are very light.

The Yellow-ridged Toucan (left) is a tropical, South American species related to the Toco Toucan. Below left: a Pied Barbet, a bird endemic to southern Africa, in acacia woodland in Etosha National Park, Namibia.

and lower branches of forest trees. Most are sedentary birds, but the toucanets, which inhabit forests at higher elevations, are altitudinal migrants.

Ten of the larger members of the family belong to the genus *Ramphastos*, and include the widespread Toco Toucan *R. toco*, 26 in. (66 cm.) long, which occurs from the Guianas south to northern Argentina. This genus has the largest and most massive bills. The Keel-billed Toucan *R. sulfuratus*, 20 in. (51 cm.) long, is one of three species whose range extends north into Mexico. Another Mexican species is the Collared Araçari *Pteroglossus torquatus*, 15 in. (38 cm.) long, also found south to Colombia and Venezuela. Araçaris are slimmer birds than the larger species, with a slender bill. Eight other species that belong to the genus *Pteroglossus* are also called Araçaris. They occur throughout much of the range of toucans in South America. The Ivory-billed Araçari *P. flavirostris*, 13 in. (33 cm.) long, is as small as the lowland toucanets belonging to the genus *Selenidera*. Those toucanets of the genus *Aulacorhynchus* occur at higher elevations to 9,800 ft. (3,000 m.). Other high altitude species are the four species of Mountain-Toucan, three of which are found at over 9,800 ft. (3,000 m.) in the Colombian Andes; the Gray-breasted Mountain-Toucan *Andigena hypoglauca* occurring up to 11,150 ft. (3,400 m.).

Toucans nest in disused woodpecker holes and in crevices in trees caused by decay. The clutch of 2 – 4 eggs is incubated by both parents, but neither sit for more than one hour at a time, as they are restless on the nest. The incubation period that lasts for at least 16 days, is followed by a slow fledging period of up to 46 days.

WOODPECKERS

Order: *Piciformes*
Family: *Picidae*
27 genera contain 204 species

It must be the dream of almost every birder to see an Ivory-billed Woodpecker *Campephilus principalis* 19.5 in. (50 cm.) long. This is probably a forlorn hope, for this, one of the largest woodpeckers, is almost certainly extinct in the United States, and the population on Cuba has been reduced to a handful of individuals. It is a black and white woodpecker, larger than the familiar Pileated Woodpecker *Dryocopus pileatus* 16.5 in. (42 cm.) long, and differs from that species by its prominent white secondaries that are even more noticeable than those on a Clark's Nutcracker *Nucifraga columbiana*. The decline of the Ivory-bill was initially due to loss of habitat in the south-eastern United States, but later, persecution from collectors took its toll.

cryptically coloured woodpecker-like birds, that earn their name from their ability to twist their necks into extraordinary positions without strangling themselves! The Red-necked Wryneck *J. ruficollis* has a scattered distribution in African woodlands south of the Sahara. The Northern Wryneck *J. torquilla* occurs across the Palearctic, where it is a summer visitor from Africa and Asia. Piculets are a group of 31 species divided between 3 genera, with 27 belonging to the genus *Picumnus*. They are found over much of Central and South America, with only a single representative in Africa and three in the Oriental region. Although they search tree trunks for food like the true woodpeckers, they have short tails and do not use them to support themselves against the tree trunk. The true woodpeckers generally spend their lives searching for food amongst the trees, although several regularly feed on the ground, often on ants. North America is home to 22 species, including the flickers and sapsuckers, several being migratory in the northern parts of their range. Western Europe by comparison has only nine breeding species excluding the Northern Wryneck, and only three of those breed in the U.K. Vagrant Yellow bellied Sapsuckers Sphyrapicus varius, the

The largest woodpecker, the Imperial Woodpecker *C. imperialis* 22 in. (56 cm.) long, once inhabited pine forests of Mexico. Due to shooting and habitat destruction there are few recent records and it might now be extinct.

There are 207 species divided into 27 genera spread through the woods and forests of the World, but absent from the Australasian region, deserts and the treeless tundras. Few species are not associated with trees; the Ground Woodpecker *Geocolaptes olivaceus* is an endemic occurring in South Africa, where it drills a tunnel in an earthen bank or even into a rock face up to 39 ins. (100 cm.) in length.

Woodpeckers are not as diverse a family as many other bird families. Except for wrynecks *Jynx spp.* and the piculets, all species conform to a standard pattern, but with considerable variation in plumages. The Wrynecks are two species of

most migratory of the North American woodpeckers, have occurred in the fall in Britain, Ireland and Iceland. Many woodpeckers are strongly patterned black or brown and white with or without red patches on the head, that sometimes take the form of a crest; some have plain white or red heads. In the Old World, several species are predominantly green and others have golden backs. The largest European species is the Black Woodpecker *Dryocopus martius*, 18 in. (45 cm.) long, whilst in Asia it is eclipsed by the Himalayan Great Slaty Woodpecker *Mulleripicus pulverulentus* at 20 in. (51 cm.). All woodpeckers have large heads and often thick necks with powerful bills. Their feet and claws are strong with most having two forward and two backward pointing toes, although the tail feathers are particularly stiff to help support the bird as it climbs trees. The exceptions are the Three-toed and the

Above left: a male Green Woodpecker from the Western Palearctic feeds his growing young. The Red-naped Sapsucker (above) of western North America is closely related to the eastern Yellow-bellied Sapsucker. It winters south in Mexico.

Black-backed Woodpeckers *Picoides tridactylus* and *P. arcticus*. The former has a holarctic distribution and the latter occurs across the northern forests of Canada and the United States.

The diet of woodpeckers is mainly insects, found in cracks and holes in trees and rotting branches, either on the tree or when fallen to the ground; they also eat fruit and nuts. The Acorn Woodpecker *Melanerpes formicivorus*, found from the western United States to Colombia, drills holes in the bark of trees in which to store acorns for the winter. The sapsuckers drill holes in the bark of trees and feed on the sap that seeps out.

Woodpeckers excavate a nesting hole and chamber which is lined with wood-chips and where 2 – 9 eggs are laid. Both birds share the incubation for 11 – 17 days. Unlike most other hole nesting species, where the female incubates at night, it is the male woodpecker that works the night shift in almost all known cases. The chicks fledge in 18 – 24 days. In many species the family remains together for some time after fledging.

BROADBILLS

Order: *Passeriformes*
Family: *Eurylaimidae*
eight genera contain 14 species.

Broadbills are a family of birds ranging from Africa to Asia, where 10 of the 14 species occur. The family is divided into eight genera of mainly forest-dwelling birds, although two

The Green Broadbill (left), an Asiatic member of its family, occurs in south-east Asia, Indonesia and Malaysia.

The Great Spotted Woodpecker (below) of the Palearctic is the most widespread of the 'pied' woodpeckers.

species, the African Broadbill *Smithornis capensis* and the Black-and-Red Broadbill *Cymbirhynchus macrorhynchus* also occur in scrub habitats. In the past Broadbills were thought to be related to the Pittas *Pittidae*, birds that are also found in Africa and Asia. However, recent investigations analysing the egg-white proteins have established a link with the Cotingas *Cotingidae* and the Tyrant Flycatchers *Tyrannidae* of the Americas.

Broadbills have particularly broad bills from which the name is derived; a bill shape shared with the frogmouths *Podargidae* and trogons *Trogonidae*. All three families are unrelated, but have evolved the same bill to feed in similar ways. All feed on insects and fruit collected off stationary objects whilst the bird is in flight. One species that deviates significantly from this strategy is the Black-and-Red Broadbill; it also feeds on the ground and includes crabs, fish and molluscs in its diet. Bill sizes vary, but the disproportionately large pink bill of the Dusky Broadbill *Croydon sumatranus* has been described as grotesque by some authors. It is the only permanently gregarious member of the family, forming groups of up to 10 birds that search for insects and fruit amongst the canopy of the forest. Other species are usually found singly or in pairs, often in the mid-stratum of the forest. The Dusky is the largest broadbill, 11 in. (28 cm.) long, and occurs widely on mainland south-east Asia and on several islands including Sumatra and Borneo. The smallest species are the Red-sided *S. rufolateralis* and Grauer's Green *Psuedocalyptomena graueri* Broadbills, both 4.5 in. (11 cm.) long. The latter species is one of the rarer African birds, restricted to the bamboo zone on two mountain ranges in eastern Zaïre and on another in the Impenetrable-Kayonza Forest of south-western Uganda. It resembles the Asian species, rather than the dull African broadbills, being green with a pale blue face. Some Asian species, such as the genus of Green Broadbills *Calyptomena* and the Long-tailed Broadbill *Psarisomus dalhousiae*, are also green and the latter is the only broadbill with a long tail. Other species are generally darker with coloured under-parts and sometimes coloured rumps and patches in the wings.

Broadbills make an untidy hanging nest with a porched entrance suspended from a branch or telegraph wire, although the Black-and-Red Broadbill chooses a branch overhanging a stream that passes through its territory. A pair of Dusky Broadbills is helped in the construction of their nest by other members of the group, but this assistance does not appear to extend to any of the domestic duties. One to eight eggs are laid depending on the species and the parents share the household chores. The rarest species are Grauer's Green Broadbill from Africa, mentioned earlier and the Wattled Broadbill *Eurylaimus steeri*, which occurs on islands in the Philippines; formerly common, there have been few recent records.

WOODCREEPERS
Order: *Passeriformes*
Family:*Dendrocolaptidae*
13 genera contain 50 species

In South America are a large number of bird species that exploit the swarms of army ants *Ecitoninae*, that frequent the forests. Amongst the mixed bird-parties that follow the ants, can be one or more species of woodcreeper. The woodcreepers occur from Mexico to northern Argentina, inhabiting forest and open woodland, from sea-level to 6,500 ft. (2,000 m.).

The fifty species of woodcreepers *Dendrocolaptidae* are divided between 13 genera. They are nondescript birds, mainly brown to rufous; some are plain dull birds, while others are well marked. One such is the Black-striped Woodcreeper *Xiphorhynchus lachrymosus*; it has pale feathers on the head, back and breast, these edged with black, giving a striking scaled effect. Woodcreepers range from 5 – 14 in. (12.5 – 36cm.) long and are slim birds well adapted for a life foraging around trees and branches; they cling to the bark with strong feet and claws, climbing jerkily, woodpecker-like. Woodcreepers have stiff tails that support the body against the tree. Their bills have evolved into a variety of shapes; the Scythebills *Campylorhamphus*, have long curved bills, some 2.5 in. (7cm.) long; other species have wedge-like bills of varying length. Woodcreepers feed on insects and other invertebrates, found as they probe the bark. They work steadily up one tree, then fly to the base of the next in the manner of the treecreepers *Certhiidae*. Those species belonging to the plain-coloured genus *Dendrocincla*, including the aptly-named Plain-brown Woodcreeper *D.fuliginosa*, specialise in following the swarms of army ants. They feed on small creatures escaping from the cracks in the bark as the army progresses along a tree-trunk.

Details of the breeding biology for several species remain to be discovered, but probably the details known for some, apply to most of the lesser known species. Woodcreepers prefer to nest in natural cavities in trees, although they may use an old woodpeckers' nest as a last resort. The clutch of 2eggs is laid in a nest of leaves and other vegetable matter. Some species are monogamous, and all domestic duties are

shared equally by the adults. In other species there is no pair bond, and the male leaves the female to get on with the chores unaided. Incubation lasts 17 – 21days and the chicks take a further 18 – 24days to fledge.

OVENBIRDS
Order: *Passeriformes*
Family: *Furnariidae*
36 genera contain 219 species.

Ovenbirds *Furnariidae* comprise a diverse family of Neotropical birds, ranging from Mexico south to Tierra del Fuego. The species belonging to the Order differ considerably from one genus to the next and occupy a wide variety of habitats, although most are woodland or forest birds. The greatest variety of ovenbirds is to be found in tropical and equatorial South America. It is interesting how the density of species shows up in the respective birdlists – at the northern end there are seven species in Mexico, whilst Colombia and Argentina boast 72 and 76 respectively; at the extreme southern end there are eight recorded from Tierra del Fuego.

No other South American family shows such variety between its members, and to cover every aspect would require a book in its own right. In size they vary from some species the size of a warbler, to others as large as an American Robin *Turdus migratorius*. The basic colours of ovenbirds are shades or combinations of brown, chestnut, cream, grey and black; some have long tails and others short. Some, such as the *Cinclodes* Cinclodes, may recall dippers *Cinclidae*; the Miners *Geositta* are terrestrial, stand upright and resemble wheatears *Oenanthe*, whilst others are compared to warblers. Two features serve to illustrate the similarities and the differences between members of the family. The diet of all species consists of insects and small invertebrates; some also eat seeds. The other feature is the great diversity in the nest-building, with nests being truly remarkable. The Ovenbirds *Furnarius* build a large oven-shaped nest, on a branch or on top of a fence-post. Miners, dig burrows in earthen banks or in sand dunes or use the old burrow. of a mammal. The Firewood Gatherer *Anumbius anumbius* builds a bulky structure of large twigs, high in a tree, whilst the largest nest assembled by any member of the family is that of the White-throated Cashalote *Pseudoseisura gutturalis*. The nesting chamber of the enclosed nest is big enough to accommodate a turkey and a man can stand on the roof without damaging it; the birds themselves are only 8.25 in. (21 cm.) long! Many genera have descriptive names that hint at some aspects of the bird's appearance or behaviour. The Ovenbirds and Miners are named after their nests; the Earth-creepers *Upucerthia* named from their furtive behaviour, which has resulted in them being some of the least known members of the Order. As expected, Tuftedcheeks *Pseudocolaptes* have tufts of feathers on their cheeks; the Tit-spinetails *Leptasthenura* and Spinetails *Synallaxis*, are tit or warbler-like birds that have long stiff pointed tails. Some species have names that suggest their habitats and behaviour, such as Reedhaunters *Limnornis*, Woodhaunters *Philydor*, Streamcreepers *Lochmais*, and Treerunners *Margarornis*. Other names like Foliage-gleaners *Automolus*, and Leafscrapers *Sclerurus* imply particular feeding methods. The nests of most species have been discovered, but as yet little is known about their breeding biology. The clutch size varies from three to nine eggs and incubation can be from 13 – 18 days, depending on the species.

ANTBIRDS
Order: *Passeriformes*
Family: *Formicariidae*
52 genera contain 230 species.

Antbirds are a large and varied family of small to medium sized birds from tropical lowland Central and South America. The total number of species varies from one book to another, for antbirds are one of the South American bird families that

The Ochre-breasted Antpitta (facing page top) lacks a long tail and belongs to the South American Antbird family. Facing page bottom: a Rufous Hornero, the National Bird of Argentina, starting to construct its oven-shaped nest.

are at the forefront of discovery; unknown birds and additions to national birdlists continue to be found in remote areas. Many species are poorly known, often because of the lack of detailed knowledge of their distribution.

The Black-hooded Antwren *Formicivora erythronotos* was rediscovered in 1987 in south-eastern Brazil, in an area of swamp near mangroves. First described in 1852, but since then there has been considerable habitat destruction in the areas where the bird had occurred; the authorities had assumed that the Black-hooded Antwren was extinct. Only after the construction of a new road, were birders able to reach the area and discover the new site. This species had belonged to the genus *Myrmotherule*, but from the field studies of the birds in the wild and analysis of the song, it has been placed in the closely related genus *Formicivora*. With increased awareness of South American birds and the loss of the forests, more man-hours are being spent on research into the indigenous bird families. Antbirds are a highly varied family, and not all are called 'antbirds', for many bear the names of other birds they resemble; examples include ant*shrikes*, ant*vireos*, ant*wrens*, ant*thrushes*, and ant*pittas*. Several similarly named are closely related, but belong to different genera. Antbirds can be found at all elevations within the forest, from the floor to the canopy. They are birds that live in the shade, and most are subtly coloured in shades of brown, rufous, grey and yellow. Some are black, and often birds show a combination of colours. Many have spots or barring on the wing coverts. Most have large heads and appear to be neckless; often the tail is short and the legs and bills are stout. They vary in length from 3 – 14 in. (8 – 36 cm.)

Antbirds are almost entirely insectivorous, but may also eat other items such as spiders and small lizards. At least 28 species follow the swarms of army ants *Ecitoninae*; they do not eat the ants, but those insects and other prey items that flee from the hordes. Other antbirds take advantage of the escaping insects, but not to the exclusion of conventional feeding methods.

The breeding biology of many species is unknown. The nest is cup- or dome-shaped, and is built either on the ground or in a cavity in a tree. The usual clutch is 2 eggs, which are incubated by both parents during the day, but only by the female at night. The incubation period lasts 14 – 20 days, and the youngsters fledge in 9 – 18 days, some leaving the nest before they can fly properly.

GNATEATERS
Order: *Passeriformes*
Family: *Conopophagidae*
genus *Conopophaga* contains eight species

Amongst many South American bird families are the eight species of Gnateaters, placed together in the genus *Conopophaga*. They resemble the Robin *Erithacus rubecula* of the Old World in appearance and in some species, colour.

Members of the family are found from Colombia to Argentina, but the greatest variety occurs in Brazil, where five of the eight species are to be found.

Gnateaters are plump, rotund birds about 5 in. (13 cm.) long, having short rounded wings and a short tail; their long thin legs give them an upright stance. Most species are brown, mixed with black and chestnut; the males of several species and some of their females have a brilliant white tuft of feathers behind the eye; these are most conspicuous when the bird becomes excited.

In humid forests they inhabit shrubs and dense

undergrowth, especially where vegetation has proliferated in the vicinity of a fallen dead tree. They are insectivorous and often stand motionless on a low branch, waiting to drop onto an unsuspecting meal, before returning to their perch.

The cup-shaped nest is constructed of leaves and other vegetable matter, and placed in vegetation close to the ground. Much remains to be discovered about their breeding biology, but often in small families, such as the gnateaters, the behaviour and habits of one species, apply to its congeners. One better-known species, the Black-cheeked Gnateater *C. melanops*, of Brazil, lays two eggs and evidence suggests that both parents share the incubation of the eggs and subsequent feeding of the young. They have been observed injury-feigning to lure a predator away from the nest. This behaviour is usually associated with shorebirds, such as the Killdeer *Charadrius vociferus*.

Many species of pitta are endangered, resulting from habitat destruction and from the activities of bird-catchers. One of the rarest species is Gurney's Pitta *P. gurneyi*, whose population in Thailand has been decimated by the indiscriminate clearance of its forest habitat. This bird formerly occurred in Burma, but no recent information regarding its present status in that country has been forthcoming.

TAPACULOS
Order: *Passeriformes*
Family: *Rhinocryptidae*
12 genera contain 30 species.

Another family of South American passerines that inhabits the forest floor comprises the Tapaculos, a family that currently consists of around 30 species split between 12 genera. They range from Costa Rica, south down the mountainous western side of the continent.

The Cotingas are another family of interesting South American birds. Top: an Andean Cock-of-the-Rock in Bolivia, and (above) a Barè-necked Umbrellabird displaying in the cloud forests of Costa Rica.

166

Tapaculos range in size from 4.75 – 9in. (12-25cm.) in length and have stout legs and feet, preferring to hop rather than fly; they have short-rounded wings and a weak flight. The largest number of species is to be found in the genus Scytalopus, small dark stubby birds, often with brown and black on the rump and flanks, that cock their tails in the manner of a Winter Wren *Troglodytes troglodytes*. This habit has given the family its name – *tapaculos* can be translated from the Spanish as 'cover your bottom' *tapa* = cover and *culo* = backside! This genus of very sedentary birds is currently intriguing researchers in South America. A birding colleague, Simon Boyes, has just returned from Ecuador, where he learned that the use of tape-recorded Tapaculos songs raised more questions than answers. Most birds respond to the play-back of the song of their own kind, but in South America, scientists are discovering that the recording of one tapaculo produces no response from an apparently identical bird in the next valley! This suggests that populations of these birds have no contact with their neighbours, often separated by a mountain ridge, they may have evolved into different species. There are many valleys!

Tapaculos are terrestrial birds, feeding on insects and sometimes seeds, scratched from amongst the débris on the forest floor with their strong feet.

The nests of tapaculos are amongst the hardest to locate. Those that build in cavities amongst vegetation on earthen banks, conceal their nests perfectly. Other species build theirs in recesses in trees, whilst yet other members of the family, dig burrows in which they nest. A clutch of 2 – 4 eggs is laid and both birds share the incubation and the feeding of the youngsters.

COTINGAS
Order: *Passeriformes*
Family: *Cotingidae*
25 genera contain 65 species.

The Cotingas *Cotingidae* is another family of South American birds that contains several apparently unrelated species. They occur from southern Mexico to south-eastern Brazil, where they frequent a range of wooded and forest habitats from lowland to montane. They are birds of primary growth, and many species are unable to adapt to the secondary growth that emerges after the clearance of the original timber. They are particularly vulnerable to habitat destruction.

The classification of cotingas is complex, and the latest situation will be clarified when *Birds of South America Vol. 2 – the Suboscine Passerines* is published. There are about 65 species that are divided into some 25 genera. Some authorities have split the Cocks-of-the-rock into a new family *Rupicolidae*, and the Becards and Tityras into another, the *Tityridae*, although others place the latter with the Tyrant Flycatchers *Tyrannidae*. The Plantcutters *Phytotomidae* and the monotypic Sharpbill *Oxyruncidae* may be added to the cotingas.

Cotingas range in size from the diminutive Kinglet Calyptura *Calyptura cristata*, only 3 in. (7.6 cm.) long, to the Amazonian Umbrellabird *Cephalopterus ornatus*, 20 in. (50 cm.) long. The Kinglet Calyptura occurs in south-eastern Brazil, where much of its former habitat has been destroyed. It has not been recorded this century, and although suitable forest occurs in the Serra das Orgaos National Park, it has yet to be seen there. The chances that this species is extinct are high, but one must not forget that the Black-hooded Antwren *Formicivora erythronotos* was rediscovered in 1987, in the same corner of Brazil, and that it too, was not recorded after the late 1800s. The Umbrellabird is one of the ornate members of the family, with a large umbrella-like crest, but one of the least colourful, being black. The male Three-wattled Bellbird *Procnias tricarunculata*, is a chestnut bodied bird with a white head, neck, throat and upper-breast. From the base of the bill hang three flaccid worm-like wattles. Some species are particularly striking; the male Lovely Cotinga *Cotinga amabilis* is an amazing blue bird with a purple belly, and equally startling is the male Snowy Cotinga *Carpodectes nitidus*, with pure white under-parts, and with a hint of grey to the upper-parts.

The diet of cotingas consists of fruit and insects, although some are entirely frugivorous. Most species are sedentary, although some move altitudinally and others wander in search of fruiting forest trees.

A variety of nests are constructed, and the clutch size is 1 – 2 eggs. In some species only the female incubates and rears the young; others share the duties and yet others have helpers. Incubation may last 17 – 28 days and the fledging period can be 21 – 33 days, quite long for a passerine.

The two species of Cocks-of-the-Rock are sufficiently different that they may belong to a family in their own right, the *Rupicolidae*. They are spectacular inhabitants of the forests of northern South America. It is the orange-plumaged males that are well-known and sadly in demand by the pet trade.

The Andean Cock-of-the-Rock *Rupicola peruviana*, the richer-coloured of the two, occurs from Colombia to Peru, in humid, wet ravines in forests, where it occurs at higher elevations than the closely related Guianan Cock-of-the-Rock *R. rupicola*. The Guianan species occurs in the Guianas, southern Venezuela and northern Brazil.

Male cocks-of-the-rock are orange-bodied birds with black wings and tails. Both species have white on the wings, most extensive on the Andean species. They have large orange crests on the forehead, that of the Guianan bird having

a dark sub-terminal band. Females are duller, brown birds and slightly smaller than the males' 12.5 in. (32 cm.) length.

The diet of cocks-of-the-rock consists largely of fruit, although the Guianan Cock-of-the-Rock has been observed following army ants *Ecitoninae* on rare occasions.

During the display, a number of male cocks-of-the-rock gathers at a communal display area known as a 'lek', similar to those used by some species of grouse *Tetraoninae*. Within the area of the 'lek' each male has its own cleared area or `court'. There he dances, and calls to attract the attention of a visiting female. Once he has achieved the object of his advances, he takes no further interest in the domestic life of the female. Alone, she builds the nest of mud, plastered on a cliff in a ravine, or in a cave or perhaps behind a water fall. Two eggs are laid and those of the Guianan species take 27 – 28 days to hatch. The nestlings of the Andean Cock-of-the-Rock fledge after 42 – 44 days in the nest. During the fledging period the young are fed on insects.

Above: a male Three-wattled Bellbird, a Cotinga, in a Costa Rican forest, calling to his mate.

MANAKINS
Order *Passeriformes*
Family: *Pipridae*
17 genera contain 60 species

Manakins are a family endemic to the forests of Central and South America. They range from southern Mexico, Trinidad and Tobago to north-western Argentina and Paraguay. The closer one travels towards the Equator, the greater the number of species encountered. Mexico has only five species listed in the field guide, Costa Rica has 10 species, whilst Colombia and Venezuela boast 25 on their lists. To the south the numbers fall away again, with Argentina having only 6 species.

Most manakins are small thickset birds that range in length from 3.5 – 6 in. (9 – 15 cm.); some males have elongated tail feathers, especially the Long-tailed Manakin *Chiroxiphia linearis* whose central tail feathers may be up to 6 in. (15 cm.) long! Most males are colourful compared with their plain female, often coloured green. There is some doubt whether four species are manakins; they are the three species belonging to the genus *Schiffornis* and the monotypic Broad-billed Manakin *Sapayoa aenigma*. These birds are not sexually dimorphic or brightly coloured, and the males do not perform elaborate display. The true affinities of these birds are unclear, for if they are not manakins they are either cotingas *Cotingidae* or tyrant flycatchers *Tyrannidae*, but which? That is the question.

Manakins are sedentary birds, that mainly eat fruits plucked from trees and bushes whilst the bird is in flight. Lesser quantities of insects are also on the menu and these are taken from leaves in the same manner as fruit.

Male manakins display at communal 'leks' to attract females. This form of display is uncommon amongst *Passerine* birds; the only South America family whose males also 'lek' are the cotingas. The result of this behaviour is that the female ends up with all the domestic duties. Most nests are cup-shaped and situated in a horizontal fork of a tree, where 2 eggs are laid. The incubation period lasts 17 – 19 days, followed by a fledging period of 13 – 15 days. Details of the breeding biology for all members of the family are insufficiently known.

Manakins of South America perform elaborate displays. Left: a male Wire-tailed Manakin engaged in a courtship dance in a Peruvian forest. Below: a Sulphur-bellied Flycatcher at its nest site in Costa Rica.

TYRANT FLYCATCHERS
Order *Passeriformes*
Family: *Tyrannidae*
109 genera contain 384 species

The tyrant flycatchers *Tyrannidae*, to which all the New World flycatchers belong, is the largest of the World's bird families; 384 species divided between 109 genera, although these figures might vary from one authority to another. It is possible that there are new species waiting to be discovered, for many species of them are plain, and similar to other closely related members; all contributing to a few field identification headaches!

Tyrant flycatchers are a varied group, ranging in length from the Short-tailed Pygmy Tyrant, which at 2.75 in. (6.9 cm.) is the World's smallest passerine, to the Fork-tailed Flycatcher *Tyrannus savana*, 14.5 in. (37 cm.) long. In general, many species are dull olive-green, but with prominent supercilliaries and wing bars; one only has to glance at plates in Hilty and Brown's *A Guide to the Birds of Colombia* to appreciate the complexities of identification of South American species. In North America the *Empidonax* flycatchers present similar problems and in this instance the situation is aggravated by the apparent regular sub-dividing of species. Does this aid identification or is it a ploy to ensure that one buys the next edition of the field-guide? Recently the Western Flycatcher *E. difficilis* has been split into the Pacific-slope Flycatcher, and the Cordilleran Flycatcher *E. occidentalis*, which is the form that occurs in the Great Basin and the Rockies.

There are numerous exceptions to the confusion, one of the more striking is the male Vermilion Flycatcher *Pyrocephalus rubinus*, a red and brown gem, that breeds in the south-western United States, south to Chile and Argentina, and out to the Galapagos Islands west of Ecuador. In South America, the ground-tyrants are more chat-like and less like flycatchers than other members of the family; they are often to be found foraging on the ground. Another distinctive part of the family are the Kiskadees *Pitangus spp.*, with striking black and white head patterns, brown and rufous upper-parts, and yellow breast and belly. These are more thickset than most other members of the family, except for the becards *Pachyramphus spp.*. The becards are large headed, bull-

necked birds with heavier bills than most other members of the family. They are traditionally categorized with the cotingas *Cotingidae*, but are now treated as tyrant flycatchers. This might not be the end of the story, for there appears to be scientific justification for placing then in a family of their own. Except for the Jamaican Becard *P. niger*, the genus occurs on the mainland, from southern Arizona and Texas to Argentina.

As with all flycatchers, the principal food is flying insects, caught in mid-air by the bird. Flycatchers are often to be seen perched at the end of a bare branch or similar exposed position, from which they make forays after passing insects. Food may also be taken from leaves, whilst the bird is in flight. The Great Kiskadee *Pitangus sulphuratus* and other large members of the family include fish, frogs, lizards and tadpoles in their diet. Some species, especially those in the tropics eat fruit and berries.

The nests of tyrant flycatchers vary from cup-shaped, to spherical or hanging nests with side entrances. Several genera nest in cavities. Nests are usually constructed by the female and she also incubates the 2 – 5 eggs; the larger clutches being laid by the northern species. Incubation lasts 14 – 20 days and during the 14 – 23 day fledging period, the nestlings are fed by both parents. In many Central and South American species the family remain together until the following breeding season.

SHARPBILL
Order: *Passeriformes*
Family: *Oxyruncidae*
the genus *Oxyruncus* contains a single species *Oxyruncus cristatus*.

The Sharpbill Oxyruncus cristatus, the only member of the genus Oxyruncus, has a discontinuous distribution in Central and South America, scattered through seven countries from Costa Rica to Brazil. Recent research would appear to indicate that the Sharpbill is an aberrant member of the cotinga family Cotingidae. It is a small forest species about 6.5 in. (16.5 cm.) long, that is sedentary and lives and breeds in the canopy of primary rain and cloud forests above 1300 ft. (400 m.) above sea level. Its plumage is green above with spotted yellowish white under-parts. An orange-red crown-stripe edged with black is probably more conspicuous on the male than the female. Sharpbills get their name from a sharp, conical bill used to extract insects and other invertebrates from the base of leaf clusters and other vegetation. The bill is well adapted for this purpose and with the aid of strong legs they feed around the tops of forest trees with the agility and dexterity of titmice and chickadees Paridae. They also eat fruit when available.

Much of the breeding biology of Sharpbills, completely unknown until October 1980, was learned when the first nest was found in primary forest in the Serra do Tingua mountains some 30 miles (50 km.) north of Rio de Janeiro, Brazil. It was discovered by D.A. Scott, just beneath the canopy of one of the tallest trees in the area, standing at about 100 ft. (30 m.) high. The nest was being built on top of a horizontal fork and straddled the branch like that of a Hummingbird Trochilidae. It was later collected for examination after the young had fledged, and found to be a shallow cup constructed from interwoven leaf stalks and dried leaves. The outside was covered with mosses, liverworts and spiders' webs held together by a substance thought to be dried saliva.

The ornithologists were able to study the site throughout most of the breeding cycle, but not on a daily basis; resulting in some doubt about the exact length of time taken over incubation and fledging. The figures show the minimum and maximum number of days that could have been taken and not the possible range for those particular activities. The attendant bird throughout was rather drab and believed to have been a female with an inconspicuous crown-stripe. The incubation period lasted somewhere between 14 – 24 days and fledging took place between 25 – 30 days later. The two young were about 5 days old, when they could be first seen and were fed a regurgitated mixture of fruit and invertebrates by the adult. When last watched they were showing signs of the juvenile plumage, which resembled that of the adult.

PLANTCUTTERS
Order: *Passeriformes*
Family: *Phytotomidae*
the genus *Phytotoma* contains three species.

The Plantcutters *Phytotoma* are a family endemic to South America. The three closely related species are solidly built, finch-like birds about the size of a Fox Sparrow *Passerella iliaca* – 7 in. (18 cm.). Because of their appearance, combined

with heavy bills, they were originally placed with the finches, but further research showed them to be more primitive *Passerines*. More recent investigations indicate that Plantcutters are probably members of the cotinga family *Cotingidae*.

They are mainly sedentary birds, found in small flocks of up to a dozen birds, that inhabit open woodland and bush country. There is some contraction of their range by birds that breed farthest south and those at the higher altitudes. They are vegetarian and eat buds, shoots and fruit; consequently in places they have learned to exploit orchards, where they can inflict considerable damage with a stout bill that has a serrated cutting edge. All three species have a prominent white wing-bar and, depending on the species, the males have varying amounts of rufous in the plumage. The Peruvian Plantcutter *P.raimodi*, 7 in. (18 cm.) long, has the most restricted range, limited to coastal Peru north of Lima. The other two species occur farther south. The larger is the Chilean or Rufous-tailed Plantcutter *P rara*, 7.5 in. (19.5 cm.) long; as its alternative name suggests, the Chilean species has rufous inner webs to the tail feathers; it also lacks the white tips to the tail of the other species. In addition to occurring in Chile, the Chilean

species reaches southern Argentina, but does not overlap the distribution of the Red-breasted or White-tipped Plantcutter *P.rutila*. Its range lies to the north of the Chilean bird in Argentina, and extends into Uruguay, Paraguay and south-eastern Bolivia.

Plantcutters build an untidy nest of thin roots near the top of a low tree or bush, in which the clutch of 2 – 4 eggs are laid. There is much to be unravelled about the breeding biology of the members of this family.

Above: a Western Flycatcher breeding in New Mexico – one of many North American birds that winter in Central America.

PITTAS
Order: *Passeriformes*
Family: *Pittidae*
the genus *Pitta* contains 26 species

The Pittas *Pittidae* are a family of birds whose distribution, in the tropical and equatorial latitudes of the Old World and Australasia, ranges from Africa, across southern Asia to the East Indies, New Guinea and Australia. They have a distinctive upright stance, resulting in other birds with a similar posture having pitta-associated names; these include the antpittas, members of the large South American family of antbirds *Formicariidae*.

Pittas are large-headed rotund birds, with rounded wings, short tails and long legs giving them the characteristic stance. They are birds of the forest floor, found in a variety of dense woodland habitats including rain, and riverine forests. Their diet includes a variety of animal and invertebrate species.

Snails are a particular favourite; the bird uses a stone or other hard object as an anvil, against which they smash the shells in the same manner as the Song Thrush *Turdus philomelos*, of the western and central Palearctic. Other prey items include crustaceans, earthworms, insects, lizards and small snakes. Pittas range in size from 6 – 11 in. (15 – 28 cm.) in length. Many species of pitta are very colourful birds, although the brightest parts are mainly on the head and under-parts; the back is plain, and depending on the species, may be blue, brown or green. To a potential predator the bird might go undetected as it feeds on the forest floor, for dappled sunlight filtering through the tree canopy above helps with camouflage. Colours of the under-parts include blue, buff, green, and red; the majority have patterned heads, usually in the form of distinct caps, eye-stripes and facial masks. Most, but not all pittas, show prominent white patches on the wing in flight and nine species have dimorphic plumages.

The greatest variety of species is to be found in Asia and the Australasian region. In the whole of Africa only two species occur; the African or Angola Pitta *Pitta angolensis* is the more widespread of the two, sparsely scattered in suitable habitats over much of sub-Saharan Africa. It is an intra-African nocturnal migrant, sometimes turning up in gardens, or flying into the windows of houses after being attracted by the lights. Several Asiatic pittas are also nocturnal migrants, including the northern populations of the Indian Pitta *P.brachyura*. The Blue-winged Pitta *P.moluccensis*, another Asiatic migrant, has occurred in north-western Australia as a vagrant. Over half the World's species of pitta, 15 species, are to be found on the islands between south-east Asia and Australia; either they are endemic or part of their distribution falls within the area.

Most pittas build a dome-shaped nest close to the ground; it is constructed of roots and other vegetable matter. Some species including the Noisy Pitta *P.versicolor* of Australia and New Guinea, place their nests on the ground. For some reason the Noisy Pitta places animal dung at the entrance to the nest, but the purpose of this is unclear. It may be to mask the scent of the nest from possible predators. There is little knowledge about the breeding biology of pittas other than the clutch size, which is usually 2 – 7 eggs. Incubation lasts 15 – 17 days, and fledging can take up to three weeks. One reason for the lack of further information, appears to be that the eggs have been collected from many of the nests when discovered.

NEW ZEALAND WRENS

Order: *Passeriformes*
Family: *Acanthisittidae*
two genera contain three species.

Of all the accounts of birds that have become extinct, perhaps the most pathetic is the loss of the Stephen Island Wren *Xenicus lyalli*, first discovered in 1894. Stephen's Island lies at the western approach to the Cook Strait which separates the North and South Islands of New Zealand. It only covers about one square mile (2.6 km2), and around the time of the bird's discovery a lighthouse was built on the island to assist shipping passing through the area. A number of specimens of the Stephen Island Wren were obtained for collections, but after completion of the lighthouse the keeper only saw the bird on two evenings as it ran amongst holes in the rocks. His cat, single-handed, exterminated the entire population! It was an extraordinary bird, for it had the smallest distribution of any known species, although sub-fossil evidence has come to light suggesting that at one time it occurred more widely on the North Island. It was a very small brown bird that ran like a mouse, and might have been the only flightless passerine; it was never seen to fly and became extinct before anything could be learned about its habits and behaviour.

New Zealand wrens are small, dumpy, wren-like birds, only about 3 –.5 in. (8-9 cm.) long, with very short tails. The family is endemic to the islands, but their exact relationship with other bird families is not fully understood, for they share similarities with the Pittas *Pittidae* of the Old World and the Antpittas *Formicariidae* of South America. Scientists believe them to be the descendants of the first land birds to colonise New Zealand during the Tertiary Period.

There are now only three species placed in two genera; of these the Rifleman *Acanthisitta chloris* is the most abundant and one of the other two, may also be extinct. New Zealand's endemic land birds have suffered badly from habitat destruction and the havoc wrought by introduced mammalian predators since the islands were colonised by Man about 1000 years ago. Over eons of time they had become highly specialised in an isolated environment, with few terrestrial enemies. The arboreal Rifleman is one of the few species that has been able to adapt and has moved into the recently developed coniferous forests, although it is not as plentiful as formerly. The Rifleman shows marked sexual differences, for the male is bright green above with off-white under-parts and a distinctive white eye-brow stripe. The female has brown upper-parts that recall the plumage of a Brown Creeper *Certhia americana*;, she is also pale below. Both species have a yellow wing bar, white tertials and a buff-tipped tail. They behave like creepers as they search for insects with a well-adapted slightly upturned bill, amongst moss and in cracks in the branches of trees.

Both the Bush *X. longipes* and the Rock *X. gilviventris* Wrens are now very rare and possibly the Bush Wren might already be extinct. They are plainer browner birds than the Rifleman, lacking the marked sexual differences and the strong contrast between the upper and under-parts, but sharing the pale eye-brow stripe. They also have a dipper-like habit of bobbing the body on landing. They spend more time feeding on the ground than the Rifleman, making them vulnerable to introduced predators. The Bush Wren is a poorly known bird that formerly occurred in remote forests on both islands, where it foraged for insects amongst foliage, but none have been seen on the North Island since 1955. The last birds belonging to a population called Stead's Bush Wren *X. l. variabilis* inhabited Big South Cape Island, although the species previously occurred on several other islands around Stewart Island off the South Island. In 1964 Black Rats *Rattus rattus*, which had escaped from a fishing boat, went through a population explosion and exterminated the remaining Bush Wrens. It is possible that birds still exist in isolated parts of the South Island. The Rock Wren is a bird of montane slopes of the South Island, where it feeds on insects and occasionally fruit found on scree slopes and amongst nearby scrub.

The breeding biology for all New Zealand wrens appears to be similar, although little is known about the Bush and Rock Wrens. The Rifleman builds a domed nest in a hole and two to five eggs are laid. Incubation is shared by the adults and lasts for 19 – 20 days, and during the fledging period of a further 24 days, off-spring from a previous brood may assist the parents.

ASITIES

Order: *Passeriformes*
Family: *Philepittidae*
two genera each contain two species.

The family, *Philepittidae* is one of the bird families that has evolved in isolation on Madagascar. They are small, confiding arboreal birds that mainly feed on fruit, berries and nectar.

The two species that make up the genus *Philepitta* are Velvet *P. castanea* and Schlegel's *P. schlegeli* Asities. They look quite unlike the related birds belonging to the genus *Neodrepanis*. The present species recall Pittas *Pittidae* with dumpy bodies and stubby tails. Their stout legs also recall those of the Pittas, but Asities are birds that live in the trees and not on the forest floor. The Velvet Asity occurs in the moist forests of eastern Madagascar, whilst the less well known Schlegel's Asity prefers denser evergreen forests in the north-western part of the island.

Both species are about 6 in. (15 cm.) long. The male Velvet becomes velvet black during the breeding season, when the yellow edges to the newly moulted feathers wear away. The black on Schlegel's Asity is confined to the head, the rest of the body being yellow green above with yellow under-parts. Both males have blue wattles over the eye and across to the top of the bill. The females and immatures of both species have olive upper-parts and the Velvet is greenish white below, whilst Schlegel's Asity shows more yellow. Little is known about the breeding biology of any of the four species dealt with here. Only the nest of Velvet Asity has been found. It was a small, pear-shaped, hanging nest containing three pure white eggs.

The genus *Neodrepanis* consists of two species, False Sunbirds, which look more like the sunbirds *Nectariniidae* of Africa, Asia and Australia, than the two other species of Asity. They are also birds of dense evergreen forest, a habitat that makes observation difficult. The False Sunbirds are the Wattled *N.coruscans* and Small-billed *N. hypoxantha*. Smaller birds than their cousins, the Wattled is 4 in. (10 cm.) long, of which an inch (2.5 cm.) is a slender curved bill. The male, with iridescent blue upper-parts, is dull yellow below and has a blue wattle around the eye. The Small-billed False Sunbird looks identical except for being slightly smaller. It is 3 in. (7.6 cm.) long with a bill of 0.75 in. (2 cm.). The females of both species are less brightly coloured. The food of the False Sunbirds is nectar and insects collected by probing their long bills into flowers.

more local distribution and only found in rain forests in south-east Queensland and north-east New South Wales.

Both species are very shy and if disturbed, will run rather than fly, for they are poor fliers. Their wings are better suited to gliding away down a slope than weaving through the trees at speed. On the forest floor they search for food in the form of crustaceans, earthworms, millipedes, beetles and other invertebrates by scratching away at the soil or rotting tree trunks with powerful legs and claws. Although ground dwellers, Lyrebirds roost in trees and the domed nest can either be on the ground or as far as 72 ft. (22 m.) up a tree. The wonderful lyre-shaped tail, used by the male in display is not fully attained until the bird is five to seven years old, by which time it will have established a territory that is vigourously defended against all comers. Within the territory the males construct a number of earthen mounds from which they sing and display their tails to attract the attention of the females, several of whom may visit the male prior to breeding. Male

The male Superb Lyrebird (left) of Australia spreads its tail to attract females and mates with any that fall for his charms.

The Small-billed False Sunbird is a rare and very poorly known bird, partially because of the similarities between the two species. It was first established as a true species in 1933, several specimens being collected prior to that date, but since then it has only been satisfactorily identified on a handful of occasions.

Along with other birds peculiar to Madagascar, their future remains insecure as long as the indigenous forests are cleared for cultivation.

LYREBIRDS
Order: *Passeriformes*
Family: *Menuridae*
the genus *Menura* contains two species

Lyrebirds are a family of ground feeding birds that are endemic to the island continent of Australia. The males are noted for their elaborate tails, spread with great effect during display. There are two species, the Superb Lyrebird *Menura novaehollandiae*, which is about the size of a Ring-necked Pheasant *Phasianus colchicus* and the slightly smaller Albert's Lyrebird *M.alberti*. The Superb Lyrebird, a brown and grey bird, is widespread in wet forests from south-east Queensland to Tasmania, where introductions took place from 1934 to at least 1941. It has been successful, but population has not spread away from the original areas. Albert's Lyrebird, more rufous in colouration with a less spectacular tail, is of much

lyrebirds are promiscuous, for mating is a brief affair and afterwards he takes no further interest in that particular female!

Breeding takes place in the austral winter and the substantial structure is built entirely by the female. She lays a single egg and carries out all the parental duties. Incubation can last up to 50 days, because she spends from three to six hours each day away from the nest during cold weather, which does not appear to have an adverse effect on the subsequent success of the nest. It is a case in Nature of an only child in a single parent family! The chick fledges after 47 days, leaving the nest before it is fully grown. It stays with the mother for up to eight months, during which time she still feeds it, although it becomes more independent as it grows older.

In former times Lyrebirds were hunted for their plumes, but now both species have full protection and the only threats come from predators, native and introduced, and from the commercial exploitation of the forests.

SCRUB-BIRDS
Order: *Passeriformes*
Family: *Atrichornithidae*
the genus *Atrichornis* consists of two species.

Scrub-birds are a family endemic to Australia. Both species, the Noisy *Atrichornis clamosus* and the Rufous *A. rufescens*, are rare birds with very restricted ranges at opposite ends of the island continent. The Noisy Scrub-bird inhabits thick coastal vegetation along a small area of the south coast near Albany, Western Australia. In the east, the Rufous Scrub-bird occurs in dense forest undergrowth along the Great Dividing Range in south-eastern Queensland and north-eastern New South Wales. It is a rare bird within its limited range, but it has never been as vulnerable as the Noisy Scrub-bird.

They are both very shy terrestrial birds that run and scramble through the undergrowth rather than fly, which they can only manage poorly. The larger, Noisy, is 8 in. (21 cm.) long, whilst the Rufous is 6 in. (16 cm.) long. The Noisy Scrub-bird has darker brown upper-parts than the red-brown plumage of the Rufous. Both species have fine black barring on the back, wings and tail, but only the males have black chest or throat markings.

The Noisy Scrub-bird breeds during the austral winter, whereas the Rufous appears to be more conventional and breeds during the spring and summer months. However, in reality both birds breed during their respective rainy seasons a continent apart.

Scrub-birds, closely related to Lyrebirds *Menuridae*, show several similarities during the breeding season. The male Noisy Scrub-bird spends much of the time singing and leaves the female to do all the work. It is the female that builds the

His personal involvement was a contributing factor in the re-siting of a new town planned for Two Peoples Bay. Later, Noisy Scrub-birds were found on Mount Manypeaks and since then both areas have been declared reserves.

LARKS
Order: *Passeriformes*
Family: *Alaudidae*
17 genera contain 75 species.

One of the loveliest sounds of an English spring is the song of the Sky Lark *Alauda arvensis*, drifting down from above, as the male song-flights above its breeding territory.

Larks are small ground dwelling birds found naturally throughout much of the World, except South America and New Zealand; although in the latter Sky Larks were successfully introduced by European settlers. There are 76 species split between 13 genera, but of these only the Horned Lark *Eremophila alpestris* occurs naturally in North America; the Sky Lark was introduced successfully to Vancouver

Below: a European Skylark – a renowned songster – feeds her hungry brood of youngsters in Britain.

domed nest close to the ground, often near a stream. Incubation of the single egg lasts up to 38 days, for like the Lyrebird, the female scrub-bird leaves the nest unattended for some time each day. She feeds the chick a wide variety of invertebrates such as insects found amongst leaf-litter and occasionally larger items such as, small frogs and lizards. On fledging, the juvenile stays with its mother for a further two to three months. The male who has one female within his territory, also mates with unattached and young females from the surrounding area.

The Noisy Scrub-bird was first described in 1843 from Western Australia, but was always a rare bird and although some specimens were collected subsequently, by 1889 it was considered extinct. A period of 72 years elapsed before the Noisy Scrub-bird was rediscovered in 1961 at Two Peoples Bay about 25 miles (40 km.) east of Albany and not far from where the species had occurred during the 19th. century. Soon after, H.R.H. Prince Philip, the Duke of Edinburgh, visited Western Australia and took a keen interest in the rediscovery.

Island early in the 20th. century. The Horned Lark is a widespread but local bird, inhabiting open fields, grasslands, prairies and tundra, from coastal to mountainous regions. It is a widespread species with three distinct populations in the Palearctic; one ranges from Scandinavia eastwards across the tundra of Siberia, another from the Middle East to Central Asia and the third in the Atlas Mountains of North Africa. Throughout much of North Africa and the Middle East it is replaced by the very similar Temminck's Horned Lark *E.bilopha*.

It is in Africa that the greatest number of lark species are to be found. No less than 67 of the 80 species either breed or spend the winter months in the Continent and out of those, 50 are endemics! The highest numbers of endemic species come from two areas – north-eastern Africa holds 11 species found nowhere else in the World, but is beaten by southern Africa with a score of 15! They are birds of open grasslands, arid and semi-arid habitats; many are found in deserts, where few other birds can exist. Some species are sedentary, while

others move to warmer latitudes for the winter months. The remaining species are nomadic, moving into areas of drought conditions and leaving when regeneration begins after the rains come.

Larks range in size from 4.25 – 9 in. (10 – 23 cm.) in length. Many species are brown nondescript birds, often with striated black upper-parts; the paler under-parts can be plain or streaked depending on the species. Some have white outer-tail feathers and some prominent wing-bars, like the Hoopoe Lark *Alaemon alaudipes* of North Africa, the Middle East and south-western Asia. This species has a long decurved bill, one of the longest of any lark. Others by comparison have short, stubby bills resembling the bills of more traditional seed-eating species. A particularly large bill belongs to the Thick-billed Lark *Rhamphocoris clotbey*, that occurs in north-west Africa and a few localities in the Middle East; its bill is as massive as that of an Evening Grosbeak *Coccothraustes vespertinus*. In South Africa occurs *Calendula magnirostris*, also known as the Thick-billed Lark and placed in the genus *Galerida* in some bird books. Although it has a heavy bill, it lacks the bulk of the North African species.

Apart from the finch-larks *Eremopterix*, the only species to differ greatly from the general lark colouration is the male Black Lark *Melanocorypha yeltoniensis*, very aptly named, that occurs in Central Asia. Finch – or sparrow-larks are a distinctive genus comprising seven species; found in the semi-arid areas of Africa and Asia, these birds have finch-like bills and are amongst the most well marked species. The males have black under-parts and heads, often with white or grey patches on the crown or cheeks; the colour of the back

Above: a Rufous-naped Lark singing in the Masai Mara, Kenya, a lark common to the African savannah. The Horned Lark (left) breeds across the northern latitudes of North America, but less extensively in the Palearctic.

173

varies from grey to chestnut, depending on the species. The species is dimorphic, with the females being much duller.

Larks eat insects and seeds of many kinds, which may fulfil all the bird's moisture requirements. One rare and localised species is Gray's Lark *Ammomanes grayi*, found only on gravel deserts of the Namib along the Skeleton Coast of Namibia. On a recent tour to that country we found them feeding by a roadside garbage dump. Never has such a rare species been reduced to the level of 'trash-bird' so quickly! Larks are ground nesting birds often making a cup-shaped of grass in a scrape set into a tuft of grass. In the hotter areas, the nest can be situated beside a clump of grass or perhaps a small rock, so that it is shaded during the heat of the day. Some species, including the finch-larks, use small stones to make a barrier to the windward side of the nest, probably to prevent the nest becoming covered by wind-blown sand. In the Arctic and temperate regions larks usually lay 4 eggs, but in the hot, arid regions a clutch of 2 – 3 eggs is usual. The incubation period usually lasts 10 – 13 days and may be carried out by both parents or just the female, depending on the species. Both parents feed the nestlings, who leave the nest prior to fledging. In some species such as the finch-larks, the youngsters leave the nest when they are as young as 7 days. This is a survival strategy, for the chances of a predator discovering and eating all the brood are considerably reduced.

SWALLOWS and MARTINS
Order *Passeriformes*
Family: *Hirundinidae*
15 genera contain 75 species

To those living in the Northern Hemisphere, swallows and martins are conspicuous harbingers of spring, with the Barn Swallow *Hirundo rustica* being one of the most widespread species. In Australia and New Zealand a similar species is called the Welcome Swallow *H. neoxena* – a charming name.

Swallows and martins occur throughout the World, except in the highest latitudes and polar regions of the Northern Hemisphere and the Antarctic; over half the species spend part of their annual cycle somewhere in Africa. By October, when our tours visit Botswana, Barn Swallows are just arriving after a breeding season in Europe, and four or five months later they are streaming north again. It is very easy to become complacent about swallows, for when they are present in large numbers one can assume that only one or two species are involved. This was particularly true during a trip one January to Jamaica, where Cave Swallows *Hirundo fulva* were common. We visited the Black River Morass on the south side of the island. Over the marshy areas were many swallows, mainly Caves, but a glimpse of a brown species made me realise that it was going to be worth a much closer look, and the next half hour or so proved to be well worthwhile. Amongst the Cliff Swallows, we found about 30 Bank Swallows *Riparia riparia* and single Barn, Tree and Bahama Swallows *Tachycineta albilinea* and *T. cyaneoviridis*, whilst nearby along a drainage ditch were 30 Northern Rough-winged Swallows *Stelgidopteryx ruficollis* – not bad for an area with supposedly only Cave Swallows.

Members of the family are all aerial-feeders that hawk insects with great skill. Because of this reliance on a seasonal food supply many species are migratory, even within a continent like Africa. Swallows usually have longer wings than martins, and often deeper forked tails. In Britain and other parts of the World the Bank Swallow is known as the Sand Martin. Blue and brown are the most frequently encountered colours, but black and green also occur in some genera. The under-parts are often paler than the upper-parts, ranging from pure white, through buff and rufous to red. Several species have white or rufous rumps and/or crowns; some have neck or breast bands. The most beautiful species must surely be the Violet-green Swallow *T. thalassina* of western North America. Swallows and martins range in length from 4.75 – 9 in. (12 – 23 cm.) and have short, but wide bills.

Swallows and martins nest in sites that conform to one of three types. It might be a nest of mud that may be an open cup or have an entrance tunnel, and some incorporate grass or

feathers; Barn Swallows and American Cliff Swallows *H. pyrrhonota* make nests of this type, and have benefited from the activities of Man, by nesting in barns and other farm buildings or beneath modern concrete bridges. The Tree and Violet-green Swallows in North America are among those that choose a natural hole, perhaps an old woodpecker site or crevice in a tree or cliff. The final type is the tunnel excavated in an earth or sand bank by the Bank Swallow, which often breeds in large colonies at suitable sites. The clutch of 3 – 8 eggs is usually incubated by the female throughout the 13 – 16 day incubation period, but both parents share the feeding of the young during the 15 – 30 day fledging period.

A number of swallows are rare or declining for a variety of reasons. The Purple Martin *Progne subis* has decreased in the face of competition for nest sites from House Wrens *Troglodytes aedon*, House Sparrows, *Passer domesticus* and European Starlings *Sturnus vulgaris*. The White-eyed River Martin *Pseudochelidon sirintarae* was discovered for the first

The Wire-tailed Swallow (left and bottom) occurs in Africa and Asia and, like many other members of the family, makes a nest of mud. The American Cliff Swallow (below) has benefited from the construction of concrete road bridges, which often provide it with good nesting sites, whilst in western Europe the House Martin (below left) prefers to nest under the eaves of houses.

175

time in 1968. It was wintering with other swallows at a reservoir in Thailand, but is a very rare bird that is not recorded annually, and its breeding grounds somewhere in central or eastern Asia are unknown. The only other member of the genus, the African River Martin breeds mainly along the banks of the Congo River and in Gabon, nesting while water levels are low. One serious threat facing the White-eyed River Martin, is the prospect of a major hydro-electric or irrigation scheme, that floods the breeding areas without anyone realising the loss.

WAGTAILS
Order: *Passeriformes*
Family: *Motacillidae*
five genera contain 57 species.

Wagtails and pipits, with their African relatives the longclaws, give the *Motacillidae* family almost global coverage except in the highest latitudes and on some of the remotest oceanic islands. The 57 species are divided between five genera, but the taxonomic position of some members of the family, certain pipits in particular, requires clarification.

The Polynesian Triller (above left), a member of the Cuckoo-Shrike family, is widespread on islands in the western Pacific. The Large Pied Wagtail (above) is an Asiatic species found in India and Pakistan. Left: a Tree Pipit, found in Britain. Most pipits are ground nesters.

Wagtails are slim, long-tailed insectivorous birds that characteristically wag their tails; they range in length from 6.5 – 7.75 in. (17 – 20 cm.). The genus *Motacilla* comprises 11 species, four of which occur in Alaska, including breeding White and Yellow Wagtails *M. alba* and *M. flava*. During the spring migration the Black-backed and Gray Wagtails *M. lugens* and *M. cinerea,* may occur as vagrants. The Gray Wagtail is a particularly elegant species with a longer tail than most. It has yellow under-parts, but the longer tail and conspicuous white wing bar, that shows well in flight, should separate it from the Yellow Wagtail. The ranges of both the White and Yellow species spread across the Palearctic. There is a variety of subspecies with breeding plumages that make one population noticeably different from neighbouring areas. Most White and Yellow Wagtails are migratory, the Yellow being the greater traveller, for it reaches South Africa during the austral summer. Other species of wagtails occur in Africa and Asia.

Pipits are birds of open country, from grasslands to mountain tops and tundra. All 36 species are similar and range from 5.5 – 7.5 in. (14 – 19 cm.) in length. Most pipits are LBJs, nothing to do with the former president I hasten to add, but the initials of an apt description – Little Brown Jobs! In many parts of the world, where pipits are plentiful, it is easy to dismiss one with a derisory "It's just another pipit." They are also slim, insectivorous birds, but without the wagtails' long

breeding species that has a foothold as a breeder in Alaska by the Bering Sea. It occurs as a rare visitor farther south down the Pacific coast in the fall, when it is distinctive, with clear, bold dark streaks down the sides of the breast and flanks. Other mouth-watering goodies that can turn up in Alaska in the spring include Olive Tree-Pipit *A. hodgsoni*, Eurasian Tree-Pipit *A. trivialis* and Pechora Pipit *A. gustavi.*

The Golden Pipit *Tmetothylacus tenellus*, found in semi-arid country in north-east Africa, shows a closer affinity to the longclaws than the pipits. It has brilliant yellow under-parts with a black breast-band, like the longclaws, but in addition has largely yellow wings and outer-tail feathers. The yellow wings are shown off to best effect during the display flight of the male.

Longclaws are larger than pipits, about 8 in. (20 cm.) long, with heavier lark-like bodies. There are eight species scattered through grassland habitats over much of sub-Saharan Africa. All have brown upper-parts, streaked with black and a black breast-band. They have coloured under-parts – orange, red and yellow. The most widespread species is the Yellow-throated Longclaw *T. croceus*, found from West to South Africa. The immediate impression given by this bird is that of a slim Eastern Meadowlark *Sturnella magna*; another case of convergent evolution.

Some wagtails nest in holes in walls, or cliffs, others nest on the ground in a tussock of grass; pipits and longclaws

Left: a Yellow Wagtail at its nest in England. This bird ranges across the Palearctic, and the European breeders of this species winter in Africa.

tail. They are essentially shades of brown and fawn, with paler under-parts and usually black or darker brown striations on the back, or under-parts, or both. They can have white or buff outer-tail feathers, that are conspicuous as the bird gets up from the grass in front of you and as it flies away, to drop down again farther on. You follow, hoping for a better view, but because the bird runs away behind cover, the second sighting is seldom better than the first. Some species, including the Red-throated Pipit *Anthus cervinus*, have a distinctive breeding plumage; others require much more attention. When it comes to pipits, birders in North America get off lightly, for only two species occur regularly. The American Pipit, formerly known as the Water Pipit *Anthus rubescens*, is found in the far north and mountainous areas of the States and Canada during the breeding season. Sprague's Pipit *A. spargueii* occurs on the grasslands of the Great Plains in the mid-west, straddling the border between the United States and Canada. But it is in Alaska, where one stands any chance of finding other pipits in North America. The Red-throated Pipit is a Palearctic

choose the latter. The nest is made of grass, lined with finer material such as animal hair. The clutch size can be up to seven eggs and the incubation, usually undertaken by the female, lasts between 12 – 16 days. Both parents feed the young, who fledge 14 days after hatching.

CUCKOO-SHRIKES
Order *Passeriformes*
Family: *Campephagidae*
9 genera contain 72 species

The cuckoo-shrikes are an Old World family of insectivorous birds that occurs throughout much of sub-Saharan Africa, Madagascar, and the Oriental and Australasian regions. They are neither cuckoos *Cuculus* nor shrikes *Laniidae*, and to make matter worse not all are called cuckoo-shrikes. The name comes from a number of species that are grey with shrike-like proportions. In particular the Barred or Yellow-eyed Cuckoo-shrike *Coracina lineata* from New Guinea, Australia and the Solomon Islands, looks very much like the Oriental Cuckoo *Cuculus saturatus*, with its barred underparts. Two species of Wood-shrike *Tephrodornis*, an Asiatic genus, strongly resemble shrikes belonging to the genus *Lanius*, complete with black mask.

There are 72 species in 9 genera, with 41 species belonging to the widespread genus *Coracina*. Most cuckoo-shrikes occur in the Oriental region, with many species being endemic to the islands of the East Indies. Others inhabit Africa and the Australasian region. They range in length from 5.5 – 15 in. (14 – 40 cm.).

Cuckoo-shrikes frequent woodland, where they are often to be found singly or in small parties, foraging in the canopy. The Ground Cuckoo-shrike *Coracina maxima* is a terrestrial species that occurs in Australia.

In general, those species known as cuckoo-shrikes are grey or black birds with or without black faces, and pale or barred underparts. The females of some look so different from their partners that they could almost be a different species. The male Black Cuckoo-shrike *Campephaga flava* an African species, is completely black except for yellow shoulder patches on some individuals. The female by comparison is scaled black and yellow. The most striking is the Golden Cuckoo-shrike *Campochaera sloetii*, endemic to New Guinea; it has a yellow body, black facial mask and tail, with black and white wings. Otherwise the most colourful members of the

form flocks or join mixed bird parties. Members of the cuckoo-shrike family are essentially insectivorous, and are amongst the few bird families to eat hairy caterpillars. Fruit is also eaten, as may larger items such as frogs and lizards.

A shallow cup-shaped nest is constructed by both adults from grasses, roots and small twigs, and bound with cobwebs. It is built on top of a branch and sometimes camouflaged with lichen. In Australia some species occupy the disused nests of other birds, in particular those of the Magpie-lark *Grallina cyanoleuca*. The usual clutch size is 2 – 5 eggs, but further details of the breeding biology are only poorly known. Some species share the incubation and in others it is just by the female, who may be fed on the nest by the male. The incubation period of some African species is 20 – 23 days, followed by a fledging period of 20 – 30 days. The young White-breasted Cuckoo-shrikes *Coracina pectoralis* are dependent on their parents for up to 3 months, but the family remains together until the following breeding season.

BULBULS
Order *Passeriformes*
Family: *Pycnonotidae*
13 genera contain 119 species

One of the most familiar of African birds is the Black-eyed Bulbul *Pycnonotus barbatus*, an olive-brown bird with a black head and yellow under-tail coverts. It is one of those

Below: a White-cheeked Bulbul in Bharatpur in India. This bird ranges from Iraq to the Himalayas.

family are the minivets *Pericrocotus spp.* an Asiatic branch of the family, that are about 7 in. (18 cm.) long. They are slim birds with long tails; most have a black, brown or grey head and back, with orange, scarlet or yellow underparts and rumps, and have a similar-coloured wing-panel and outer tail feathers. Closely related to the minivets are the trillers *Lalage spp.*, a genus of nine species that ranges from the Philippines to Australia, and east to Samoa in the Pacific. Trillers are mainly black or brown and white, some with barred underparts.

Most cuckoo-shrikes are sedentary or move only locally, but some northern populations of certain Asiatic species migrate southwards in the fall. During the winter minivets,

annoying birds, that when not seen clearly, can sometimes be confusing to the unwary. The situation is aggravated by the species' great vocal ability.

Bulbuls are an Old World family of 119 species divided into 13 genera. It ranges over much of Africa except the Saharan area, the Middle East, southern and south-east Asia and the islands of the East Indies. Several species have been introduced to other parts of the World; the Red-whiskered Bulbul *P. jocosus*, an Asiatic bird, was deliberately introduced to south-eastern Australia in 1880. In the United States, a feral population has become established in south-eastern Florida following the escape of cage birds.

Bulbuls were considered to be related to the cuckoo-shrikes *Campephagidae* until recent research involving DNA analysis; it now appears that bulbuls are more closely related to drongos *Dicruridae*, and perhaps the orioles *Oriolidae* and starlings *Sturnidae*. On Madagascar the Tylas-vanga or Kinkimavo *Tylas eduardi*, usually treated as a bulbul, is now placed with the endemic vanga shrikes *Vangidae*.

Bulbuls range in length from 5 – 9 in. (13 – 23 cm.); they are short winged birds with long full tails, and strong, yet slender bills. The appropriately named finchbills *Spizixos* have heavier bills, but are otherwise obviously bulbuls. The family is not a colourful one, most species are shades of yellow-olive to brown, and may have black and white head patterns; some show patches of pure yellow or red, and a number have crests.

Bulbuls are birds of woodland habitats from tropical forests to arid scrub. Of the 57 African species, 35 inhabit the lowland tropical forests of Zaïre.

Most bulbuls live on a diet of berries and soft fruit, others eat buds and nectar and some are insectivorous. Bulbuls are a sedentary family, although some species may move locally.

Bulbuls make a cup-shaped nest of twigs, grass and other vegetation, sited in a bush or a tree. The clutch size, depending on the species, is 1 – 5 eggs. With some species the eggs are incubated by the female, who may be fed by the male while on the nest; in others the duties are shared. Incubation lasts from 12 – 14 days and the youngsters fledge 10 – 17 days later.

The Common or Dark-eyed Bulbul (above) ranges over much of Africa. Left: a Brown-eared Bulbul in its nest in Japan. These birds will also occur in China and Korea.

LEAFBIRDS and IORAS
Order: *Passeriformes*
Family: *Irenidae*
three genera contain 14 species.

Leafbirds are a family of 14 species, small to medium arboreal birds that range from Pakistan to the Philippines and the East Indies. They belong to three families: the Ioras *Aegithina*, the Leafbirds *Chloropsis* and the Fairy-bluebirds *Irena*; the genera differ considerably from one another.

The Ioras are about 6 in. (15 cm.) in length, the largest being the Great Iora *A. lafresnayei*, 6.5 in. (16.5 cm.) long, which occurs in south-east Asia. It is lacks the prominent white wing-bars, characteristic of the other ioras. The members of this genus have green or black upper-parts with yellow or green under-parts. Ioras occur throughout much of the range of the Leafbird family; they are mainly insectivorous and frequent a variety of woodland habitats.

Leafbirds are birds of the forest canopy, found mainly in south-east Asia and Indonesia. The largest species is the Great Green Leafbird *C. sonnerati*, 8 in. (20 cm.) long, and found both on the mainland and islands. Like the other leafbirds it is green, ideally coloured for a life searching for insects and fruit amongst the foliage of trees. Some species have black throats, lacking in others, and all but the Himalayan population of the appropriately named Orange-bellied Leafbird *C. hardwickii* are sedentary. In the mountain forests that species is an altitudinal migrant.

Above left: a member of the arboreal Leafbird family, this female Fairy Bluebird inhabits Asiatic woodlands. Left: a Rufous-backed Shrike watches for prey from a perch in Bharatpur, India.

The Blue-backed Fairy-bluebird *I. puella*, 10 in. (26 cm.) long, occurs from India to south-east Asia; and with the Blue-mantled Fair-bluebird *I. cyanogaster* of the Philippines, forms an allopatric pair. They are forest birds and can be nomadic in their search for fruit outside the breeding season. Occasionally they may leave the forest to forage around areas of cultivation, or reach 6,500 ft. (2,000 m.) in montane forests; but they do not breed at such altitudes.

Members of the family lay 2–3 eggs in a cup-shaped nest, which in the case of the Common Iora *A. tiphia*, is constructed by both adults from grass and vegetable fibres, bound into the fork of a tree with cobwebs. Both share the 15 day incubation period, with the female working the night shift, and both parents tending the young. Little is known about the breeding biology of leafbirds, and from the scant information on the Blue-backed Fairy-bluebird, the female constructs the nest and incubates the eggs, although both parents feed the nestlings.

SHRIKES
Order *Passeriformes*
Family: *Laniidae*
12 genera contain 79 species

Any day when one sees a shrike is a good day! They are predatory passerines with hooked bills, that recall small raptors. Often they can be easily watched, sitting on prominent perches looking for food, which might take the form of beetle, bee, small bird, mammal or reptile. Most northern species impale prey on thorns and on barbed wire. Not all are as obvious, for amongst the colourful African bush-shrikes *Telophorus* are some arboreal species that are difficult to see. Many shrikes are birds of open bush country, but the bush-shrikes and the puff-backs *Dryoscopus* are amongst the species inhabiting woodland and forest habitats.

There are 82 shrikes belonging to 13 genera, but only two occur in North America, the Northern and Loggerhead Shrikes *Lanius excubitor* and *L. ludovicianus*. The British Isles fares even worse, for the Red-backed Shrike *L. collurio*, once widespread, may soon be faced with extinction as a breeding species. The reason is attributed to climatic changes over the last 100 years, for in Britain most summers have been too damp for this species. In the winter the Northern, or Great Grey as it is known, is a visitor in small numbers from mainland Europe, and during migration periods three other species occur as uncommon visitors. If one wants to see shrikes, then Africa is the place – 68 species are endemic and three more winter regularly south of the Sahara. Authorities differ in the composition of the family, some exclude the helmet-shrikes *Prionops*; these are included here. Recently there have been suggestions that the wattle-eyed flycatchers *Platysteirinae* are aberrant shrikes, but for the time being the accepted classification is preferred.

The Northern or Great Gray Shrike (above), circumpolar in distribution, is a winter visitor to areas south of its breeding range. Left: a Bay-backed Shrike, another Indian species, in Bharatpur.

Most shrikes are long-tailed birds, and appear neckless with large heads and stout, hooked bills. They range in length from the Brubru *Nilaus afer* 5.5 in. (14 cm.), a widespread African bird, to the southern African race of the Long-tailed Shrike *Corvinella melanoleuca*, whose 14 in. (35 cm.) tail gives it a total length of 20 in. (50 cm.). The Brubru, the helmet-shrikes and the puff-backs lack the longer tails of other shrikes, and forage for insects amongst woodland foliage. In arid areas of Namibia and Angola lives the White-tailed Shrike *Lanioturdus torquatus*; this is a striking black and white species with a short tail and long legs, that hunts for its insect prey in both bushes and on the ground, where it hops with an upright stance.

With few exceptions, adult shrikes are usually immaculate birds, often black and white, sometimes with shades grey and/ or rufous in the plumage. The bush-shrikes are brightly coloured with green upper-parts and yellow beneath, some having areas of black, grey, orange and red. One of the most beautiful is the Crimson-breasted Shrike *Laniarius atrococcineus*, another dry-country species from the south-western corner of Africa. It is black above with a white wing-patch and has crimson under-parts. A rare colour-form exists, where the crimson is replaced by chrome yellow.

The Red-backed and Lesser Grey Shrikes *L. minor* are long-distance migrants, breeding in the Palearctic and wintering as far south as southern Africa. Other migrants travel shorter distances, but most are sedentary, and of those the majority occur singly or in pairs. In woodlands the helmet-shrikes occur in small foraging parties.

Shrikes build cup-shaped nests of grass, twigs and other vegetable matter, often lined with softer material, and located in a variety of sites from bushes to trees. The clutch size ranges from 2 – 7 eggs depending on the species, and the incubation period lasts from 12 – 18 days. Both birds share the duty in some species, but in many cases incubation is by the female alone. Both parents feed the nestlings during the 12 – 20 day fledging period. Helpers from their social group assist a pair of helmet-shrikes in nest-building, incubation and the feeding of the nestlings. In most other bird families involving helpers, their part is to feed the chicks.

VANGA SHRIKES
Order: *Passeriformes*
Family: *Vangidae*
11 genera contain 14 species.

When the ancestors of the Vanga Shrikes, probably some species of helmet shrike *Prionopidae*, arrived in Madagascar they found an island with a great variety of habitats and little competition from other birds. This left the door wide open to evolution and over the thousands of years that have passed since they arrived the Vanga Shrikes have become the most successful group of colonists.

Vangas have evolved in a similar way to the Darwin's Finches of the Galapagos, where birds arrived on an isolated group of islands without any serious competition from other species. From a common stock they were able to fill the various habitats that were available and diversified to exploit the vacancies and avoid competition. There are 14 species, if one includes the Tylas-vanga or Kinkimavo *Tylas eduardi* formerly classed with the bulbuls *Pycnonotidae*, split between 11 genera. These species now occupy the ecological niches filled by more familiar birds in other parts of the World.

Bill shape is one of the greatest differences between the species. The Helmet Bird *Euryceros prevostii* has evolved a large bill that resembles that of the Smooth-billed Ani *Crotophaga ani*, found from Florida to South America, whilst the Sicklebill has developed the curved bill and crevice-probing feeding method of the Wood Hoopoes *Phoeniculidae* found extensively on the African mainland. Another niche that needed to be filled was that of an arboreal creeping bird, occupied by the treecreepers *Certhiidae* and nuthatches *Sittidae* elsewhere in the World. The Coral-billed Nuthatch *Hypositta corallirostris* fills that gap on Madagascar; having evolved to behave like a nuthatch, it Looks like one, although the two families are unrelated.

Vangas occur throughout Madagascar in a variety of

The Loggerhead Shrike (left and below) is a widespread species which winters in the United States, flying there from its northern breeding areas. Shrikes often watch for prey from prominent perches, and nest in thorn bushes. Bottom: a striking White-tailed Shrike in Khorixas, Namibia. This bird is endemic to the dry south-west of Africa.

habitats where they form small flocks to search for food amongst trees and bushes. Their diet includes insects, tree frogs and reptiles. Some species are found in the damp evergreen forests of the eastern side of the island, whilst more adaptable species such as the Chabert Vanga *Leptopterus chabert* and the White-headed Vanga *L. viridis* inhabit the western woodlands and the arid scrub of the south-western corner of Madagascar. The Blue Vanga *L. madagascarinus* is the only species to have extended its range beyond Madagascar, colonising home, two islands in the Comoro group to the north.

Vangas have mainly glossy black or blue upper-parts and white under-parts. Some species have patches of grey or brown and some, including the White-headed Vanga and the Sicklebill *Falculea palliata*, have white heads. The plumage of the male and female of some species is identical, whilst very different in others. They vary in size from the Red-tailed Vanga some 5 in. (13 cm.) long to the Hook-billed Vanga *Vanga curvirostris* which is 12 in. (30 cm.) long.

The breeding biology of the Vangas is poorly known with only a handful of nests found. The clutch size is usually three or four eggs. It appears that both adults share in the domestic duties and with at least one species, the Chabert Vanga, non-breeding birds act as helpers.

On the island of Madagascar, where so much of the indigenous forest and woodland has been destroyed, many forms of wildlife are in decline including three species of Vanga. Van Dam's Vanga *Xenopirostris damii* occurs in only one area, part of which falls within the Ankarafantsika Nature Reserve. Recent sightings suggest that it is present in quite good numbers within its very limited range. The outlook is not as healthy for Pollen's Vanga *X. polleni* or Bernier's Vanga *Oriolia bernieri*, for neither have been recorded with any regularity in recent years.

WAXWINGS
Order: *Passeriformes*
Family: *Bombycillidae*
two genera contain four species.

The Waxwing family *Bombycillidae* consists of four species in two genera, although some authorities also count the Silky Flycatchers *Ptilogonatinae* that include the Phainopepla *Phainopepla nitens*. However, recent analysis of the egg-white protein has shown that they are unrelated and I have treated them separately.

The true waxwings *Bombycilla* are birds of northern latitudes, spread across North America and Eurasia, although it is only the Bohemian Waxwing *Bombycilla garrulus* that is of Holarctic distribution. In the United States this bird breeds mainly in north-western Canada and Alaska, usually spreading farther south during the winter months and occasionally across to the Eastern Seaboard. In the Palearctic it breeds from northern Norway eastwards, with birds wandering south in winter.

In some years the population irrupts out of the normal winter range and large numbers can appear elsewhere. The exact reasons for this behaviour are not fully understood, but the mostly likely explanation is an imbalance between the population (high) and the food supply (low) within their usual range. During these irruptions hundreds of birds can travel as far west as the British Isles, where these colourful birds create considerable interest. They arrive in gardens and city parks and systematically strip the red berries from trees and shrubs. Hawthorn *Crataegus oxyacanthoides*, Holly I*lex aquifolium* and Cotoneaster *Cotoneaster sp.*, are particularly attractive to Bohemian Waxwings.

Of the other two waxwings the Cedar *B. cedrorum* occurs in North America, breeding across southern Canada and the northern United States. During the winter months, birds move south and may reach the West Indies or even Panama, if the weather farther north is particularly severe. Perhaps the name Japanese Waxwing *B. japonica* is a misnomer for the species breeds in north-eastern Siberia. During the Fall the species leaves the breeding area and moves south to winter in China, Korea and Japan, where it is a common visitor north to Hokkaido.

Waxwings are about Starling *Sturnus vulgaris* size, 7 in. (18 cm.) long. The Bohemian is the largest and the Cedar Waxwing is the smallest, although the differences are only a matter of millimetres. The name 'Waxwing' comes from the curious scarlet tips to the secondaries. These appendages are waxy and look like small blobs of sealing wax. This is found on the Bohemian and Cedar Waxwings, but the red on the secondaries of the Japanese Waxwing is nothing more than conventional red tipped feathers. The plumage is soft and silky and all species look similar, with a warm grey-brown body colouring, rather more chestnut on the head and grey on the lower back and rump. They all have crests, less prominent on juvenile birds, with black through the eye and beneath the chin. The Japanese Waxwing has a red band across the end of the tail, but in the other species this is bright yellow. Common features seem to be well mixed between the three species, for the under-tail coverts on the Bohemian and Japanese are chestnut or red, and white on the Cedar Waxwing!

Pairing of birds takes place amongst the winter flocks, so that the pair-bond is firmly established by the time birds arrive at the breeding areas. Display is highly ritualized with the male and female passing a small object to and fro between them. In the display of the Cedar Waxwing, a berry is used and it ends when one or other bird eats the offering! The Bohemian performs a similar display, but the token is not eaten as it is not always an edible object. Waxwings breed singly or in small groups in conifers, mainly Spruce *Picea sp.* and occasionally in Birch *Betula sp.* The nest of twigs, moss and lichen, with a soft lining, is built by both birds. A clutch of 3 – 7 eggs is laid and incubated, again by both, for 15 – 17 days. During his 'spare' time, between territorial duties, the male feeds the incubating female.

Studies have not shown that she reciprocates. The chicks fledge after 19 – 22 days during which time they are fed regurgitated insects by both parents. After leaving the nest the family stay together for at least three weeks.

The final species is the sole member of the genus *Hypocolius*. The Grey Hypocolius *H. ampelinus* is an aberrant waxwing found in south-western Asia, occasionally wandering to India, North Africa and the Middle East. It is a bird, recalling a Northern Shrike *Lanius excubitor*, being 10 in. (25 cm.), long. The male has a soft grey plumage with a narrow black band running from the bill, through the eyes to the nape at the back of the head. The wings are largely black, with white tips to the primaries and the long tail has a black terminal band. The female is pale grey-brown with the black and white on the wings reduced to the tips of the primaries.

It occurs in arid lowlands, usually found in areas with palm trees and scrub such as in river valleys and flood plains, where it can find fruit, its staple diet. Insects are also eaten; often caught when the bird drops from an overhanging perch to catch the prey on the ground. Some insects are captured in mid-air by fly-catching.

The Bohemian Waxwing (above) is the most northerly and widespread of the three waxwing species.

During the breeding season the Grey Hypocolius is loosely colonial. Both birds build the nest of twigs, grasses and vegetable-down in a dense bush or tree or even at times in the bases of palm tree fronds. The clutch is 4 – 5 eggs and incubated by both birds, although mostly by the female, for about 14 days. Both parents tend the young feeding them a mixture of regurgitated fruit and insects. Once again the female does most of the work!

SILKY FLYCATCHERS

Order: *Passeriformes*
Family: *Ptilogonatinae*
three genera contain four species.

The four species of Silky Flycatcher range from south-western United States to western Panama. They have traditionally been placed by taxonomists with the waxwings *Bombycillidae*, but detailed studies of the egg-white protein and other characteristics have shown that this is not the case. Further investigations may reveal a relationship closer to the solitaires *Myadestes*.

The species are split between three genera and perhaps the most familiar is the Phainopepla *Phainopepla nitens*. The species is found from southern California across to western Texas and south to central Mexico. Anyone travelling around the arid areas of the south-western States, will have noticed male Phainopeplas conspicuously perched on roadside bushes. The name comes from two Greek words meaning 'shining cloak'; very apt as the male has silky, glossy black plumage and white wing patches. The female, dull grey with greyish white wing patches and a comparatively inconspicuous bird, gave rise to an earlier belief that male Phainopeplas outnumbered the females! The main source of food is berries, especially mistletoe, but it is while hawking insects from a prominent perch on a bush or small tree that the males attract attention.

Nest building starts in February and construction is all, or almost entirely by the male. Two to three eggs are laid in the small cup made of leaves and other plant material, bound together by spiders' webs and lined with hair and down. Incubation, with the male working most of the day shifts, lasts 14 – 15 days and the young fledge at about 19 days with parental duties being shared.

The two species that make up the genus Ptilogonys are the Grey *P. cinereus* and the more southerly Long-tailed *P. caudatus*, Silky Flycatchers from the mountains and highlands of Mexico and western Panama respectively. The Long-tailed Silky Flycatcher is about 9.5 in. (24 cm.) long, and over half of that, 5 in. (12.7 cm.) is tail! The Grey is the same length, but the tail is an inch (2.5 cm.) shorter. Both species have crests and are mainly grey with black wings and black and white tails. In both, the crissum is dull yellow and in addition the male Long-tailed has an olive-yellow head. The food is mainly insects, berries and fruit and outside the breeding season parties of a dozen or so birds can be found together.

The final species is the Black and Yellow Silky Flycatcher *Phainoptila melanoxantha*, 8.5 in. (21 cm.) long, which shares the same range as the Long-tailed Silky in Costa Rica and western Panama. It is the only species without a crest and is more thrush-like. The male is glossy black; the rump, sides and crissum are yellow and the breast is olive-green.

PALMCHAT

Order: *Passeriformes*
Family: *Dulidae*
the genus Dulus contains a single
species *Dulus dominicus*.

The Palmchat *Dulus dominicus*, a West Indian endemic species, is found on the island of Hispaniola and the off-shore islets of Gonâve and Saona. It is a social bird, widespread on the islands, where it avoids dense rain forest and high altitude.

Palmchats are about 8 in. (20 cm.) long with olive-brown upper-parts, green wings and heavily streaked buff coloured under-parts. They are probably related to the Waxwings *Bombycillidae*, but have rougher plumage and heavier bills. They forage through the trees, often in flocks, in search of food which consists of fruit and blossoms.

They prefer lower elevations, and are often associated with Royal Palm, where a communal nest of twigs is built. The nest is more like an apartment block than a regular nest as it can be as much as 10 ft. (3 m.) high and 3 ft. (1 m.) across! It is occupied by several pairs, each with an entrance hole that leads along a tunnel to their individual nesting chambers. When not used for breeding the structure is used as a communal roost. Trees are used at higher elevations where palms do not grow. Because of difficulties in studying life in the massive nest very little is known about the breeding cycle other than the clutch consists of 2 – 4 heavily spotted eggs.

DIPPERS

Order: *Passeriformes*
Family: *Cinclidae*
the genus *Cinclus* contains five species

Dippers, related to Wrens *Troglodytidae*, supremely adapted to a life along the swift, oxygen rich streams of mountain and uplands areas, occur across the Palearctic and the Americas. They are a bird often seen by walkers and hikers in those lonely places, where one feels close to Nature. Dippers fly up-and down-stream as one walks or watches, stopping on a boulder in the torrent and characteristically bobbing, whilst flashing the white nictitating membrane. This membrane is the third eyelid, possessed by birds and usually transparent. Why it should be so conspicuous in dippers is not known. Dippers are the only truly aquatic *Passeriformes* and unlike many other water birds they have not evolved webbed feet. They search for invertebrates, mainly insect larvae, beetles, small crustaceans, fish fry and tadpoles, in the currents and among stones and boulders of the fast flowing streams. From suitable rocks they walk into the water and search for food below the surface. When swimming below the surface they do not use their feet, but fly with short, sharp wing beats. Returning to the surface, they bob up like a toy being released from the bottom of a child's bath and swim or walk ashore or dive again. When swimming on the surface dippers use a combination of the currents and very rapid leg movements to reach their destination. As a rule dippers are non-migratory, but in latitudes and elevations where the habitat becomes completely unsuitable during the winter freeze, birds move to lower stretches of stream or river. On the west coast of Scotland White-breasted Dippers *C. cinclus* feed around rocks along by the seashore during periods of severe cold weather.

The American Dipper *Cinclus mexicanus* is a plain grey bird, 7.5 in. (19 cm.) long, which occurs from Alaska south into Panama. In North America it is a western bird in the United States not extending farther east than the eastern foothills of the Rocky Mountains. Pairs are scattered along the streams at regular intervals, but one does not have to walk miles to see and enjoy dippers. During a visit to Utah in 1989 we drove north up Logan Canyon, seeing several birds standing on boulders in the river. The highlight came during a lunch stop at one of the turn-offs in the Canyon. Only yards away on the opposite bank of the rocky stream stood three young dippers on wet, moss covered stones. They impatiently waited for food and, having only left the nest a day or so previously, were mainly grey with buff coloured under-parts and bobbed in true dipper fashion. As soon as an adult appeared, flying low and fast on a blur of grey wings, they would call excitedly displaying a wide orange gape. They were being fed by both parents, one was working up and the other downstream.

The domed nest would have been of mosses and other vegetable material under rocks or the roots of a tree overhanging the river or perhaps close to a waterfall. Such nests blend so well with the surroundings that they can only be found by watching the bird fly straight into the round entrance on the side. Artificial sites are used and in 1989 we found several pairs feeding young in nests under road bridges that crossed

Facing page: a White-breasted Dipper pauses by a swift-flowing stream in Britain; its nest of hungry youngsters is concealed nearby.

rivers in Grand Teton and Yellowstone National Parks. The nest is built by both birds and incubation of the clutch of 3-6 eggs is carried out mainly by the female for 13 – 16 days. The young birds fledge after 18 – 20 days and become fully independent after a further period of up to 18 days. American Dippers can have two broods each year, but less unlikely in the northern part of the range.

In South America are two species of dipper; the Rufous-throated *C. schulzi* and the White-capped *C. leucocephalus* Dippers frequent streams and rivers flowing down the Andes. The White-capped is the most widespread South American species, occurring from Colombia and Venezuela south to Bolivia. It is a small dipper 5.5 in. (14 cm.) long; a dark brown bird, it has as expected a white cap. There is a patch of white on the back together with a white throat and breast. The back is dark on birds found in northern Colombia, which also have less white on the under-parts. White-capped Dippers have not been recorded swimming under water. The little known Rufous-throated Dipper occurs farther south on the eastern side of the Andes in southern Bolivia and north-western Argentina. It may be declining as a result of streams and rivers becoming polluted by mining activities in the area. Like the American Dipper it is a grey bird, but has a rufous throat.

The remaining two species occur in the Palearctic. Most widespread is the White-breasted Dipper *C. cinclus*. Its range extends eastwards from Ireland to Tibet and central Asia. In Britain, and in most countries of western Europe it is called 'The Dipper' or the equivalent in the respective languages. The name is used without qualification, but A.C. Bent called the American Dipper 'The Dipper', when he wrote *Life Histories of North American Nuthatches, Wrens, Thrashers, and their Allies*. Modern books about North American birds all call the bird 'American Dipper', so perhaps the Europeans could become a little less insular by acknowledging the existence of other dippers by calling their bird the White-breasted Dipper! The White-breasted Dipper is 7 in. (18 cm.) long and is a dark brown and black dipper with a white throat and upper-breast. Those birds from Britain have chestnut-brown lower breasts and bellies, darker on birds from western Scotland and Ireland, while Continental birds have black bellies. Single birds of this, the nominate race, known as the Black-bellied Dipper *C. c. cinclus*, occasionally stray across the North Sea to eastern Scotland and England during the winter. The breeding biology and behaviour of the White-breasted Dipper closely matches that of the American and other species. The last species found in the Palearctic is the Brown Dipper *C. pallasii* of the Himalayas, north-eastern Asia and Japan. It is an all dark brown bird, the juvenile having a scaly appearance, and at 8.5 in. (22 cm.) is the largest of the five species of dipper.

WRENS

Order *Passeriformes*
Family: *Troglodytidae*
16 genera contain 61 species

In the spring of 1953, James Fisher and Roger Tory Peterson undertook an epic 30,000 mile (48,000 km.) journey around North America that was to result in the superb book *Wild America*. One of the first bird's songs to help James Fisher feel at home was that of a Winter Wren *Troglodytes troglodytes* singing in Newfoundland. This dumpy songster is only 4 in. (10 cm.) long and breeds across North America and the Palearctic. It is absent from the far north and only occurs in the southern United States during the winter months, and of the World's 61 species of wren, the only one to occur outside the Americas.

Characteristically wrens are brown stubby birds with cocked tails that are brown but once one looks beyond the genus *Troglodytes*, so the birds become more strikingly marked, although none could be described as colourful. Of the North American species the Cactus Wren *Campylorhynchus brunneicapillus* of the dry south-west is the largest and most boldly marked, with striated upper-parts, barred wings and spotted throat and breast. Similar species occur in Central and South America, but the most distinctive wren to be found in those areas is the White-headed Wren *C.*

albobrunneus, with its white head and under-parts, dark brown back, wings and tail; it occurs from central Panama to south-western Colombia. An aberrant wren is the Black-capped Donacobius *Donacobius atricapillus*; it is the least wren-like of the family and has previously been treated as a mockingbird *Mimidae*. It is the largest member of the wren family at 8.5 in. (22 cm.) long, but there are several contenders, including the Winter Wren, for the smallest at 4 in. (10 cm.) in length.

Wrens live in most habitats between Canada and Tierra del Fuego. They are entirely insectivorous, feeding on a diet of insects and their larvae, spiders and other small invertebrates. Being so dependent on a specialised diet they readily succumb

The Winter Wren (above) is the most widespread member of its family and, with a circumpolar distribution, it is the only wren occurring outside the Americas. The House Wren (left) ranges from southern Canada to Argentina and the Falkland Islands.

to the effects of cold weather, and so the populations of several North American species, and the Scandinavian population of the Winter Wren, migrate south or to the coasts in the fall.

Wrens construct a nest of vegetable fibres; the males of some species build several nests, one of which is selected and lined with soft material by the female. Most are dome-shaped with a side entrance and sited in hollows in banks or amongst vegetation. Both the male and female Cactus Wrens build untidy grass nests, often large conspicuous structures sited in cactus bushes. Cactus Wrens are monogamous, unlike other species who may practice polygyny. The wrens in temperate regions lay 6 – 10 eggs, whilst their tropical relatives produce a clutch of only 2 – 4 eggs. Incubation lasts for 12 – 20 days and is undertaken by the female. The chicks fledge in 12 – 18 days; if the male has not gone off with another bird, then he helps the female rear the young. Young Cactus Wrens from previous broods help their parents rear and feed the subsequent brood.

Salvador. The legs are strong, and the bill may be short, as in the Northern Mockingbird, or curved as in several thrashers, including the California Thrasher *T. redivivum*. Mockingbirds inhabit scrub, bushes and small trees; some thrashers are found in cactus deserts. The diet of the mockingbird family includes various insects and fruits. They forage for food in the vegetation or on the ground.

Nests made by members of the family are cup-shaped and usually constructed by both birds from twigs and lined with softer material such as hair. It is sited in a bush, or in the case of the Sage Thrasher *Oreoscoptes montanus*, in Sagebrush *Artemisia tridentata*. Le Conte's Thrasher *T. lecontei*, must be tough, for it is one of the few species to nest in the spiny bushes of various species of cholla cactus *Opuntia spp.* The clutch of 2 – 5 eggs is incubated by both parents of most, if not all, species for 12 – 13 days until hatched, although the female may do more than her fair share. The chicks fledge in 12 – 13 days and during that time are fed by both parents; some tropical species may take longer.

MOCKINGBIRDS
Order *Passeriformes*
Family: *Mimidae*
12 genera contain 30 species

ACCENTORS
Order: *Passeriformes*
Family: *Prunellidae*
the genus Prunella contains 12 species

The Gray Catbird (above left) breeds over much of southern Canada and the United States except for the dry south-west. The Hedge Accentor or Dunnock (above) leads a quiet life in the gardens of Britain.

Mockingbirds are a New World family that includes several species found in North America, namely the widespread Northern Mockingbird *Mimus polyglottus*, the Gray Catbird *Dumetella carolinensis* and Brown Thrasher *Toxostoma rufum*, and a further six species of thrasher that occur in the south and western states. Birds of the family occur from southern Canada to Tierra del Fuego. Recently, the Black-capped Mockingthrush *Donacobius atricapillus* has been removed from the family Mimidae and placed with the wrens *Troglodytidae*, and is now known as the Black-capped Donacobius.

Members of the mocking bird family range from 8 – 13 in. (20 – 33 cm.) in length. They are short-winged birds with long-tails and a plumage that is often shades of brown or grey, with black and rufous in some species; some have striated under-parts and others are plain. Two more colourful members are the Blue, and Blue and White Mockingbirds, *Melanotis caerulescens* and *M. hypoleucus*; the former is endemic to Mexico and is blue-grey with a black mask, and the latter, a similar bird but with white underparts, occurs south to El

Accentors are small birds found over much of the Palearctic region, except for most of North Africa and the extreme north of Siberia. They are placed in the Order of Passerines next to the mockingbirds and thrashers *Mimidae*, but recent DNA studies have determined an affinity with the Old World weavers *Ploceinae*.

Most of the twelve species breed in mountainous areas and descend to lower altitudes during the winter months. The greatest diversity of species is in an area that includes Tibet and the Himalayas, where seven species occur, some in the tree-zone, some in alpine meadows and others residing above the tree-line.

Widespread in western Europe is the Hedge Accentor or Dunnock *Prunella modularis*, 6 in. (15 cm.) long; it is a common bird of woodland, hedgerows, city parks and gardens, besides montane areas. This very drab bird with brown upper-parts and grey beneath might appear to be dull and uninteresting as it shuffles along, mouse-like, amongst the flower beds and edges of the lawn, but it has a great sex life! Most birds with unconventional domestic arrangements are consistent, but

187

Hedge Accentors prefer variety! In addition to conventional pairings, one finds a breeding territory held by a male and more than one female; two males and a single female or perhaps a group involving several males and females!

The most widespread species is the Alpine Accentor *P. collaris*, 7 in. (18 cm.) long; it breeds in mountains above 3300 ft. (1000 m.) from Spain and the Atlas Mountains of North Africa east to the Himalayas. It is brighter and more well-marked than the Hedge Accentor, as are many of the other species. The Black-throated Accentor *P atrogularis*, 6 in. (15 cm.) long, inhabits montane coniferous forests and scrub; a smart bird with buff under-parts, black cap, lores, ear-coverts and throat.

Accentors build a cup-shaped nest of grass and other vegetable materials, which they line with a soft material such as hair or wool, depending on availability. This is either in a bush, amongst rocks or on the ground. Incubation of the 3 – 6 eggs lasts for 12 – 13 days, although this may take longer for the high-altitude species. This duty is shared by a pair of Alpine Accentors, but only by the female Hedge Accentor, whose mate helps feed the nestlings during the 12 – 13 day incubation period. If the relationship involves an additional male, he also helps with feeding if he mated with the female.

Blackbird *T. merula*. The introductions took place in 1862, and were so successful that the two species are now amongst the most numerous of the country's birds.

The family is a varied, one comprising 312 species divided between 48 genera, and ranges from 4.75 – 11 in. (12 – 28 cm.) in length; they are well-proportioned birds. The plumage of many is shades of brown, grey and rufous, besides black and white; some species have conspicuous patches of blue and red. Amongst the colourful members of the family are the rock thrushes *Monticola spp.*. The Blue Rock Thrush *M. solitarius*, lives in rocky and mountainous areas from south-western Europe to Malaysia. Thrushes and chats occur in a wide variety of habitats, from tundra, through woodlands and forests at all elevations, to the barren deserts such as the Namib in south-west Africa.

The larger species are the thrushes which belong to 13 genera including *Turdus*. In North America, the American Robin *T. migratorius*, a thrush not a robin, occupies a similar niche to the Blackbird of the Palearctic. The latter is also a thrush, and not related to the New World blackbirds *Icteridae*. Both are familiar birds of lawns and gardens as well as wooded areas. The northern populations of both these species are migratory. Several genera include a number of species

THRUSHES and CHATS
Order: *Passeriformes*
Family: *Turdinae*
48 genera contain 312 species

One of the best songsters in the British Isles is the Nightingale *Luscinia megarhynchos*, immortalised in song by the one that sang in Berkley Square. The lyrics resort to a certain degree of poetic licence, for the Nightingale is a bird of bushy scrub and secondary woodland, habitats absent in Central London.

The Nightingale is a member of the widespread family of thrushes and chats *Turdinae*, found throughout the World except for the Antarctic and New Zealand. However, in New Zealand the early European settlers introduced several songbirds to remind them of home, and these included two thrushes – the Song Thrush *Turdus philomelos* and the

Many fine songsters have a dull plumage, and the Nightingale of Europe and western Asia (above) is no exception. The Song Thrush (left) of the Palearctic is larger than New World thrushes.

188

with brown upper-parts and the paler under-parts are spotted. These species typify thrushes to many people and in North America are represented by the New World thrushes *Catharus*. Smaller birds than their Old World counterparts, they are migratory with only the widespread Hermit Thrush *C. guttatus* present in the United States during the winter, and then only in the southern states.

The chats form the larger part of the family, and it is to this group that the familiar bluebirds *Sialia* with their rufous and white under-parts belong. In the eastern and western United States, north into southern Canada, the Eastern and Western Bluebirds *S. sialis* and *S. mexicana* form an allopatric pair. The Mountain Bluebird *S. currucoides*, also a western species, is the most beautiful of chats, with its sky-blue upper-parts, and subtly paler below. Chats are mainly found in the Old World, but if one visits Alaska during the breeding season, there is the chance of seeing the other species that breed in North America. The Bluethroat *Luscinia svecica* breeds in scrub thickets in the tundra, elsewhere it ranges across much of the Palearctic from Scandinavia to north-eastern Siberia. It is a migratory species wintering in Africa, India and south-eastern Asia. The other chat that breeds in Alaska is the Northern Wheatear *Oenanthe oenanthe*, one of the most

The Seychelles Magpie Robin (above left), one of the world's rarest birds, is confined to the island of Frégate. The Cliffchat is an African member of the family. Above: a male Cliffchat at Lake Nakuru, Kenya. After a winter in Africa, the Northern Wheatear (left) flies north to breed in areas from Alaska westwards to north-eastern Canada.

widespread species; it also breeds in north-eastern Arctic Canada and Greenland, in addition to most of the Palearctic. It is a familiar bird in Britain along coastal footpaths, and in hilly and mountainous country, its white rump flashing distinctively. Indeed, the name is a corruption of the Anglo-Saxon 'white-arse.' It is a long-distance migrant, with almost the whole population including those breeding in Alaska, Arctic Canada and Greenland, wintering in Africa. They occur in a belt across the continent south of the Sahara, yet mainly north of the Equator except in East Africa where they occur south to northern Zambia.

Thrushes and chats eat insects, earthworms and other invertebrates; snails feature high on the menu of the Song Thrush, who has favoured stones – 'anvils', on which to smash the shells. During the fall and winter many include fruit and berries in their diet. One of the familiar signs of the fall in Britain, is the annual invasion of Fieldfares *T. pilaris* and Redwings *T. iliacus* from Scandinavia and Iceland. They are attracted by the bright berries of trees and shrubs such as the Hawthorn *Crataegus oxyacanthoides*, it is also worth leaving fallen fruit on the ground for the birds during the winter months.

Thrushes and chats build sturdy cup-shaped nests from vegetable materials including grasses, moss and roots, which some species line with mud and others with hair and feathers. It is invariably built by the female, while the male is singing and defending the territory. Nest sites vary from forks in branches to hollows in earthen banks, holes in trees and walls, and in the case of the Northern Wheatear in old rabbit burrows. At home we have a Blackbird that regularly nests on top of a roll of wire fence-netting. The female incubates the clutch of 2 – 6 eggs during the 12 – 15 day incubation period, and also broods the chicks for the first few days after hatching, although both parents feed the nestlings during the 12 – 15 day fledging period.

One of the rarest species is the Seychelles Magpie Robin *Copsychus sechellarum*, endemic to the island of Frégate in the central Seychelles. It is a black chat with white shoulder patches, and has little fear of Man. It searches for food amongst the leaf-litter and soil disturbed by Giant Tortoises *Testudo gigantia*. Magpie Robins were formerly more widespread within the islands, but being a confiding, terrestrial-feeding bird, it was an easy prey for the feral cats and rats that spread from settlements. When I first visited Frégate in 1977, the World population of this attractive bird stood at 39 individuals; by my next visit in 1988 this was down to only 20. The situation looked grim, but a keen ornithologist, Jan Komdeur, was employed by the International Council for Bird Protection (ICBP) to study the surviving birds. I was fortunate to return 12 months later, and was thrilled to find that under Jan's management the population had increased from 20 birds to 26; a very encouraging improvement. Through his research Jan discovered that the more time the birds have to spend collecting food, the lower the chances of breeding success. Supplementary feeding proved to be the key, so he persuaded the local inhabitants of the island to catch cockroaches during the night. The following morning these were placed close to occupied nest sites where they were discovered by the Magpie Robins, who therefore had to spend less time foraging. Now that some of the Magpie Robin's secrets have been unlocked, perhaps there is cause for cautious optimism for its future.

Left: a Mountain Bluebird in Montana. This is perhaps the most beautiful of the North American bluebirds.

The Robin (above) of Britain and Europe has given its name to red-breasted birds throughout the world.

LOGRUNNERS

Order: *Passeriformes*
Family: *Orthonychinae*
eight genera contain 19 species

Logrunners are a family of small terrestrial birds that all occur in the Australasian region, except for the Malaysian Rail Babbler *Eupetes macrocerus* that resides in south-east Asia, Borneo and Sumatra. Of the remaining 18 species, nine are endemic to Australia and eight to New Guinea, and one, the Spine-tailed Logrunner *Orthonyx temminckii*, has one population in eastern Australia and another in New Guinea.

The Logrunners, who give their name to the family, are ground feeding birds, found searching for food amongst the leaf-litter and other debris on the floor of their rain forest habitat. The Spine-tailed Logrunner, 7 in. (18 cm.) long, has mottled rufous-brown, black and buff upper-parts, with a grey face and a strong black mark running down the side of the neck and breast. The under-parts are white and the female has a rufous throat. The larger Chowchilla or Spalding's Logrunner *O. spaldingii*, 9.75 in. (25 cm.) long, occurs in northern Queensland; it is black with white under-parts and just like the only other member of the genus the female has a rufous throat. The shafts of tail feathers of both species have become spiny tips. Also found in Australia are the two species of Whipbird and the two Wedgebills that comprise the genus *Psophodes*. These are duller birds, with crests that recall some of the Asiatic bulbuls *Pycnontidae*. The Whipbirds occur in coastal scrub and other habitats along the eastern and southern coasts of the continent. The Western Whipbird *P.nigrogularis*, 9.5 in. (24 cm.) long, was formerly thought to be a much rarer bird, until birders became familiar with the ventriloquistic call and discovered it at several new sites in southern Australia. Inland they are replaced by the Whipbirds, 8 in. (20 cm.) long, which frequent scrub and acacia in arid and semi-arid country. The Ajax Quail-thrush *Cinclosoma ajax* occurs in New Guinea, but the other four members of the genus inhabit dry and wet forests, in scrub along ridges or along dry watercourses in Australia. Quail-thrushes are slender birds with disproportionately short legs, ranging from 7 – 11 in. (18 – 28 cm.) in length. They are a mixture of rufous, black, grey and white. Both sexes have prominent white eyebrows and malar stripes, but the females are duller, lacking the black throat and breast patterns of the males. They are shy and secretive birds and when disturbed often freeze, or suddenly fly like a quail *Coturnix*.

Several of the New Guinea species are more colourful than their Australian relatives, which is often the case, for birds inhabiting forests need to be more brightly coloured. The two species of Melampitta *Melampitta* contradict this pattern, for both are black; they inhabit montane forests, and differ considerably in size - the Lesser Melampitta *M. lugubris*, 7 in. (18 cm.) long, is dwarfed by the Greater Melampitta *M. gigantea*, 11.5 in. (29 cm.) long!

The nest, made of twigs and grass, of most members of the family is either on the ground or sited low in bushes or ferns. One exception is the Green-backed Babbler *Androphobus viridis*, found on the Snow and Weyland Mountains in western New Guinea, whose nest can be situated up to 13 ft. (4 m.) in vegetation. Some of the other New Guinea species and the quail-thrushes make a cup-shaped nest of grass and other materials in a depression on the ground, often sheltered by an overhanging rock. Logrunners make a dome-shaped nest, with a side entrance, from twigs; this is situated on the ground or on a bank or low stump. The clutch size of 1 – 3 eggs, depends on the species, but beyond this much has still to be learned about the breeding biology of these birds.

BABBLERS
Order *Passeriformes*
Family: *Timaliinae*
50 genera contain 257 species

The Wren-Tit *Chamaea fasciata* is the only North American representative of the babblers *Timaliinae*, one of the largest of the Old World bird families. The Wren-Tit is a wren-like bird with a long tail, 6.5 in. (17 cm.) in overall length, and found only along the Pacific coast of the United States and northern Mexico.

The family comprises 257 species in 50 genera, and of these about 200 occur in Asia, including the East Indies where many species have evolved in isolation. In Africa there are 49 species of which 8 are endemic to Madagascar, whilst Australia has only 6 species. Babblers are birds of the warm temperate and tropical regions, where they range in habitats from tropical rain forests to deserts, although in the latter, babblers are always associated with scrub and thickets.

This a very variable family, with some species resembling thrushes *Turdinae* and others, including the Wren-Tit, more lightly built, and appearing wren or warbler-like. They range in length from 4 – 13.75 in. (10 – 35 cm.). Most babblers are brown, grey and cream, some with strongly patterned heads, and others that are spotted or streaked; some species have tufted crests, the most colourful belong to a handful of Asiatic genera including the Shrike-babblers *Pteruthius spp.*. It is their shape and appearance that varies greatly, and in this respect they resemble the South American antbirds *Formicariidae*. The smaller species are so like the Old World Warblers *Sylviinae* that they must have caused taxonomists a few headaches in their time. The terrestrial Wren-babblers *Spelaeornis spp.* are dumpy, short tailed, wren-like birds with an upright stance recalling the antpittas, whilst the larger

Top: a Blue-capped Ifrita – a logrunner endemic to New Guinea. The White-crested Laughing Thrush (above left) is a striking babbler that ranges from the Himalayas to Indonesia, and the Eastern Whipbird (above) is an Australian Logrunner found from Queensland to Victoria.

Scimitar-babblers *Pomatorhinus spp.* are long slim birds with decurved bills, and resemble the North American thrashers *Toxostoma spp.*. These are all Asiatic babblers, but the Jungle-babblers *Turdoides spp.*, the thrush-like members of the family, occur in both Asia and Africa. Several species stand out as distinctive, but the White Crested Laughing Thrush with its brown and chestnut body, white head and breast, with prominent white crest and black facial mask, is the most striking. The other members of the genus are amongst the most well-marked of the babblers.

Babblers are mainly sedentary birds, although several Himalayan species are altitudinal migrants. The diet of many is insectivorous, supplemented by fruit, seeds, and in some cases, nectar. Some species join mixed bird parties, but in some, such as the Jungle-babblers, the social group is of particular importance. Noisily they can be found foraging amongst the litter and in bushes, but at other times they rest quietly in shrubs mutually preening one another; this behaviour is known as 'allopreening'.

Babblers build either cup or dome-shaped nests, depending on the genus; some such as that of the Arrow-marked Babbler *T. jardineii* are built by several members of the social group. Nests are usually in a bush, in thick vegetation or in a few instances on the ground. The clutch of 2 – 6 eggs is incubated for 13 – 16 days by both adults; the chicks are fed during the fledging period, which lasts a similar length of time, by their parents and helpers, and often leave the nest before they can fly well. They can remain dependent on the group for food for up to four weeks after fledging and stay on as members of the group for a year or more.

The 19 species are divided into 3 genera, with 17 species belonging to the genus *Paradoxornis*; they are brown-bodied birds and all have either brown, grey or rufous heads. Except the Short-tailed Parrotbill *P. davidianus*, all have long tails, and with the exception of the Bearded Reedling or Bearded Tit *Panurus biarmicus*, whose bill is small and conical, all have stout heavy bills, from which the family earns its name. The Bearded Reedling is the most widespread member of the family, ranging from England across the whole of the Palearctic to eastern China. Together with the Chinese Parrotbill *Paradoxornis heudi*, it inhabits reed beds; they are the only members of the family not to occur in bamboo thickets.

The Chinese Parrotbill is the rarest member of the family, and until recently, was thought to be restricted to the vast reed beds of the Lower Yangtze, one of the most densely populated parts of the globe. The effect of the human population on an endemic species with such a restricted range and habitat was unknown, because of the political difficulties in obtaining information. In 1972, a population of Chinese Parrotbills was discovered by Lake Khanka in the U.S.S.R.; later, further populations were found in China and Mongolia in 1983 and 1987. This parrotbill is particularly vulnerable, when faced with the loss of its habitat in the form of drainage schemes.

The other parrotbills live in and around the bamboo zone, with several species occurring above 10,000 ft. (3050 m.). Parrotbills range in length from the diminutive Short-tailed Parrotbill 3.5 in. (9 cm.) long, to the comparatively massive Great Parrotbill *Conostoma oemodium*, 11 in. (28 cm.) long.

Parrotbills are gregarious birds, and feed on a variety of insects and seeds, with the larger species also eating berries.

PARROTBILLS

Order: *Passeriformes*

Family: *Panurinae*

three genera contain 19 species

The Parrotbills are an Old World family, centred on the Far East, in particular China, which is included in the range of 18 species. The exception is Gould's Parrotbill *Paradoxornis flavirostris*, found only in the eastern Himalayas and western Burma.

They are mainly sedentary birds, although those in the higher latitudes move altitudinally in spring and fall. Over the last twenty-five years the Bearded Reedling has undertaken irruptions in the fall, to colonise new reed beds.

The nest is built amongst reeds or grass, and in the case of the Bearded Reedling, is constructed by both adults from dead vegetation. It is lined by the male with softer material. The usual clutch size for the true parrotbills is 2 – 4 eggs, but the Bearded Reedling lays 5 – 7 eggs. The incubation period lasts for 12 – 13 days by both parents. The youngsters leave the nest between 9 – 12 days, and even before they can fly, they are able to scramble amongst the surrounding reeds and grasses.

Above: a female Bearded Reedling feeds its young in a reedbed in England. This bird, the most widespread member of the Parrotbill family, ranges as far as eastern China.

PICATHARTES

Order: *Passeriformes*
Family: *Picathartinae*
the genus Picathartes contains two species

In the equatorial rain forests of West Africa are two of that continent's most unusual passerines. They are the Picathartes, or as they are sometimes called 'Rockfowl'. They are related to the babblers *Timaliinae*, although in the past have served time with crows *Corvidae* and starlings *Sturnidae*.

The two species are the White-necked Picathartes *Picathartes gymnocephalus* and the Grey-necked Picathartes *P. oreas*; both are poorly known and localised birds, about the size of a large thrush and with a bald head. The White-necked Picathartes is known to occur only from Guinea east to Togo, whilst the Grey-necked species appeared to be restricted to the Cameroon and Gabon, until 1987 when it was discovered in eastern Nigeria. They are both sedentary species and have evolved in a very specialised habitat, for they are amongst the very few birds that are entirely dependant on caves for their existence. They inhabit large caves with wide entrances and appear to favour those with running water to maintain a high humidity. Their natural rarity is due to the restricted availability of their habitat, but this has been exacerbated by the demands made on the species by zoos and collections; the locations of the limited number of colonies are well-known by the local trappers, although during recent years hitherto unknown colonies have been discovered.

The Grey-necked Picathartes has grey upper-parts, a white belly and black wings, but the most striking feature is the bald head; this species has a red nape, blue forehead and black sides to the head. The White-necked Picathartes has white under-parts and neck and a largely yellow bare head with a black nape. Structurally both are very similar, with quite long legs. They obtain most of their food by searching through the large deposits of bat dung on the floor of the caves for cockroaches and other insects that are associated with such a habitat. It is possible that Picathartes have evolved a bald head for reasons of cleanliness, for like the bare-headed larger vultures they might have permanently dirty heads otherwise. Those species of vultures are often the first at the dead animal, and with their heavier bills open up the carcass if it has not been torn apart by a predator. The species with feathered heads come in later when the dirty work has been completed.

Picathartes spend much of their time feeding in the cave or in thick vegetation near the cave's mouth. During the heat of the day they retire to preen and a siesta, before feeding prior to settling to roost as the light fades in late afternoon.

A swallow-like nest of mud and grass, lined with coarse vegetable material, is built on a dry rock-face and two, sometimes three, eggs are laid. Few details of the breeding biology are known, other than incubation is shared by both parents.

For the continued survival of these two fascinating species, it is essential that the protection offered by Ghana is extended to all those countries where the Picathartes are known to occur, and that the forests around their breeding areas remain undisturbed and intact.

GNATCATCHERS

Order: *Passeriformes*
Family: *Polioptilinae*
3 genera contain 14 species

The Gnatcatchers *Polioptilinae* are closely related to the Old World warblers *Sylviidae*, and should probably be in that family rather than being treated on their own. Even within the family the systematics are in a state of flux, for recently the Californian race of the Black-tailed Gnatcatcher *Polioptila melanura* has received specific status and is now known as the Californian Gnatcatcher *P. californica*. It has darker grey under-parts, a different call, and occurs in denser habitat than the Black-tailed species. An armchair 'tick' for listers.

There are 14 species in the family and 11 of these belong to the genus *Polioptila*. This genus ranges from the United States to Argentina. Gnatcatchers are slim, long-tailed birds 4–5 in. (10–13 cm.) in length, that are mainly shades of grey with paler under-parts. Some species have black caps and/or black tails with varying amounts of white showing on the underside of the tail. They have the slender bill of insectivorous birds and occur in a variety of wooded and scrub habitats. Most species are sedentary, although northern populations of the Blue-gray Gnatcatcher *P. caerulea* migrate south in the fall.

Two other species belong to the genus *Microbates* and occur from Nicaragua to Brazil and Peru. The Long-billed Gnatwren *Ramphocaenus melanurus*, the only member of its genus, occurs from Mexico to Brazil. The three gnatwrens are more wren-like than the gnatcatchers, with longer bills and shorter cocked tails. They are essentially brown birds with paler under-parts, plainest being the Long-billed Gnatwren. The other two are more distinctive; the Half-collared Gnatwren *Microbates cinereiventris* has rufous cheeks and a speckled necklace, whilst the Collared Gnatwren *M. collaris* has a striped facial pattern and a black breast band. They tend to be inconspicuous birds that inhabit forests and adjacent margins, and may have closer affinities with other New World bird families rather than the gnatcatchers.

All members of the gnatcatcher family build cup-shaped nests in trees, which may be up to 80 ft. (24 m.) above the ground. The nest is constructed by the pair and made from cobwebs, hair, grasses and fine vegetation. The Blue-grey and Black-tailed Gnatcatchers sometimes recycle material from old nests, and it is possible that other less well-known members of the genus do likewise. Both adults share the 13–17 day incubation of the clutch of 3–5 eggs. They also share the feeding of the nestlings during the 11–14 day fledging period.

OLD WORLD WARBLERS

Order: *Passeriformes*
Family: *Sylviidae*
64 genera contain 341 species

The Willow Warbler (above), one of the commonest warblers in western Europe, ranges east to Siberia and winters as far away as South Africa.

Compared with the Wood Warblers *Parulidae* of the New World, the unrelated Old World Warblers *Sylviidae* are a fairly dull family, although in a group of 341 species divided between 64 genera there are some brighter members. The family occurs across the World except the Americas and the extreme northern latitudes of the Palearctic. In much of north-western Europe they form the greatest variety of annual migrants.

Compared with the wood warblers of the Americas, the Old World species vary considerably in shape and appearance, but all are slim birds with thin bills, characteristic of insectivorous species. They frequent a wide variety of habitats from the northern forests to arid desert areas.

Within the family there is a number of well-defined groups, amongst which the leaf warblers *Phylloscopus* are one of the most widespread. Their spring songs are some of the sweetest of the summer visitors to northern latitudes. One of the most widespread is the Arctic Warbler *P. borealis* that breeds from Scandinavia to Alaska, one of three members of the family to breed in North America. In the British Isles it occurs as a vagrant in the fall, for its migration route takes it south-east from Scandinavia to south-east Asia and the Philippines. It is similar to many other members of the genus, having olive-green upper-parts and it is paler below. Among the identification features are the pale superciliary and wing-bar, and at 5 in. (12.5 cm.) in length it is one of the larger members.

Another large group comprises those warblers that frequent reed-beds, marshes and areas of rank grass and bush. Several genera are involved, one of the largest being the genus *Acrocephalus*. Many are browner than the Leaf-warblers, but most have paler under-parts. Some, such as the Lanceolated Warbler *Locustella lanceolata* and other members of its genus, have striated upper-parts. The Lanceolated Warbler occurs as a spring vagrant to the western Aleutians.

A group of warblers that occur from western Europe to China are the scrub warblers; they are particularly associated with the Mediterranean and the Middle East, where all 18 species either breed or pass through on their migration. Some species are sedentary, but many western populations winter in Africa where the Common Whitethroat *S. communis*, a trans-Saharan migrant, was one of the first species to suffer from the droughts in the Sahel region.

Several genera of grassland warblers that occur in warm temperate and tropical grasslands include a family of notoriously difficult species. These are the Cisticolas *Cisticola*, pronounced *sis-tick-ola* and not *sis-ti-cola*, small, often short-

Left: a Willow Warbler in Britain feeds its young in its domed nest, whilst a Reed Warbler (facing page), also in Britain, broods its young during a shower. Both are insectivorous summer visitors to Europe from Africa.

tailed warblers, that have rufous-brown upper-parts heavily striated with black, and pale under-parts. Many are very similar and afford only the briefest glimpse; not all can be separated on habitat and distribution. Song is an invaluable aid, but of course they do not always sing to order!

Africa and Asia are home to some of the more brightly and better marked species that are found in a variety of forest and scrub habitats. The genera involved include the apalises *Apalis* that have almost gnatcatcher *Polioptilinae* proportions,

and the eremomelas *Eremomelas* who resemble leaf warblers in outline. The crombecs *Sylvietta* are small, almost tail-less birds, that search the bark and foliage of trees and bushes, giving the appearance of nuthatches *Sittidae*.

The wren-like tailorbirds *Orthotomus* are named for their habit of sewing leaves together to enclose the fabric of the nest. All but the Red-capped Forest Warbler *O. metopias* of Tanzania and northern Mozambique occur in Asia from India to the Philippines and Indonesia.

Above: a female Blackcap calling in alarm. She can be distinguished from her mate by her rufous cap — the male has a black cap.

The Golden-crowned and Ruby-crowned Kinglets *Regulus satrapa* and *R. calendula*, are the other members of the Old World Warblers that breed in North America. They are very small warblers 4 – 4.25 in. (10 – 11 cm.) long and both have counterparts in the Old World, one of which, the Goldcrest *R. regulus*, ranges from the British Isles to Manchuria.

Elsewhere in the World a variety of other species occur, including a number in Australia, New Zealand and the Pacific islands where most are endemic.

Old World Warblers nest in a variety of places, but always concealed. Some nest in specialized situations; for example, the Reed Warbler *Acrocephalus scirpaceus* weaves a nest between the stems of the Common Reed *Phragmites communis*. Temperate species lay 3 – 7 eggs, whilst their tropical relatives produce 2 – 4 eggs. Incubation is usually undertaken by both adults and lasts for 12 – 14 days, and the fledging period, during which both birds feed the nestlings, lasts for a further 11 – 15 days. Some youngsters leave the nest before they fledge, and most are dependant on their parents for a week or more after their first flight.

A number of species are threatened, both from introduced predators and habitat changes, so it makes a pleasant change to come across a conservation success story. The Seychelles Brush Warbler *Acrocephalus sechellensis* was a threatened species, occurring only on the granitic island of Cousin in the central Seychelles. In 1968 the island, which is also an important seabird colony, was purchased by the International Council for Bird Preservation. The Brush Warbler population was dangerously low, standing at under 50 birds; with careful management the bird had increased to such an extent, that by 1988 over 450 were present. Shortly before I visited the islands that year, 29 birds were translocated to the nearby island of Aride. Within days the birds were settling into their new home and establishing territories. Twelve months later when I was next fortunate to visit the Seychelles, the Brush Warblers on Aride had doubled!

AUSTRALIAN CHATS
Order *Passeriformes*
Family: *Ephthianuridae*
2 genera contain 5 species

The systematics of several endemic Australian bird families have undergone recent changes and the five species of Australian Chat *Ephthianuridae* are now in a family of their own. They were formerly part of the Australian Warbler/Wren *Malurinae* complex, although they do not resemble other members of that family. Laboratory investigations suggest that they may be related to the honeyeaters *Meliphagidae*, for like that family, the Australian Chats have brush-tipped tongues, although so far, only the Crimson Chat *Ephthianura tricolor*, has been noted eating nectar.

Australian Chats are birds of a variety of habitats. The White-fronted Chat *E. albifrons* inhabits the low vegetation growing in salt-marshes along the coasts and in wet fields inland. Other species occur inland, some in semi-arid habitats; the Gibberbird *Ashbyia lovensis*, the only member of its genus, frequents the stony flats of the Lake Eyre drainage system. This habitat is known as 'gibber', and gives the 'Gibberbird' its name.

These chats resemble the chats *Turdinae* of the Old World, the Gibberbird standing upright like a wheatear *Oenanthe sp.*. They walk or run rather than hop, swaggering starling-like. In flight they have an undulating flight and often fly high when flushed. Australian Chats are all about 4.75 in. (12 cm.) in length, with quite long legs and the thin bill of a bird that is essentially an insectivore. The males are more brightly coloured than their mates and they give the members of the genus Ephthianura their names; those not already mentioned are the Orange Chat *E. aurifrons* and Yellow Chat *E. crocea*.

Australian Chats feed mainly on insects, but will also take seeds. The Crimson Chat frequents flowering trees, being the only member of the family known to take nectar as part of its diet. In the non-breeding season there is a tendency for chats to form nomadic flocks, often involving more than one species.

During the breeding season, which often follows the rains, Australian Chats form loose colonies, within which the male defends the territory of a particular pair. The female Crimson Chat constructs the cup-shaped nest of grass and other vegetable fibres, lined with hair and other fine materials, and it is probable that the females of the less well-known species build similar nests. That of the Gibberbird is placed on the ground, a site dictated by the barren habitat, whilst the other species select a site low in a bush. The usual clutch size is 3 eggs and studies have shown that a pair of Crimson Chats share in the incubation of the eggs and the subsequent feeding of the nestlings. The incubation period averages 13 days and youngsters fledge 14 – 15 days later. All species, but the poorly known Yellow Chat, practice 'injury-feigning' to draw a predator away from the nest. Few passerine species employ this strategy, although it is typical of several shorebirds and wildfowl.

The Fernwren (above), despite resembling a typical wren, is actually an Australian Warbler and occurs in north-east Queensland.

AUSTRALIAN WARBLERS
Order *Passeriformes*
Family: *Acathizidae*
11 genera contain 66 species

The warblers that inhabit the Australasian region and parts of south-east Asia, belong to a family that has recently been split from the Australian Wrens *Maluridae*. The precise composition of the family is still a matter of conjecture, for some authorities suggest that two genera, *Mohoua* and *Finschia*, endemic to New Zealand, belong to the whistlers

Pachycephalinae. They build cup-shaped nests, unlike the domed nests of the rest of the family. At present the family comprises 11 genera that contain 66 species.

The overall range of the family extends from Thailand to New Zealand, but distribution centres on Australia with 37 species, and New Guinea home to 20; many are endemic. Most species are nondescript, and resemble the Old World warbler *Sylviidae* but lack the variety of plumages. The smallest is the Weebill *Smicrornis brevirostris*, 3 in. (8 cm.) in length. This tiny yellow bird, endemic to Australia, is the smallest of all species inhabiting the island continent. The largest members of the family are also Australian; they are the three species that comprise the Bristlebirds *Dasyornis*, largest of which is the Rufous Bristlebird *D. broadbenti* 10.5 in. (27 cm.) long. Most however, are about midway between these extremes.

The majority of Australian warblers are sedentary and found in a variety of habitats from montane forests to arid country. The Rock Warbler *Origma solitaria* is an exception, for it inhabits rocky sandstone and limestone areas in south-eastern Australia. Some species are terrestrial, and others are to be found amongst the foliage of trees and bushes. Their diet is mainly insects and small invertebrates, although the Rufous Bristlebird eats fruits and berries in season. An interesting aspect of behaviour is that of the Pilotbird *Pycnoptilus floccosus*, whose distribution overlaps with that of the Superb Lyrebird *Menura novaehollandiae*. The two species occur in south-eastern Australia, where the Pilotbird feeds on small items exposed by the larger Lyrebird as it scuffs around on the forest floor in search of its own food.

Australian Warblers build with grass, roots and other soft vegetation, an enclosed nest with a side entrance. It may be woven between twigs in a horizontal fork in a bush or suspended from a branch. The nest of the Weebill, made of vegetable down, grass and cobwebs, is described as resembling a 'baby's woollen bootee!' Two–four eggs are laid, incubation lasts for 18 – 24 days and the nestlings fledge some 15 – 18 days later. Details of the breeding biology of many species is inadequately known.

AUSTRALIAN WRENS
Order *Passeriformes*
Family: *Maluridae*
6 genera contain 23 species

The family of Australian Wrens *Malurinae* has been split into three separate families. The Australian Warblers *Acathizidae* and the Australian Chats *Ephthianuridae* are families in their own right. The position is still clouded, for the genus *Dasyornis* is placed with the wrens in one Australian field guide and with the warblers in another!

Australian Wrens are small long-tailed birds; the 23 species divided between 6 genera are all endemic to Australia and New Guinea. They range from 4.5 – 9 in. (11.5 – 23 cm.) in length; smallest is the White-winged Fairy-wren *Malurus leucopterus* and the largest being the Black Grasswren *Amytornis housei*. Both are Australian endemics, together with another 16 members of the family; the remaining species inhabit New Guinea. The fairy-wrens *Malurus* and the emu-wrens *Stipiturus* are the more colourful members of the family, with the White-winged Fairy-wren, all blue except for the wings, one of the most striking. They occupy a variety of habitats from rain-forests to scrub and grasslands, where they live on a diet of insects, other invertebrates and seeds. Fairy-wrens live in social groups, non-breeding members acting as helpers to the breeding pairs. The emu-wrens are noteworthy, for they have only six tail feathers! The grass-wrens *Amytornis* are comparatively nondescript birds that mainly frequent more arid habitats than the other members of the family; the Grey Grasswren *A. barbatus* occurs in swamps. All run well and are some of the most difficult of Australian birds to see. Grasswrens take a greater percentage of seeds in their diet than other members of the family.

The nest of most species is dome-shaped, made of grasses and other vegetable matter, and situated in a low bush. Snakes are significant nest-robbers. Two to five eggs are laid and incubated by the female for 13 – 16 days. Fledging takes place some 12 – 14 days later.

OLD WORLD FLYCATCHERS
Order *Passeriformes*
Family: *Muscicapinae*
29 genera contain 156 species

The Old World flycatchers are a family comprising 156 species in 29 genera that occurs throughout much of the Old World, the Australasian region and out into the Pacific as far as Samoa. Only five species breed in Europe, and one other, the Brown Flycatcher *Muscicapa latirostris* has occurred as a vagrant. Three species have arrived in Alaska as vagrants, and it is highly likely that other Asiatic species will turn up there in time.

These flycatchers range in length from 4 – 8 in. (10 – 20 cm.), of which many are drab grey or brown birds, usually with paler under-parts. The most colourful are undoubtedly

Both the Eastern Yellow Robin (above) and the Pale Yellow Robin (left) are Australian representatives of the Old World Flycatchers and both are restricted to eastern forests.

The Spotted Flycatcher (left) is a familiar summer visitor to Europe and Asia from wintering areas as far distant as South Africa. Its name is derived from the spotted plumage that distinguishes the juvenile birds.

the blue Asiatic members of the genus *Muscicapa*, and the Australian robins *Petroica* which are black, red, and white, but are not really robins. In the early days of discovery any bird with a red breast was a 'robin'.

Flycatchers usually frequent wooded habitats, although some inhabit semi-arid areas, including the Marico Flycatcher *Bradornis mariquensis*, found in *Acacia* scrub in southwestern Africa. Many are sedentary, although northern and higher altitude species are migratory, for otherwise they would be unable to find sufficient insects. One of the longest migrations within this family is that of the Spotted Flycatcher *M. striata* which breeds across the Palearctic to western Asia. The European population breeds as far north as the Arctic Circle in Scandinavia and winters in Southern Africa; that from Asia winters in East Africa.

Flycatchers feed primarily on winged insects and as their name suggests, they often catch their prey in mid-air. Some species forage for prey amongst the foliage and branches, whilst others, such as the Marico Flycatcher, drop to the ground from a low perch to catch their prey which includes ants and termites. Several species also include small quantities of fruit and nectar in their diets.

A variety of nests are constructed in the shape of cups and domes, usually situated in a crack in walling or in trees; some species also nest in disused Woodpecker holes. In western Britain, the Pied Flycatcher *Ficedula hypoleuca* readily uses nest boxes placed in deciduous woods. This species may lay up to 10 eggs, but 2 – 5 is more normal. In some species incubation is shared, and in others by the female alone. The eggs hatch in 10 – 15 days and the youngsters fledge over a similar period, during which time they are fed by both parents.

WATTLE-EYED FLYCATCHERS
Order *Passeriformes*
Family: *Platysteirinae*
5 genera contain 25 species

The family of wattle-eyed flycatchers *Platysteirinae* are a family of small African birds that occurs widely in various woodland habitats, south of the Sahara. Traditionally they are treated as part of the Old World flycatcher complex, but recently friends in southern Africa have told me that they may be an aberrant group of shrikes *Laniidae*.

The family comprises 25 species, divided into 5 genera; the largest number, 15 species, are placed in the genus *Batis*. Typical is the Chinspot Batis *B. molitor*, 4.75 in. (12 cm.) in length. It is an attractive, restless bird, with grey upper-parts and white below. The wings are black and white, black ear-coverts and lores surround a staring yellow eye. The male has a black breast band, which is chestnut on the female. The name comes from the chestnut spot on the chin of the female. They occur, often in pairs, amongst small bushes and scrub, where they utter a distinctive three note call to the tune of the children's rhyme 'three blind mice'.

Slightly larger are the wattled-eyed flycatchers *Platysteira*, seven species that usually occur in more heavily wooded habitats than the batis. They vary in size from the tiny Yellow-bellied Wattle-eye *P. concreta* 3 in. (7.5 cm.) to the Black-throated Wattle-eye *P. peltata* 5 in. (13 cm.) in length.

Members of the family, like arboreal shrikes, search for

insects, caterpillars and larvae amongst the foliage of bushes and trees, and occasionally catch flying insects flycatcher-fashion.

The nest is a small cup-shaped structure, tidily made from vegetation and bound with cobwebs, often lined with soft materials. Two eggs are laid; incubation is shared by the wattle-eyes, but only by the female batis. The incubation period lasts for about 17 days and the young fledge 14 – 17 days after hatching. During the fledging period they are fed by both parents and remain dependent on them for at least one week after leaving the nest.

The Gray Fantail (left) is an Australian species and belongs to a family that ranges from India to the Pacific.

FANTAIL FLYCATCHERS
Order: *Passeriformes*
Family: *Rhipidurinae*
the genus Rhipidura contains 40 species

The Fantail Flycatchers are a family of 40 species that all belong to the genus *Rhipidura*, occurring from India to the Philippines, through the islands of Indonesia and New Guinea to Australia and New Zealand, and on many of the islands of the eastern Pacific east to Western Samoa. It is on the islands within the range of the family that many individual species have evolved, giving rise to the high number of members within the sole genus of a family. This may suggest that the colonisation of the region by fantails is a comparatively recent event, for although there has been considerable specific diversification, no other genera have arisen.

Fantails are plump birds ranging from 5.5 in. (14 cm.) to 7.75 in. (20 cm.) long, depending on the species. Subtly coloured birds, fantails are mainly a mixture of two or more colours, from a palette that includes black, blue, brown, buff, grey, rufous, white and yellow. Fantails are mostly restless birds that fan or flick their long, broad fan-shaped tails from side to side or up and down, often displaying white outer feathers or white tips. They have short legs and feed both in bushes and trees and on the ground. The Willy Wagtail *R. leucophrys*, not a proper wagtail *Motacillidae* I hasten to add, prefers to feed on open ground and can be found feeding on insects disturbed by the feet of grazing cattle, in the same way that the true wagtails feed in pasture.

Fantails are mainly sedentary birds, although those species in the extreme north and south of the family's range withdraw to lower latitudes during the colder months. They live in a variety of woodland and bush habitats including mangroves, where the aptly named Mangrove Fantail *R. phasiana* of Australia occurs. Until recently this species, was treated as a race of the Grey Fantail *R. fuliginosa*, a widespread species throughout the island continent.

The cup-shaped nest, built from moss, grasses and other vegetable matter, is usually coated with spiders' webs on the outside and situated in a fork of a branch or placed on top of a horizontal branch. Some species incorporate a hanging tassel to the base of the structure. The clutch of 2 – 4 eggs is incubated for 12 – 14 days and the nestlings take 13 – 15 days to fledge. Little is known about the allocation of parental duties, although in a pair of White-throated Fantails *R. albicollis*, a widespread Asiatic species, nest building and incubation are known to be shared by both birds. It is likely that the equal distribution of labour applies to most members of the family.

MONARCH FLYCATCHERS
Order *Passeriformes*
Family: *Monarchinae*
17 genera contain 72 species

One of the Old World families of flycatchers is the Monarch Flycatchers *Monarchinae*, that occurs in Africa, southern and south-east Asia, and part of the Australasian region. It is a varied family comprising 72 species divided into 17 genera that frequent forest and woodland habitats. Although it is a widespread family in distribution, three-quarters of the species

are endemic to various islands between the Philippines and New Guinea, and across the Pacific to Hawaii.

This family is perhaps the Old World equivalent of the tyrant flycatchers of the Americas, and like many of that family they are species with a pronounced angle or slight crest to the back of the head. It is a varied collection of birds, but unlike the tyrant flycatchers there is generally a greater degree of plumage differences, with many being colourful but not garish. Most species are between 5 – 8 in. (12.5 – 20 cm.) in length, but the male paradise flycatchers *Terpsiphone* have central tail feathers that are 12 in. (30 cm.) or more long. These are the most of the spectacular monarch flycatchers, the tail feathers of the males fluttering behind them in flight. The African and Asiatic Paradise Flycatchers *T. viridis* and *T. paradisi* have black heads and chestnut upper-parts and tails; both have an incredible white colour phase which retains the black head. In contrast, the male Seychelles Black Paradise Flycatcher *Terpsiphone corvina* is a glossy blue-black, relieved by a powder-blue eye-ring. Female paradise flycatchers have much shorter tails than their partners, but still longer than other members of the family.

The largest genus is known as the Monarchs *Monarcha*, they occur in New Guinea, Australia and neighbouring islands. They are dumpier, slightly more round-headed than other members of the family, and their plumage is a combination of black, white, grey and brown. One of the most striking exceptions to this colouring is the Golden Monarch, a black and yellow bird with a small white tear-drop below the eye.

Monarch flycatchers are mainly sedentary, but some species migrate within a limited area and some that breed at high elevations move to lower altitudes when not breeding.

The Wattle-eyed Flycatcher (above) from East Africa is the subject of an identity crisis – is it a flycatcher or, perhaps, an aberrant shrike?

Members of the family join or form mixed bird parties; most are insectivorous, with their prey either being caught in mid-air or by foraging amongst foliage.

Monarch flycatchers construct neat cup-shaped nests of vegetable materials, bound with cobwebs and lichens. It may be sited in a vertical fork, suspended from a horizontal fork, or placed near the end of a branch, which is where the nests of the Seychelles Black Paradise Flycatcher are to be found. This flycatcher is endemic to the island of La Digue, but very rare; small boys with catapults are blamed for the decline of this species. Members of the family lay 1 – 4 eggs, but the breeding biology of many species is unknown. Both adults share the incubation of the eggs for 14 – 17 days, and both tend the nestlings who fledge some 12 – 18 days later. The work is not always shared equally, for in a number of cases the female builds the nest and undertakes most of the incubation, often as much by choice as necessity. I was once watching a female Seychelles Black Paradise Flycatcher incubating, when she left to feed. The male immediately came in and settled on the eggs, a minute or so later he was driven from the nest by the female, anxious to resume her duty.

bird occurs from Indonesia, where it is centred on the Moluccas, in southern and eastern Australia, and the Pacific from the Bismarck Archipelago to Fiji. It is markedly dimorphic; the female is generally a dull grey-brown bird with paler under-parts, but the male has an olive-green back, yellow under-parts and nape, black head and breast band and white throat. It occurs on dozens of islands throughout its vast range and on almost every island a different subspecies has evolved, resulting in a total of 73 subspecies; no other species shows this degree of variation.

Many members of the family are plain, such as the Sandstone Shrike-thrush *Coilluricincla woodwardi*, one of the Australian species. It is a mainly terrestrial bird, usually found about sandstone cliffs in north-western Australia. The diet of most members of the family comprises insects. An exception is the White-breasted Whistler *P. lanioides*, a greyer bird than the Golden species and has pale under-parts and a rufous nape; it often eats crabs found in mangrove swamps. The Mottled Whistler *Rhagologus leucostigma*, from New Guinea, and the Buff-throated Thickhead *Hylocitrea bonensis*, of Sulawesi, are fruit-eating.

WHISTLERS

Order: *Passeriformes*
Family: *Pachycephalinae*
10 genera contain 47 species

Whistlers are a varied family of small passerines that mostly occur in the Australasian region. They range from south-east Asia, the East Indies, New Guinea, Australia, and various islands east to Samoa in the Pacific. The largest genus, *Pachycephala*, contains 29 species. Of the 47 members of the family only 15 species, belonging to four genera, inhabit Australia.

Whistlers are robust birds, that range in length from 5 – 11 in. (12.5 – 28 cm.). They occur in a variety of woodland habitats, from rain forests to mangrove swamps and from woodland to arid scrub.

Some species are colourful, one of the most widespread being the Golden Whistler *Pachycephala pectoralis*. This

The breeding biology of members of the family is inadequately known. The Whistlers and Shrike-thrushes of Australia construct cup-shaped nests in the forks of trees; terrestrial species nest amongst rocks. Depending on the species, the clutch size varies from 1 – 4 eggs.

No member of the family is yet sufficiently rare to give cause for concern, but destruction of their wooded habitat threatens a number of species.

LONG-TAILED TITS

Order *Passeriformes*
Family: *Aegithalidae*
three genera contain 7 species

Members of the Long-tailed Tit family *Aegithalidae* are busy, active little birds that are to be found in feeding flocks, searching the foliage of trees and bushes for insects. The

The Long-tailed Tit (above) is a widespread species in the Palearctic and has the longest tail of the Tit family.

seven species are divided between three genera; five belonging to the genus *Aegithalos*; the other two species are in the monotypic genera *Psaltria* and *Psaltriparus*. The most familiar species are the Long-tailed Tit *Aegithalos caudatus* of the Palearctic and the Bush Tit *Psaltriparus minimus* of North and Central America.

Members of this family are small, dumpy birds, that appear to have no necks. They are insectivorous, with a small bill. The plumage of true long-tailed tits can include black, brown, grey, pink and white. The Long-tailed Tit, 5.5 in. (14 cm.) long, has a 3 in. (7.5 cm.) tail that is more than half its length. This bird has the longest tail of the family, whose other members are more conventionally proportioned.

These birds occur in forest and woodland habitats, from the British Isles to China, the most widespread species being the Long-tailed Tit. The other species occur from Afghanistan to China, where they are often associated with mountain ranges. The smallest member of the family, the Pygmy Tit *Psaltria exilis*, 3 in. (8 cm.) long, a nondescript grey species, is the also the smallest bird occurring on the Indonesian island

of Java; it is endemic to montane forests over 3,280 ft. (1,000 m.). The sole representative in North America is the Bush Tit 3.5 in. (9 cm.) long. This bird inhabits scrub and woodland from British Columbia, Canada, south through the western United States to Guatemala. Formerly, the North American population was treated as two species, the greyish Common Bushtit and the distinctively marked Black-eared Bushtit, but now they are lumped as one.

They build dome-shaped nests, from feathers, lichens and mosses, intricately woven together, in a bush or tree. Over two thousand small feathers have been found in the nest of a Long-tailed Tit. The clutch may consist of 4 – 12 eggs and are incubated for 13 – 14 days by the female. Both parents feed the young during the 15 – 16 day fledging period. The family stay together for several weeks afterward, some remaining as a flock through the winter.

The Golden Whistler ranges from the East Indies to Australia, and is also found on islands in the western Pacific. Many different sub-species have evolved on the islands. Above: a male Golden Whistler in Australia. The Rufous-naped Whistler (left) is endemic to the montane forests of New Guinea.

PENDULINE TITS
Order *Passeriformes*
Family: *Remizidae*
four genera contain of 10 species

Penduline Tits *Remizidae* are small chickadee-like birds, mostly found in the Palearctic and Africa, but one species, the Verdin *Auriparus flaviceps* occurs in the south-western United States and northern Mexico.

Members of the family occur in a variety of habitats. The Masked Penduline Tit *Remiz pendulinus*, lives in trees and bushes along the margins lakes and waterways, across much of the temperate Palearctic, except for parts of western Europe. Birds belonging to the genus *Anthoscopus*, which is endemic to Africa, inhabit dry scrub, whilst the Verdin, a similar species, inhabits desert scrub. The Fire-capped Tit *Cephalopyrus flammiceps*, from the Himalayas, northern India and China, is a bird of evergreen forests. Some species are nomadic; the Masked Penduline Tit, which is extending its range into Western Europe, has occurred as a vagrant in the British Isles.

These are tiny birds; most are 3.5 – 4.5 in. (9 – 11 cm.) long. The Masked Penduline Tit is a well-marked bird with a grey and chestnut body, and a grey head with a black 'bandit-like' mask. The African species are plainer, usually grey-brown birds, found in small flocks searching for insects as they wander through the bush. The juvenile Verdin resembles these species, but the adult has a grey body with a yellow head and chestnut shoulders.

The Palearctic and African species build nests of soft material, such as the down from willow flowers, suspended from the end of a slender branch, where it swings in the breeze. The African Penduline Tit *Anthoscopus caroli*, and the other members of the genus, constructs a nest has a conspicuous entrance and chamber, with a cap-like lip above. The apparent nesting chamber is a false one, for a narrow slit in the lip conceals the entrance to a passage leading to the actual nest. The Verdin makes an equally remarkable nest in a thorn bush. It appears large for the size of bird and is constructed from thorny twigs, over 2000 were counted in one nest, and lined with feathers. Depending on the species, the clutch size is between 3 – 10 eggs, which are incubated by the female for 12 days. The young fledge after 16 – 18 days and some species are assisted by helpers.

The Common Nuthatch (left), with its strong claws, is a typical bird of deciduous woodland in western Europe.

TITS and CHICKADEES

Order: *Passeriformes*
Family: *Paridae*
three genera contain 47 species

Chickadees are delightful, busy little birds, found in a variety of North American habitats from New York gardens to the Rockies, but not necessarily the same species. The name 'chickadee' is applied to some members of genus *Parus* in North America; others are 'titmice'; elsewhere in the World, these small birds are known simply as 'tits'. The 47 members of the family belong to three genera, 45 of which constitute the genus *Parus*. The remaining two species belong to the monotypic genera *Melanochlora* (1), *Sylviparus* (1).

Tits are a widespread family found in a variety of wooded habitats, from northern forests and willow scrub to acacia savannah, in many parts of the World. They are absent from the extreme northern latitudes, from South America and from the Australasian region.

They are small insectivorous birds, often rotund and usually between 4.5 – 5.5 in. (11 – 14 cm.) in length, the exception being the Sultan Tit *Melanochlora sultanea*, at 8 in. (20 cm.) long; it dwarfs other members of the family. The Chickadees are mainly grey-brown birds with paler underparts, brown or black caps, and bibs contrasting with white cheeks. The Mountain Chickadee *Parus gambeli* is the greyest species and the only one with a white stripe over the eye; during the breeding season this can become worn and comparatively indistinct. The titmice are evenly-coloured greyish birds with crests, but only the Bridled Titmouse *Parus wollweberi*, has a striking black and white head pattern which resembles the Crested Tit *P. cristatus* of the western Palearctic. All the North American species are a combination of black, shades of brown, buff, grey, rufous and white; elsewhere blue, green and yellow are often the dominant colours.

Several members of the family have become friendly garden birds during the winter months, readily coming to feeders for peanuts and fat. During recent years the Tufted Titmouse *P. bicolor* has been able extend its range in northeastern North America as result of the increased use of feeders in suburban areas in winter. It is essential that birds are not fed

nuts and other supplementary foods during the breeding season. At that time of the year, adults must feed their youngsters natural, highly-nutritional and easily digested food, such as caterpillars and grubs. Some tits, and similar sedentary insectivores, supplement their diet during the winter months, when there are fewer insects, with seeds and other vegetable matter.

Tits are hole-nesting birds; often those garden species will use a nest-box placed on the side of a tree or wall. Usually the nest is in a hole in a tree, a stone wall, or crevice in a rock face. In North America, the Black-capped Chickadee *P. atricapillus*, and in the Palearctic, the closely related Willow Tit *P. montanus*, excavate nest-holes in rotten tree-trunks; formerly these two were thought to be conspecific. Some tropical tits lay 3 – 4 eggs, but those in more northerly latitudes may lay more; the Blue and Great Tits *P. caeruleus* and *P. major* may lay up to 12 – 14 eggs in a good breeding season. Breeding

The Blue Tit (above), a common member of the Tit family in Europe, frequently breeds in nestboxes.

success depends on the availability of an abundant food supply. Usually both parents build the nest of moss and hair, but only the female incubates during the 13 – 14 day incubation period. During the 15 – 20 day fledging period, both parents tirelessly feed their growing brood, who still are dependent for at least a week afterward.

NUTHATCHES

Order: *Passeriformes*
Family: *Sittidae*
three genera containing 25 species

During the very cold winter of 1983-84 my family and I spent Christmas with relations at Mount Vernon, just outside New York. Knowing that I was interested in birds they set up a feeder on the patio, where one of the first birds to take advantage of their hospitality was a delightful White-breasted Nuthatch *Sitta carolinensis*. It landed on the peanut holder and held on upside-down as it hammered away to extract a nut through the wire mesh. Such birds become very tame and

down tree trunks as easily as up. During the winter months many species turn to foraging for seeds and small nuts. The only exceptions to the tree-climbing behaviour are the rock nuthatches, who run around rock faces with the same ease as their arboreal relatives explore trees and branches.

In North America there are three nuthatches besides the White-breasted mentioned earlier – the Red-breasted *S. canadensis*, and an allopatric pair, the eastern Brown-headed *S. pusilla*, which is replaced in the west by the Pygmy Nuthatch *S. pygmaea*. Most species are sedentary, but the Red-breasted Nuthatch moves south in the fall and in 1989 a vagrant that arrived in eastern England caused great excitement amongst birders.

In Europe the Common Nuthatch *S. europaea* extends from the British Isles eastwards across the Continent to Asia, where it reaches the farthest limits of its distribution in China. The western Mediterranean holds two very localised and rare species of nuthatch. On the island of Corsica lives the Corsican Nuthatch *S. whiteheadi*, found only in the pine forests that are threatened by forest 'management' where some 2,000 pairs remain. Even rarer is the recently discovered Algerian Nuthatch *S. ledanti*. In 1975 a Belgian scientist, Jean-Paul Ledant, discovered a hitherto unknown species of nuthatch in forest

confiding as one watches from the warmth of one's lounge. All too often people continue to feed their garden birds throughout the breeding season, when the adults should be feeding their young nourishing insects and caterpillars. These are soft items and, unlike nuts, easily digested by chicks and young birds. There have been instances of nestlings being fed nuts and killed by kindness!

Nuthatches are birds of the temperate Northern Hemisphere, evolving in Asia where the greatest variety of species is to be found. They range in length from 4 – 8 in. (10 – 20 cm.), yet all species look quite similar, small birds with blue-grey upper-parts and white to rufous under-parts, depending on the species, and for the same reason varying amounts of black on the head. They have strong pointed bills, thick necks, short, but strong legs and feet and a short tail. Nuthatches are found in woodlands, where they search for insect food in cracks and crannies in the bark; they can climb

on top of a mountain at Kabylia. The following year he returned on an expedition led by M. Vielliard, who named the species after its discoverer. There are only about 70 pairs in the forest that covers 3,460 acres (1400 ha.) on a single mountain top.

Nuthatches nest in holes in trees; some of the smaller species excavate their own, others use a natural hole, or nest box, the entrance of which they may reduce in size using mud. The Rock Nuthatch *S. neumeyer*, of south-eastern Europe and western Asia, uses the same principle to reduce the size a hole in a rock face, but in addition builds a short entrance tunnel. The only other species to do this is the larger Eastern Rock Nuthatch *S. tephronota*. Incubation, in some species if not all, is carried out by the female for 14 – 15 days. The fledging period lasts for 22 – 24 days, and during this time both parents tend the young, who will become independent after a further 8 – 12 days.

The White-breasted Nuthatch (above left) is a widespread breeding species in North America and can be attracted to garden feeders. The Mountain Chickadee (above), with its distinctive white eyebrow, occurs in the western United States and Canada.

203

Another rock dwelling member of the family is the Wallcreeper *Tichodroma muraria*, 6.5 in. (17 cm.) long, an elusive bird of the mountainous regions of southern and eastern Europe and Asia. The most striking features of this bird are the broad crimson and black wings with white spotted primaries. It has a grey body and the male has a black chin and throat that is white on the female and immature birds. They have a thin decurved bill that enables them to extract insects from small fissures. In winter those living in the northern and higher parts of the range withdraw to more clement surroundings. The nest is sited in a crack or hole in a rock face or wall, where the female builds a nest of material that includes grass, moss, roots and wool. She then incubates the clutch of three to five eggs for up to 19 days, during which the only help she receives from the male is a regular supply of food. Both parents feed the nestlings during the fledging period of 28 – 29 days.

The remaining members of the family inhabit New Guinea and Australia. Formerly split into two genera, all three Sittellas are at present placed in the genus *Daphoenositta*. They look like small nuthatches, but this may be a case of convergent evolution; recent DNA studies suggest that they are related to a family of flycatchers *Pachycephalinae*, which occurs in the same part of the world. Unlike nuthatches they do not nest in holes, but make a nest from bark, lichens and spider-webs, set in the fork of a tree like the flycatchers. They also share similarities in eggs and juvenile plumages; further studies will be required to establish the relationships. The Australian species, the Varied Sittella *D. chrysoptera*, 4 in. (11 cm.) long, is an extremely variable bird, each subspecies differing, yet interbreeding with its neighbour. Some have black heads, others white; some have striated under-parts while others are plain. Small wonder that at one time several species were thought to be involved. The other two species are endemic to New Guinea, although the Papuan Sittella *D. papuensis* may be conspecific with the Variable. The Black Sittella *D. miranda* occurs in montane forests from 6,500 – 11,500 ft. above sea-level (2,000-3,500 m.).

TREECREEPERS

Order: *Passeriformes*
Family: *Certhiidae*
two genera contain seven species

The seven species of treecreeper or creeper are split into two genera, six belonging to the genus *Certhia*; the remaining species is the Spotted Creeper *Salpornis spilonotus*.

The treecreepers *Certhia* inhabit deciduous and coniferous woodlands and forests across North America and the whole of the Palearctic from Ireland to Japan. They are small brown birds, about 5 in. (12.5 cm.) in length, streaked buff and black on the upper-parts, and white to brown, depending on the species, below. Just like the woodpeckers *Picidae*, Treecreepers have stiff tails that give support while they are climbing up tree trunks or along branches with their small but strong, claws and feet. They have very fine decurved bills with which they extract their prey of insects and other small invertebrates, from crevices in the trunk and branches or from behind flaking bark. Treecreepers work their way up a tree as they search for food and then fly to the base of the next tree and start all over again.

The most widespread species is the Common Treecreeper *C. familiaris*, which ranges the width of the Palearctic. Some authorities consider this bird to be conspecific with the Brown Creeper *C. americana*, that occurs over much of the United States and southern Canada, either as a breeding bird or as a winter visitor. The range of the Brown Creeper extents beyond the States south to Nicaragua. The Common Treecreeper is a bird of almost all woodland habitats in the British Isles, but in parts of mainland Europe it competes with the very similar Short-toed Treecreeper *C. brachydactyla*. Where the two species overlap, the Common Treecreeper usually inhabits conifers and at higher altitudes than its relative which prefers the lower broad-leaved woodlands and forests. The greatest variety of species is to be found in Central Asia where three other species occur. These species include the Brown-throated or Sikkim Tree-creeper *C.*

discolor; with its grey under-parts it is the darkest species and occurs in deciduous woodlands from Nepal to south-east Asia.

Usually treecreepers nest behind some loose bark on a tree trunk, in a deep crack in the trunk or behind ivy. The nest of grass, moss and roots is lined with softer materials such as feathers and wool. Incubation of the three to eight eggs is mainly by the female for 14 – 15 days; both parents feed the young during the 14 – 16 day fledging period, although the young of some Asiatic species may take 21 days to fledge.

The Spotted Creeper, 6 in. (15 cm.) long, from Central India and sub-Saharan Africa south to Zimbabwe is slightly larger than the treecreepers, and is blackish, heavily spotted with white. It has the same decurved bill, but does not use its tail for support against tree trunks; the tail feathers are not stiffened like those of its more northerly relatives. Unlike the concealed nest of the treecreepers, the Spotted Creeper makes a deep-cupped nest of bark, spider-webs, lichen and other soft materials in the fork of a tree. Little is known about the breeding biology other than the clutch of three eggs is incubated by the female and during that time she is fed by the male.

PHILIPPINE CREEPERS

Order: *Passeriformes*
Family: *Rhabdornithidae*
the genus *Rhabdornis* contains two species

Philippine Creepers *Rhabdornithidae*, are a family of two small birds endemic to the Philippines. The larger Plain-headed Creeper *R. inornatus* occurs in mountainous forests above 3000 ft. (900 metres) on Leyte, Luzon, Mindanao, Negros and Samar. At lower elevations on these islands and on the smaller neighbouring islands of Bohol, Dinagat and Masbate lives the Stripe-headed Creeper *R. mystacalis*.

Both species are straight-billed birds frequenting rain forests, margins and clearings. They forage for insects and occasionally fruit in the outer canopy of trees, and at times climb tree trunks as their name suggests.

The breeding biology of Philippine Creepers is poorly known, for nests have yet to be found, although the Stripe-headed Creeper probably uses holes in trees.

AUSTRALIAN TREECREEPERS

Order: *Passeriformes*
Family: *Climacteridae*
two genera contain 7 species

Traditionally the Australian Treecreepers have been classified with the other tree-climbing passerines, nuthatches *Sittidae* and treecreepers Certhiidae, but recent studies of the DNA of these birds have shown that they are related to the bowerbirds *Ptilonorhynchidae*, lyrebirds *Menuridae* and scrub birds *Atrichornithidae*, all families that are indigenous to the Australasian region.

They are small tree-climbing birds, 6 in. (15 cm.) long; a little more thick set than treecreepers and their tails lack the stiffening that enable the other species to support themselves against the tree trunks. As with the nuthatch-like sittellas, this is a case of convergent evolution. They are mainly brown birds with striated under-parts and a prominent wing bar that varies from cream to rufous, depending on the species. The Black-tailed Treecreeper *Climacteris melanura* has dark under-parts; the male has a scaled throat, whilst the throat of the female is white. The other major deviation from the standard pattern is the Rufous Treecreeper *C. rufa*. The male has a rufous face and scaled under-parts, whereas the female is entirely rufous below.

The White-throated Treecreeper *Cormobates leucophaea* differs in several ways from the other members of the family and has recently been split into a distinct genus. Unlike the other species it has shorter legs, and has a straighter and thinner bill. It is a bird of rainforests in eastern and south-

Facing page: a Common Treecreeper returns to its nest, in a crack in a tree trunk, with a beak full of grubs for its young.

eastern Australia; its greater vocal abilities and conspicuous display suggest that it evolved in a confined environment where such attributes were essential to establish territories and pair-bonds. This species roosts on branches and trunks, whereas the others roost in hollow branches. The female White-throated Treecreeper builds a nest of bark, lined with softer materials in a hollow branch or trunk. The long incubation period of the two to three eggs lasts for 23 – 25 days. A pair of White-throated Treecreepers has an old fashioned conventional relationship, whilst most other species of Australian Treecreepers are communal and more than one male will feed the incubating female.

The other members of the family inhabit woodland and are scattered across the island continent with little or no overlapping of distribution; one species the Papuan Treecreeper *Climacteris placens* occurs discontinuously in montane forests on the island of New Guinea. Birds belonging to this genus build a nest of grass and bark, lined with fur or hair in a hollow tree, stump or fence-post. Some species such as the Brown Treecreeper *C. picumnus* build their nests on a foundation of cow, horse or kangaroo dung! Two to three eggs are laid and the incubation period of 16 – 18 days is considerably shorter than the White-throated Treecreeper; this is a generic difference and nothing to do with the additional insulation provided beneath the nest!

FLOWERPECKERS

Order: *Passeriformes*
Family: *Dicaeidae*
six genera contain 50 species

Flowerpeckers are a family of small, mainly fruit-eating birds, that occur in Asia and Australasia. They range from India and south-east Asia down through Indonesia to Australia. The greatest number of species found in a limited area are the 13 that occur in the Philippines, 11 of which are endemic. A further 11 species inhabit New Guinea and its offshore islands and are also endemic. Other endemic flowerpeckers are

resident on islands from Indonesia to the Solomon Islands. Flowerpeckers frequent a variety of wooded habitats from rain forests to suburban gardens.

Most species range in length from 3 – 6 in. (8 – 15 cm.), only the Crested Berrypecker *Paramythia montium* is larger, 8.25 in. (21cm.). This species, the only member of its genus, is one of those endemic to New Guinea. Flowerpeckers and their relatives are short-tailed birds, some have fine bills, rather warbler-like, whilst others are heavier, such as the Thick-billed Flowerpecker *Dicaeum agile*. This is one of the most widespread members of the family ranging from northern India across to North Vietnam and south to Timor, just north of Australia. This species belongs to the largest genus in the family, which includes a number of colourful birds. Several, including the Thick-billed, are plain, but others such as the Scarlet-backed Flowerpecker *D. cruentatum* are much brighter.

Most flowerpeckers eat a mixture of fruit and insects; the berrypeckers of New Guinea feed entirely on fruit. The Mistletoebird *D. hirundinaceum*, an Australian species, feeds mainly on mistletoe and does not inhabit areas such as Tasmania, where this food item is absent. Most species are sedentary, with the notable except of the Mistletoebird that is nomadic in its search for fruiting mistletoe.

Most flowerpeckers build hanging nests of vegetable matter and cobwebs that resemble those of the sunbirds *Nectariniidae*; some New Guinea species build cup-shaped nests. The clutch of 1 – 4 eggs is usually incubated by both adults for 12 days, they then tend the nestlings for 15 days until they fledge. The breeding biology is unknown for several of the more remote species.

Above left: at Naro Moro, in Kenya, a male Northern Double-collared Sunbird feeds alongside a subdued-coloured female. The male Seychelles Sunbird (above) is more dully coloured than most members of the family, with iridescence confined to his throat.

PARDALOTES
Order: *Passeriformes*
Family: *Pardalotidae*
the genus *Paradalotus* contains five species

In Australia lives an endemic family of small passerines, the Pardalotes *Pardalotus*, that have traditionally been placed with the flowerpeckers *Dicaeidae*. After studies of the egg-white protein and DNA, it is possible that they are a family of Australian origin rather than an off-shoot of the Oriental flowerpeckers; as a result, they have been split from the flowerpeckers and placed in a family of their own. The five species include three that have been lumped with the Striated Pardalote *P. striatus*, to form a species that occurs over most of the continent.

They are small, stubby, thick-necked birds, with short bills, and range from 3 – 4.75 in. (8 – 12 cm.) in length. They vary considerably in plumage; most have white spotting on the upper-parts that gave them the popular name of 'diamond birds'.

Pardalotes frequent a variety of wooded and forested habitats, where they are almost exclusively insectivorous.

They are hole-nesting birds, breeding in chambers at the end of tunnels excavated in an earthen bank. Sometimes the Forty-spotted *P. quadragintus* and the Striated Pardalote, nest in holes in trees. The two species are often found nesting close to one another, but it seems that the Forty-spotted Pardalote nests colonially, to prevent the domineering Striated species from taking over their nest sites. There are gaps in the knowledge of the breeding biology of some species. The clutch size may be 2 – 5 eggs, although 4 is the usual number. The female builds the nest and incubates the eggs. Both parents feed the nestlings.

SUNBIRDS
Order: *Passeriformes*
Family: *Nectariniidae*
five genera contain 118 species

Anyone visiting Africa for the first time might be forgiven for thinking that the small birds with thin bills and iridescent coloured plumages of blue, greens, purples and yellows were some kind of hummingbird. Unfortunately they are not, for the hummingbirds *Trochilidae* of the New World are members of the *Apodiformes*, an Order of birds that includes the swifts. Sunbirds *Nectariniidae* are passerines, and from their pedigree their closest relatives include the Asiatic family of flowerpeckers *Dicaeidae*, but recent work on the family suggests a relationship with the Old World weavers *Ploceinae*. The apparent similarity between sunbirds and hummingbirds is an instance of convergent evolution, where certain feeding methods have dictated similar evolutionary requirements. Sunbirds lack the hovering ability of the hummers, and have not developed the same dependence on particular plant species. They are busy birds that are often so involved with their search for insects and nectar from favoured flowers, that they can be oblivious to human presence.

The 118 species of sunbirds are divided between 5 genera. Sunbirds range throughout most of Africa where the family evolved, and the greatest number of species occurs through the Middle East into Asia and to Australia. Once away from Africa, where 78 are endemic, the variety declines markedly. Asia holds 35 endemics and several other species occur in more than one continent.

Sunbirds are amongst the most colourful of the Old World birds, with wonderful iridescent plumages of many colours which dazzle the eye as they catch the sunlight. Usually the

Below: a male Kenya Violet-backed Sunbird near Lake Baringo, Kenya.

male is considerably more colourful than his mate, but some species, usually those that solely occur in forests, are amongst the plainest in colour. They range from 3 – 6.25 in. (8 – 16 cm.) in length, some having elongated central tail feathers; all have short rounded wings. The bill, although always fine, varies in length; whilst others, such as those of the spider-hunters *Arachnothera* of south-east Asia, are long and curved. Short billed species often cheat by piercing the corollas of flowers to reach the nectar, thus not serving as pollinators. Several species form distinct groups within a genus, such as the double-collared sunbird complex of Africa, which involves several closely related species. The males belonging to the group have dark green upper-parts and purple and burgundy breast bands. Some species differ in size and are often separated by habitat, latitude and altitude.

The typical sunbirds make pendulous nests from cobwebs and soft vegetable material, yet they are strong enough to withstand the weight of a young cuckoo *Chrysococcyx sp.* Usually two eggs are laid and incubated for 13 – 15 days; the nestlings fledge after 14 – 19 days. Spider-hunters sew their nests to the undersides of leaves, either in the form of a cup or a tube which incorporates the leaf as a roof.

WHITE-EYES

Order: *Passeriformes*
Family: *Zosteropidae*
11 genera contain 85 species

Sometimes it is hard to fathom the reasoning behind the naming of some bird families, but with the White-eyes there is no such problem. Most members of the family Zosteropidae have a clear white eye-ring, easily visible in most species at close range, without binoculars.

not in the normal way, where unrelated families have distinct similarities. With the white-eyes the problem lies with one species evolving to look like another. An example is the little known Annobon White-eye Z. *griseovirescens*, found only on the island of Annobon, in the Gulf of Guinea off equatorial Africa. This bird is reported to look identical to the equally local Christmas Island White-eye Z. *natalis*, found only on Christmas Island in the eastern Indian Ocean. The extreme similarity is the evolutionary result of demands enforced on related birds by their habitat and environment. Birds belonging to the other 10 genera are similar.

Some species of White-eye are highly migratory and form flocks on completion of the breeding season. The Silver-eye Z. *lateralis*, from Tasmania and south-eastern Australia was thought to be nomadic, but an intensive banding programme has shown that it migrates north to Queensland. In June 1856, flocks of Silver-eyes appeared on the west coast of New Zealand near Wellington. Those colonists have since spread throughout the country, and are now the commonest passerine.

White-eyes make a cup-shaped nest of grass, other soft material and cobwebs, suspended in the fork of a bush or branches of a tree. Two to four eggs are laid; incubation and the other domestic duties are shared by both parents. The youngsters may be fed by their parents for up to two weeks after fledging.

The rarest white-eye is the White-breasted White-eye Z. *albogularis*, found only in remnants of the rain-forest on Norfolk Island, Australia. Formerly common, a population of under 50 birds was recorded in 1982. It has suffered from the feral cats that roam the island, and has been possibly affected by direct competition from the Silver-eye, which colonised the island in 1904.

Probably the next species in the rarity league is to be found in the remnants of the indigenous montane forests of Mahé, the principal island in the Central Seychelles. The Seychelles White-eye Z. *modesta*, a greyer bird than those white-eyes of Africa, can be one of the harder endemic birds to find. During

The Silvereye (left) is a common Australian member of the White-eye family of small, active birds. The White-cheeked Honeyeater (above) occurs in south-western and eastern Australia. A brush-tipped tongue enables it to feed on nectar.

White-eyes are warbler-like passerines that are mainly green, yellow or grey, with the fine bill of an insectivorous species and about 4.75 in. (12 cm.) in length. There are around 85 species, placed in 11 genera, the majority belonging to the genus *Zosterops*. The situation is far from clear, for there is a host of species and races scattered from Africa to India, and down through south-east Asia to New Zealand, continuing out to Samoa in the Pacific. Mainland Africa is home to four *Zosterops* species, and its off-shore islands host a further nine. But once in Asia the situation is different, with 50 found as far east as Samoa. Many species are restricted to island groups, where different races have developed on the various islands in the area. Convergent evolution has taken a hand, but

a tour in 1988 we had been trying to find the bird during the day without success. One last try led us up a rough track to what appeared to be some old farm buildings. When I showed an elderly gentleman the illustration in the field guide, he shook his head gravely and gestured that the view from the other side of the main building would compensate. It was a lovely view, looking down on Victoria Harbour. But far more exciting was the unfamiliar song coming from a bare fruit tree above. Only feet away was a male Seychelles White-eye in full song; so, quietly we retreated and brought the rest of the party along to share both views. One thing about birding, it is always full of surprises!

HONEYEATERS
Order: *Passeriformes*
Family: *Meliphagidae*
Sub-family: 36 genera contain 169 species

Wallace's Line is not marked on maps, but is significant nevertheless. During the break up of the great continent, Gondwanaland in geological times, birds evolved in isolation in Australia, as that part of the world headed up towards south-east Asia. In the 19th. century a British naturalist, Alfred Wallace (1823 – 1913), realised that a number of families of mammals and birds of Oriental origin met those of Australasian origin. The demarcation line known as Wallace's line, passes south of the Philippines, between Borneo and Sulawesi, and Bali and Lombok; only on Sulawesi is there any significant overlap.

The Honeyeaters are a diverse family of Australasian origins, for only the widespread Brown Honeyeater *Lichmera indistincta* and the Bonin Island Honeyeater *Apalopteron familiaris* occur east of Wallace's Line. The relationship of the Bonin Island Honeyeater to other members of the family is not 100% certain, so that the Brown Honeyeater which has crossed 18 miles (30 km.) of sea between Lombok and Bali, may in reality, be the only honeyeater outside Australasia. The Sugarbirds *Promeropidae* of southern Africa have been treated as honeyeaters in the past, but are now in a family of their own.

The Eastern Spinebill (left) is a Honeyeater which is endemic to Australia; it occurs in the east of the country.

Honeyeaters vary considerably, but all are slim, many with proportionally long tails. The smallest is the Pygmy Honeyeater *Oedistoma pygmaeum*, a plain, short-tailed, olive-coloured bird that resembles a sunbird and is under 3 in. (7.5 cm.) long. It is the smallest of New Guinea's birds and one of the smallest passerines in the World. At the other end of the scale is the Helmeted Friarbird *Philemon buceroides*, 14.5 in. (37 cm.) long and one of the least attractive species, with an unfeathered black head. This and other members of the genus occur in both Australia and New Guinea. The others belonging to that genus also have bare heads and several other species have areas of brightly-coloured bare skin around the face. There are several sunbird-like honeyeaters, the scarlet and

209

black members of the genus *Myzomela* are particularly conspicuous, with the all-red Red Myzomela *M. cruentata* being locally common with other species at flowering trees. Most other members of the family are plain shades of brown, grey, olive or yellow; some have black, white or yellow patterning on the head, looking extremely similar to one another. Many species have decurved bills, and several display tufted plumes on the throat and sides of the head; these are most elaborate on the throat of the Tui *Prosthemadera novaeseelandiae* of New Zealand. This is a glossy black bird, its plumage having given rise to the local name of 'Parsonbird', for obvious reasons.

Honeyeaters are social birds that search for food in small flocks; during the breeding season some species are colonial. They wander in search of suitable flowering or fruiting trees, and some species undertake short migrations whilst others are

Above left: a male Cape Sugarbird in South Africa, where members of the family are often to be found on or near Protea blooms. The Yellowhammer (left) is a bunting that occurs across the Palearctic. In Britain it is often found in hedgerows.

just nomads. Their diet is of insects and nectar, and to enable them to extract the nectar from blossoms they have evolved a brush-tipped tongue. Several larger species are frugivorous and may inflict considerable damage to orchards in Australia; those inhabiting rainforests are also fruit-eaters.

A cup-shaped nest is built, and situated often high in a bush or tree. The clutch size is 1 – 4 eggs, the larger clutches being laid by the larger species. In New Zealand the Stitchbird *Notiomystis cincta* may lay up to 5 eggs. The incubation period lasts 12 – 17 days and the fledging period takes a further 10 – 16 days. Many species enlist the aid of non-breeding adults to help them feed their youngsters.

A number of honeyeaters are sufficiently rare to give cause for concern, but none as much as the Bishop's Oo and the Kauai Oo *Moho bishopi* and *M. braccatus*, two Hawaiian species that are amongst the rarest birds in the World. The Bishop's Oo was rediscovered in 1981 having been last recorded in 1915, and the Kauai Oo has declined during the present century to only a handful of individuals.

SUGARBIRDS

Order: *Passeriformes*
Family: *Promeropidae*
the genus Promerops contains two species

It may seem strange that the Sugarbirds *Promerops*, two species found in southern Africa, should have been included in the family of honeyeaters *Meliphagidae*, essentially Australasian in origin and distribution. The relationship of the sugarbirds with other bird families had been the subject of speculation until DNA analysis entered the field of research. Sometimes laboratory investigations have answered such questions, but they have also raised queries that challenge many long-held opinions. Research into the ancestry of the sugarbirds has shown that they are probably related to the starlings *Sturnidae*.

Sugarbirds are the only bird family endemic to the area known as Southern Africa; this region covers that part of Africa lying south of the Zambezi to the east, and the northern border of Namibia to the west. There are two species, the Cape Sugarbird *P. cafer* and Gurney's Sugarbird *P. gurneyi*. The Cape Sugarbird occurs only in a habitat rich in endemic plant species, known as *fynbos*. This is confined to an area of South Africa from Cape Town to Port Elizabeth and ranges from sea-level to mountains. *Fynbos* where the *Protea* is a dominant plant are particularly attractive to the Cape Sugarbird, but the quality of the *fynbos* is being diluted in some areas. Introduced plants, with no natural enemies to hold them in check, may take over the habitat at the expense of the *Proteas*. In turn the Cape Sugarbird suffers, for the lives of plant and bird are intertwined. The Sugarbird needs the nectar that the flowers provide and the flowers need the bird for pollination. Gurney's Sugarbird, a similar species, has a more extensive range, occurring from eastern South Africa north to Zimbabwe and Mozambique, but usually resides at higher elevations, although some populations migrate altitudinally in winter. In the Eastern Highlands of Zimbabwe it has learned to exploit the growing number of *Protea* plantations. Sugarbirds also feed on the nectar of several other families of flowers, as well as insects and spiders. They may wander when not breeding in search flowers in bloom.

Sugarbirds are slim birds with brown upper-parts, streaked darker, white and rufous below, with yellow under-tail coverts. They have long curved bills, but it is the exceptionally long tail feathers, especially those of the males, that are the most striking aspect of the family. The Cape Sugarbird is the larger of the two species, and the male with a full-grown tail can be 17 in. (44 cm.) long; the tail accounts for more than half the length.

The female builds an untidy cup-shaped nest in a *Protea* bush from grass, twigs and other vegetable material. This is lined with the down collected from a seeding *Protea* flower. Two eggs are laid, which she incubates for 17 days, after which she is the main provider of food for the chicks during the 19 day fledging period. The young birds remain dependant on their parents for at least three weeks after leaving the nest.

BUNTINGS and their allies
Order: *Passeriformes*
Family: *Emberizinae*
72 genera contain 282 species

Although this family is named after the buntings of the Old World *Emberiza*, it is of New World origins, where especially in South America, the greatest diversity of species occurs. Members of family are essentially seed-eaters, that are found throughout the world except parts of south-east Asia, and the entire Australasian region, where introductions have taken place in New Zealand.

The group includes the juncos, longspurs, the New World sparrows, South American finches and seed-eaters and the towhees. Members of the family occur from north of the Arctic Circle to the Equator, and inhabit almost every habitat from forests to deserts; some are solitary, others form flocks of their kind or join mixed flocks with other seed-eating birds. It is a large family of 282 species in 72 genera. Overall the group ranges in length from 4 – 9 in. (10 – 23 cm.), but mainly the family members are sparrow-size. They are all finch-like birds that are essentially terrestrial feeders, although trees and bushes provide song perches and nest sites for many. Some are colourful and distinctive, whilst others, including many of the North American sparrows, may appear to the uninitiated, dull, drab and not particularly distinctive unless one can see them well. They come in a host of colours, shades and patterns, and in general all have conical seed-eating bills, some heavier than others. /cont.

It was the bill shapes of the Galapagos finches, or as they are now known 'Darwin's finches', that provided Charles Darwin with one of the most important clues in his investigation into the theory of evolution. There are 14 species that belong to four genera, and all bar one, the Cocos Finch *Pinarolaxis inornata*, occur on various islands within the Galapagos. The Cocos Finch occurs on Cocos Island lying 400 miles (650 km.) north east of Galapagos, and belongs to Costa Rica. When Darwin visited the islands in 1835, he realised that the finches had descended from a common ancestor, and had evolved to fill the range of ecological niches unexploited by the few other birds that inhabited the islands. The bill sizes vary from the fine bill of the Warbler Finch *Certhidea olivacea*, to the grosbeak-like bills of some ground finches *Geospiza spp.*. The Warbler Finch is insectivorous, whilst the ground finches crack seeds; the Vegetarian Finch *Platyspiza crassirostris* eats buds, and the cactus finches include nectar in their diet. The Mangrove and Woodpecker Finches *Camarhynchus heliobates* and *C. pallidus*, are unique for they use a cactus spine or a fine twig to extract larvae from holes in branches. The population of the Sharp-beaked Ground Finch *G. difficilis* on Wenman Island, feed on the blood of boobies *Sula spp.* extracted from the bases of the feathers on the larger birds' backs.

Other members of the family are far more conventional as they feed on seeds of all shapes and sizes; many species feed their nestlings on insects and larvae. Whilst many are sedentary, or only wander locally in search of food, populations of others are migratory, especially those that breed in northern temperate latitudes.

Nests of grass, twigs and other vegetable matter are sited in trees, bushes or amongst vegetation on the ground. The

clutch of 2 – 7 eggs is laid and incubation is by either the female or shared by both adults; as with many families it is the tropical species that lay the smaller clutches. Nestlings fledge in 12 – 14 days, but for safety reasons some may leave the nest earlier than this.

PLUSHCAP
Order: *Passeriformes*
Family: *Catamblyrhynchinae*
the genus *Catamblyrhynchus* contains a
single species *Catamblyrhynchus diadema*

The Plushcap, or Plush-capped Finch *Catamblyrhynchus diadema* as it was formerly known, is a rare and very poorly understood bird from South America. It is the sole member of its family and looks finch-like, with a stubby seed-eating bill, but is related to Tanagers *Thraupinae*.

It is a non-migratory species found along the Andes from Venezuela, south through Bolivia to north-western Argentina. The Plushcap, 5.5 in. (14 cm.) long, has a bright yellow forehead and crown of plush-like feathers. The upper-parts are dark grey and the sides of the head and under-parts are chestnut. It occurs in the lower stratum of humid montane forests and their margins; most frequently found around bamboos *Chusquea*, on which it feeds in a manner recalling titmice and chickadees *Paridae*, using its bill to probe into stems and leaf nodes. Conventional feathers on the forehead and crown of the Plushcap would be continuously dishevelled as a result of this method of feeding, so the special yellow plush-like feathers probably evolved to overcome the problem.

Details of the breeding biology of the Plushcap are unknown.

Two North American relatives of the Buntings are the Dark-eyed Junco (top) and the Rufous-sided Towhee (above). Both belong to sub-species that occur in the western United States.

CARDINALS and their allies

Order: *Passeriformes*
Family: *Cardinalinae*
15 genera contain 46 species

One of the most distinctive of North American birds is the male Northern Cardinal *Cardinalis cardinalis*, all red with black around the eyes and throat. Females and juveniles are browner.

The Cardinal belongs to a family of 46 species divided into 15 genera, that occur from north-eastern Canada to Argentina. As might be expected not all are known as cardinals, for the family includes buntings, some grosbeaks, saltators and the Dickcissel *Spiza americana*, a finch-like bird that is a summer visitor to the eastern United States. North of Mexico, ten members of the family breed, but only two, the Northern Cardinal and the closely related Pyrrhuloxia *Pyrrhuloxia sinuatus*, a species of the dry south-west, are resident throughout the year. Amongst the migrants are the Rose-breasted and Black-headed Grosbeaks *Pheucticus ludovicianus* and *P. melanocephalus*, and the Indigo, Lazuli and Painted Buntings *Passerina cyanea*, *P. amoena* and *P. ciris*. The greater number of species belonging to the family occur in tropical Central and South America. The cardinals

and their allies inhabit a variety of woodlands and their margins, to dry semi-arid scrub.

Members of this family range in length from 5 – 8.75 in. (12.5 – 22 cm.). The largest and heaviest are the grosbeaks and saltators *Saltator spp.*, the latter including some of the least colourful species. Most males of the family are more colourful than the females, they range from all blue, of which there are several, to the all red male Northern Cardinal. Other species are combinations of colours and patterns. These birds have conical seed-eating bills, lightest in some South American Cardinals and heaviest in the grosbeaks. Cardinals and grosbeaks are well-built birds, with the cardinals, saltators and some grosbeaks having longer tails. Most cardinals have prominent crests.

They feed on a diet of seeds and other vegetable matter including berries, and may eat insects at certain times of the year.

A nest, usually loosely woven of twigs, strips of bark and grass, is sited in a bush or tree; the Dickcissel sometimes nests on the ground. For reasons best known to itself, the Blue Grosbeak *Guiraca caerulea* usually includes a cast snake skin in the construction of its nest. The clutch size is usually 3 – 5 eggs. The breeding details of some are unknown, but the Northern Cardinal female incubates her eggs for 12 – 13 days, during which time she is fed away from the nest by the male. In the Rose-breasted Grosbeak *Pheucticus ludovicianus* the pair share the incubation for 12 – 14 days. While they are on the nest both birds, although particularly the male, sing. Perhaps it helps pass the time! Fledging takes place after 9 – 15 days and young Northern Cardinals go off with their father, while mother gets on with another brood. Cardinals usually rear two to three, sometimes four, broods in a breeding season. Mortality must be high, for otherwise we would be overrun with Cardinals.

This page: male Cardinals. The Red-crested Cardinal (top) occurs in South America, from Bolivia to Argentina. The Northern Cardinal (above) is a familiar North American species found from southern Canada to Mexico. The female Northern Cardinal is browner in colour.

TANAGERS

Order: *Passeriformes*
Family: *Thraupinae*
60 genera contain 246 species

One of the most colourful and varied of the New World bird families are the Tanagers *Thraupinae*, a family whose distribution ranges from Canada to central Argentina and northern Chile, via Central America and the Caribbean. By far the greatest variety occurs in the tropical Andes; Colombia for example is host to 160 species, whilst Chile is home to only four.

The family comprises 246 species contained within 60 genera, although this varies slightly from one authority to another. The systematics of some genera are unclear, but following *The Birds of South America Vol.1*, the Swallow-Tanager *Tersine viridis*, the conebills, flower-piercers and honeycreepers are all treated as tanagers. Discoveries are still being made, for recently the Sira Tanager *Tanagar phillipsi* was discovered in a remote area of montane forest in eastern Peru; other species have been added to the national lists as more and more research takes place in the Neotropical region.

Tanagers are woodland and forest birds, although generally absent from the deepest jungle. When not breeding many species join with other birds to form mixed bird flocks. Tanagers can be found at all elevations in an area, although very few species can be considered ground feeders. In shape and structure most tanagers are ordinary looking birds, with strong insectivorous-type bills. The crowning glory of the family is that they are amongst the most colourful bird families; however, females are usually plainer. Most tanagers are small birds about 4 – 7 in. (10 – 18 cm.) long; the largest is the *Buthraupis*, the Hooded Mountain-Tanager *B. montana* of Andean forests from Venezuela to Bolivia is 9 in. (23 cm.) in length. Four species breed in North America, the most widespread being the Scarlet and Western Tanagers *Piranga olivacea* and *P. ludoviciana*; all four are migrants that winter in Central and South America.

There are two groups placed with the tanagers that differ considerably from other members of the family. These are the conebills and flower-piercers, and the honeycreepers. The former have sharp bills, and although being colourful, lack the brilliance of the true tanagers. Most honeycreepers are also colourful and have decurved bills, some resembling the Old World sunbirds *Nectariniidae* in shape.

The diet of most tanagers is mainly fruit, although the majority eat varying quantities of insects. Some species join mixed parties of insectivorous species as they wander through the forests. Others, including the Sooty Ant-Tanager *Habia gutteralis*, a Colombian endemic, join the antbirds that follow the swarms of army ants *Ecitoninae*.

Tanagers build cup-shaped nests in trees or bushes, only a few species nest in earthen banks. The Swallow-Tanager nests in holes in walling, or in one dug in an earthen bank by the female. The Euphonias *Euphonia spp.* and the closely related Chlorophonias *Chlorophonia spp.* build ball-shaped nests with side-entrances, situated by some species in recesses in earthen banks, and high in trees by others. The clutch varies in size with the species from 2 – 5 eggs; the incubation period lasts from 12 – 18 days, although the breeding biology of all species is not fully known. The length of the fledging period is interesting; for a family as large as the tanagers there is inevitably some variation, but in this case the explanation is straightforward; those species that nest in low bushes fledge in 10 – 13 days, whilst those that nest high in trees take up to 24 days. This is a survival strategy that gives those nesting in more accessible sites a greater chance of success.

WOOD WARBLERS

Order: *Passeriformes*
Family: *Parulidae*
25 genera contain 117 species

The wood warblers *Parulidae*, are amongst the most attractive of the spring migrants that arrive in 'waves' in March and April in the United States and Canada. The distribution of the 117 species, divided between 25 genera, extends from Alaska to northern Argentina. Most of the North American breeding species are migrants, withdrawing to the southern states, the Caribbean, Central and South America in the fall. This family of warblers is New World in origin, and unrelated to the warblers *Sylviidae* of the Old World. During the fall migration period, 16 species have occurred as vagrants in the British Isles.

They are slim insectivorous birds, and with a few exceptions are smart and often brightly coloured; some could even be described as multi-coloured. A few North American species are plain, but the Tennessee Warbler *Vermivora peregrina* in particular resembles the Leaf-warblers *Phylloscopus* of the Old World. Members of the family range in length from 4.25 – 7.5 in. (11 – 19 cm.); several species fall into the smaller size bracket, whilst the largest is the Yellow-breasted Chat *Icteria virens* that occurs from south-western Canada to Mexico. Most wood warblers occur in a variety of habitats, from tropical rain forests to arid scrub and from sea-level to mountains.

They are often to be found searching for food amongst foliage, although some, such as the Ovenbird *Seiurus aurocapillus* and the Louisiana and Northern Waterthrushes *S. motalcilla* and *S. noveboracensis*, are mainly terrestrial.

The diet of wood warblers is mainly insects and other invertebrates. At certain times of the year some also eat berries.

A wide range of nest sites is chosen. Many, especially the tropical species, nest on the ground or in a recess in an earthen bank. Others nest in bushes and trees; a Wilson's Warbler's *Wilsonia pusilla* nest that I found in Yellowstone National Park, Wyoming, was amongst flood-water debris at the base of a small bush. The nests of Lucy's and the Prothonotary Warblers *V. luciae* and *Protonotaria citrae* are constructed in crevices in trees. The female, with the male often attending, builds a cup-shaped nest. The clutch size varies. The northern species lay from 3 – 5 eggs, which are incubated from 11 – 12 days by the female. She feeds the young throughout the fledging period, with help from the male increasing in the later stages. The Black-and-White Warbler *Mniotilta varia* has been recorded with a fledging period of only 8 – 10 days, whilst most others take a little longer. After they have flown the nest, some are tended by the female and others by the male for up to two weeks before becoming fully independent. The tropical members of the family lay 2 – 4 eggs, that are incubated for 13 – 17 days, and the nestlings fledge in 12 – 15 days.

The greatest threat to the North American wood warblers which winter in Central and South America is the continuing destruction of primary tropical forest, where many species occur. They seem particularly dependent on this type of habitat, and are unable to adapt to areas of secondary growth. During the next few decades alarming declines may take place in the populations of many species we currently consider common. In the United States one of the rarest is Kirtland's Warbler *Dendroica kirtlandii*. It breeds in a very specialised habitat, large areas of Jack Pine *Pinus banksiana* between eight and twenty years old in Michigan. These areas occur because of natural regeneration after fire has swept through older forests. This habitat exists elsewhere, but Kirtland's Warbler has taken a fancy to Lower Peninsular Michigan, and after breeding it spends its winter vacation on the Bahamas. Judging from the lack of records along the migration route, it would appear to fly non-stop. The species has probably never been particularly common, but the population is declining steadily because nests are being parasitised by the Brown-headed Cowbird *Molothrus ater*. A cowbird eradication programme has increased the breeding success of the warbler, but the population has yet to show a significant recovery and stands at about 200 pairs. Unknown factors must be involved, but until scientists can unravel the complete picture, the future of this species cannot be assured.

Amongst the other rare species are Bachman's Warbler *V. bachmanii* and Semper's Warbler *Leucopeza semperi*. Bachman's Warbler was formerly a common breeding species in an area that included Missouri, Kentucky, Arkansas, Alabama and South Carolina, but little is known about its present status. It winters in Cuba and the Bahamas, but there have been few reported sighting in recent years. One of five wood warblers endemic to the West Indies is Semper's Warbler, found on the island of St Lucia, but it has not been recorded since 1972. It breeds at or just above ground level, and is vulnerable to predation by the introduced mongoose.

HAWAIIAN HONEYCREEPERS
Order: *Passeriformes*
Family: *Drepanididae*
16 genera contain 20 species

The systematics of the Hawaiian Honeycreepers or Finches is complex to say the least; some books list 12 species and other works list as many as 24! Perhaps the most authoritative list is to be found in the *Field Guide to the Birds of Hawaii and the Tropical Pacific* by Pratt, Bruner and Berrett. They list 29 species of which 10 are extinct or probably so, 11 more are endangered and the remaining eight range from abundant to uncommon. Several species that are not extinct have already been extirpated from some islands within their range. The exact number of species varies from book to book, as some authors split or lump together species. One thing on which they all agree is that this is a remarkable family of small birds.

The family has evolved from the colonisation of the islands by a single species of North American finch thousands of years ago. Of the surviving species it is suggested that the Laysan and Nihoa Finches *Telespyza cantans* and *T. ultima*, 6.5 in. (17 cm.) long, resemble the original colonist most closely. These species are endemic to the islands of Laysan and Nihoa, and an attempt to establish a second population of the latter species on French Frigate Shoals in 1967 failed. These species are yellow, but the colours of other species include red, green and black. The most elaborate plumage of the surviving species is sported by the Crested Honeycreeper *Palmeria dolei*, 7 in. (18 cm.) long. This endangered species now occurs only on Maui; it has a black plumage streaked and spotted with grey and red, giving much of the body a scaly effect. It has a rufous patch on the nape and a pale tufted crest on the forehead.

The evolutionary diversification has occurred elsewhere with other species; in the Galapagos Islands Darwin's Finches *Geospizinae* have exploited a variety of habitats and on Madagascar, the Vanga Shrikes *Vangidae* have exhibited the same ability. In neither of these instances has such a great variety of species evolved as amongst the islands of the Hawaiian group. On Hawaii the birds were able to specialize to a very high degree, in an environment comparatively free of predators and other harmful influences. The variation in bill shapes shows the extent to which this took place; some species, such as the now extinct Hawaii *Mamo Drepanis pacifica*, 9 in. (23 cm.) long, have a long sickle-shaped bill for probing the native flowers for nectar. This species was last seen in 1899 on the island of Hawaii, but it was the brilliant yellow rump and crissum that led to the species' decline over the earlier centuries. The plumage was used to decorate the cloaks and ceremonial robes of Hawaiian chieftains that were made from the skins of another now extinct Hawaiian species, the Hawaiian O'o *Moho nobilis*, a species of honeyeater *Meliphagidae*. Other honeycreepers are insectivorous with warbler-like bills, but other insectivores have developed a multi-purpose bill; the Akiapolaau *Hemignathus munroi*, 5.5 in. (14 cm.) long, chisels into soft wood with its short, lower mandible and uses the longer decurved upper mandible to extract wood-boring insects or grubs from within the cavity. Other species eat fruit, seeds and snails, whilst the Laysan Finch is omnivorous and is purported to have survived extinction by turning to a diet that included the eggs of seabirds, after the introduced Rabbits *Oryctolagus cuniculus* destroyed the native vegetation. The same rabbits were partially responsible for the demise of the last Laysan Honeycreepers *Himatione sanguinea freethi*. This bird was a race of the Apapane *H. s. sanguinea*, one of the commonest surviving honeycreepers on the larger Hawaiian Islands. The Laysan race inhabited an island that had virtually become a desert by the 1920s, as a result of the destruction of the natural vegetation by the rabbits. During a severe gale and dust storm in 1923 the remaining three individuals were simply blown off the face of the earth. The decline of the Hawaiian Honeycreepers began with the arrival of Man, who colonised the islands from Polynesia around 400 AD. As soon as the native vegetation, on which so many species depended, was cleared for cultivation and introduced plants began to displace the indigenous species, the Honeycreepers were squeezed out.

Extinction was inevitable for a number of species and the same threat hangs over many of those currently considered to be endangered. Another factor was the introduction of the Mosquito *Culex quinquefasciatus* that provided the link between the native birds and those introduced by man. The Hawaiian birds had little or no resistance to disease and the lowland species in particular soon contracted avian malaria and pox.

Little is known about the breeding biology of many species in the family. Most of the known nests are cup-shaped and made of twigs, lined with softer materials and situated in a tree. Some species have been found nesting in holes in trees and the Nihoa Finch uses cavities in rocks. The closely related Laysan Finch, thought by some to be conspecific, nests in tussocks of grass. The clutch size is usually 1 – 3 eggs, and during incubation the female leaves the nest to be fed by the male.

VIREOS
Order: *Passeriformes*
Family: *Vireonidae*
four genera contain 45 species

The vireo family *Vireonidae* occurs over much of temperate North America, Central America and tropical South America, south to northern Argentina. It is believed to have evolved in the New World, but recent DNA analysis suggests that there might be a relationship with several Old World families, including the cuckoo-shrikes *Campephagidae* and the drongos *Dicruridae*.

The family comprises 45 species divided between 4 genera and occurs in a range of woodland and scrub habitats. Most species have predominantly olive-green upper-parts, and yellow and/or white under-parts. The darkest species, and aptly named, is the Slaty Vireo *V. brevipennis* of Mexico. Several species have conspicuous superciliaries, eye rings and/or wing-bars. They range in length from 4 – 6.5 in. (10 – 17 cm.), and many resemble heavily built Wood Warblers (Parulidae). Least well-marked are the Greenlets *Hylophilus*, a genus found in Central and South America. Two other genera also occur in the same region; they are more colourful and are the heavier-billed members of the family. Two species belong to the peppershrikes *Cyclarhis* and three others to the shrike-vireos *Vireolanius*. The Rufous-browed Peppershrike is a widespread species in woodland and scrub habitats from central Mexico to north-western Argentina. The shrike-vireos are three species that usually occur in wetter forests from Mexico to Brazil and Bolivia. Some authorities place both these genera in families of their own, but the more recent books include them with the vireos.

The largest number of species belonging to a single genus within the family are the true vireos *Vireo*; there are 26 species, of which 13 occur in North America. All but Hutton's Vireo *Vireo huttoni* which is found along the Pacific coast and south-western States, are migratory. The Thick-billed Vireo *V. crassirostris* occasionally turns up as a vagrant to the Florida Keys. The most widespread, the Warbling Vireo *V. gilvus*, is a bird that occurs over much of the United States and southern Canada. Recently, the form of the widely occurring Red-eyed Vireo *V. olivaceus* that occurs in south-east Texas has received specific status and is known as the Yellow-green Vireo *V. flavoviridis*. In western Europe, the Red-eyed and Philadelphia Vireo *V. philadelphicus* have occurred as vagrants in the British Isles.

Members of the vireo family are primarily insectivorous, but several species, including the Red-eyed Vireo, eat mainly fruit in their wintering areas of South America. In South America, the Tawny-crowned Greenlet *H. ochraceiceps* is one of the bird species to feed on insects disturbed by swarms of army ants.

The nests of members of the vireo family are built by both adults from vegetable matter including bark, grass, and rootlets.

A clutch of 2 – 5 eggs is laid and incubated for 11 – 16 days; the nestlings fledge in 12 days. Both parents share the domestic duties, and the youngsters finally become independent 20 – 30 days after fledging.

The Black-capped Vireo *V.atricapillus*, a small, dark-headed species found in Oklahoma, Texas and northern Mexico during the breeding season, is declining and causing concern. The decline is largely due to nest parasitism by the Brown-headed Cowbirds *Molothrus ater*. Some cowbirds discover Black-capped Vireo nests with fresh eggs and lay their egg immediately, whilst others destroy existing clutches to prompt them to lay afresh. Cowbird eggs hatch within 10 – 12 days, several days earlier than those of the vireo. Sometimes the adult vireos loose interest in incubating their own eggs, being too involved with feeding the young cowbird who ejects the other eggs. If the vireo eggs hatch after the cowbird's egg, the youngsters may weigh only one-tenth of that of the cowbird. They are too small to compete for food and inevitably die. This is such a serious problem that the future of this species is far from secure throughout its range.

striking family of black, orange and yellow birds found mainly in North and Central America. Most blackbirds, grackles and cowbirds are mainly black. A conspicuous exception is the Yellow-headed Blackbird *Xanthocephalus xanthocephalus*, a familiar North American species, where it is associated with marshes during the breeding season. The meadowlarks *Sturnella spp.* are also members of this family; five other species belong to the genus besides the two that occur in the United States and eastern Canada. The last species to mention is the Bobolink *Dolichonyx oryzivorus*, whose male is a striking finch-like black bird with a straw-coloured nape, white shoulders and rump.

Icterids feed on a diet of fruit, seeds, insects and other invertebrates. The Brown-headed Cowbird *Molothrus ater*, used to feed on insects disturbed by Bison *Bison bison* as they wandered the Western United States. Since the decline of the Bison, it has found a widespread alternative in cattle, although the first Cowbirds I saw were around the feet of the Bison in the Bronx Zoo!

The nests and breeding habitats vary within the members

ICTERIDS and their allies
Order: *Passeriformes*
Family: *Icteridae*
23 genera contain 93 species

In spite of the term 'bird-brained', birds are remarkably intelligent. During a visit to Disney World at Orlando, Florida, I was amazed to watch the antics of the blackbirds and grackles. Every time we gave them popcorn, they took it to the nearest water to wash off the salt. I suppose they had learned the hard way!

Icterids *Icteridae* occur in forest and open habitats throughout the Americas, except the highest latitudes of North America. It is a varied family of 93 species divided into 23 genera. They have conical, probing bills, longer than the stubby bills of seed-eaters. The family includes the New World blackbirds and orioles.

Icterids range in length from 6 – 20 in. (15 – 53 cm.) in length. The largest species belong to the oropendolas *Psarocolius spp.* from Central and South America. They are large, almost crow-like birds, with a pointed bill and yellow outer-tail feathers. Slightly smaller, but similar are the caciques, which are mainly black, with red or yellow patches on the wings or rump. The New World orioles *Icterus spp.*, are a

of the family from the cup-shaped nest of the Bobolink to the pendulous nests of the oropendolas. The clutch size varies from 2 – 6 eggs, depending on the species, and is incubated for 12 – 15 days by the female alone. Both parents feed the nestlings during the fledging period of 10 – 35 days. The cowbirds are parasitic breeders; they have been described as promiscuous, with courtship and mating being brief encounters. In Louisiana and Texas the Black-capped Vireo *Vireo atricapillus* has declined dramatically as cowbirds have spread through its range, for the young intruder ensures that it is the only chick to survive.

FINCHES
Order: *Passeriformes*
Family: *Fringillidae*
19 genera contain 122 species

Finches are a family of colourful seed-eating birds that are widespread in the Americas, the Palearctic and Africa, but largely absent from the Oriental and Australasian regions. Most species are sedentary, but those with populations in the higher latitudes migrate south in the fall; others move irregularly when food shortages and adverse weather dictate.

This page: two male North American Icterids. The Red-winged Blackbird (above left) occurs widely and is so abundant in places that it reaches pest proportions. Above: a Yellow-headed Blackbird in Grand Teton National Park.

Finches occur in a great variety of wooded and scrub habitats from lowlands to mountains, forests to semi-arid areas, and from high northern latitudes to the Equator. They range in length from the Lesser Goldfinch *Carduelis psaltria* 4.5 in. (11 cm.) long, one of three North American goldfinches, to the Pine Grosbeak *Pinicola enucleator* 9 in. (23 cm.) in length, which has a Holarctic distribution. Most northern and South American finches are colourful; unusually it is the African seedeaters *Serinus spp.* that let the side down. The largest genus in the family is that of the seedeaters, serins and canaries, but none of the 31 species occur in North America. The Canary *S. canaria*, the best-known member of the genus, is a popular cage-bird. Next come the 24 species that belong to the genus *Carduelis*, which contains several familiar species, including the American Goldfinch *C. tristis*, the Pine Siskin *C. pinus* and the redpolls. Coniferous forests in many parts of the Northern Hemisphere are home to the Red Crossbill *Loxia curvirostra*, one of four species that have evolved specialised crossed mandibles that enable it to extract seeds from cones. The Scottish Crossbill *L. scotica* is the only species endemic to the British Isles, where it is confined to the pine forests of northern Scotland. The Parrot Crossbill *L. pytyopsittacus* of the pine forests of the northern Palearctic has the heaviest and strongest bill. At the other end of the scale the Two-barred Crossbill *L. leucoptera* occurs in northern larch forests, and

often lining it with hair and other soft materials. The nest is usually sited in a tree or bush. The clutch of 3 – 6 eggs is incubated by the female; the male feeds her as she sits on the eggs. The incubation period lasts about 14 days and the nestlings take a similar length of time to fledge. The male feeds the family, while the female broods the youngsters, but as their feathers begin to appear, she helps to feed the ever-growing brood.

WAXBILLS
Order: *Passeriformes*
Family: *Estrildidae*
27 genera contain 129 species

Waxbills *Estrildidae* are a family of small seed-eating birds often to be found as cage-birds; many are colourful. They are an Old World family that inhabits the warm temperate and tropical regions of sub-Saharan Africa, Asia and Australia. Over half the species in the family occur in Africa, and nearly one third inhabits the Australasian region. One of the widespread African species, the Common Waxbill *Estrilda*

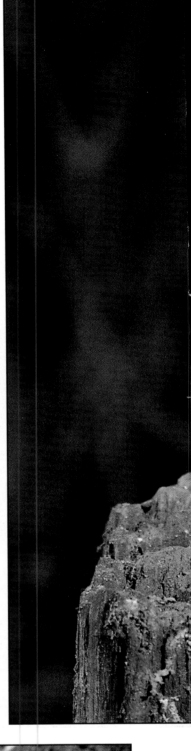

requires a lighter-weight bill. This form of specialisation reaches its greatest development in the Galapagos Islands, where Darwin's Finches have evolved. Their relationship with other bird families is lost in the mysteries of time, although no doubt DNA analysis will prove something. Howard and Moore (1980) and other authors place them with the buntings and New World sparrows *Emberizinae*.

The House Finch *Carpodacus mexicanus*, is a member of a genus that occurs mainly in Central Asia and the Far East. In North America it was found from south-west Canada to Mexico until about 1940, when birds were liberated on Long Island, New York. Since then, and partially due to the provision of food in garden feeders during the winter months, it has thrived and now occurs in many eastern states.

Finches are essentially seed eaters, although many species feed their youngsters nutritious soft-bodied insects and larvae during their early days. Most species have conical-shaped bills that have evolved to crush seeds. Some species, including the American Goldfinch and the Pine Siskin, have developed finer bills to extract thistle seeds. The Northern Bullfinch *Pyrrhula pyrrhula* can be a pest in orchards in spring, where it feeds on buds. It is the female finch that builds the cup-shaped nest from grasses, lichens and other vegetable matter,

astrild, has been introduced to South America and several islands in the Indian and Pacific Oceans.

The Waxbill family comprises 129 species divided between 27 genera and range in length from 3.25 – 5.25 in. (8.5 – 13.5 cm.). They occur in a variety of habitats from woodland to savannah, and are often to be found in small, sometimes mixed flocks feeding on the ground or sitting in the shade on a branch of a small bush, preening. Some, including the Quail-finch *Ortygospiza atricollis*, a species found in open grassland in Africa, is often so wary that the small feeding flocks are not easy to watch properly. Other species are confiding, and offer excellent opportunities to watch them at close range on lawns and in gardens. They are pretty birds that come in all colours and shades, some with spots and others barred on parts of their plumage. Some such, as the Quail-finch, appear almost tail-less and others, including the Violet-eared Waxbill *Uraeginthus granatinus*, have long tails.

Most species are sedentary, although the populations of some undertake seasonal movements stimulated by the rains. The main item in the diet of the family is grass seeds, although some forest species found in tropical Africa, such as the Grey-headed Negro-finch *Nigrita canicapilla*, are insectivorous; others may take insects during the breeding season. They are

Above left: a male American Goldfinch – one of the most striking North American finches – and (far left) a male Chaffinch – a colourful representative of the Finch family from the Palearctic. The fine bill of the Spruce Siskin (above), also of the Palearctic, is used to extract seeds from cones, whilst the Red Crossbill (left) uses its crossed mandibles to prise open cones.

Left: a male Madagascar Fody in the Seychelles, where the species was introduced in about 1860.

Below left: a male African Masked Weaver constructing a hanging nest of grass. Below: a male Red-collared Widow in his striking breeding plumage, in Kenya.

a mainly sedentary family, although it is possible that some species undertake regular seasonal movements during the dry season; others are nomadic.

Waxbills and other birds that inhabit the same areas of the World, often regulate their breeding cycle to coincide with the rainy season to ensure an abundance of food after the eggs hatch. The male gathers grass and similar materials, which he takes to the nest site, where the female carries out the construction of the domed nest. It may be sited in grass or in a bush or tree. In Australia, several species, including the Painted Firetail *Emblema pictum*, which occurs in arid areas, nest on the ground. Northern Australia is home to the Gouldian Finch *Erythrura gouldiae*, a bird of open woodlands and grasslands, that breeds in holes in trees or in termite mounds. The clutch of 4 – 6 eggs is incubated by the adults for 10 – 14 days depending on the species, and during the 14 – 21 day fledging period both adults feed the chicks by regurgitation. The young may be dependent of their parents for up to two weeks after fledging.

WEAVERS

Order: *Passeriformes*
Family: *Ploceidae*
22 genera contain 155 species

Weavers *Ploceidae* are an Old World family noted for the construction of their nests, especially those made by some of the true weavers *Ploceus*. The true weavers also include the fodies *Foudia*, the malimbes *Malimbus* and the queleas *Quelea*. Within the family there are several other groups. These include the Old World sparrows *Passer* and rock sparrows *Petronia*, widely distributed throughout the Old World. The snow finches *Montifringilla* are a Palearctic genus, whilst Africa is home to several genera closely related

adds flowers! While the grass is still green the males hang at the entrance, fluttering their wings and making a scratchy sound that is their feeble attempt at song. Once a female is attracted she lines the nest, and lays 2 – 6 eggs which she alone incubates for up to 14 days. The males help to feed the young during the 15 – 20 day fledging period.

One of the most abundant birds in the World is the Red-billed Quelea *Q. quelea* of Africa. This species of weaver breeds in vast colonies that may cover several acres of thorn-bush in areas of savannah. Only where they come into conflict with man's agricultural activities do they inflict damage; elsewhere they provide food in abundance for raptors and other species, such as the Marabou Stork *Leptoptilos crumeniferus*. Queleas are nomadic when not breeding, and they can decimate crops of rice, wheat and other cereals. Considerable time and effort goes into various control measures, but without significant effect. In one year an

to the weavers, including buffalo, sparrow and social weavers, bishops, widows and whydahs.

The weaver family comprises 155 species divided between 22 genera, found from montane forests to deserts, and includes some of the commonest and most abundant land birds. They are mainly seed-eating birds with stubby conical bills, although insects form a supplementary part of the diet of many species.

Some are colonial breeders and many form non-breeding flocks with other species. The majority occurs in Africa, especially those belonging to the largest and most colourful genus *Ploceus* – 59 species of true weavers. Only seven weavers occur in Asia, and in general they are not as brightly coloured as most of their African relatives. Many have large amounts of yellow or orange, some have black masks or hoods. Females are duller birds and with many closely related species they can be hard to separate in the field. The males weave hanging nests of grass suspended from the ends of branches. Some Asiatic species add mud to the fabric, and to this the Black-throated or Bengal Weaver *P. benghalensis*

estimated 183 million Queleas were destroyed in South Africa; they are avian locusts. In one tree within a colony, as many as 500 hundred nests have been counted. The nest, constructed by the male, is a ball of woven grass, with a side-entrance. The usual clutch is 2 – 4 eggs, which is incubated for 10 – 12 days. Both adults share the duty during the day, but on particularly hot days no incubation takes place; the female always works the night shift. Both parents feed the nestlings during the 11 – 13 day fledging period.

Another interesting African weaver-related bird is the Sociable Weaver *Philetairus socius* of the dry south-west. These birds build a huge colonial nest that recalls a thatched roof, where many pairs have individual entrances and nesting chambers. The nest is often in an *Acacia* tree or built around the crossbars of a telegraph pole at the roadside. To protect the inhabitants from intrusions by predators, such as snakes, the Sociable Weavers place forward-pointing grass stems along the entrance passage. Quite often an African Pygmy Falcon *Polihierax semitorquatus* will take over a nesting chamber

Above: a Golden Weaver, another African weaver, in Tsavo National Park. This bird is often found on or near waterside vegetation.

for its own use, and is tolerated by the colony who appreciate the protection afforded by the presence of the raptor. Two to four eggs are laid by a hen weaver and incubated by both adults for 13 – 14 days. The fledging period lasts 21 – 24 days and during which time the adults are often assisted by a helper.

Another African genus includes the smart bishops and widows *Euplectes*. Black is the main colour of the males who may also have various red or yellow patches on their body plumage, and some have coloured areas on the wing-coverts. They perform conspicuous displays, especially elaborate in the widows who have long flowing tail feathers; Jackson's Widow *E. jacksoni* is the only member of the family to perform at a 'lek.' These tail feathers are longest in the appropriately name Long-tailed Widow *E. progne*. In its striated buff-coloured non-breeding plumage this bird is only 8.5 in. (22 cm.) in length, but in full breeding dress the tail may increase the total length to 24 in. (60 cm.)

The most widespread member of the whole family is the House Sparrow *Passer domesticus*. It now occurs over much of the inhabited world, following in Man's footsteps. Some populations have been the result of deliberate introductions and others have resulted from birds that stowed away on board ship! The House Sparrow is an opportunist. They, and other members of the genus, breed in a variety of natural and artificial sites, where an untidy nest of grass is constructed. All domestic duties are shared, although the female carries out most of the incubation of the 2 – 7 eggs, which hatch after 12 – 14 days. The fledging period for the House Sparrow averages 15 days, whilst that of the Cape Sparrow may take as long as 25 days.

The least typical members of the family are the whydahs and widow-finches or indigo-birds *Vidua*. These are small stubby birds, although male whydahs have elongated tail feathers that double or treble their length. In non-breeding plumage the males resemble the buff and black females. The unusual feature of these birds is that they are parasitic, laying their eggs in the nests of various Estrildid finches. The various members of the genus have particular hosts and the mouth patterns of their chicks match those of the host species.

STARLINGS

Order: *Passeriformes*
Family: *Sturnidae*
24 genera contains 108 species

The European Starling *Sturnus vulgaris*, an inquisitive and noisy bird, has been introduced from Europe and Central Asia, to North America, South Africa, Australia and New Zealand. They reminded the settlers of home, but no doubt their descendants now wish they had not felt so homesick, for Starlings have adapted to their new environments so well that they have become agricultural pests. The first European Starlings in North America were about 60 birds released in Central Park, New York in March 1890, followed the following year by 40 more birds. Both these were successful and by 1904 they had spread to Connecticut and New Jersey. South and west they spread; Alabama fell in 1918, by 1926 they were breeding in Texas and in 1942 they had reached California. By that time Starlings had already made their way into north-eastern Mexico, colonised in 1935; to the north they reached Alaska during 1952.

In other parts of the World the Common Mynah *Acridotheres tristis* was introduced, often initially in an attempt to control agricultural pests such as locusts *Locustidae*. However, you cannot tell a bird what it may or may not eat, and in many places the Mynahs themselves found an abundance of food in the crops, so they in turn became a pest. Being a boisterous character it also had an immediate adverse effect on many indigenous bird populations.

In their native range members of the Starling family *Sturnidae* occur from western Europe to the Far East, south into Indonesia, and throughout much of Africa where some 45 species are recorded. The 108 species are divided between 24 genera; they range in length from 6 – 17 in. (16 – 45 cm.), with the tails of some African species accounting for more than half the birds total length. Starlings are sturdy birds, often

having an upright stance with the tail nearly touching the ground; they usually run or walk with a swagger, rather than hop.

Starlings occur in a wide variety or habitats, although invariably they are associated with trees and to a lesser extent rocks; such habitats offer sites for breeding and roosting. Most starlings are sedentary, but northern populations of such species as the European Starling and the attractive pink and black Rose-coloured Starling *S. roseus*, move to warmer climates in the fall, where some form huge roosts that can be counted in hundred of thousands or even millions. During the day birds from the roost disperse in small flocks to the surrounding countryside, where they forage for food before returning from all directions during the late afternoon to the roost.

The Bali Starling (left), endemic to Bali, is very rare as a result of pressures from the cagebird trade.

Starlings and the closely related mynahs come in many colours, although many have to a greater or lesser extent a black or blue iridescent plumage. Some species are grey and others may have an orange lower breast and belly, such as the Superb Starling *Spero superbus*. Several African species are black or dark grey that display red or chestnut wings in flight. Also from Africa comes the beautiful Golden-breasted Starling *Cosmopsarus regius*, a long-tailed species with a blue head and upper-parts and a golden lower breast and belly.

One of the rarest species is the Bali Starling or Rothschild's Mynah *Leucopsar rothschildi*. It is mainly white with a shaggy crest, black primaries and a black terminal band to the tail; around the eyes there is a patch of bare blue skin. This species was formerly widespread on the island of Bali, but the population is now down to an estimated 180 birds, largely due to the demands made by the cage-bird trade. Recently the Black-winged Starling *Sturnus melanopterus* has started to expand its range and is competing with the Bali Starling for nest sites.

Starlings are omnivorous birds, and it is this aspect of diet that has enabled the European Starling and the Common Mynah to be such successful colonists. Both these species can become agricultural pests, for their diet and that of other species includes fruit and insects; some also eat seeds, nectar

The Common Starling (facing page) has been introduced by man to many parts of the world. In some places it is considered to be an agricultural pest. The Greater Blue-eared Starling (above) is one of many colourful African members of the family.

and pollen. The Jungle Mynah *Acridotheres fuscus* of Asia is an important pollinator of many species, the pollen adhering to the tufted feathers on the bird's forehead as it passes from flower to flower. In Africa the Wattled Starling *Creatophora cinerea* is a gregarious species that forms nomadic flocks; these follow the plagues of locusts that periodically swarm across the continent. Africa is home to two aberrant starlings that have evolved a very specialised feeding behaviour, they are the Red-billed and Yellow-billed Oxpeckers *Buphagus erythrorhynchus* and *B. africanus*, birds that feed on ticks and other parasites on the skin and in the wounds of game animals. It is not uncommon to see ten or more oxpeckers, sometimes of both species, feeding up the neck of a giraffe *Giraffa camelopardalis*. In cattle producing areas, oxpeckers are unpopular because of the damage caused to the beast's hide by their labours.

They nest in holes, often in a tree, which may be a natural crevice or one excavated by a barbet *Capitonidae* or

The Figbird (above) is a close relative of the Orioles and occurs in Australasia. Above left: a Black-headed Oriole – an African member of the family – in the Okavango Delta, Botswana. Common Starlings (left) find nest holes in a variety of sites, including dry-stone walls.

woodpecker *Picidae*; alternatively the birds may choose a crack in a rock-face. The European Starling often nests under the eaves of houses, or in nest boxes if the entrance hole is large enough. In Asia the Bank Mynah *A. ginginianus* lives up to its name, and excavates a burrow about 20 in. (50 cm.) long in an earthen bank. This is one of several colonial species, with a large number of pairs breeding in close proximity at a suitable site. Another colonial species is the appropriately named Woodpecker Mynah or Grosbeak Starling *Scissirostrum dubium* of Sulawesi and its neighbouring islands, where a suitable tree may be honeycombed with holes as a

colony moves in to breed. The Superb Starling is a hole-nesting species that sometimes builds a ball-shaped nest in an acacia or a bush. Usually a bulky nest is constructed inside the cavity, often the male making the nest and the female applying the soft furnishings of hair or feathers. A clutch of 1 – 6 eggs is laid and both birds share duties during the 11 – 18 day incubation period. The nestlings fledge 18 – 30 days later, during which time they are fed by both parents; they may not become independent for another week or more. Several species enlist the aid of non-breeding helpers to feed the young.

ORIOLES

Order: *Passeriformes*
Family: *Oriolidae*
two genera contain 25 species

Another instance of confusing the uninitiated, comes in the naming of the Orioles. The Old World family of Orioles *Oriolidae* is unrelated to the New World family, which belongs to the group that includes the American blackbirds and grackles *Icteridae*. The Old World Orioles *Oriolus* are 24 species of arboreal birds of forest and woodland habitats. They range from western Europe to Central Asia and down to south-east Asia; some species are also found on many islands from the Philippines to New Guinea and Australia, and throughout much of sub-Saharan Africa. The greatest diversity

The breeding biology for several obscure species is unknown, but is probably similar to the more familiar members of the family. The nest of the European Golden Oriole is a cup of grass and other vegetation. Often located near the end of a horizontal branch, it is woven securely to a fork in the bough by the female, who usually builds the nest unaided. The clutch of 2 – 4 eggs is incubated by both parents during the 14 – 15 day incubation period. Fledging lasts a similar length of time.

The Figbird is similar in appearance to the widespread orioles, but with the striking difference of having bare skin between the eye and the bill, red in the male. Restricted in its range, it occurs only in Australia, New Guinea and the offshore islands of Timor and Wetar. During a recent reappraisal of the family, four species of figbird were lumped together under the unqualified name of Figbird. Sometimes when the 'powers that be' start playing around with the systematics of a family, species are split and 'listers' can add one or two new birds, without leaving home, but when closely

occurs on the islands off south-east Asia, where eight species are endemic; by comparison the whole of Africa has only seven breeding species. The Figbird *Sphecotheres viridis*, the only member of its genus, occurs in New Guinea and Australia.

Orioles, well proportioned birds, vary in size from 8 – 12 in. (20 – 30 cm.) in length. They are arboreal feeders and in spite of being brightly coloured can be remarkably hard to see as they search for insects and other food items amongst the canopy of the trees. Males are brighter than the females and come in three basic colours – yellow, red and black. Those species that are yellow have black on the wings and tail, and usually have black on the head. An exception is the Green-headed Oriole *O.chlorocephalus*, found in montane forests from Tanzania to Mozambique. It lacks black in the plumage, but besides yellow, has a green head and back with blue-grey wings. The plumage of several Asiatic species is maroon or red instead of yellow; the Black Oriole *Oriolus hosii* of Borneo has chestnut under-tail coverts, but is otherwise all black. Females of all species are less well coloured.

Many orioles are sedentary, but others migrate southwards. European Golden Orioles *O. oriolus*, the most widespread species, reach as far as South Africa during the northern winter.

related species are lumped together they lose one or two! The Figbird occurs in a variety of wooded habitats, ranging from rain forests to city parks and gardens, where it eats mainly fruit. It builds an untidy nest, compared with the neatly woven nests of the orioles; in fact one can look at the nest from below and see the silhouette of the three eggs through the fabric.

DRONGO

Order *Passeriformes*
Family: *Dicruridae*
two genera contain 20 species

Anyone visiting Africa on a safari tour will soon see a glossy black bird perched on bushes at the roadside; now and then it flies from its perch after a passing insect, displaying a shallow fish-tail as it swoops in pursuit. This is the Fork-tailed Drongo *Dicrurus adsimilis*, one of three species found on the African mainland. Sometimes they ride on the back of a herbivore such as Black Rhinoceros *Diceros bicornis*, and chase items

Above: an incubating Yellow Oriole in Australasia. It is perhaps inappropriately named, being predominantly green. Orioles weave their nests between the branches of trees.

of prey that the animal disturbs as it wanders through the grass of the savannah.

Drongos form a family of 20 species divided into two genera that occur in tropical areas of the Old World. The majority belong to the widespread genus *Dicrurus*, whilst the Papuan Mountain Drongo *Chaetorhynchus papuensis*, the only member of its genus, is endemic to New Guinea. They range from Africa, across Asia from Iran to southern China, and through the East Indies to Australia. The Black Drongo *D. macrocercus*, introduced to the Marianas Islands from Taiwan in 1935, is now a widespread bird of lowlands. Of the seven species that occur in Africa four species are endemic to the Malagasy region, and in Asia where the remaining 13 species are to be found, another four do not occur on the Asiatic mainland.

Most species of drongo have a glossy black plumage, except the appropriately named Grey and White-bellied Drongos *D. leucophaeus* and *D. caerulescens*; the majority also have a distinctive forked tail. The flycatcher-like, Square-tailed Drongo *D. ludwigii* that occurs in forests of sub-Saharan Africa is one exception. The family ranges in length from 7 – 15 in. (18 – 38 cm.), but the elongated tail streamers of the Lesser Racket-tailed Drongo *D. remifer* add a further 20 in. (51 cm.) to its 10.5 in. (26.5cm.) length; those of the Greater Racket-tailed *D. paradiseus* are not as long.

Drongos are mainly insectivorous, feeding on a great variety of species; they may also eat nectar, and have been recorded taking small vertebrates including birds, lizards and mammals. At Okaukuejo, a rest camp in Etosha National Park, Namibia, a Fork-tailed Drongo regularly catches insects attracted by the flood-lights that illuminate the water-hole after dark.

A pair of drongos share in the building of the shallow saucer-shaped nest, also with the incubation of the 3 – 4 eggs and the feeding of the nestlings. The breeding biology of some is still poorly known, but studies have shown that the Fork-tailed Drongo raises two to three broods in a season.

Above: a Fork-tailed Drongo, a familiar African bird, conspicuous as it perches to seek out insect prey.

WATTLE-BIRDS
Order: *Passeriformes*
Family: *Callaeidae*
two, possibly three genera, *Callaeas* and
Creadion each contain a single species,
whilst *Heteralocha* may not be extinct.

Many of the indigenous land birds of New Zealand have shared the fate of many species that evolved elsewhere in isolation. They have been unable to adapt to the changes to their habitats wrought by Man, or have suffered as a result of his persecution or predation by introduced species such as cats and dogs.

The Wattle-birds are a family endemic to the native forests that formerly covered vast tracts of New Zealand. The family now consist of two species, the Kokako or Wattled Crow *Callaeas cinerea* and the Saddleback *Creadion carunculatus*. Until 1907 a third member of the family occurred on the North Island; this was the Huia *Heteralocha acutirostris*, considered now to be extinct, but reports over the years are hard to ignore.

Of the surviving species, the larger species is the Kokako, 15 in. (38 cm.) long, a dark grey bird with olive-brown wings and back, that originally occurred in the forests of both of the main islands and also on Stewart Island, lying south of the South Island across Foveaux Strait. Birds on the North Island have distinctive blue fleshy wattles at the sides of the stout bill, whilst those on the birds from the South Island are largely orange. It is a vegetarian species that feeds on flowers, fruit and leaves. When searching moss-covered branches it may be looking for insects, but this has not been substantiated. The Kokako works its way up tree trunks and branches before descending to the next tree with a long glide. It was a locally common bird, but even by 1880 it had shown a marked decline. There have been so few reports of Kokako on the South Island that it may be extinct, although the subspecies survives on Stewart Island where recently it has been rediscovered after being thought to be extinct for some thirty years. The North Island race appears to be in a healthier position. The large nest is constructed of twigs in the fork of a tree and lined with moss and other soft materials. Incubation of the three eggs appears to be by the female, although both parents feed the young. Incubation lasts for about 25 days, with fledging taking a little longer.

The other species of Wattle-bird is the Saddleback, a black bodied bird 10 in. (25 cm.) long with a chestnut back, wings and under-tail coverts. It has a sharp black bill which it uses to find insects, invertebrates and fruit on the forest floor. The nest is in a hollow tree or in dense vegetation, often close to the ground, where it is unfortunately accessible to the predations of such introduced mammals as rats. Two eggs are laid and incubated by the female. The male feeds her during the incubation period that lasts for about 21 days and afterwards both birds feed the nestlings. Families stay in groups for several weeks after fledging. The Saddlebill, formerly widespread on both the main islands, declined dramatically from the late 19th. century onwards, but thanks to conservation efforts still survives on a handful of rodent-free islands off-shore. The South Island race remained on three of the South Cape Islands off Stewart Island, but in 1964, rats, that had escaped from a fishing boat, went through a population explosion. Just in time, Saddlebacks were successfully translocated to vermin-free islands nearby, for in a matter of months the South Cape population had crashed from being numbered in thousands to just a handful! Unfortunately a race of the Bush Wren *Xenicus longipes*, known as Stead's Bush Wren *X. l. variabilis*, which formerly occurred on several neighbouring islands including Stewart Island, failed to survive the predations of the rats and within a year had become extinct.

And so there is the Huia – does it survive? I would like to think so, for in recent years a number of birds, previously thought to be extinct, have reappeared thanks to the persistence of an enthusiastic generation of field ornithologists. In New Zealand several species have been rediscovered after being 'lost' for years. A prime example is the Takahe *Notornis mantelli*, a very large flightless gallinule, unrecorded from

1898 until its rediscovery in 1948. Similarly, the large terrestrial parrot, the Kakapo *Strigops habroptilus* and the Saddlebill have been rediscovered on Stewart Island in recent years. So what is the chance of the Huia returning from the dead? The Huia is a large black bird 18 in. (45 cm.) with orange wattles and unmistakable white tips to the tail feathers, that occurred in the southern half of the North Island. It was these feathers, so highly prized in ceremonial dress of Maori chiefs, that were to contribute to its demise. Hunting for its feathers by Maoris and later for its unique bill by Europeans was too much. The male and female Huias have different shaped bills, a feature that has not evolved in any other species of bird. The male has a sharp white bill, similar in shape to that of the Saddlebill, but the female has a long, curved one like the wood-hoopoes *Phoeniculidae* of Africa and probably likewise used to probe holes and cracks in trees for insects and their larva. Dissimilar shaped bills suggest different feeding methods, although it is not known for certain if the male and female Huia had separate diets.

History appears to have closed the door on the Huia when the last authenticated sighting took place shortly after Christmas 1907. Perhaps not quite, for there have been occasional reports from its traditional range since that time, but none with sufficient credence for the authorities. In 1970 Margaret Hamilton, writing in *Birds*, the magazine of the Royal Society for the Protection of Birds, gave such an account in an article entitled 'I thought I saw a Huia bird'. Ms Hamilton describes how, during a habitat study of native bush during 1961, she saw a black bird, with a prominent white-tipped tail flying away through the New Zealand Beech Trees *Nothofagus fusca*. It was about the size of the parrot, the Kaka *Nestor meridionalis* that she had been watching earlier. She was familiar with the resident species of the forest and it was not until a few days later that she found her bird illustrated in a book. Without doubt it had been a Huia, but the evidence, although taken seriously, was insufficient for the record to be officially accepted. Perhaps one day the enigmatic Huia will be shot by Man once more, not with a gun, but a camera.

MAGPIE-LARKS
Order: *Passeriformes*
Family: *Grallinidae*
the genus *Grallina* contains two species

There are two species of Magpie-larks, *Grallinidae*, a family endemic to Australasia. The Australian Magpie-lark *Grallina cyanoleuca* and the New Guinea Torrent-lark *G. bruijni* were formerly classified with the Mud-nest Builders; the White-winged Chough *Corcorax melanorhamphos* and the Apostlebird *Struthidea cinerea*, are now placed in the family Australian Mud-nesters *Corcoracidae*. All four species build similar bowl-shaped mud nests, but recent studies of DNA have showed that the birds should be split into separate families, although for the time being they are still adjacent in the order of Classification. The Magpie-larks show a strong resemblance to the Monarch Flycatchers *Monarchinae*, and in particular the Australian Magpie-lark looks like a large edition of the White-eared Monarch *Monarcha leucotis*. It is possible that further scientific investigations might produce closer affinities between these families than between the Magpie-larks and the Mud-nesters.

The Australian Magpie-lark, a bird of open habitats, is widespread in suitable areas throughout the Continent, but to breed, it requires a good supply of mud and therefore is absent from the great deserts of Western Australia. It is 10.5 in. (27cm.) long and has a striking pied plumage that gave it part of its name. The sexes differ slightly in their plumages, although both have black and white wings, head, and tail, with a white belly and rump. The male has a white patch over the eye and the female a white forehead, chin and throat. Juvenile birds are similar to the male, but in addition have the white chin and throat of the female. The bill of the adult is white, but black on juvenile birds.

Australian Magpie-larks feed on the ground and strut like Starlings *Sturnus vulgaris*, searching for insects and other invertebrates, which include ticks and freshwater snails that often harbour the liver fluke, both agricultural pests. It is a bird that has been able to extend its range, as a result of agriculture requiring permanent water supplies for irrigation and for the watering of livestock.

Breeding takes place during the rains, which fall in the summer in the northern states and during the winter in the south of Australia. Birds inland tend to breed when there is available water and mud. Unseasonal rains prompt non-breeding birds into action and during a particularly good rainy season two or even three broods will be reared. The nest, a mixture of mud and grass placed near the end of a horizontal branch, is lined with feathers, grass and wool. One to four eggs are laid, although the usual clutch is three. Both parents incubate and feed the young during the 20-day fledging period, after which the family stays together for several weeks before the juveniles leave to join a wandering flock of other young Magpie-larks that can contain as many as 3000 birds.

The New Guinea Torrent-lark, also pied, but slightly smaller than its Australian cousin, lives along the swift, montane streams in the highlands of Papua New Guinea, where it is an active bird feeding on insects. This is a difficult habitat to study birds and as a result little is known about its breeding biology.

AUSTRALIAN MUD-NESTERS
Order: *Passeriformes*
Family: *Corcoracidae*
two genera each containing a single species

Until recent DNA studies showed that they were unrelated, the White-winged Chough *Corcorax melanorhamphos* and the Apostlebird *Struthidea cinerea*, were placed in the family *Grallinidae* with the two species of Magpie-larks. Both families are endemic to Australia, where they construct similar nests made of mud.

The White-winged Chough occurs in eastern and south-eastern Australia, with a narrow band occurring along the coastal belt of the Great Australian Bight. It is a bird of dry forest and scrub and has spread into introduced woodlands and agricultural land where it can be found around farms, in poultry enclosures and in crops. It has also extended its range into introduced forests and wooded suburbia. The White-winged Chough bears a striking resemblance to the unrelated Choughs *Pyrrhocorax sp.* of the Palearctic. It is a medium-sized bird as large as an American Crow *Corvus brachyrhynchos*, 17.5 in. (45 cm.) long, with black plumage and black and white wings. It has a long decurved bill and a red eye. The White-winged Chough lives in groups made up of a dominant male, several females and the offspring from the previous breeding season. All members of the group help with the building of the nest and later help brood and feed the chicks. The bowl-shaped mud nest also includes vegetable matter and fur to help bind the mud together and act as lining. It is built on a horizontal branch at least 20 ft. (6 m.) up a tree. The usual clutch is three to five eggs, but if more than one female lays, this number can be as high as nine. However, the size and strength of the nest is such that no more than four nestlings fledge. The species is largely sedentary, but family groups may join others to exploit an abundance of food.

The Apostlebird is smaller than the White-winged Chough, being 12 in. (30 cm.) long, with a grey body, brown wings, a full black tail, short legs and a stout, short bill. The appearance of the bird recalls the Babblers *Turdoides* of Africa and Asia. The two families are not related, but both are ground feeding birds that have evolved similar characteristics. Apostlebirds occur in eastern Australia, inland from the coast and in a small area of the Northern Territories. They are birds of dry open forest, woodland and scrub near water, essential for the mud needed to construct their nests. The mud is combined with grass to provide strength and more grass provides a dry lining. Like White-winged Choughs, Apostlebirds live in family groups and all members help with the construction of the nest, incubation of the eggs and feeding of the nestlings. The nest, sited on a horizontal branch, can be 10 – 65 ft. (3 – 20 m.) above the ground and usually contains a clutch of two to five eggs, but this can be more if more than one female is involved. After the young have fledged, the party usually comprising six to ten birds wanders in search of food that includes grain

and insects. They are garrulous, quarrelsome and restless and sometimes, when a particular food item is abundant in a limited area, Apostlebirds gather to form flocks that number in the hundreds.

WOOD-SWALLOWS
Order: *Passeriformes*
Family: *Artamidae*
the genus *Artamus* contains 10 species

Wood-swallows belong to a genus of birds that evolved in Australia, where five of the ten species occur. Two of the remaining species are widespread; the Ashy Wood-swallow *Artamus fuscus* occurs from India eastwards to Indo-China, and the White-breasted Wood-swallow *A. leucorhynchus* ranges from Indonesia and Borneo to the Philippines, south through New Guinea to Australia and east across the Pacific to the islands of New Caledonia and Fiji. The last three

species have very restricted ranges – the White-backed *A. monachus* found on Sulawesi, the Greater *A. maximus* occurs on New Guinea, and the Bismarck Wood-swallow *A. insignis* inhabits New Britain.

Some species are resident, others migratory and two of the Australian species, the White-browed *A. superciliosus* and the Masked Wood-swallow *A. personatus* are nomadic. They form mixed flocks that wander widely after the breeding season, although it is unusual for either species to breed in the same site in consecutive years.

The exact relationship between the Wood-swallows and other bird species has still to be discovered, for although they usually catch their diet of insects in flight, they also can catch them like a shrike *Lanius sp.* Their shape in flight recalls a European Starling *Sturnus vulgaris*, yet they fly with the ease and grace of a swallow *Hirundo sp.* Perhaps one day modern technological analysis may provide the answers.

Wood-swallows are 5 – 9 in. (12 – 23 cm.) long and characterised by their long, triangular shaped wings, their graceful flight and soaring ability. They are well-built birds with stout bills and most species are plain – grey, white or brown, some with black masks. Two species are more striking than most. The White-browed Wood-swallow has a blue-grey head, chest and upper-parts, contrasting with a chestnut breast and belly. The White-breasted Wood-swallow has a dark grey-brown head, chest and upper-parts, whilst the breast, belly and rump are white.

All species breed in loose colonies. The nest is placed in a hollow or recess in the top of a tree trunk or a broken branch, sometimes at the base of a palm leaf. It is a rough cup of twigs roots and grass and as a rule there is no lining. Both birds build the nest together and share the incubation of the 2 – 4 eggs.

The White-breasted Tree Swallow (above) is the most widespread of its family, ranging from the East Indies to Fiji.

Left: a Gray Butcherbird at its nest. This is the smallest member of its family and is endemic to Australia.

The Pied Currawong (below and below left) is a large relative of the Butcherbirds and is a species endemic to the eastern side of Australia. It differs from the Black Currawong in that it has a distinctive white section at the base of its tail.

The incubation period lasts 12 – 16 days and the fledging period a further 16 – 20 days. Five species have been recorded benefiting from 'helpers' during the rearing of the offspring; it might be possible that some of the other species may do likewise.

BUTCHERBIRDS
Order: *Passeriformes*
Family: *Cracticidae*
three genera contain ten species

This family of crow-like Australasian birds consists of three genera; there are six species of Butcherbird *Cracticus*, three of Currawongs *Strepera*, whilst the Australian Magpie *Gymnorhina tibicen* is the sole representative of its genus. They are not related to crows *Corvidae*, but are a distinctive family centred on Australia and New Guinea. Eight of the ten species occur in Australia, of which five species are endemic; the other three species inhabit both Australia and New Guinea. The remaining two species, the Black-headed *C. cassicus* and the White-rumped *C. louisiadensis* Butcherbirds, are endemic to New Guinea.

Butcherbirds include some of the smaller members of the family ranging from the Grey Butcherbird *C. torquatus*, 9.5 in. (24 cm.) long, to the Black Butcherbird *C. quoyi* 18 in. (45 cm.) long. Apart for the obvious exception of this species, the others are pied, with or without grey in the plumage. They occupy a wide variety of habitats from tropical rain forests to

scrub and farmland. Both the Pied and the Grey are widespread over much of Australia and the latter is allopatric with the Black-headed Butcherbird *C. cassicus*, of New Guinea. These two may be conspecific and if proved by further studies, would reduce the Black-headed to a subspecies of the Grey Butcherbird. The diet of butcherbirds consists of invertebrates, small birds, mammals and reptiles, besides fruit and seeds. Their name comes from the habit, shared with some shrikes Lanius, of stashing uneaten food on thorns in the fork of two branches.

Currawongs are larger than the butcherbirds and are all about 18.5 in. (47 cm.) long. The Currawongs are all closely related and are darker than most butcherbirds, having a dark plumage with white patches. Darkest of the three species is the Black Currawong *S. fuliginosa*, which unlike the Black Butcherbird is not entirely black, having a white tip to the tail and white in the wings. It is restricted to Tasmania and islands in the Bass Strait. The other two species, the Pied *S. graculina* and Grey *S. versicolor* Currawongs, only occur in eastern and southern Australia respectively. Currawongs are birds of open woodland; they have a more varied diet and are habitual robbers of other birds' nests. A partiality to fruit has resulted in them being a pest in orchards when they gather in flocks after the breeding season. However they appear to be one of the major predators of stick insects which may defoliate eucalyptus trees.

The Australian Magpie, 17 in. (44 cm.) long, is another pied member of the family, though the plumage and the name are the only similarities with the Black-billed Magpie Pica pica. Like the currawongs, they have a varied diet and also inhabit open woodland. Australian Magpies have a complicated social life. A communal territory is held by a

The Fawn-breasted Bowerbird (above left) is a poorly known species from eastern New Guinea and Queensland. Bowerbirds construct a variety of bowers. MacGregor's Bowerbird (above) of New Guinea, for example, constructs a 'maypole', whilst the Satin Bowerbird (left) builds an 'avenue'.

number of birds; there is a dominant male, but no definite pairing with one particular female. Several females can be expected to be on nests within the territory. The male is a good songster and from this comes the alternative names of Bell Magpie and Piping Crow. Most of the domestic duties are undertaken by the female.

Information on the breeding biology is rather patchy. The nest, in a tree or perhaps on a telegraph pole in more open country, contains two to five eggs, depending on the species. Incubation, by the female alone, lasts 20 – 23 days and during this time the male provides her with food. Fledging takes 28 – 31 days and afterwards the youngsters can be fed by other members of the group.

BOWERBIRDS
Order: *Passeriformes*
Family: *Ptilonorhynchidae*
eight genera contain 18 species

Some of the most elaborate structures made by birds are built by members of the bowerbird family *Ptilonorhynchidae*, of Australia and New Guinea, where they inhabit woodland, rain and cloud forests up to 13,100 ft. (4,000 m.) above sea-level. There are 18 species belonging to 8 genera; 9 species are endemic to New Guinea, 7 endemic to Australia and the other two occur in both areas.

Three species belong to the genus *Ailuroedus*, the Catbirds; they differ in several aspects from the rest of the family. These Catbirds are unrelated to the Gray Catbird *Dumetella*

authorities. New Guinea is also the home of the third member of the genus, the White-eared Catbird *A. buccoides*. Being a lowland forest species it does not overlap with the Spotted Catbird that can be found in the central mountain ranges up to 3,000 ft. (914 m.) above sea-level. The Green Catbird builds cup-shaped nests of twigs and leaves in trees, sometimes as much as 100 ft. (30 m.) above the ground. Being monogamous, the male defends the territory, feeds the incubating female and then helps with the rearing of the youngsters. The diet of adult catbirds is fruit, especially figs, and seeds. The young birds are fed fruit and also nestlings of other birds.

Most bowerbirds are also birds of rain and cloud forests, although the members of the genus *Chlamydera* occur in riverine woodland and more open habitats, thus enabling the Spotted Bowerbird *C. maculata* and the Great Bowerbird *C. nuchalis* to occur farther inland than other species. Bowerbirds range in size from 8.5 – 15 ins. (22 – 38 cm.) in length and vary considerably in colour. Some species are markedly dimorphic, whilst other species are duller, but may have a coloured crest at the back of the head. The dimorphic species include the iridescent black Satin Bowerbird *Ptilonorhynchus violaceus*, the striking black and yellow Regent Bowerbird *Sericulus chrysocephalus* and the predominantly yellow Golden Bowerbird *Prionodura newtoniana*. Several species are polygamous, and in human terms could be described as down-right promiscuous. The bowers, built by the males, help to attract the females; the bigger the bower, the more successful the male will be in seducing and mating with any females that enter his territory! The plainer species have coloured crests, and the larger the crest the more successful the male. Some species, such as the Satin Bowerbird, build 'avenues' of twigs, held upright by a mixture of saliva and fruit pulp. This

carolinensis of North America, which belongs to the Mockingbird family *Mimidae*. The Australasian Catbirds form monogamous pairs. They are well-built birds, 12 in. (30 cm.) long, with stout bills and predominantly green plumages with the amount of black and white, varying between the species. They frequent rain forests; the Green Catbird *A. crassirostris* occurs in eastern Australia, whilst the closely related Spotted Catbird *A. melanotis* of north-eastern Queensland, is also widely distributed in New Guinea. These two species are considered to be conspecific by some

is lined with grass and decorated with coloured objects, usually blue. Other species construct tall structures, known as 'maypoles'; that of the Golden Bowerbird can be up to 10 ft. (3 m.) high. Yet others build large bowers that resemble thatched huts.

Independently the female builds a cup-shaped nest of twigs and leaves in a tree. Alone she incubates the clutch of 1 – 2 eggs for 19 – 25 days. The chicks fledge 18 – 22 days later, but do not become independent for a further 60 – 80 days.

Above: a female Satin Bowerbird.

BIRDS OF PARADISE
Order: *Passeriformes*
Family: *Paradisaeidae*
20 genera contain 43 species

For centuries, generations of tribesmen in the remote mountainous forests of New Guinea have worn head-dresses made from the incredible plumes of the male birds of paradise. These colourful and uniquely shaped feathers are unsurpassed in the world of birds.

The forty-three species of birds of paradise are divided between 20 genera, and occur exclusively in the Australasian region, where all but four species are endemic to New Guinea and its offshore islands. Of the remainder, two species of Riflebird *Ptiloris* are endemic to north-eastern Australia, whilst the Magnificent Rifleman *P. magnificus* and the Trumpet Manucode *Manucodia keraudrenii* occur in the north of the Cape York Peninsula, Queensland, and in New Guinea.

The years of persecution and more recently habitat destruction have taken their toll on the populations of these spectacular birds. Perhaps increased awareness of the birds and the island, resulting from a developing tourist industry, will help to preserve a great natural asset.

Not all birds of paradise have evolved the spectacular plumages, as is popularly supposed. Those species belonging to the genus *Cnemophilus* are smaller than many and exhibit the family's ancestral relationship with the bowerbirds

The Ribbon-tailed Astrapia (above) is a monogamous bird of paradise and the male tending the young. Above left: detail of the breast shield of a male Carola's Paroita, and (left) a male Crested Bird of Paradise. These species are to be found in New Guinea. Facing page: a female Victoria Riflebird has a more understated beauty than the iridescent males of the species. This bird is endemic to north-east Queensland, Australia.

Ptilonorhynchidae. Several others are black with yellow wattles, the most extreme being the rosette-like wattles around the eyes of Macgregor's Bird of Paradise *Macgregoria pulchra.* This species has yellow primaries with black tips, that show in flight as large yellow patches contrasting with an otherwise black plumaged bird. Others have elaborate head plumes, those of the King of Saxony Bird of Paradise *Pteridophora alberti* being 16 in. (40 cm.) long, compared with the bird's length of 9 in. (23 cm.). Some show elongated wire-like central tail feathers, others have incredibly long tail feathers, especially the Ribbon-tailed Astrapia *Astrapia mayeri.* This, a small bodied bird, has two long white tail streamers that give it a total length of 53 in. (135 cm.). Often when one thinks of birds of paradise, it is perhaps unwittingly those belonging to the genus *Paradisaea* that spring to mind. In a family of superlatives these come out on top, they are the yellow and green headed species with trailing orange, pink and yellow plumes, such as the Raggiana Bird of Paradise *P. raggiana.* The male birds of paradise with elaborate plumes are

CROWS and JAYS
Order: *Passeriformes*
Family: *Corvidae*
26 genera contain 112 species

Legend states that Britain will never fall as long as there are Ravens in the Tower of London, and as a child I believed the story to the letter. My faith in the story was shattered when I visited the Tower for the first time, and realised that of course they couldn't leave – their wings had been clipped!

The species of raven involved is the Northern Raven *Corvus corax,* one of the most widespread members of the crow family. It occurs across the Northern Hemisphere, south to Panama in the Americas and to North Africa in the Palearctic region. It is a bird of often rugged and mountainous country, where its deep croaking call is a familiar sound to

The Steller's Jay (above left), with its distinctive crest, ranges from western Canada south to Nicaragua. The Black-billed Magpie (right) ranges across the Palearctic and into western North America and is a notorious and persistent robber of eggs and nestlings from the nests of other birds.

polygamous and display to one and all; the plainer species are monogamous, with the males participating in all domestic duties other than incubation.

Many species are well studied because of their spectacular display, but there is still much to be learnt about other aspects of their domestic lives. The diet varies from species to species, but the family as a whole feeds mainly on berries, fruit, nuts and insects, and other forms of animal life, including frogs and the nestlings of other birds.

The bulky nest is usually cup-shaped, made of twigs and other vegetable material and located in the fork of a tree, although the King Bird of Paradise *Cicinnurus regius* chooses a hollow in a tree. The Crested Bird of Paradise *Cnemophilus macgregorii,* and perhaps other closely related species, builds domed nests. While the brightly coloured male of a polygamous species displays for all he is worth, the drab female constructs the nest, lays a clutch of 1 – 2 eggs, which she incubates for 17 – 20 days and then tends the nestlings who fledge 3 – 4 weeks later. In the monogamous species the female incubates unaided, but the males help with nest building and the feeding of the young; they may also brood the chicks during their early days of life.

many, from backpackers seeking solitude in the wilderness to sightseers along the rim of the Grand Canyon.

There are 112 species belonging to the family *Corvidae,* divided between 26 genera, and it is to the largest genus *Corvus* that the Northern Raven belongs. Most true crows are black, although several, including the Jackdaw *C. monedula* of the Palearctic, have a black and gray plumage. Some races of the gray and black Hooded Crow *C. corone,* also of the Palearctic, are plain black. Some species have a pied plumage, one of the most striking being the aptly named Pied Crow *C. albus* of Africa. Members of the genus vary in size from the Northern Raven 24 in. (61 cm.) long, to the much smaller Jackdaw 13 in. (33 cm.) long. Most of the family are associated with a variety of woodland and forest habitats; only the two choughs *Pyrrhocorax spp.* found on cliffs and mountains in the Palearctic are the exception. They are also among the few black members of the family not to belong to the genus *Corvus,* although unlike the true crows they have coloured bills as their names show – the Red-billed and Yellow-billed Choughs *P. pyrrhocorax* and *P. graculus.*

The Americas are home to many members of the crow family, with the most colourful species, the jays, being

particularly well represented. Many of them are blue, brown, green or purple. In South America there are 15 species, but the greatest variety occurs in Central America, where there are 20 species, 15 of which are endemic. The United States and Canada have six species; the Blue and Gray Jays *Cyanocitta cristata* and *Perisoreus canadensis* are endemic. The striking black and white Black-billed Magpie *Pica pica* occurs in the western half of North America, but is widespread across the Palearctic. The only other member of the genus is the Yellow-billed Magpie *P. nuttalli*, endemic to California. In Spain and Portugal lives the Azure-winged Magpie *Cyanopica cyana*, a bird with an interesting distribution, for the only other area where it occurs is the Far East, an example of a relict population. One other North America member of the family is Clark's Nutcracker *Nucifraga columbiana*; a soft gray bird with black and white wings and tail, it is a familiar bird to picnic sites in the mountainous western states and provinces.

Most members of the family have an omnivorous diet, with some being opportunist feeders. They feed on berries, fruit, seeds and insects, as well as carrion, eggs, young birds and mammals. Generally such species as the crows and ravens are scavengers and some, including the jays and

The Scrub Jay (above) occurs in the western United States and Mexico, and also forms an outlying population in Florida.

233

Facing page: a Gray Jay in Colorado, a common inhabitant of the northern and western coniferous forests of North America. Left: a Clark's Nutcracker, and (below left) two Common Ravens, both in Yellowstone National Park. The Nutcracker's range is restricted to the Rocky Mountains area, whereas the Raven is circumpolar in its distribution.

nutcrackers, store food in the fall for the forthcoming winter. Some species nest in colonies; these include the Rook *C. frugilegus* of the Palearctic, a gregarious species that nests high in the canopy of tall trees. Others are solitary and although many nest in trees, some choose sites in a variety of locations. Ravens and crows sometimes nest on cliff-ledges, besides regularly nesting in trees; choughs nests in caves, or in cracks in rocks or ruins; and the ground jays nest on the ground or in holes in banks, depending on the species. The cup-shaped nest is usually built by both birds and made of twigs, lined with hair or other soft material. Some species such as the Black-billed Magpie, build an enclosed nest of twigs with a side entrance and line the base of the interior with mud, before adding fine grass and roots. Up to 8 eggs are laid by the northern species, but the jays of Central and South America only lay a clutch 2 – 4 eggs. Incubation ranges from 16 – 22 days, whilst fledging takes place some 20 – 45 days later, depending on the species. Generally the female incubates and broods the young chicks. She is fed by the male whilst incubating the eggs and brooding the chicks. She only helps feed the young as they become older.

GLOSSARY

Aberrant A bird that in some way is not typical of its species or family.

Adult A mature, fully developed bird, capable of breeding.

Aerial A bird that spends the vast majority of its life in flight.

Aerial feeder A bird that obtains its food whilst in flight, for example swallows hawking insects.

Allopatric Species or families that are closely related but found in different geographical areas.

Arboreal Relating to or living in trees.

Boreal Forest The coniferous tree belt that stretches across the northern continents, south of the Arctic Tundra. It is often referred to as the 'taiga'.

Casque An enlargement on the upper surface of the bill in front of the head as in most hornbills, or on the top of the head as in cassowaries.

Clutch A group of eggs laid at one breeding period.

Congeners Birds of the same genus.

Conspecific Two or more sub-species that may superficially look noticeably different but belong to the same species.

Convergent Evolution The result of demands enforced on different species or genera by food and living conditions, resulting in unrelated species sharing characteristics.

Coverts Feathers which protect the base of the wing and tail feathers.

Crèche A gathering of mobile chicks, as in penguins.

Crepuscular Active at dawn and dusk, rather than in full darkness.

Cryptic Camouflaged plumage, often a mixture of brown, buff or black with mottling or barring, or other characteristics that provide concealment.

Dimorphic The difference in appearance between a male and female of a species in plumage, size and structure.

DNA Deoxyribonucleic acid – the key to genetic inheritance.

Diurnal Active during the day.

Echo-location Sophisticated form of navigation used by a number of cave-dwelling birds including the Oilbird and cave swiftlets.

Eclipse Non-breeding plumage of birds; it is usually applied to ducks, when the drake in particular assumes a less conspicuous plumage whilst moulting its flight feathers.

Endemic A species that occurs only in a restricted area.

Facial disc A disc-like formed face, as with the owls.

Feral A domesticated species that has become wild.

Fledging period The time taken by a young bird from hatching to flying.

Frontal shield Unfeathered fleshy or horny forehead which goes down to the base of the upper mandible.

Frugivorous Fruit eating.

Gizzard A part of the stomach with muscular walls that grind down the food; some birds purposely swallow grit or small stones which lodge in the gizzard to help this.

Guano Excreta of fish-eating sea birds, which is collected commercially in Peru, Chile and South Africa.

Gular Pertaining to the throat.

Habitat The environment in which a certain bird lives.

Hawking Catching prey in the air.

Helper Non-breeding birds who assist breeding birds of their own species, to raise their young.

Holarctic Region The Nearctic and Palearctic regions combined.

Hood A distinctive coloured area covering the head.

Immature Fully grown but not in full adult plumage nor sexually mature.

Irruption An irregular migratory movement of birds due to shortage of food in their usual area.

Juvenile A young bird in its first full plumage.

Lore The area between the eye and the bill on either side of the head.

Malagasy Region The faunal region formed by Madagascar and its surrounding islands.

Migration The regular movement of birds from one point of the world to another and back.

Mirror The white on black wing-tips of certain gull species.

Molt The regular renewal of feathers.

Monogamous Having a single mate for one or more breeding seasons.

Monotypic A genus of a single species.

Montane Relating to mountains.

Nestling Describes a young bird in the nest, from hatching to flight.

Orbital ring A narrow fleshy ring around the eye.

Palearctic The area covering the whole of Europe, Asia north to the Himalayas and Africa north of the Sahara.

Parasitize To lay eggs in the nest of other species, leaving the latter to raise the young.

Pelagic Living out at sea apart from when breeding.

Pellet The indigestible remains of prey, such as feathers, hair, scales and bones which are regurgitated in a mass.

Piracy One species that robs another of its food eg. jaegers.

Polyandry Where a female mates with two or more males. There is usually role reversal, with the male incubating the eggs and tending the nestlings.

Polygamy Where a male mates with two or more females.

Polygyny Occurs in a species where one bird may mate with more than one individual.

Race See sub-species.

Raptor A diurnal bird of prey.

Ratite The name "Ratite" is given to the group of flightless birds found mainly in the Southern Hemisphere eg. ostriches, emus, cassowaries and kiwis. They are flightless because they lack the breast bone to which the powerful flight muscles are attached.

Scrape A shallow depression scraped in the ground for use in place of a nest.

Sedentary A bird resident in the same area throughout its annual cycle.

Sibling Species Species which are closely related and believed to have separated in recent times.

Striated Streaked.

Sub-adult A bird not in full adult plumage.

Subspecies A sub division of species,

Talon Claws of a predatory species, usually those of an owl or raptor.

Terrestrial A ground-dwelling species.

Vagrant A bird occurring far beyond its normal range.

Wetlands Marshes, either salt or fresh water and sloughs.

Facing page: a male Mistletoe Bird feeding its young. This bird is a member of the Flowerpecker family and occurs throughout Australia.

PICTURE INDEX

Facing page: a male Superb Fruit Dove from
Australia on its nest; the female of the species
is greener in coloration.

ACKNOWLEDGMENTS

A book that covers the birds of the world, cannot be written solely on the experience of one person, so I have supplemented my knowledge with help from many field guides, handbooks, monographs and reference books. I am grateful to the researchers and authors of those works.

The greatest help and encouragement has come from my wife Elizabeth, who has always been there to help in so many ways; from endless cups of coffee to reading text and correcting manuscripts on the word-processor. My father, Frank, was a tremendous help with research as deadlines approached. I should like to thank Lawrence Holloway of Ornitholidays, Bognor Regis, for the many opportunities he has given me to watch and study birds in wonderful parts of the world, and for his checking and constructive criticism of the manuscript of this book. Simon Boyes, a fellow Ornitholidays' leader has given useful advice on South American birds; George Green and Moira Adie have helped in various ways; Gillian Lythgoe of Plant Earth Pictures and Andrew Preston of Colour Library Books have been a great source of encouragement and advice. Elsewhere Colin Bell and Ian Davidson (Wilderness Safaris, Johannesburg), Brian Graham, Ronnie Crose, Lloyd and June Wilmot (Botswana); Robert Sutton (Jamaica), Jan Komdeur (ICBP/Seychelles) and Rhett Butler (Zimbabwe) are among many who have given me the benefit of their local knowledge.

A special thank you is due to our sons Tim and Roger, who have been so long suffering while we worked on the book.